Roman Fever

Roman Fever

Influence, Infection and the Image of Rome, 1700–1870

Richard Wrigley

Yale University Press
New Haven and London

Designed by Charlotte Grievson
Printed in China

Library of Congress Cataloging-in-Publication Data

Wrigley, Richard.
Roman fever : influence, infection, and the image of Rome 1700–1870 / Richard Wrigley.
pages cm
Includes bibliographical references and index.
ISBN 978–0–300–19021–2 (cl : alk. paper)
1. Rome (Italy) – Description and travel. 2. Influence (Literary, artistic, etc.)
3. Travel – Health aspects – Italy – Rome. 4. Rome (Italy) – Social conditions – 18th century.
5. Rome (Italy) – Social conditions – 19th century. I. Title.
DG809.W75 2013
945.6′3207–DC23
2012029246

A catalogue record for this book is available from The British Library

CONTENTS

ACKNOWLEDGEMENTS

This book has deep roots, and a widely dispersed circle of gratitude and indebtedness. Kerry Downes's teaching inspired an enduring enthusiasm for Rome, specifically its Baroque architecture. Thinking about the status of Roman architecture as a model probably lies behind a curiosity about the nature of influence, and its various idioms. While researching in Oxford and Paris, Rome was never far away, thanks to Francis Haskell and Jon Whiteley. The idea to start a study of influence as a phenomenon intrinsic to Rome's role as an art centre was generously supported by Alastair Laing, which led to my first visit to the British School in Rome, and new horizons in conducting research abroad, and thinking, by virtue of exploring the city, what artistic influence added up to. At a time when my research was focused on revolutionary France, an invitation from Chloe Chard to speak in a seminar series on artists and travel prompted a speculative paper, which then turned into an article in the volume she edited with Helen Langdon, *Transports: Travel, Pleasure and Imaginative Geography*. Chloe's example as an innovative and brilliant writer on travel, and a stimulating interlocutor, has been irreplaceable. At Oxford Brookes University, I had the good fortune to meet George Revill, who generously and energisingly opened doors onto the kinds of thinking and research which went on under the sign of historical and cultural geography.

I acknowledge the award of an Arts and Humanities Research Council Research Leave Scheme grant, and the funding of research leave during time at Oxford Brookes University and the University of Nottingham. Colleagues at these institutions have been supportive of the necessary absence while researching and writing. Several libraries have been indispensable: I offer boundless thanks to the librarians and staff at the Wellcome History of Medicine library, Leeds University Library, the Académie de France in Rome, the Bibliothèque Nationale de France, the Courtauld Institute of Art, the Paul Mellon Centre for Studies in British Art, London, and the Yale Center for British Art, New Haven. Like many scholars, I applaud all those enlightened institutions that have been willing to make their images available without charge.

I benefited greatly from having been granted a Visiting Scholarship at the Getty Research Institute, Los Angeles; while there I was lucky to have Karen Gunterman as a resourceful and industrious research assistant; and also to have a sympathetic group of contemporaries, including Tim Benton, and Peter Burke. The award of a Fellowship in Anglo-Italian studies by the Paul Mellon Centre for British Art allowed me to spend six months as a resident of the British School in Rome. This was a transformative time for working through some crucial primary material and developing ideas that have grown into this book. As are all those who stay there, I am indebted to the staff of the School for making possible exemplary conditions for working and being in Rome. During my time at the British School in Rome, I was blessed with a group of friends with whom to explore the city: Piers Baker Bates, Louise Camrass, Simone Chung, Michael Kruger and Anne Ronayne, Juho Laitinen, Tom and Yuki Lamb, Darren Marshall, Denis Masi and Suzy Giblin, Christine Morrow, Sista Pratesi, Corinna Riva, Xavier Salomon, Simone Shu-Yeng Chung, Alex Thein, and Geoff Uglow. I should mention a memorable evening at the American Academy in Rome, when David Soren spoke about his excavations of the infant cemetery at Poggio Gramignano, and Frank Snowden on his book, then in preparation, *Conquest of Malaria*, with contributions from the floor by the distinguished malariologist Mario Coluzzo. Also present was Gilberto Corbellini, who kindly welcomed me to the Istituto della Storia della Medicina, University of Rome. It is a great pleasure to recall the generosity of Marco Fiorilla at the Biblioteca Lancisiana. Mentioning the American Academy obliges me to thank Piers Bakers Bate for support beyond the call of art-historical duty, on an evening that began listening to a lecture on seventeenth-century Florentine plague, but ended at Salvator Mundi. With Dave Atkinson, discussions of Roman streets, their politics and salubriousness, extended to the Stadio Olimpico. It was also at the British School in Rome that I met Lisa Beaven, whose work on Claude and the campagna has been inspirational. At the Bibliotheca Hertziana, Christoph Frank was a genial cicerone; in the company of Angela Windholz, Georg Schelbert and Giampaolo, Dopolavoro ATAC's challenging clay courts provided a counterpoint to bookstacks.

To the many people who have given me references and pointed me towards new ideas, or just put up with interminable monologues on bad air, I extend sincere thanks (some specific debts of gratitude are signalled below and in the notes):

Agnès Bouvier, for precious Flaubertian assistance; Susanna Caviglia-Brunel; Matthew Craske; Maarten Delbeke; Frédérique Desbuissons; Michael Erwee, for his help in Rome; Dario Gamboni and Johanna Weiss; Margaret Morgan Grasselli for invaluable help with Hubert Robert; Brian Grosskurth; David Jackson for his advice on Aleksandr Ivanov; James Kearns for kindly assisting with Gautier; Frank MacMahon for *Daisy Miller*, no less; Archie Maconnel briefed me on the eucalypt; Sarah Maconnel provided Dickensian advice; David Marshall, for allowing me to use some of his photographs of Roman rubbish plaques; Kathy Mclauchlan generously shared several valuable references arising from her work on the French Academy in Rome in the nineteenth century; Katherine Rinne; Clare Robertson for photographic help; Alex Mancey Barratt and Charlotte Wright have provided medical sounding boards.

I am indebted to Jay Clarke for suggesting and making possible a visit to Bruce and Dee Lundberg's remarkable collection of Roman photographs. It is a particular pleasure to thank Bruce and Dee for sharing their collection, including the reproduction of some works in this book.

Several people read the manuscript at various stages and offered indispensable suggestions for reshaping and improving it. Stephen Bann and Stephen Daniels both provided thought-provoking and encouraging advice. I am especially grateful to John Bonehill for agreeing to read the manuscript, and offering valuable and much needed comments. I should also acknowledge the usefulness of a variety of challenging comments from readers for presses who preferred not to publish this book. Fortunately, thanks to Gillian Malpass, this is now appearing under Yale's imprint; at Yale, Charlotte Grievson calmly and deftly steered the text, images and author towards the finished article.

Pleasurable as it is to gather these acknowledgements together, completing this book brings with it a larger, more personal sense of retrospect. During the several years of researching and writing it, I lost my mother, my beloved great aunt, Alice Abell, and my brother Michael. In more ways than I perhaps fully understand, this book is written in their memory. Over several years, Penelope Curtis has heard more about *mal'aria* and its cultural repercussions than anyone should have to bear. Her patience has been exemplary, and I dedicate this book to her with love and gratitude.

INTRODUCTION

This book started out with a simple question: what did influence mean during the eighteenth and nineteenth centuries as applied to artists' and travellers' experience of Rome? Although neither unaware of nor uninterested in the more general ramifications of influence as an art-historical topic, my interest in it, and the shape of the book that has resulted, has grown out of working on (and in) Rome. A more comprehensive account of changing ideas concerning transmission and assimilation of artistic knowledge in and from Italy would need to range more widely through comparative attitudes to other cities, and would inevitably come up with different conclusions. Be that as it may, the meanings of influence articulated here have emerged from a study of the ideas and circumstances which were thought to explain the idiosyncratic nature of Rome and the effects it produced. It was clear from the outset that past thinking about Rome as a stage for the working out of influence was premised on the belief that there was something unique about the city, and more specifically that this could be explained in terms of the city's relation to its environment. The combination of exceptional artistic resources, a strangely bleak surrounding countryside, and a notoriously changeable and at times inhospitable climate created a potent but unpredictable milieu awaiting artists who journeyed to Rome in order to realise its promise of transformation. I have tried to suggest how these different components worked together, and fed into narratives of the journey to Rome and its consequences.

Rome was and remains an exceptionally appropriate place in which to think about influence and art. From the origins of the Grand Tour in the seventeenth century to its replacement by modern tourism, the 'Eternal City' was the preordained climax of an Italian journey. Rome's credentials as the home of ancient grandeur reduced to picturesque ruination were unassailable, albeit that Naples, Pompeii and Herculaneum had a seductive southward pull. Its status as a treasure house of great Renaissance and seventeenth-century art was reinforced and thrown into relief by the framework of dispersed but sublime antique remains. In the earlier nineteenth century Rome became the quintessential Romantic city – its ruins stimulated melancholy reverie, less about the fall of a great civilisation than introspective ruminations, interspersed with laments over the smothered aspirations of Italian nationhood. Even after its reinvention as national capital in 1871, its accumulated symbolic significance provoked ambivalence if not outspoken resistance to modernisation. Yet the city's cultural capital continued to remain highly valued. If Rome had been an early exemplar of museum culture, at one and the same time home to innovative museums and a museum city par excellence, its status as a unique repository of art and architecture was further intensified by an unprecedented phase of accelerated urban expansion and modernisation.

Influence is usually thought of as a matter of the transfer of visual knowledge or information, and fits within well-worn art-historical models of change or development. *Roman Fever* is made up of an interlocking set of studies and argues that ideas of influence should be detached from this kind of matching and making, and rather rethought in contextual terms, acting through an ambient, immersive dimension as much as being the result of conscious ambition be that individual or institutional. Adopting such an approach follows from trying to understand what range of meanings influence and its workings had in the period studied in this book.

It is immediately apparent that, as applied to art, influence has predominantly been construed as an inherently pathological process; indeed, ambiguity between artistic and medical language and concepts seems to be almost invariably present. The journey to, and encounter with, Rome engendered altered states of mind and body, which frequently descended into collapse and crisis. This predicament endowed narratives of arrival and discovery, usually expected to involve a thrill of accomplishment, with a sense of risk and the threat of failure; in its milder manifestations this might take the form of temporary disarray and disorientation, but could lead to more disturbingly painful reaction.

Explanations for this were sought in terms of a general theory of the impact of air, situation and local climatic conditions. This type of cause had been familiar as part of attempts to explain the collapse of the ancient city of Rome. In modern times the Roman climate was notorious for the seasonal curse of 'bad air', or *mal'aria*. That this caused various problems for travellers and artists was a commonplace, but one which modern art history has tended to ignore, despite the well-established recognition by social and medical historians of the devastating effects of what in modern terms is understood as malaria throughout Rome and across southern Italy. Artistic engagement with the Roman landscape turns out to be particularly problematic, as the source of the tainted atmosphere's noxious ingredient was habitually identified with the *campagna* and especially the Pontine marshes. Traversing these spaces was risky and involved juggling with local knowledge as to the respective presence of picturesque sites and models, and entrenched 'bad air', a threat which was all the more unsettling in so far as it was recognised to be on the move.

Similar problems were attendant on navigating the city and its variegated topography of infection, exacerbated by prevailing insanitary conditions. The abstract notion of influence and the pursuit of artistic betterment was a different matter when the urban fabric itself, caked in human waste, was not only repellently foul but also reputed to be contagious, and through whose spaces circulated an invisible poison, all the more unnerving for being capricious in its changing distribution. As a place where influence was put into practice, Rome emerges as rife with obstacles, deterrents and threats, even before the business of making sense of art had begun.

Central to my account is an emphasis on the crossover and overlap between influence as both a cultural and medical term. Such shared conceptions of the dependence of cultural expression and health on physical conditions remind us of the different, much closer, relations that obtained between artistic and scientific theory and practice compared to later professional and disciplinary distinctions. 'Roman fever' refers to one of the names for the indigenous illness caused by 'bad air', expressing the widely held belief that this was a quintessentially Roman problem. The phenomenon of 'bad air' derives from the miasma theory of the environmental causes of disease, which was dominant throughout the period covered, and indeed lingered on even after the discovery of the true nature of malarial fever. *Roman Fever* draws attention to something which is abundantly present in primary sources but has almost entirely been ignored in cultural historical studies focused on Rome.[1]

I explore the idea of Rome as a place of heightened artistic experience in relation to its parallel reputation as an environment blighted by 'bad air' (*mal'aria, aria cattiva*). What caused 'bad air', and how did its pervasive presence inform the image of the city as a place of transformation, and more especially as a place for the viewing and making of art? The complexity required of any attempt to interrelate medical and cultural history is demonstrated by virtue of the brilliant synthesis achieved in two recent studies. Robert Sallares brings his scientific expertise to bear on the history of malaria in ancient Rome (*Malaria and Rome: A History of Malaria in Ancient Italy*, Oxford and New York, 2002). Frank Snowden offers an account which is at once social and cultural in the sense that he constructs an account of malarial research through an analysis of the professional community in Rome in the early twentieth century (*The Conquest of Malaria: Italy, 1900–1962*, New Haven and London, 2006). While Sallares brings early modern material into play in his study, his subject is ancient Rome; Snowden is concerned with modern Italy. In terms of the history of medicine, *Roman Fever* deals with the two centuries which preceded the discovery of the true nature of malaria at the end of the nineteenth century.

Matters of historical change are addressed as and when appropriate in each chapter, rather than there being a single chronological sequence. That said, certain important questions regarding ideas of what it was to encounter and experience Rome, the long-running debate on its climate, and the abiding problem of the causes and effects of bad air are set out as they were articulated in the eighteenth century, before following these through into eighteenth- and nineteenth-century landscape imagery and the unpalatable aspects of the city, which reputedly remained unchanged throughout the whole period. In terms of medical perspectives, the survival of papal authority for Rome and its surrounding area provides good reason to take the long view. Medical ideas themselves, of course, evolved during this period, but the core beliefs regarding the interconnectedness of climate, topography and the crucial role of air remained remarkably persistent. This is not to say that they were simply reiterated, based on uncritical faith in archaic theory: it is more a question of a certain respect given to ideas which proved to be resilient despite continued empirical attempts to locate and isolate the essential pathogen behind the deadly effects of miasma or 'bad air'. The period covered corresponds to a series of interrelated cultural historical episodes, which give different meanings to the currency and reputation of 'bad air' and its repercussions.

In some ways this is an 'anti-Grand Tour' book – a working title I rejected was 'The Dark Side of the Grand Tour', partly because it was too closely modelled on John Barrell's *Dark Side of the Landscape*, but also because the book follows through into the later nineteenth century. It aims to get away from assumptions about Roman travel as an extension of the history of collecting (although it is true that this could be construed as an adjunct to what might be called the infrastructure of influence), and also from the focus on the rediscovery and interpretation of antiquity. Equally, Rome as a Romantic destination has all too often been confined to canonical authors, defined by their literary responses and reinventions, and downplayed if not ignored contextual investigation. In so far as certain familiar texts also appear here, it is hoped that their ideas and words are given different meaning, both by being juxtaposed with lesser-known writers and artists, and more importantly by being situated within what might be called an aesthetics of the environment, or more accurately environmental blight.

Aspects of the history of travel are combined with art-historical and historical (primarily medical) perspectives. Nonetheless, this is a book written by an art historian. Thinking about the making and reception of works of art is central to how I have approached the Roman environment. In a sense, it is precisely the question of how we envisage that environment as a place for encountering and responding to art and monuments which I have tried to rethink. I engage more directly with paintings, prints and photographs in the last two chapters, respectively on landscape imagery and the problems posed by Rome's insalubriousness for artists and travellers. Being able to follow through the ideas and issues surrounding Rome's 'bad air' in terms of how this impinges on the making and meaning of works of visual art is a deliberate structural priority. That said, there is meant to be a continuous thread running through successive chapters: the underlying ambiguity in attitudes to Rome's atmosphere and its effects, whether inspirational or incapacitating, scientifically enigmatic or politically scandalous.

My material is predominantly French and British but includes an eclectic range of other sources, corresponding to the cosmopolitan character of Rome as a cultural crossroads. Such an emphasis derives in part from the project's origins in my previous studies of French art. However, my holistic approach provides an alternative to the prevalent willingness to confine French art's history within national boundaries. There is also the fact of two prolonged French occupations under the First and Second Empires (1809–14, 1851–70), providing an exceptional opportunity to study and analyse the climate and environment as a broader administrative and especially military adjunct to the well-established presence of French artists in Rome. On the other hand, I am all too conscious that, even as regards France and Britain, there are many artists, writers and travellers who do not appear in these pages: it is an open question as to whether further accumulation of material would change the essential argument. Indeed, the various Italian, Russian, German, Swiss and American sources I occasionally draw on have not provided inherently different versions of Rome, so to speak; rather, they reinforce the sense that there were remarkably consistent and widely diffused habits of thought and imaginative templates by means of which the journey to Rome was anticipated and recounted, and that one respect in which this shared vision was bound together was through ideas on climate and hygiene. Moreover, the sense of cosmopolitan sharing in artistic matters was also echoed in the scientific and medical spheres, allowing for occasional accusations of chauvinism.

That said, there are, of course, national narratives and contexts which give particular significance to being in Rome: for example, the renewal of British travel after the Napoleonic wars. More particularly, wherever appropriate I give due weight to Italian, primarily Roman, texts and commentators, who shared concerns and a sense of vulnerability when it came to the ambient insalubriousness of their city, as well as wishing to stand up for the city's reputation and counter any threat to tourism and its economic benefits. As we will see, the Romanness of Roman fever was a moot point; paradoxically, the idea that the city was home to a localised form of disease was harder to dismiss precisely because of the deep-rooted belief in Rome's artistic uniqueness.

INFLUENCE: BETWEEN MAGIC AND MALADY

In a shadowy church, a man sits drawing (fig. 1). His curiously elongated chair is perched upon two shallow wooden platforms; a sketch book rests on his knees and the back of the chair in front of him. He looks up at a mural, his pencil still pressing on the sheet of paper. We only see a fragment of the painting he studies – the lower body of a man who pivots on his right leg. Beneath the mural an empty easel is propped against a font; to the left a chair has been pushed out of the way, as if recently vacated. A dog stands in the doorway, just as alert as the artist but more interested in whatever is going on outside. Within the doorframe, the paper is left white, and in places rubbed clean, to create an effect of bright sunlight. Although he has kept his kerchief on, his loosened stockings suggest his state of absorption or else might be a concession to the summer heat. In the centre of the drawing beneath the open door a tricorne hat is propped up, as if it was intended to remind the viewer that it belongs to Hubert Robert, the otherwise invisible artist who has made this image.

We are too far away and too obliquely positioned to be able to see anything of the image he has created in his sketchbook, and Robert only includes the lower right corner of the painting being studied. But as anyone familiar with the history of painting in the eighteenth century would have recognised from the fragment that is visible, we are in Rome. The draughtsman sits before Domenichino's *Flagellation of St Andrew* (1609) (fig. 2) in the Oratorio di Sant'Andrea, in the grounds of San Gregorio Magno al Celio (fig. 3). The figure whose body we see, and which seems to be the object of the draughtsman's attention, is indeed that of the executant of the saint's brutal punishment. The absence of an inscription implies that this would be recognised.[1] The abbreviated depiction of Domenichino's painting suggests familiarity not indifference.

In so far as the drawing's *mise-en-scène* would have been recognised by those familiar with Rome, it would also have been a reminder of a celebrated seventeenth-century debate over the relative merits of the two artists whose murals face each other in the oratory, Domenichino's *Flagellation* and Guido Reni's *St Andrew led to Martyrdom*. According to Bellori, Annibale Carracci thought Domenichino's picture was better, and cited the enthusiastic gestures made by a woman as she explained the picture; Algardi

FACING PAGE: Hubert Robert, *Draughtsman copying Domenichino's Flagellation of St Andrew (1608) in the Oratario di Sant'Andrea, Rome*, detail of fig. 1.

1 Hubert Robert, *Draughtsman copying Domenichino's Flagellation of St Andrew (1608) in the Oratorio di Sant'Andrea, Rome*, 1763, red chalk, 32.9 × 44.8 cm. Thaw Collection, Pierpont Morgan Library, New York, 1981.74.

disagreed, saying Reni's work was better executed.[2] Whatever the balance of opinions in the seventeenth century, Domenichino's painting was to retain its artistic authority through the eighteenth century.[3]

In 1788, the director of the Académie de France, Ménageot, organised a copy to be made by Jean-Baptiste Desmarais of what he considered 'one of the beautiful things that there are in Rome'.[4] Moreover, he observed how much it had deteriorated since his first visit to Rome in 1769; he predicted that in fifteen years it would have disappeared, 'for this beautiful fresco is deteriorating every day'. Desmarais's copy would therefore become a precious document of a work which was 'a great lesson in drawing, thought and expression'.[5] Poussin's high regard for Domenichino would have encouraged a respectful attitude on the part of later French artists. François-Marius Granet, for example, made a drawing on this subject (fig. 4).[6]

Hubert Robert shows us a nominally sacred space which has been appropriated for the study of art. This is made more obvious in another drawing by Robert which includes three artists in the oratory, two facing the Domenichino, one the Reni (a figure

2 Domenichino, *Flagellation of St Andrew*, 1609, fresco, Oratorio di Sant'Andrea, San Gregorio Magno al Celio, Rome.

3 Oratorio di Sant'Andrea, San Gregorio Magno al Celio, Rome, interior.

4   François-Marius Granet, *Poussin and Several Figures before the Works of Reni and Domenichino*, 1843, pen and ink and pencil, 25 × 38 cm. Louvre, Paris, inv. 26928.

who has been identified as Robert himself) (fig. 5). Deanna Petherbridge characterises this scene as 'an artist sneaking a view of another artist'.[7] I see it as a much more care-fully orchestrated study. Both drawings evoke the process of learning from past art. However, in the New York drawing, Robert's gaze is turned away from the mural towards the artist, who is set before the entrance corner of the church. It is he not the mural that is the centre of attention. Or more precisely, it is the active engagement of an artist in 'a great lesson in drawing, thought and expression'. Robert's image focuses on a moment of concentrated scrutiny, which stands for a more comprehensive engagement with Rome's artistic resources. Yet there is something about the distorted shape of the chair on which he sits, and the confusing tangle of his legs, which seems to express a sense of the strain and effort involved in this act of making artistic contact. Confronting the old masters was not, this drawing seems to tell us, a straightforward matter.

    We might take this further and read the drawing as a documentary aperçu of an art-ist's engagement with a seicento model, and connect it to attitudes to copying such art in the academic milieu of mid-eighteenth-century France. Thus, Victor Carlson quotes

5   Hubert Robert, *Three Draughtsmen in the Oratorio di Sant'Andrea*, 36 × 50 cm. Formerly Paul Bureau collection sale, Galerie Georges Petit, Paris, 20 May 1927, cat. no. 13 (ill.).

the *Encyclopédie* on the French Académie Royale de Peinture et de Sculpture, and declares that the drawing 'illustrates [its] philosophy of art as it was put into practice'.[8] Copying was indeed an integral part of the educational obligations of artists and students in Rome, and an exemplary means to ensure close-up contact with great art of the past, thereby intensifying the kind of transfer of knowledge and technique which could be achieved. 'It is here only', judged Stephen Weston, 'that artists of all denominations and degrees may find something congenial with their talents, however diversified and extraordinary, and work after originals still superior to their most favourite ideas of perfection'.[9] The question of quality was in fact problematic. As we saw with Domenichino, some Roman murals might have deteriorated, such that copying was particularly directed to the best preserved examples; moreover, access to works was by no means automatic, and even then it was often not possible to move paintings from dark locations to be able to copy them effectively.[10] In the early eighteenth century, Jonathan Richardson (senior) took this to extremes by arguing that English artists had no need to make the journey to Rome, because paintings in native collections were of a better quality and condition.[11] Even in France, the examples of Jouvenet and Lesueur, whose achievements were agreed to be impressive despite having failed to undertake Italian journeys, combined with the plentiful presence of excellent Italian art and antique sculptures, could be cited so as to question the need for an academic outpost in Rome.[12] But copying was also associated with a certain servility, either to the academic framework within which it was stipulated,[13] or to the merely mechanical business of faithfully recreating another artist's work. Joshua Reynolds, addressing his peers but referring to how students should organise their studies, called it 'a delusive kind of industry', which risked becoming almost an end in itself.[14]

In order to complete the image, it is not so much the drawing the artist is making which we need to imagine, but rather the motive and expectations which lie behind his intense gaze and studied draughtsmanship. The making of drawings after past art occurred for various reasons – for some a form of academic duty, but for more mature artists the opportunity to accumulate a valuable 'harvest' (*moisson*) which they would be able to exploit for the rest of their careers.[15] This sense of a process of learning and assimilation is a consequence of the veneration of Rome as the destination of an artistic pilgrimage. In one sense the essence of a pilgrimage is to complete the journey, to arrive. But in the case of Rome as the destination for hundreds of artists, travellers and tourists, it was what followed the crossing of a symbolic threshold which was more consequential. At root, drawings such as the one Robert shows us being made were the physical manifestation of a long-cherished compulsion to take possession of canonical images. To this extent, we can read Robert's drawing as providing an emblematic way into the somewhat elusive and amorphous notion of influence of art on artists. How are we to understand influence as being translated into forms of practice and response within the particular conditions of Rome in the eighteenth and nineteenth centuries?

When, in 1881, at the age of 40, Renoir went to Rome, the very sarcasm of his comments illustrates the durability of this scenario – but also its vulnerability to being taken for granted. He declared: 'I have suddenly become a traveller, and the fever to see the Raphaels has overcome me. I am in the process of swallowing my Italy'[16] – as if he was submitting to the taking of medicine. Yet he was all too conscious of the art-historical mechanism he was conforming to: 'I want to see the Raphaels Monsieur, the Ra, the Pha, the els. After that if anyone's not happy....I bet they'll say I have been influenced!'[17] Despite Renoir's dismissive tone, his remarks point to the way that influence was a cliché of artistic education, and Rome was its *locus classicus*.

In art-historical writing, influence has remained a commonplace if undertheorised notion which has been invoked to explain how art changes its nature according to the impact on artists of other art, thereby effecting some kind of mimetic adjustment or transformation. Yet, the way influence is used is more often obfuscatory than elucidatory, in so far as it is employed to describe the results of a purported interaction, rather than to account for how and why this might have taken place. This seems particularly to apply to the way assimilation of Italian Renaissance art was presumed to be not merely desirable but inevitable, premised on its innovative reputation.[18] It was for this reason that Michael Baxandall rightly denounced influence as a 'curse of art criticism'.[19] He argued that influence is habitually employed to imply that works of art themselves exert an active force, whereas the reverse is a more plausible way of understanding such interactions: being influenced is usually the result of conscious choice. In literary studies, encouraged by Harold Bloom's example in *The Anxiety of Influence*, the topic has had sustained attention.[20] Bloom provided the prime model for Norman Bryson, whose contribution to art-historical writing emerged out of a fertile and eclectic phase of Cambridge literary studies. In his revisiting of the canonical passage from David to Delacroix, Bryson adapted then current forms of literary theory to painting in order to give an account of tradition and its discontents. But, as Brian Grosskurth observed, his combination of semiotic and psychoanalytic methods ignores the textual specificity of Bloom's analysis, and fails to take account of the ways in which contemporary artists and commentators articulated and worked with and within the nature of tradition.[21] To this extent, despite the injection of new vocabulary into the conventional notion of influence, Bryson's account remains a matter of perspicacious decoding: the recognition of sources is essentially a way in to the symbolic labyrinth of Lacanian visuality.[22]

In some recent art-historical writing, the word itself seems to have become almost repressed, as if to engage with an outmoded concept risked being compromised by association with an embarrassingly untheorised concept.[23] In so far as influence has attracted the attention of cultural historians more generally, it has tended to be censorious. 'Influence' was singled out for criticism by Michel Foucault as one of the illusory 'unquestioned continuities' which helped to sustain the purported discursive unity of the history of ideas. For Foucault, this was one of a series of conventions which contributed to the propping up of a fundamentally bogus mode of historical analysis. The 'notion of influence', he remarked, connects 'individuals, œuvres, ideas or theories' in a way that is nothing less than 'magical', as if it operated on so fundamental a level of causality as not to require explanation – if not, indeed, to be beyond explanation.[24] Foucault's censure is particularly relevant to the historical study of art, music or literature, in which influence can be seen to do a lot of invisible work linking artists and artworks. Influence works in terms of a reciprocal process: the power of the image or object which exerts its influence, and the artist's vision or sensibility which absorbs this nourishment to fuel its transformation or reinvention. Influence leaves the figure of the artist in limbo, deprived of agency – unless this is understood as having been displaced onto the level of unconscious drive, or functioning like some irresistible osmotic – indeed automatic – mechanism. When an author or artist is unidentified, artworks become little more than transparently legible symptoms of the impact of a given influence: the common presence of a particular motif stands as evidence of broader patterns of contact or connectedness across time and space.

For artists in the eighteenth century, however, Italy was indeed a place of magic. In 1776, Thomas Jones wrote ecstatically of his discovery of the Roman countryside: 'Every scene seemed anticipated in some dream – It appeared Magick Land.'[25] Jones's 'dreams' were, of course, shaped as far as landscape painting was concerned by his schooling in Richard Wilson's classical prospects. For Stephen Weston, 'Rome, whither I shall suppose myself indued with magick enough to transport my reader, is the very soul of Italy for a virtuoso.'[26] Nowhere else could compare to Rome as an 'artistic paradise', declared Edward Lear.[27] The ailing David Wilkie purred at the experience of at last finding himself in 'a land of fancy and imagination'[28] – between the realm of the artist's creative mind and the spectacle by which he was surrounded, all barriers seem to have been dissolved. This sleight of hand whereby nature is almost miraculously made up of art seemed to offer an environment in which the artist had merely to open his eyes, and to absorb and record what lay revealed before him.

Rome's magical reputation makes it an ideal place to revisit the notion of influence. By virtue of its status as a key destination for artists who either aspired, or were required, to learn fundamental lessons from their forebears, the journey to and sojourn in Rome has generated an abundant literature. This allows us to analyse the relation between contemporary ideas of what influence was, how it was meant to work, and how it played out in practice, in terms of the experience of a wide range of individuals. Throughout our period, Rome sustained a reputation as a place of transformation which was at once biographical and artistic. By focusing on the lived experience of artists, and how this was transcribed into letters, journals, reports, essays and books, we are brought closer to a consideration of the environment within which these professional activities were played out. In opening out a reconsideration of influence in this way, we need first to take account of its climate, an extremely important aspect of Rome as a site for viewing and making art, which had a profound effect on the health and sensibility of its inhabitants, transient or permanent. Artistic taste might ebb and flow, but Rome's relentless climate spared nobody.

If Rome was a city uniquely blessed by its classical past and the surge of creativity which defined the Renaissance, it was also cursed with a disturbingly inconsistent climate and a well-founded reputation for being at times dangerously unhealthy. In the eighteenth and nineteenth centuries, Rome's climate was a matter of perplexing concern, because the benign effects of its mild winters and spring were compromised by excessive heat in the summer, and most damagingly by chronic outbreaks of fever in the autumn, attributed to the *mal'aria* which both caused and gave its name to this type of illness. Rome also bore the legacy of a once great civilisation which centuries before had withered and now survived in ruins scattered across the city and its *campagna*. Why Rome had such a contrary climate and hazardous propensity to infect its visitors, and whether this was the cause or consequence of the former empire's collapse, exercised historians, administrators and medical writers alike.

Rome had also acquired a reputation as one of the dirtiest cities in Europe, a condition which many held as being directly responsible for its appalling public health problems. Bearing this in mind, it seems entirely appropriate to think of Rome as a place where putting 'influence' into practice engaged different levels of experience, whether artistic inspiration or prophylactic self-preservation, but was always directly related to the physical condition of the city – its air, light, humidity, winds and general salubrity.

As we will see, the formulation of these ideas depended crucially on assumptions and observations about the idiosyncratic character of the Roman atmosphere, more specifically its air, and what caused the dramatic contrasts of benign and damaging qualities of which it was capable. What is particularly interesting is that scientific and cultural ideas about the nature and effects of the Roman climate share a considerable degree of common ground. On the one hand, we find that scientific discourses provide a model for theories of cultural creativity and differentiation; on the other, the vocabulary and metaphorical register of the language of science was well stocked with an eclectic array of cultural references, be they poetic quotations, or literary sources used as quasi-scientific evidence, or merely evidence of a struggle to find the right terminology with which to pin down phenomena which were intractably elusive.

In antiquity, influence had originally referred to the astrological theory that heavenly bodies determined climatic variation, which in turn acted upon the human body according to an individual's constitution, that is, their balance of humours (melancholic, phlegmatic, sanguine, choleric).[29] This meaning survived well into the eighteenth century, notably in medical usage;[30] at the same time there was a shift of emphasis towards a more physically focused, so to speak terrestrial, conception of the body's dependency on environment and climate.[31] Jean-Jacques Menuret de Chambaud's article on 'influence' in the *Encyclopédie* sets out clearly the move away from astrology and its mystifications towards the more solid ground of observable phenomena. This is exemplified in the attention he pays to the effects of the sun and moon on air, and therefore on health. He also argues for investigation of weather as a way of understanding more precisely the incidence of disease, following but refining the primordial precepts of Hippocrates.[32]

However, by the middle of the century, the Italian form of the term had acquired a pathological meaning with a specific Roman connection. The word 'influenza' achieved an international currency after a virulent epidemic in Rome in 1743;[33] thereafter it also came to mean disease in a general sense. It was not until the mid-nineteenth century that 'influenza' came to refer to a specific sort of disease.[34] In addition, influence was used metaphorically to point to a form of pathological collective behaviour, what the *Oxford English Dictionary* terms 'an attack of some general prostration'. Even Bloom, in his reinvention of poetry as the 'anxiety of influence', restricts the sphere within which influence operates to the entity of the individual writer, as they craft their prose and verse out of, or rather in spite of, the onerous residue of the past. But Bloom goes further and states, 'Influence is Influenza – an astral disease.' He almost paraphrases Goethe's 'Classic is health, Romantic sickness': 'If influence were health, who could write a poem? Health is stasis.'[35] The link between cultural influence and disease is reiterated in the second edition, whose preface he entitles 'the anxiety of contamination'.

It is revealing to compare the usage of influence with that of contagion – that is, at a time prior to the evolution of the modern medical sense of contagion – as this brings out the comparable spectrum of meanings, and therefore the contiguity of varied applications in different kinds of discourse.[36] The *Oxford English Dictionary* lists eight different meanings under contagion, but these essentially consist of two: the communication of disease and the metaphorical notion of infectiousness. As summed up by Gabriel-François Venel in the *Encyclopédie*, contagious diseases were those which were transmitted by some form of direct contact, or at one remove via clothes and furniture or other infected objects, or by means of the air which was able to carry 'miasmas or morbific seeds' over considerable distances. He observed that it was precisely this dimension which generated more elaborate ideas and spawned 'ingenious metaphors', by virtue of having no method of being disproved, a predicament which showed no sign of being resolved. Yet ultimately the 'first origin or the womb of miasmas' was as unknown as their nature.[37] Thus, contagion could be invoked while having no understanding of what it was that threatened to be transferred by contact. In early nineteenth-century medical discourse, a distinction was made between contagion and infection. As we will see later, the problem of Rome's 'bad air', which is central to this book, was usually not linked to contagion, in the sense of a disease which was likely to be passed from one person to another through close contact. The meaning given to infection fits better with the broadly environmental approach to 'bad air' as an ambient, social and inescapable phenomenon. In the early nineteenth century, Armstrong preferred to think in terms of infection, 'a local taint, or contamination of the air', external to the body, rather than contagion, which he equated with something originating from within the body; yet in both cases, he insisted on the elusiveness of 'the mode of primary generation'.[38]

Eighteenth-century medicine was not unique is relying on an eclectic repertoire of metaphors to offset its diagnostic limitations. Contagion as metaphor has a wide range (and has been the subject of many recent studies).[39] For example, Hume, in his discussion of climate and its possible role in shaping manners, treats contagion as something social: 'The human mind is of a very imitative nature; nor is it possible for any set of men to converse often together, without acquiring a similitude of manners, and communicating to each other their vices as well as virtues.' That is, it is a matter of process, not of taste or moral choice: 'The propensity of company and society is strong in all rational creatures; and the same disposition, which gives us this propensity, makes us enter deeply into each other's sentiments, and causes like passions and inclinations to run, as it were, by contagion through the whole club or knot of companions.'[40] The 'as it were' signals Hume's consciousness of the different meaning he is giving to contagion: something not harmful, but rather a more neutral mode of transmission, like disease only in as much as it is to do with an experience which, for better or worse, cannot be resisted. The related term infection shares this ambiguous usage; James Elmes expressed the complete degree of identification between Poussin and his prime artistic model by observing that 'the air of antiquity which breathed over all his works seemed to have infected even his person and his features'.[41]

In art language, however, the link to disease is usually accentuated to make censure explicit. Thus, the abbé Leblanc, writing in 1753 of the bad example of Borromini in seventeenth-century architecture, conceived of taste and style in terms of epidemic and remedy: 'In a time when the contagion had become almost universal, were we not obliged to certain artists of a happier and wiser genius finally to have returned us to true taste, which is that of the antique?'[42] Charles-Nicholas Cochin (who had a more qualified attitude to the antique as model), writing in the 1770s, warned against succumbing to the potentially dangerous 'contagious' manner of Pompeo Batoni and Anton Raphael Mengs.[43] For de Staël, the beauties of Italian poets had been fostered by language, climate and imagination, circumstances which could not be recreated elsewhere, 'whereas their faults are very contagious', which should be a matter of concern for visiting artists.[44] Evoking the corrupt nature of artistic imitation in the second half of the seventeenth century, Quatremère de Quincy claimed that only landscape painting had preserved its purity and was free from the prevailing general 'contagion'.[45] Consistent with this medicalised conception of artistic propriety, in 1796 the continued existence of the Académie de France in Rome was urged, despite the comprehensive abolition of royal academies, so as to safeguard the French School from becoming mannered, dessicated and impoverished. Government rewards directed at artists studying in Paris were not enough to ensure this: 'The preventative as the models are beyond the Alps.'[46] However, by the mid-nineteenth century, the Académie de France itself could be considered to be inimical to the authentic experience of Roman art. In 1851, Pierre Petroz complimented Ernest Hébert on the robustness of his artistic temperament, which had protected him from being overcome by 'the stupifying influence of the Villa Medici'.[47] Viewed from across the Channel, French art could be identified as a source of disease. Reviewing the state of British art in the early nineteenth century, in 1841 Benjamin Robert Haydon judged, 'We escaped the contagion of David's brickdust which infected the continent, and the [Nazarenes'] frescoes at Munich are but a branch of the same Upas tree.'[48]

Rome itself was so to speak on the receiving end of contagion, in so far as, in the opinion of Hester Piozzi, 'the rage for antiquities' seemed to have spread its 'contagion' over northern peoples, the same ones who had destroyed the city centuries earlier, but who had now succumbed to this rampant modern malady.[49] And Byron found even the prospect of entering Rome distasteful because of the surfeit of tourists who were busy debasing the élite preserve of the Grand Tour, rendering the city 'pestilential with English' – a social and cultural affliction to which he had no immunity.[50]

The viability and power of the metaphoric register of contagion takes on a more specific and powerful meaning when we consider eighteenth-century ideas concerning the nature of disease and its transmission, more specifically with regard to the presence and impact of one of the most distinctive ingredients in the Roman environment – 'bad air'. Moreover, in so far as contagion implies a sense of physical contact, all its inherited ambiguity in terms of risk of disease informs accounts of direct physical engagement with the fabric of the city and its topographical setting. If the exhilaration of arrival was habitually expressed in gestures of literally embracing the Eternal City and taking hold of it – whether clambering over monuments, fondling statues[51] or picking up antique fragments – in doing so travellers also exposed themselves to the lurking threat of infection from the Roman environment. Indeed, for many commentators the allure of antiquities, monuments and the superabundant array of artistic riches was only incompletely capable of disguising the degree to which the city was dirty and unhygienic. This ambiguity could result in a disturbingly polarised state of mind and body, oscillating between fascination and repulsion.[52]

A review of narratives of arrival and encounter suggests that it was more normal for visitors to experience disarray and crisis than to saunter in a state of untroubled or self-congratulatory enthusiasm amongst Rome's ruins and artworks. In part this has to do with the sheer burden of expectation weighing upon those who set out to experience at first hand Rome's unrivalled riches. On the one hand, the profusion of things to see and the difficulty to resist the impulse to see as much as possible as quickly as possible engendered disorienting overload. On the other hand, Rome was surprisingly, not to say shockingly, messy and decrepit. Considering the vicissitudes of arrival and the *Sturm und Drang* engendered by the obligation to make sense of the city leads to an exploration of the significant role played by the physical environment in altering states of mind and body. Chief amongst the factors which were held to be responsible for the impact of environmental conditions was climate, at once a general predisposing envelope and a particularised local equilibrium.

Rome's climate turns out to be extremely important precisely because it was challengingly problematic. It was an object of debate as to whether or not it should be held to be responsible for the decline of the great city of antiquity. Was the local climate so inhospitable as to have eventually undermined the city's vast expanse of prosperous and magnificent buildings? Or was it the historical decline of the Roman Empire which had led to the neglect and deterioration of the environment? And yet, travellers also bear witness to a belief that Rome's atmosphere must have contained some special ambient factor which had stimulated the remarkable artistic achievements which were everywhere to be seen. Based on prevailing medical ideas of the central importance of air as an expression of the particular combination of local conditions, which in turn shaped physical constitution and character, Roman air was presumed to contain some magical artistically inspirational ingredient.

However, as historians of the decline of Roman civilisation had recognised, the city had also long been home to 'bad air'. This has had a curiously uneven historiography. In writings on Rome by local commentators and travellers, the problem of bad air was so chronic that it provoked long-running discussion on its causes and nature. Yet the failure to establish its identity and therefore to reduce or remedy its noxious presence at times gave it the status of a banal if disagreeable phenomenon. To the extent that it was a staple aspect of a visit to Rome, it lost some of its threatening reputation. Nonetheless, in terms of medical accounts, there is a clear sense that local commentators sought to claim bad air as a contingent problem, and to refute the too easily recycled accusation that it was in some way inherent to the city and its surrounding countryside. Whatever its causes, bad air impinged in numerous ways on the experience of the city, and on the business of viewing artworks and antiquities. I try to show how pervasive this problem was and the various ways it feeds into the mindsets and behaviour of Roman visitors, in ways which are developed further in chapters 5 and 6, where the repercussions for making art in and of the city and its *campagna* are pursued.

Rome was approached via the *campagna*, a zone which was thought of as being continuous with the city in several respects. The neglected state of the *campagna* was blamed as one of the principal sources of bad air, but it was also revered as the site of inspiration par excellence for landscape painters in search of a beauty at once ideal and palpable, antique and contemporary. As much as anything, the *campagna* was described as empty; this strange and to outsiders unanticipated absence of life and incident encouraged more than it deterred imagined scenes of past prosperity and idyll. The city, by contrast, not only suffered from an excess of accumulated artistic objects and sites, but these had become enveloped in a combination of the detritus of centuries and less august quotidian rubbish. Together, these had the effect of blocking and frustrating the access and movement of visitors, not just by being a physical impediment, but also because of the stench from a lack of sanitation. Influence as an abstract idea turns out to require a degree of endurance and tolerance when negotiating a decrepit and unsavoury urban fabric. Like the *campagna*, the city's labyrinthine old streets obliged visitors to put their resolve to the test, as they sought close contact with monuments and artworks without succumbing to contagion from years of encrusted filth.

2

SUCCUMBING TO ROME

From the sixteenth century until the later nineteenth century, Rome held a talismanic place in the European and later North American imagination as a destination of artistic pilgrimage. Papal largesse had made Rome a dynamic international entrepôt, attracting artists and architects in search of work, training and fame. Viewed from the eighteenth century, and in terms of increasingly elaborate art-historical perspectives, Rome took on a double importance as home to incomparable antique remains – many of which had emerged from or were still embedded in its ground – and some of the most revered modern artistic masterpieces, which had been made in and remained an integral part of the fabric of the city. The belief that Rome was the most valuable site for artists' study, at once fundamental and advanced, was systematised by the spread of academies in the later eighteenth century. From 1666, French artists had been able to compete for the Prix de Rome, which brought with it an extended period in the Académie de France. As *pensionnaires* of the king, they were expected to perfect their art through study, a cornerstone of which was the copying of examples of important art, before returning as accomplished artists to practise in France.[1] In these terms, the experience of Rome was less a matter of individual experiment and negotiation than sharing in a collective duty. Such identification of the individual artist and the institution was later to be highly productive of tension, conflict and divergent views on the independence of the artist. Rome's reputation as a place of transformation was sufficiently inclusive that it could be considered an essential element in ensuring proper academic progress, and also as offering a means to escape from such prescribed orthodoxy.

Yet already at the beginning of the eighteenth century, the idea of Rome as an unequalled repository of historic masterworks became intensified, insofar as contemporary Italian artistic life was recognised to be no more than a shadow of its former self. In 1708, Poerson, director of the French Académie, judged that Rome's reputation only survived through the works of dead artists.[2] Foreign artists were more inclined to think of themselves as timely successors to a faltering tradition, remedy for which was to be found through study of the antique, and less likely to seek guidance from leading Italian masters.[3] A version of this in the mid-nineteenth century was Beavington Atkinson's

FACING PAGE: Henry Fuseli, *The Artist in Despair before the Remains of Antiquity*, detail of fig. 6.

claim that Italy was only just capable of sustaining a 'school of Art, especially in sculpture, which neither malaria can kill, the stiletto stab, nor tyranny extinguish'. Whatever it was that had elicited great achievements in times past had faded: contemporary circumstances combined to stifle native artistic creativity. In Beavington Atkinson's review of the Italian showing at the 1862 International Exhibition, the spectacle of these latecomers elicited 'a world of sympathy' rather than admiration.[4] Of course, this was never anything other than a matter for polemical assertion and rebuff, in past commentaries as in contemporary art history.[5] An extreme form of such scepticism was the rejection of the benefits of travel, specifically to Italy. In Britain, champions of sedentary chauvinism were not in short supply.[6]

An Italian visit was equally desirable for those non-artists who aspired to underwrite their authority as arbiters of taste – or at least to be conversant with what passed for taste. In the age of the Grand Tour, and with the expansion of tourism that followed the end of the Napoleonic wars, the experience became a stock subject for authorship. What had been refined in the mid-eighteenth century as a specialised digest of sites defined by the presence of works of art which were allocated varying degrees of approval and intended for the guidance of professional artists and their patrons, as in C. N. Cochin's *Voyage*, was adapted to the more abbreviated forms of guidebook which proliferated in the early nineteenth century.[7] Reading others' accounts, as well as resorting to more programmatic guidebooks or pretending to abjure them, was an integral part of the idea of travelling. More generally, the myth of Italy was recycled and transformed in several hundred published texts, as well as in correspondence and private accounts.[8] Indeed, the idea of travel became almost inseparable from the act of writing about it, or more precisely the idea of writing about it. Before setting foot in Italy, Stendhal inscribed a notebook 'A TOUR THROUGH SOME PARTS OF ITALY IN THE YEAR 1811', ready to receive his *récit de voyage*.[9] As a matter of course, Edward Gibbon had prepared himself in similar fashion, but his travel journal ran out of steam in Florence, and then remained entirely blank once he encountered Rome.[10] Clearly, there was something about the encounter with Rome which seemed to choke the flow of touristic notation. Nonetheless, whether in the itineraries of world-weary Romantic *littérateurs*, or the most unreflecting of tourists embarking on a routine trip to the Warm South, Rome's aura as an essential destination was remarkably enduring.

THE BURDEN OF EXPECTATION

A measure of the power of Rome's cultural authority was the degree to which it could be disablingly inhibiting. This is nowhere more clearly evident than in remarks made in anticipation of the journey. An Italian journey, centred on Rome, was the fulfilment of a long-nurtured ambition at once individual and collective – in the case of younger artists, they would have absorbed from their seniors a mixture of treasured recollections or a frustrated sense of inadequacy from not having made the trip. As long as it remained an imaginary destination, consciousness of not having been there could acquire a pathological degree of intensity. For Benjamin Robert Haydon, the prospect of a journey was intimidatingly disturbing: 'A Tour of Italy seems on the whole to unhinge the mind.' The fact that Rome was a place 'in which the greatest human efforts…now lie in ruins creates a melancholy sensation of the futility of all human attempt.'[11] When Auguste Creuzé de Lesser contemplated a visit to Italy, he was disturbed by 'an involuntary shudder, a sort of mysterious discomfort'. Later he reflected that his intense expectations had only been exorcised once he had arrived in Rome itself: 'It was necessary to enter Rome for us to be healed of Rome.'[12] Looking back on his 'Italian journey', Goethe finally felt able to admit to the crippling combination of anticipation and inadequacy his not having been to Italy had produced: 'Now, at last, I can confess a secret mania of mine. For many years I did not dare look into a Latin author or anything which evoked an image of Italy. If it happened by chance, I suffered agonies.'[13] Such anguished equivocation regarding the status of Italy as at once alien but indispendable survived into the later nineteenth century. Hans von Marees confessed to Adolf von Hildebrand in 1872: 'How great my longing for Italy is, I cannot even explain, but I am aware that in this longing there is something pathological. Italy is, as it were, within us, and until we are able to express it in a clear way for others, we cannot hope to find inner peace.'[14]

Henry Fuseli left two drawings which illustrate his complex and turbulent feelings about Rome. The better-known image is usually given the title 'The artist in despair before the remains of antiquity'. However, this is a twentieth-century title, and would be better replaced by a description which acknowledges the play on words which is being illustrated, albeit that it expresses profound anxieties. Given that the artist changed his name from 'Füssli', meaning 'little foot', to Fuseli after arriving in Rome, the image is more convincingly read as an emblematic illustration of the sense of crushing inferiority he experienced having arrived in the city; the etiolated and melancholy figure seated, as if in a state of subjection, by the giant foot of Constantine in the Capitoline museums is humbled and rendered sightless by his monumental neighbour (fig. 6). This personalised reading of the drawing should surely take precedence over the more familiar one focused on generic neoclassical reverence for antiquity, as expressed in the modern title.[15] Fuseli was later to paraphrase the predicament shown in his drawing in a Royal Academy lecture on 'Invention': 'an idea of genius borrowed by mediocrity, tears all associate shreds, it is the giant's thumb by which the pigmy offered the measure of his own littleness.'[16]

Fuseli's other drawing corresponds to his departure from Rome (fig. 7). In 1778, writing from Lugano to James Northcote to apologise for not having stayed in Rome to meet him, Fuseli explained the extreme emotions it caused: 'What would have been friendly to you would have been death to me; and self-preservation is the first duty of the eighteenth century. Madness lies on the road I must think over to come at you; and at the sound of Rome, my heart swells, my eye kindles and frenzy seizes me.'[17] In the

6   Henry Fuseli, *The Artist in Despair before the Remains of Antiquity*, 1778–80, red chalk and sepia wash, 42 × 35.2 cm. Kunsthaus, Zurich, inv. no. 1940/144.

7 Henry Fuseli, *Caricature of the Artist leaving Italy*, 1778, pen and ink, 24.5 × 19.3 cm. Kunsthaus, Zurich, inv. no. 1938/668.

drawing which accompanied this letter he shows himself in the guise of a contorted colossus who shits on Switzerland, having already deposited a turd upon France; England is inhabited by mice labelled 'B. West', 'Romney', 'Oz Humphry'; above, a winged phallus, implicitly detached from the artist's loins, takes flight for Italy. Italy is the land of visceral destabilisation, activating a new state of being in which physical lust and intellectual yearning are intertwined. That Fuseli is able to reinvent himself in the image of a revered antique model does nothing to dilute the memory of Rome as the site of profound personal transformation: his chosen alter ego is the Laocoön, the archetype of epic suffering.[18]

DREAMS

Symptomatic of the power of attraction exerted by Rome is the variety of dream metaphors it spawned, as if the conscious image of the city as a repository of great art was accompanied by a more profound undercurrent of fantasy and uncertainty. The sculptor John Gibson felt that to journey to Rome, 'the great University of sculpture', was his destiny. 'Rome was ever in my thoughts, and I became harassed by anxiety, and often passed sleepless nights.' A dream provided an emblematic prefiguration of the achievement of his longings: 'I was wandering in solitary isolation when a colossal eagle darted down upon me, and took me up in the air' – Rome was conceived of as existing in another, higher dimension.[19]

On the eve of arrival, dreams of Rome were experienced with renewed intensity. Charles Dupaty had the not unfamiliar experience of arriving late at night, and having to wait for daylight to reveal to him the city he had longed to see. He described himself as being assailed in his fitful sleep by the concert of ideas that attached to Rome: 'Centuries, emperors, nations, all that this vast word Rome contains of greatness, the imposing, the interesting, the frightening, emerged successively, or at the same time, and surrounded my soul.'[20] So strange was the kaleidoscopic dream experienced by James Johnson after his first day of sightseeing that he characterised it as a 'Dervise' vision.[21] Sir Humphrey Davy's 'Vision', reports J.J. Tobin, who accompanied him on the travels which he hoped would restore his shattered health, was based on a dream he had had in which he found himself borne through the firmament from planet to planet. He recalled that the dream was a consequence of 'a highly interesting and animated conversation that he had held with two friends in the Colosseum at Rome, on the grandeur and decay of nations and the mutability of religions'.[22] In Davy's dream, the great ruin has become an emblematic space for a kind of transcendant and therapeutic imagery.

If such Roman dreams were little more than a figure of speech, they were no less metaphorically potent. On arrival, 'dreams' were tested by physical encounter. In 1817, Franz Horny expressed his pleasure at the unblemished beauty of the Roman *campagna* by calling it a 'genuine dreamland'.[23] But the discrepancy between expected ideal and mundane reality sometimes left artists and travellers in a state of bewildered denial. Heading south towards Rome, the painter François-Marius Granet dismissed the first Italian towns he entered as lacking any correspondence with 'the noble Italy we had been dreaming of with much relish'.[24] Yet, in his advice to a young artist about to depart for Rome, Charles-Nicolas Cochin, engraver and author of an influential *Voyage d'Italie* (1758), wrote reassuringly that, although Italian art could take on the forbidding dimensions of 'a frightening phantom' while envisaged in Paris, once on Italian soil it seemed considerably less intimidating. When Italian painters' works were seen in broad daylight they were proved to be mere mortals – not only could they be observed to make mistakes, but the art they produced offered a healthy diversity of manner, which encouraged a reassuring idea of comradely parity such that 'one could have been one of these masters, each according to their inclination'.[25] Indeed, at the turn of the eighteenth and nineteenth centuries, in one respect Italian art was genuinely becoming a shadow of its former self, in the sense of succumbing to a process of physical deterioration. Charlotte Eaton found only 'the vestiges of the matchless frescoes of Domenichino and Guido – The spectres of painting, "the ghosts of what they were"'.[26] Approaching Rome from Palestrina, John Middleton's mind overflowed with ideas of ancient Rome, but the remains he saw around him had almost 'crumbled into dust'; as he passed through the Porta Maggiore, he 'awoke as from a dream of the past'.[27] When Edward Gibbon arrived in Rome, he found that the image he had acquired from books 'fell infinitely short' of the reality he encountered; he passed into a dream state – a 'dream of antiquity'.[28] Such an association of Rome with a dream state was also a way of remembering the city: on his departure Degas surveyed the *campagna* and fixed in his mind an image of 'the Italy of our dreams! Yellow plain, corn cut – mountains grey with night falling at their feet, hazy mountains truly azure blue....'[29]

Yet insisting on Rome as occupying an otherworldly state could attract criticism precisely for the way this occluded proper observation. Thus, Winckelmann chided superficial students of antique sculpture who believed that the lack of an artist's name on a statue meant it was from a later period: this, he retorted, 'was only thought by people who saw Rome in their dreams or, like youthful travellers, in a month' – the two being on a par in his judgement.[30] But, even once in Rome, the willingness to follow prescribed itineraries rendered the state of reverie into which visitors liked to believe they found themselves more of a cliché than a mind-expanding experience. As Walter Benjamin drily observed: 'Does not dreaming itself follow well-trodden paths in Rome?'[31]

Experience of the city was strongly associated with the oneiric and otherworldly. When Granet at last arrived, he was taken off by moonlight to visit the Pantheon and Coliseum, where he and his companions wandered 'like shades', as if having entered an otherworldly realm.[32] Madame de Staël, prefiguring *Corinne*, liked Rome at night and by moonlight above all because of the way such conditions seemed to reanimate the city's antique identity: 'Everything which intrudes upon the Antique is stilled and the ruins reassert themselves.'[33] As Thomas Jones explored the *campagna*, he seemed to have left ordinary reality behind and be living a dream with which he had long been familiar.[34] Such reference to dreams and phantoms might seem to be a cliché, but they also point to a recognition that the desire to see Rome could be so powerful that it interfered with rational, conscious thought, and indeed spectatorial sangfroid.

Another traveller who dreamt of Rome at the very end of the nineteenth century before setting foot there was Sigmund Freud. Freud had been a regular visitor to Italy, but persistently postponed going to Rome, despite his intense desire to do so, and his expectation that it might stimulate his scientific thinking. As he wrote to Wilhelm Fliess in 1899: 'Learning the eternal laws of life in the Eternal City would be no bad combination.'[35] He recognised that his delay in visiting Rome was 'deeply neurotic': 'The wish to go to Rome had become in my dream life a cloak and a symbol for a number of other passionate wishes.'[36] Following Freud's own analysis of his Roman dreams, his avoidance of the city was tied up with his unresolved wish to free himself from the shadow of his father, and also his as yet unconfirmed belief that he was on the verge of a profound discovery.[37] Only once these obstacles had been resolved did the road to Rome lie open.

The importance invested in the encounter with Rome is expressed in the way the moment of physical or geographical arrival is described as equivalent to the crossing of a threshold. Beyond this threshold lay the promise of experiencing at first hand an array of long-venerated objects and images which were expected to be the means to achieving artistic initiation and fulfilment. Such ideas were intertwined with the moment of actual entry into Italy itself. Noel Humphreys lamented the at times comical 'spontaneous devotion paid to the first sod of Italian soil, which [the traveller] is so anxious to reach that he cannot enjoy the present'. He describes a party of young Englishmen, visiting the St Bernard pass, who 'forgot their becoming admiration' when told that the Italian frontier was no more than one hundred yards away: 'They rushed forward, passed the boundary mark, and were in – Italy, and though knee-deep in snow, and surrounded by dense grey atmosphere that frequently shrouds the summits of the Alps, imagined a moderated temperature and purer air – it was actually Italy; and there is a magic in the name alone, that, to an ardent imagination, fills out the dreams of genial climate and cerulean skies.'[38]

CROSSING THE *CAMPAGNA*

Crossing the *campagna* was as much a symbolic transition as a practical matter of accomplishing the final leg of a journey. As John Shearman noted, one version of this was the way Raphael's Villa Madama was used as a staging post prior to formal entries for important visitors, a ritual which carried over into purely artistic journeys.[39] As applied to Rome's surrounding *campagna*, the perception of having reached a transformative threshold also acquired a spiritual significance. A pious visitor like the young Florence Nightingale might accentuate the sense of an itinerant vigil about to reach its climax: 'In the dark – the earth was sending forth her fragrance of night like an incense to heaven, for the Campagna is covered with thyme – the stars were all out – there was a solemn silence, not a trace of habitation, all desert solitude, and we were feverish and very tired, which increased the likeness of the Valley of the Shadow [of Death].'[40]

For most northerners the final stage of the road to Rome led across what, since the sixteenth century, had become the bleak landscape of the *campagna*. The area had for long been depopulated because of malaria; it also had a bad reputation for bandits.[41] In the earlier eighteenth century, employing an empirical spirit of observation, Charles de Brosses had asked rhetorically: 'Do you know what this famous campagna is? It is a prodigious and relentless quantity of small, sterile, barren hills, absolutely deserted, sad and horrible to the last degree.'[42] The bleakness of the *campagna* was perhaps emphasised in order to dramatise the sudden revelation of the first sight of the city. 'It is impossible', wrote Chateaubriand, 'for me to tell you what one feels, when Rome appears suddenly in the middle of its empty realms....it has the air of having risen for you, from the tomb in which it lay.'[43] 'Empty realms' nicely expresses the political vacuum felt to exist in Rome at this time, and also the opportunity it gave to articulate commentators such as Chateaubriand to fill this space with their own imaginative inventions or memories.

Berlioz was one of many to recount his moment of visual encounter with Rome by means of the insouciant intermediary of the coachman: 'The *vetturino* said to me all of a sudden with a nonchalant air, while pouring himself a glass of wine: "Ecco Roma signore" [There is Rome, sir]. And without turning, he showed me with his finger the cross of St Peter's. These few words effected in me a total revolution; I do not know how to express the trouble, the sense of being gripped, which the distant view of the eternal city caused in me, in the midst of this immense desolate and bare plain....In my eyes everything became great, poetic sublime.'[44] Helped by his blasé coachman, Berlioz rehearsed the ritual of Roman revelation, willingly succumbing to a transformation of his state of mind and physical alertness before he set eyes upon the city itself. Such conventional stories of the thrill of contact acquired a poignant irrecoverability once the city was cleansed and modernised in the later nineteenth century. Thus, Augustus Hare, the editions of whose *Walks in Rome* chronicle the city's progressive expansion, its many new buildings, and the scrubbing of old ones, included a section on 'Arrival in Rome' in the form of a catalogue of such expostulations, in order to underline that they were no longer merited.[45]

Yet, as the doctor Jean-Baptiste Michel observed, a state of being overcome created an ambiguous substitution: everything about Rome 'commands enthusiasm' and 'forces admiration', but this had the effect of disguising or compensating for 'the realities which are lacking'.[46] Whether considered from the point of view of the provision of practical necessities or the less tangible behaviour of sensibilities and imaginations, arriving in Rome was comprehensively destabilising. Paillot de Montabert, who had 'sighed...for a long time after Italy, this promised land of the artist', resolved to travel to Rome from

America to seek out 'the mysteries of art'. Arriving at last after a long and perilous transatlantic voyage, at the sight of the city's walls, he fainted.[47] As recounted by Carpentier, it is precisely the ambiguity as to whether Paillot's collapse was merely a matter of physical exhaustion, or rather a form of ecstatic shock, which illustrates the intense but troubled nature of Rome's reputation. Certainly, other travellers gave precedence to more sinister dimensions of the city's reputation. Dr Bérard noted, almost approvingly, how 'most of those who arrive at Rome's threshold only do so trembling, forewarned by I know not what antagonistic voice which accuses the holy city of being a perpetual seat of fever and death!'[48]

Travellers' itineraries varied – some made a hurried descent to Rome, some worked their way thoroughly down the peninsula, others approached via Naples.[49] Whichever route they took, few arrived in pristine condition. The abbé Barthélemy described the 'excess of inconceivable exhaustion' brought on by the hot sun, dust and lack of sleep on his journey to Rome. Nonetheless, having achieved his goal, he congratulated himself on his resilience, impressed by this evidence of how intensely he desired to reach his destination: 'But nothing discourages me; I feel as if I would go to the end of the world if need be.'[50] Florence Nightingale performed a ritual cleansing – 'scoured myself, and cleansed myself from the dust of many days' – once she arrived to prepare for her first visit to St Peter's.[51]

So eager was Charles Dupaty to set eyes upon Rome that he was unable to focus properly on what was, at last, before him: 'I had to begin by wandering from one side to the other, to get rid of this initial impatience to see [everything], which always prevented me from looking.'[52] Delécluze self-deprecatingly recalled the slightly ridiculous aspect of his initial deflation: 'In the morning I had desired too intensely to arrive in Rome, for my impressions to be able to retain their freshness. I entered the suburb of this city as I would have crossed Passy.'[53] Indeed, after four days, he had still not come to terms with the place, and found the city 'a chaos…of admirable things and very ugly objects, of monuments from every century', whose debris appeared like 'different layers of earth which time and natural revolutions had accumulated on the surface of the globe'.[54]

DISENCHANTMENT

Such a high pitch of anticipation was bound to lead to cases of disenchantment and a consequent disorientation. Statements of surprise that the charisma expected of great cities had failed to materialise were commonly intended to puncture overinflated reputations, and are hardly exclusive to Rome. Jean-Jacques Rousseau, for example, notoriously exploited this strategy in his recollection of arriving in Paris; his terse reaction signalled a resolute rejection of the false gods of metropolitan culture.[55] Others recorded the tiresome impediment of obligatory passage through customs which interrupted the anticipated transition of entering into the spectacle of Rome. Stendhal warned that the first sentiment likely to be experienced in Rome was not 'divine enthusiasm' but impatience at this bureaucratic obstacle.[56]

The idea that Rome's treasures had been entombed by layers of modern dross was a common way of explaining the confusing first impression of the city, in which antiquities were found to be encumbered, if not wholly obscured, by modern accretions. The laments for Rome's lost greatness with which French Renaissance humanists had greeted the modern city they actually found as the culmination of their journeys was echoed in the eighteenth century by Dupaty: 'No, this city, this is not Rome; it is its corpse; this countryside, where it sits, is its tomb; and this populace, which swarms in its midst, worms which devour it.'[57] The motif of the tomb is linked with two related themes: the necessity of seeing beyond contemporary decrepitude and imaginatively summoning up or resurrecting a picture of ancient Rome in its prime, and the suggestion that Roman antiquities were still in some mysterious but palpable sense animate. However, by the mid-nineteenth century, Théophile Gautier was of the view that all Italy was an 'ossuary of dead cities', disconnected from the redemptive presence of antiquity's life-giving force,[58] a sentiment reiterated by Marinetti in the 1909 Futurist manifesto, where he denounced Italy's 'numberless museums that covered her like so many graveyards'.[59] An artist such as Frederic Leighton, whose Roman experience failed to live up to expectations, condemned the city as 'the grave of art'.[60]

Rome was bound to seem unsettling if visitors actually found themselves carried away by a desire to see everything while in a state of exhaustion. Yet precisely such a transition seems almost to have been a form of initiation rite for newcomers to the Académie de France.[61] Having arrived already fatigued by his journey, Vien was immediately dragged off by his confrères to see the sights, with the consequence that he promptly collapsed. The ensuing indisposition was only alleviated by a spell of recuperation outside the city, away from the dangerously excessive lure of Rome's hallowed works of art.[62] When Prud'hon arrived in Rome in 1785, he was seized on by Gagneraux, 'who made us run at full pelt the whole day long, such that in three days we had seen all Rome and most of its churches'.[63] In 1818, Léopold Robert wrote to his friend Brandt that, having arrived in Rome, he could not stay still and ran everywhere.[64] Stendhal had observed that, during their first days in Rome, tourists tended 'to run like children towards everything which seemed curious to them'.[65] Of his first day in Rome on 28 June 1803, Chateaubriand no less, wrote simply: 'I was running the whole day.'[66] Gasping for epistolary breath, Henry James exclaimed: 'At last – for the first time – I live! It beats everything....I went reeling and moaning thro' the streets, in a fever of enjoyment.'[67] The abrupt transition from Rome as imaginary pilgrimage destination to a palpable environment clearly induced an accelerated rush of experience both physical and psychological.

From the security of Paris, Saint-Yves recommended the salutary effects of what he called 'the intoxication of the marvels of Italy', but *in situ* this state of exhaltation was frequently as debilitating as it was disturbing for the artists concerned.[68] Stendhal described this state as follows: 'Where to find words to depict the perfect happiness savoured with delight and insatiably by a sensitive soul until reaching a state of annihilation and madness?'[69] It was perhaps easier for non-artists to revel in a liberating sense of spectatorial gratification, since they were not obliged to clear their minds and restore a sense of calm suitable for the more humdrum business of making artworks. However, in *Middlemarch*, George Eliot describes how intensely but perplexingly Dorothea was overcome by a surge of feelings: 'All this vast wreck of ambitious ideas, sensuous and spiritual, mixed confusedly with the signs of breathing forgetfulness and degradation, at first jarred her as with an electric shock, and then urged themselves on her with that ache belonging to a glut of confused ideas which check the flow of emotion.'[70]

For Viollet-le-Duc Rome was 'a tremendous stimulant' – addictive and engendering a hyperactivity that threatened to seriously damage health.[71] In order to evoke the physical and mental exhilaration that he had experienced in Rome, Viollet compared this to a 'fever of art', but one to which he nonetheless willingly submitted as it was 'so fecund in progress'. Viollet also likened his Roman sojourn to 'an interior tempest, indeed cruel and violent',[72] and suggested that the experience was 'a terrible cauldron from which one must emerge pure' – a kind of purifying trial by endurance.[73] He was all the more ruefully bemused to find himself eventually overcome by 'a stupefaction, a complete self-debasement', as he had conscientiously prepared himself for his Roman experience by studying antiquities and ancient and modern history.[74] Considered in this way, a phase of disequilibrium was endured as a necessary rite of passage from which artists ought to emerge purged of ingrained habits, with nonetheless the risk that they might find themselves dangerously demoralised. The history painter Julien de Parme had recounted a similar giddiness and six months of debilitating indecision after his arrival in 1760.[75]

Rome presented a dilemma to Joseph Wright. He had in part hoped a Roman sojourn would improve his health, but the 'salutary' climate's effects were offset by the unmanageable state of hyperactivity which he experienced: 'My attention and application [are] continually engaged with the amazing and stupendous remains of antiquity; and so numerous are they, that one can scarce move a foot but the relics of some stupendous works present themselves.'[76] Yet, the following year, as he reluctantly prepared to leave, he reflected on the mixture of inadequacy and self-injury which Rome had provoked: 'Notwithstanding, I have been very industrious, more so perhaps than has been consistent with my health, yet shall I leave many things that I covet much to have.'[77]

When in Rome, George Romney devoted himself to 'intense and sequestered study' to such a degree that his biographer William Hayley imputed 'those deplorable infirmities, that over-clouded the evening of his day, to his great want of … self-command'. Although he was 'very singularly addicted to that honorable yet perilous, kind of intemperance, the intemperance of study!' and 'avoided all farther intercourse with his travelling companion, and with all the other artists of his country, who were then studying in Rome', he yet made himself aware of their 'proper professional conduct'. Ironically, this included Joseph Wright, who, as we have seen, had his own Roman health problems. According to Romney, Wright 'had laid the foundations of those cruel nervous sufferings which afflicted his later years, by excess of application during his residence at Rome'.[78]

It is revealing to compare this propensity to overwork with the measured approach employed by more mature and grounded artists such as Turner and Ingres. Turner notoriously refused to give his address to anyone when he finally arrived in Rome in 1819, and exhaustively surveyed the city and its countryside, accumulating several hundred drawings.[79] Writing to his prospective father-in-law, M. Forestier, Ingres sought to convey a picture of himself as methodical but above all selective, both in the interests of professional productivity but also as a necessary means to avoid being overwhelmed: 'There is probably much to profit from in Rome, but I have my own scale of beauty which allows me to accept or leave aside a thing as beautiful or not, which means that the extracts that I am making here will be less numerous but judiciously chosen. But I always hope to come away with a fine harvest. Up to now, I have not done much, and it is impossible to do otherwise: without this, one would work without discernment and all to no purpose. The beauties of all types are here one on top of another and one is numbed from looking; only little by little does one recover from astonishment and see well.'[80]

SEEING CLEARLY

According to Charles-Nicolas Cochin, if the reputation of Italian old master and antique art had been intimidatingly exaggerated in Paris, based on the esteem given to revered but remote artists and their works, once in Italy it became clear that these hallowed figures from the past could be approached on a more accessibly human scale. Rather than having unswervingly maintained an impeccable academic rectitude, they could be seen to have moved between different styles with uneven success. To this extent, artists' experience of finding themselves on classic soil could have the result of liberating them from a state of inhibiting apprehension.[81] This certainly was one fundamental justification for making the journey. In the view of André Thouin, writing of his 1796 trip, the special effects of Italy were not only to enable artists' sensibilities to awaken, but also to qualify them to discriminate between authentic works of antiquity and bogus local artistic distractions: 'Having left France without knowing either the sites or the productions of their own country, seduced on arriving by Italian charlatanism as much as by the sight of the monuments of antiquity, their eyes seem to open for the first time to nature and to art.'[82]

The case of François Boucher illustrates the highly charged stakes involved in an artist's encounter with Rome, and also the way that retrospective prejudice can stand in for a lack of contemporary documentation. The time Boucher spent in Italy (1728–30) is usually described as unproductive; that he failed to be inspired by Rome's master-pieces was a measure of the limitations of his sensibility and his talent. This failure is either ascribed to his stubborn and arrogant spurning of the great masters of the past in preference for his own ready-made style, or else more charitably put down to illness. In fact, given that eighteeth-century and subsequent accounts of his Italian visit were based on extremely fragmentary evidence, we might see the latter explanation as an extension of the idea that the beauties of art in Rome caused Boucher physical discomfort.[83] In the literature of artistic travel, physical illness and resistance to the desirable influence of Italian and antique art are complementary. Thus, to invoke Boucher's illness was not to excuse his failure to carry out the canonical Italian experience. Rather, Boucher's indisposition can be seen as the ultimate demonstration of his artistic failure, transposed onto a physiological level. Seen in this light, his reaction was the most unequivocal testimony to the deficiencies of his sensibility, expressed through the physical dimension of his health.

The passage from resistance to revelation is nowhere better illustrated than in Jacques-Louis David's account of his first Italian experience. On the eve of his departure for Italy in 1775, David was reportedly warned: 'Don't go to do Rome, like so many others. Try not to be ruined by it, keep continually in your mind your charming composition of Seneca.' David confidently replied: 'The antique will not seduce me, it lacks spirit, and isn't stirring!'[84] Yet, the artist himself recalled that, as he descended the Italian peninsula towards Rome, he was overwhelmed by the gulf between his ignorance and the array of great art he encountered, later describing himself as 'giddy from all the beauties' which surrounded him.[85] Nonetheless, David then engaged in an initial bout of overwork which led to a 'state of collapse'; Vien, the director of the Académie, prescribed a trip to Naples to remove him from this compulsive devouring of Rome's overcharged artistic spectacle.[86] In a sense, this is an explicit challenge to the efficacy of the Académie as an institutional framework for guiding artists towards reform of their sensibility and creative skills. Personalising the narrative emphasises the merits of self-discovery and independence. Rather than assuming that artists should assimilate their identity to that of the established values enshrined in the antique and the great Italian masters, style was coming to be understood as essentially self-made – indeed, in some circumstances as equivalent to the realisation of the self.[87]

However, earlier models for the way Italy could and should reshape artistic sensibility relied on powerful physical metaphors which reflected a sense that the body was susceptible – indeed, vulnerable – to the effects of the environment. In 1755, Robert Adam urged his younger brother James to depart for Italy as soon as possible: 'Every day's delay is losing time and of dangerous consequence as you suck in prejudice which with pain you will quit.'[88] Robert recommended the services of Clérisseau, 'whose Soul, Body and Guts are tinctured' with the spirit of Rome and its architecture.[89] Rome had an irresistibly invasive power – as David's overconfident repudiation had acknowledged.

In 1796, Fuseli invoked the transformative benefits of Italian experience more tersely, when he regretted that Thomas Lawrence had not 'gone abroad for some time and return[ed] *new*', as if exposure to a different environment would without fail transform the artist and his art.[90]

FRIENDS

Dedication could descend into anti-social misanthropy. At first, David himself sought solitude far from his comrades because of his apprehensive state of mind.[91] Yet, accounts of David's subsequent discovery of the true path, including his own, were to stress the crucial involvement of other artists as supportive catalysts. At different times, David identified Peyron and Quatremère de Quincy as having initiated him into the beauties of antique art.[92] However, in both cases such interaction is applauded as exemplifying an alternative to academic communality.

A similar commitment to individual integrity and comradeship can be found in Delacroix's letters on the prospect – unrealised – of an Italian trip in 1821. 'I am overcome three or four times a month by a strong desire to emigrate to Italy. I have given up taking a chance on the Academy's prize. As I do not wish to go to Italy to eat well and live in a palace, I am also capable of living simply as I do here.'[93] In 1822 he acknowledged: 'This idea won't let go of me…friendship, friendship and Rome!'[94] Italian wanderlust was still gnawing away at him in 1826: 'In Italy!' he exclaimed to Soulier, 'I am not thinking of going there without you. It is one of my most cherished dreams.'[95] Géricault, who had earlier made the trip at his own expense, explained to Dedreux-Dorcy, who was to have accompanied him: 'I only lack a good friend with whom I could live and work.'[96] Géricault regarded the academic regime at the Villa Medici as inimical to artistic success for similar reasons. Students spent five years shielded from true artistic challenges, complacently consuming a 'bourgeois cuisine…which fattens their bodies and destroys their souls'.[97] His own experience had deliberately eschewed such institutionally cushioned conditions; it was in Rome that he supposedly exclaimed 'only suffering is real' – whether we take this to mean that it was Rome which had brought this recognition, or that in Rome the only real thing is suffering.[98] Such discomfort might nonetheless be deemed salutary, as by Gustave Planche, who saw Géricault's Roman episode as crucial for his artistic emancipation. Only inferior artists feared the lessons awaiting them.[99] However, in Planche's view, the crucial encounter was with Roman reality as refracted through the verismo of Caravaggio. It was precisely Géricault's commitment to a synthesis of art and life which bolstered his newly won independence from Davidian academicism.

Close friendship was an alternative to and compensation for living outside the community of the Académie. Isolation provoked Prud'hon to dismiss Rome's artistic resources: 'Everything here is nothingness for me.…Farewell my friend, a letter from you would do more for my tranquillity than all these ruined beauties';[100] yet he subsequently established a cocoon of discontented industriousness.[101] For David d'Angers, the personal was inflected by the ruefully political: he spurned 'these palaces, these monuments that conquerors' pride had raised to tell posterity that their ideas were as great as the world.…But what I am not going to find, are my friends.'[102]

However, such close friendship and solidarity could appear from the outside as exclusive. Stendhal reported the common view that the *pensionnaires* existed in a state of parochial isolation from Roman society – and by implication were also at one remove from the art that surrounded them. 'The young artists based in the Villa Medici form, one is told, an oasis which is perfectly isolated from Italian society and where there reign despotically all the little conventions which caused the arts in Paris to wither.'[103] In 1826, Schnetz reported to Navez that, although there were still many French painters in Rome, they no longer seemed to share a sense of amicable cohesion: 'There no longer exists amongst them the same solidarity as in your time; there are coteries; and in this respect, Rome has lost much of its attraction.'[104] That artists formed in Paris might resist the idea that Rome was a superior place to take their professional knowledge to another level was hardly surprising; indeed, it could be seen as threatening precisely because it had the power to wash away both established habits and novel visions. As Révoil wrote to Granet in 1804: 'I fear your Rome like the plague!' – the voice of an artist who had created an alternative frame of artistic reference which he did not want overpowered by heavier, weightier old master works.[105]

THE DIVIDED SELF

Following David's example, the first generation of his pupils was to push the pursuit of individuality towards a more extreme cult of originality in both style and behaviour. The two most signal examples of this shift are Jean-Germain Drouais and Anne-Louis Girodet, each interestingly different in the way they resolved the demands of artistic authority and autonomy, clearly expressed by their respective Roman trajectories.

The case of Drouais is more drastic in that he lived out his conflict with authority – that is, with the Académie and with David – to an extent that interfered with his ability to work successfully. He had isolated himself so insistently that Ménageot, director of the Académie in Rome, was worried that his 'unfortunate mania of living like a savage' might be contagious. As suggested by Régis Michel, Drouais's painting of the wounded and abandoned Philoctetes may be read as a neurotic projection of his own sense of isolation and suffering.[106] However, although he was less than happy in the academic milieu of Rome in the 1780s, Drouais nonetheless had no problems engaging with the antique. As Michel noted, unlike David's allegedly troubled route, Drouais's starting point was a willing and informed state of mind. To this extent, his indisposition could be understood as the result of a pathologically unresolved attempt to disengage himself from the authority of the Académie and his master, rather than as the consequence of a crisis of doubt about his ability to reap the benefits of Rome's artistic resources.

Girodet's espousal of an aesthetic of originality was more calculated and less self-destructive. His express intention to fashion his own peculiar brand of sensibility, and then adopt it as a standard against which to assess the revered art of the past, is manifest in his ostentatious dawdling on arrival in Rome and his refusal to submit to the customary initiatory stampede.[107] However, the degree to which this was a matter of projecting a certain persona in a preconceived plan to stand out from his peers is less clear when we consider the comments of Ménageot, the Académie's director. He noted that Girodet had trouble acclimatising, but nevertheless hoped that, if he took proper (unspecified) precautions, he could protect himself from the 'very dangerous' and frequent fevers which were everywhere in Rome during what was proving to be a harsh summer. This was because of not just the heat but also a debilitating sirocco wind.[108] In asserting his resolve not to compromise himself by conforming to academic routine, Girodet seems to be trying to insulate himself from both the rigours of the climate and a sense of institutional imposition. Writing to Gérard about the Académie in Rome, he insisted: 'If this is a digest of the world's school, it seems to me that the lessons are highly off-putting; they will not change my moral being, they will only influence my outer layer or envelope.'[109] Revealingly, he points up a deliberately dissimulative stance, which is premised on a belief that his core sensibility could proceed independently of external appearances. The alignment of inner and outer layers of identity with levels of personal and social authenticity is found in a more constructive, self-improving and indeed self-congratulatory vein in Goethe's account of his interaction with Rome: 'I am very well and more and more finding out who I am, learning to distinguish between what is really me and what is not. I am working hard and absorbing all I can which comes to me on all sides from without, so that I may develop all the better from within.'[110]

UNDERSTANDING RAPHAEL AND MICHELANGELO

According to the connoisseur and theorist Roger de Piles, to experience a state of initial incomprehension was almost a necessary indication that one was dealing with truly great works of art; this was certainly the case with Raphael's Stanze – works which, in terms of a Roman itinerary, were to be seen above all others.[111] More prosaically, Lalande blamed disappointment with Raphael on the physical conditions of display – a combination of bad lighting, unsympathetic rooms and the monotony created by a succession of too many pictures.[112] The Académie's director Guillaume Lethière contrasted the earlier freedom of access to the Stanze, where scaffolding was permanently available for artists to study and copy, with the greater difficulties the *pension-naires* in his charge experienced in 1812.[113] Despite Lalande's matter of fact explanation as to why the Vatican's collection of some of Raphael's supreme masterpieces failed to impress, this episode was considered to be one of the most momentous rites of passage in the encounter with Rome – for both the protagonist's self-esteem and public reputation. Seeing these works in the Vatican was equivalent to arriving at an inner sanctum, and was thus a defining moment in a pilgrimage to 'the great temple of the arts'.[114] To this extent, the occasion was associated with cliché, misunderstanding and disappointment.

On the one hand, according to Cochin, writing on the academic advisability of the journey to Italy, 'although all those who see them cry out with admiration, most only do so because they have heard it said that these are admirable things. Most works by this great master do not cause such sudden astonishment.'[115] On the other hand, for Reynolds, reactions to Raphael involved a more tangled and fraught narrative. After recounting the story that the guard in the Vatican was continually approached by people asking where to find the Raphaels having just walked past them, Reynolds confessed his own initial deflation at finding himself unmoved before these venerated works. He was, however, reassured by estimable 'brother artists' that he was not unusual. Indeed: 'that those persons only who from natural imbecility appeared to be incapable of ever relishing these divine performances, made pretensions to instantaneous raptures on first beholding them. This was one of the most humiliating things that ever happened to me. I found myself in the midst of works *executed upon principles with which I was unacquainted. –* I felt my ignorance, and stood abashed.'[116] The lesson that Reynolds drew from his humiliation in the Stanze was the necessity of disciplined looking: 'The excellence of his style is not on the surface, but lies deep; and at first view is seen but mistily.' Those who anticipated an immediate glow of recognition, 'as if it were to be expected that our minds, like tinder, should instantly catch fire from the divine spark of Raphael', understood little of art or the real nature of artistic sensibility.[117]

Caylus adopted more high-flown language, in which he compared Raphael's elusive stature to a form of natural force:

> Do not worry if you do not yet find Raphael to be all that he in fact is. Know that the sun will rise for you, that you will awaken in the most beautiful place in nature, that everything will dazzle you, and that the most colourful flowers or objects which are nearest to you are the only objects by which you will be struck, and that you will not be so struck by the great effects of air and sky, and that finally, in this state of bedazzlement, the great phenomena of nature must escape you. I hardly dare admit how long I had no doubt of the beauties and sublimity of this same Raphael, and [yet] for how long I only saw his faults. Don't be in a hurry: one day you will be illuminated by a flash of light; then you will see and you will see well.[118]

Caylus's imagery evokes religious conversion: artists saw the light not of revealed faith but of artistic truth – a light that at first might well be dazzling. Somewhat more clinically, David later likened his initiation to the beauties of Raphael and antique art to the removal of a cataract from his eye.[119]

When Fragonard confronted the giants of Michelangelo and Raphael, the state of high emotion produced resulted in a relapse into chronic inactivity that lasted several months. According to Alexandre Lenoir, the artist recollected this traumatic episode in the following terms: 'The energy of Michelangelo seared me; I experienced a feeling that I cannot express; seeing the beauties of Raphael I was moved to tears, and the pencil slipped out of my hand; in the end I remained, for a few months, in a state of indolence that I was no longer able to overcome; that was before I began to study the painter who gave me cause to hope to be their equal one day and that is how I became interested in Barocci, Pietro da Cortona, Solimena and Tiepolo.'[120] The response of Natoire, the Académie's director, was to prescribe that Fragonard apply himself to copying a work that ought to compensate for his shortcomings, namely Pietro da Cortona's *Ananias restoring St Paul's Sight* (1631, Santa Maria della Conciliazione) – given the context, an entirely appropriate theme, but there seems no suggestion that any sense of irony was intended.[121] Yet this account of Fragonard's impotent recoil from these great works seems formulaic, a repetition of Boucher's alleged warning that Raphael was 'very depressing' and Michelangelo 'frightening'. 'Believe in them, but don't attempt to imitate them or you will become as chilling as ice,' he told Christian von Mannlich.[122] In 1773–4, Fragonard's travelling companion, the wealthy *amateur* Bergeret de Grancourt noted that only art students were capable of deriving profit from the works in the Sistine Chapel, which he himself found rebarbative.[123]

In the early nineteenth century, Géricault is reported by his biographer Charles Clément as having experienced a similar reaction to Michelangelo: 'He trembled before the great masters of Italy, and hence doubted himself, taking a long time to settle down after this upset.'[124] Stendhal famously experienced an 'attack of nerves' when looking at and writing about Michelangelo.[125] He was reminded of the extremity of harrowing emotion he had experienced on the retreat from Moscow. In 1851, Flaubert claimed he would have rather painted the *Last Judgement* than been the victor of battles, even Marengo.[126] More prosaically, according to family tradition, Joseph Wright of Derby 'contracted an affliction of the liver' from lying on his back on the cold floor of the Sistine Chapel, which later prevented him from working 'for months at a time'.[127] Malone reports that Joshua Reynolds damaged his hearing by working too close to a stove 'by which the damp vapours of that edifice were attenuated, and affected his head'.[128]

EPIPHANY OR CRISIS

The encounter with Raphael and Michelangelo increasingly formed part of a more psychological expectation of Rome as a place of profound personal transformation. This is in contrast to the tendency to celebrate the pleasurable inevitability of self-realisation in Rome, whether through the enhancement of social status and worldliness, the acquisition of prestigious objects, or the satisfying pleasures of Romantic melancholy. In this respect, Goethe's unequivocal declaration is as misleading as it was later to be paradig-matic: 'In Rome I have found myself; for the first time I am in harmony with myself, happy and reasonable.'[129] 'I count a second birthday, a true rebirth from the day I entered Rome'.[130] However, the account Goethe gives in *Italienische Reise* is tidied up both in its form and in its autobiographical accuracy. Rather, we should see such nar-ratives – especially those which quote Goethe – as formulaic reworkings of a hallowed norm.[131] The same is true of Byron. He might exclaim: 'it beats Greece – Constantino-ple – everything – at least that I have ever seen.'[132] But he did so as a conscious alterna-tive to repeating ready-made opinions from Eustace, Forsyth and other guidebooks which he was fully aware of.[133]

This sense of situating oneself in Rome through other external co-ordinates, whether rejected or embraced, applies to Chateaubriand, who found a sense of temporal stasis: 'The place is suited to reflection and reverie: I return into a past life; I feel the weight of the present, and I seek to divine my future.'[134] The sense of rejuvenation, experienced as a feeling of incomparable harmony between self and surroundings, can also be found in a letter describing the expectation and realisation of a Roman visit in 1846 by Jacob Burckhardt, then a young would-be professor.[135] However, a triple sense of time could make Roman reality a challenging experience. Once again, Viollet-le-Duc took the trouble to explain to his father how in Florence as in Rome he found himself negotiat-ing between past, present and future: 'You cannot imagine how Italy develops the taste one has for history. Here one lives triply: one lives in the present, in the future (for the imagination being constantly in movement, creates and improves what it sees), and above all in the past; I seem to spend whole days where I am outside of the present moment; I *drift* in the past, and these, I assure you, are moments of an inexpressible sweetness; nothing distracts me here and everything, on the contrary, tends to cast me back into a poetic past.'[136]

Stendhal is not unusual in insisting on the pathological potential of the experience of Italy in general and Rome in particular, even while he celebrates the unique scope for pleasure and aesthetic gratification. In his letters and texts written during his earlier residence in Rome, Stendhal gave ample recognition to the way an excess of enthusiasm could be so overwhelming that it resembled madness.[137] And, unlike Goethe, he readily concedes his fundamentally troubled and unresolved relation to the city, or rather that this has taken a newly deepened dimension. His autobiographical text *Vie de Henry Brulard* opens with a subtle homage to Rome's climate and sensual power: 'This morning, 16th October 1832, I found myself at San Pietro in Montorio, on the Gianicolo, in Rome, it was splendidly sunny. A light, hardly perceptible sirocco wind carried some small white clouds above Monte Albano: a delicious warmth filled the air, I was happy to be alive.'[138]

Stendhal was evidently on the terrace outside the church, looking eastward across the city. He describes himself leaning against a wall, taking in the pleasures and memo-ries offered by the sight of 'all Rome ancient and modern, revealing itself to me'. His posture, at once relaxed and poised, is emblematic of a mode of viewing in which physical stasis allows a form of active panoramic scanning. The sight of particular buildings and places called to mind numerous personal and artistic reminiscences. Realising that he is about to be fifty, Stendhal asks himself what he has achieved, and finds himself overcome by doubts. Dissatisfaction is signalled by a shift of location, to the steps of St Peter's. There he spends 'an hour or two' in a dreamy introspective state set off by the realisation that he was unsure what his life amounted to. Although he would seem to be reworking the trope of a visitor overwhelmed by the building's mighty façade, in fact he literally and metaphorically turns his back on it, such that it provides an existential stage set rather than a majestic feat of engineering and papal self-glorification.[139]

PAINFUL SELF-RENEWAL

If, for Stendhal, Rome turned out to be a place for middle-age taking stock, this was no less disturbing than the angst and self-doubt experienced by young artists. Viollet-le-Duc provides a lucid and candid account of the stages in his journey of self- and professional discovery. When he reviewed his sojourn in Rome in a letter to his father, he emphasised that the slow progress he admitted that he was making was not for want of trying. We may see this desire to reassure as the result of his guilt at his separation from an ailing parent and the knowledge of the need to ensure that his sojourn was fruitful, thus laying the foundations for a successful subsequent career in Paris. It was, he explained, too easy to suppose that, once in Rome, an artist or architect would effortlessly assimilate the city's artistic resources. In practice the experience was more drawn out, complex and distressing:

> You should not, dear father, take the discouragement that I have experienced at Rome as madness or weakness. It is impossible to remake oneself all of a sudden in this great city: in the middle of this meeting point of all the ages, before one can choose a path, much time can pass. Here, it is necessary to form one's taste, recommence one's studies from their foundations so to speak, and begin again with good faith and the submission of a school boy. I would consider anyone who did not undergo this revolution in Rome as not capable of being an artist.[140]

Conceding that prior artistic education had been misguided involved a double criticism at once political and personal – of the institutional framework and the artist himself. Self-renewal could not be isolated from the larger context, nor was this process painless: 'This internal wrenching, this obligatory abandonment of some of the systems that one took for truth under the artificial influence of Paris, cannot take place without some discouragement and without some regrets when one sees how long one has been living in a *quasi-truth*.'[141]

It was indeed a chastening, if not devastating, admission to concede how traumatic the encounter with Rome had proved to be. The abbé Barthélemy recalled the state of abjection to which he had been reduced by recognising Rome's unsurpassed resources; he was overcome and struck dumb: 'Rome has changed all my ideas; it overpowers me; I can express nothing of this to you.'[142] 'You cannot understand how much my journey has humiliated me; I have seen so many things I knew nothing of, that it seems to me mad to compliment oneself on some superficial knowledge.'[143] Diminution of self was an unpalatable experience. For Flaubert, to find himself surrounded by so many masterpieces was terrifying and crushing: 'One feels smaller even than in the desert.'[144]

Rome's reputation for inducing different kinds of destabilising effect and state of mind and body was often articulated through a recurrently pathologised vocabulary. Allan Cunningham evoked Wilkie's state of excitement: 'He felt that the marvels of Rome kept his mind in a sort of slow fever of admiration.'[145] Amaury Duval recalled how the winter he spent in Rome 1834–5 had been taken up with the 'feverish' visiting of its museums.[146] Not without a certain irony, Renoir declared that 'I have suddenly become a traveller, and overcome by the fever to see the Raphaels.'[147]

Recalling his return to Rome in 1828 as ambassador, Chateaubriand described his uncomfortable state of mind. At first he felt a distaste because of the disagreeable sense that everything he remembered had changed. But 'the fever of ruins' was so insidiously powerful that it overcame his homesickness, such that he was able to revel in the love of solitude once again: 'On my arrival in the eternal city, I felt a certain displeasure and for a moment I felt that everything had changed; little by little, the fever of ruins overcame me, and I ended up, like thousands of other travellers, adoring what had at first left me cold. Nostalgia is the regret for one's native country: on the banks of the Tiber one also has homesickness, but it produces an opposite effect to the usual: one is seized by love of solitariness and by disgust for the homeland.'[148] This oscillation between love and hatred of homeland was an equivalent for changing attitudes to art, sometimes ebbing and flowing in perturbingly contradictory ways. 'It is for love of fine art that one comes to Rome, and there', as Stendhal soberly predicted, 'this love abandons you, and as usual, hate is very close to replacing it.'[149]

The idea that artists and travellers were predisposed to a pathological state of mind when in Rome, or at least were likely to pass through one while adapting more or less successfully to their new environment, can be seen to have been reinforced by the expectation of odd behaviour coming to be associated with the stereotype of the Romantic artist. Indeed, it was at this period that illness of some sort came to be an almost obligatory symptom of being an artist.[150] Antisocial behaviour, abnormal sensibility and physical deterioration – often cultivated – were coextensive. As Goethe noted with a terseness borne of painful self-knowledge: 'Classic is health, Romantic sickness.'[151]

No one characterised the ambiguous and potentially disastrous prospect that faced artists confronting Rome better than Hazlitt in his essay, 'English Students at Rome'. 'Rome is of all places the worst to study in, for the same reason that it is the best to lounge in. There is no end of objects to divert and distract the mind....if he ever wishes to do anything, he should fly from it as he would from the plague....You have no stimulus to exertion, for you have but to open your eyes and see, in order to live in a continued round of delight and admiration.'[152] Inhabiting a world where great art was commonplace did not ensure that the modern artist would produce suitably ambitious or resolved works, unless serious study was engaged in. Rome, 'the great metropolis of art', was likely to have the effect on 'those who take up their abode there' of rendering them 'ignorant, conceited, and superficial'.[153] But the predicament of a superabundance of art by which to be creatively aroused and from which to study was complicated by a more intangible yet inescapable threat, which united the city's historical legacy with its blighted atmosphere: 'There is a species of malaria hanging over it, which infects both the mind and the body. It has been the seat of too much activity and luxury formerly, not to have produced a correspondent torpor and stagnation (both in the physical and moral world) as the natural consequence at present.'[154]

Hazlitt was relentlessly pessimistic about the fate awaiting young artists who arrived in Rome full of long-cherished hopes: 'The fever of youthful ambition is turned into a cold ague fit. There is a languour in the air; and the contagion of listless apathy infects the hopes that are yet unborn.'[155] Creativity follows the same rhythm as the rise and fall of a fever, leaving the artist inert, drained and demoralised, without anything productive to show for this state of suffering. Yet ultimately, Hazlitt asserts, Rome itself is to blame for the seemingly inescapable likelihood of failure.

What lies behind these mixed metaphors and dire warnings? To what extent were they based on an informed awareness of the physical character of the city and its surroundings, or are they merely an elegant restatement of a forbidding set of received ideas? How far were such evocations of states of mind and sensibility the invention of artists and travellers, be they splenetic, chauvinistic or disenchanted, or do they rather bear some tangible relation to the experience of the Roman environment? Clearly, there is a strong sense in which the picture projected of Rome's essential identity presumes there to be an intimate connection between prevailing ambient conditions and their inhospitable character, and the deleterious effect this could have on imaginative and psychological well-being. In order to understand the ways in which such anxieties were instilled by aspects of the city of Rome and its surroundings, the following chapter will consider ideas about the role of climate in determining health and a disposition towards artistic creativity. Rome's climate emerges as a highly ambiguous and perplexing phenomenon. This will lead to a more focused review of the presence of 'bad air' – *aria cattiva* or *mal'aria* – an insidious but deeply entrenched component of Rome's physical environment.

3

'SOMETHING IN THE AIR': CLIMATE AND INSPIRATION

Contemporary ideas on Rome's climate can help us to understand the prominence of crisis, disarray and destabilisation in reactions to the city as being more than merely a matter of artistic sensibility and its disruptions. Despite the tendency amongst modern scholars to assume that climate was progressively losing its appeal as an explanatory framework for cultural and physical diversity in the eighteenth and nineteenth centuries, the case of Rome suggests that it remained very much alive. Indeed, contemporary theories of climate provide the key to understanding the coexistence of Rome's special status as a site for artistic inspiration and achievement and simultaneously as an intimidating physical environment marked by a disturbing changeability particularly associated with the dreaded sirocco.

The idea that the relative healthiness of a place depended on the specific combination of its air, prevailing winds, provision of water, and the general lie of the land was formulated in Hippocratic texts.[1] This holistic sense of the effects of topography and climate dominated thinking well into the nineteenth century. The Hippocratic belief that the nature of a place's air influenced health was extended to include the development of a people's character and their forms of language. By extension, climate and environment were understood to hold the key to understanding historical cycles of cultural efflorescence and decline. This was especially the case in relation to Rome and its long and eventful history. Within these commentaries, Rome's air in particular recurs as a compelling if frustratingly ambiguous topic.

The problem of Rome's air is already apparent in the way Vasari treats it as a phenomenon which, even in normal circumstances, could promote or interfere with artistic activity. On the one hand, he was convinced of the important role air played in fostering artistic achievements. When Vasari sought to explain why it was in Florence that the best artists were produced, and therefore why the Renaissance there was pre-eminent above all other cities' achievements, he cited three causes. First, 'the censure freely expressed by so many persons and in such various modes, for the air of the city gives a natural quickness and freedom to the perceptions of men'. Second, the need to work hard in order to survive given the high cost of living in a city which was not self-sufficient. Third, 'which is, perhaps, not less effectual than the other two, is the desire for glory and honour, which is powerfully generated by the air of that place'.[2] Seen in this light, assertions of the city's artistic supremacy can be seen to be no more than a recognition of a naturally ordained state of affairs. On the other hand, none other than Michelangelo left Florence for Rome, complaining that the air did not suit him. Although Roman air had a reputation for being difficult to cope with, it seemed not to upset the great man. Vasari dealt with this anomaly by seeing it as further evidence of Michelangelo's indomitable constitution.[3] The authority of Vasari and the mystique surrounding Michelangelo may have helped to sustain this form of explanation. Although André Chastel judged such an aerial theory of culture too simple (and inconsistent) to merit extended analysis, as if it devalued the intellectual and artistic achievements of Renaissance artists, it nonetheless remained remarkably influential.[4] As late as 1910, we find Julia Cartwright invoking a distinctive Florentine 'atmosphere of culture' to explain the unique artistic identity of the city, and modern art historians have not been immune to lapses into obsolete metaphor.[5]

A further problem with the environmental explanation of Renaissance achievements was how to deal with the undeniable subsequent decline of Italian art. Eighteenth-century Italian art was almost universally agreed (by non-Italians) to be inferior to its Renaissance and seventeenth-century predecessors.[6] The reasons for this manifest degeneration prompted much speculation, and were an extension of enquiries as to why the city of Rome, the heart of a great civilisation, had declined so lamentably since its heyday. As we will see, ideas as to what had happened and why were closely linked to a belief in the powerful effects of climate in general and the nature of the Roman climate in particular. Writing in the *Encyclopédie* in 1755, D'Alembert sought some form of physical explanation for the plight of Italian art, but confessed bafflement: 'Is it to physical or moral causes, or the combination of one or the other, that we should attribute the state of languor in which painting and sculpture are currently in Italy?...Is it the lack of rewards, encouragement and emulation which are lacking?'[7] His answer was to use an organic metaphor which relied on a sense of resignation before the fickleness of nature: 'Is it not rather a caprice of nature, which, as regards talent and genius, amuses itself, so to speak, from time to time opening mines which are then closed for centuries? Some of the great painters of Italy and Flanders lived and died in misery: some were persecuted, far from being encouraged. But nature plays with the injustice of fate and of that of men; she produces rare geniuses in the middle of barbaric peoples, as she makes precious plants grow amongst savages who are oblivious to their value.'[8]

In 1773, Jean-Baptiste-Antoine Suard reflected on the general problem of artistic cycles of decline and recovery, but confessed himself perplexed. There appeared to be no consistent pattern of social or political circumstances behind these transformations, and he found himself forced to wonder whether, in fact, 'the genius of the arts is a kind of moral epidemic?'[9] The marquis d'Argens, in support of his rejection of Italian artistic supremacy, could do no better, and invoked nature's unbidden miraculousness: 'You will surely ask me what is the reason for these changes, and how the famous schools of Rome, Bologna and Venice have suddenly dried up. I would reply to you that it is with great men who excel in the arts as with those lights in the sky which only appear in certain seasons, or like prodigies which only appear after several centuries.' In the end he concluded that 'superior genius' came from 'Heaven'; thus, the glories of French art under François I had been 'like a brilliant flower which blossoms and fades in a single day'.[10]

However, the comparison of artists to plants – relying on the plausible idea that both were extremely sensitive to their environment – had a wide currency which continued well into the nineteenth century. Such metaphoric usage facilitated shifts between the biological, the individual and the historical. Cultural change could thereby be equated with a natural process. In 1760, the Surintendant des Bâtiments, the marquis de Marigny, wrote to the artist Charles-Joseph Natoire, then director of the Académie de France à Rome, about the newly arrived Hubert Robert: 'Redouble all the cares you are taking in the cultivation of so fine a plant that will be an honour both to you, as Director, and to the arts in France.'[11] For the medical practitioner and theorist P.J.G. Cabanis, analysing the relations between man's physical and the moral dimensions, people responded as fully as plants to climate and environment, indeed more subtly.[12] With specific reference to Rome and its decline, Alphonse de Lamartine compared the Italian 'genius' to a 'plant which grows, likes the brambles of the Coliseum, more vigorously on ruins than in furrows'. After witnessing a literary conversation in Florence in which Italy's great achievements were reviewed and Alfieri's patriotic opinion quoted ('the human plant is born stronger and more robust in Italy than elsewhere'), he commented somewhat ambivalently: 'The ashes of the centuries are fertile like those of fires.…I feel that the air of this country is literary, and that one might be able to deny it freedom, but never genius.'[13]

CLIMATE IN QUESTION

In his *Réflexions critiques sur la poésie et sur la peinture* (1719), which relies on a comparison of ancient and modern culture, the abbé Dubos gave one of the fullest and most influential accounts of the historical significance of climate's role in shaping cultural activity. In relation to the exceptional creativity associated with Italy, Dubos developed an organic metaphor provided by Fontenelle in a text which also considers the relative merits of ancient and modern societies:

> Different ideas are like the plants and flowers which do not grow equally well in all sorts of climates. Perhaps our French land is not suited to reasoning like the Egyptians, no more than palm trees; and, without going that far, perhaps the orange trees which do not do as well here as in Italy, show that in Italy one has a certain

type of spirit which we do not exactly have in France. It remains certain that by the linkage and reciprocal dependence which there is amongst all parts of the material world, differences between climates which are evident in plants, must extend to brains, and have some effect.[14]

As Clarence Glacken noted, Dubos omits Fontenelle's next qualification, to the effect that 'art and culture can exercise a much greater influence upon brains than upon the soil, which is of a harder and more intractable nature.' It is clear that Dubos wished to promote the idea that Italy's benign climate was propitious for the making of art – even Italy's peasants 'are poets and musicians, because the keen and serene air of these regions refines their blood'.[15] In part such ideas were based on the claim that Italy had a climate and natural resources which were capable of prodigious productivity, but the modern science of agriculture was so poor that this was wasted.[16] Conceived in this light, artistic activity had a biological foundation, which in turn was sensitive to prevailing climatic conditions.

Dubos's analysis of the Roman climate sought to reconcile traditional claims made for its stimulation of artistic activity with the observation that modern Italian art had declined. Thus, he explained Romans' change of character from that of their ancient predecessors in terms of a change of climate: modern Rome was warmer, no longer subject to the hard winters described in ancient testimonies. However, any apparent advantages of these more clement conditions had been effaced by a new problem arising from the political and physical collapse of the city. The sewers and drains which had been created under every street and pavement in Rome, and which had formerly been flushed thanks to the water brought to the city by its system of aqueducts, had crumbled, partly because of the destructive actions of barbarian invaders. Water now entered this wrecked sewer system from above but could not escape, creating a build up of stagnant water. In the summer, extreme heat increased the rate at which corrupted air seeped out, rendering it even more harmful. This, Dubos argued, had initiated the notorious problem of Rome's bad air. That this was a potent source of illness was demonstrated by the effects on excavators who ill-advisedly opened such cavities: 'The stink and infection which emerge from them often give them fatal illnesses.'[17] In addition, in the environs of the city, deposits of alum, sulphur and arsenic contributed noxious emanations to the atmosphere.[18] Neglect of cultivation and lack of drainage had further exacerbated the situation.[19] For Dubos, faithful to a Hippocratic model of 'airs, waters, places', the primary factor in altering the physical constitution of the inhabitants of a particular location was its air. The nature of a place's air was decisive in directly determining the character of a population's blood, and therefore its internal organs – hence the significance of Rome's contaminated air, which was responsible for the physical deterioration of the city's inhabitants.

Dubos's analysis of the physical causes and cultural effects of the change in the Roman climate was developed further by Montesquieu.[20] Montesquieu's interest in climate and its effects on physical and social phenomena is well known through his *L'Esprit des lois*, but, as Robert Shackleton pointed out, it was not until after his visit to Italy in 1729 that these ideas developed seriously. Moreover, Montesquieu's ideas on this subject were informed by his interest in the numerous reports of Rome's insalubrious air to be found in the guidebooks which he read in preparation for his travels.[21] 'Starting with an examination of the specific problem of Roman air,' writes Shackleton, 'enlarging his ideas by reading, by observation, and by experiment, he arrives in the end at his general theory of climatic influence.'[22] Montesquieu also took up the physiological dimension to the association of enhanced artistic activity in Italy, suggesting that 'the high temperatures of the south and east stimulated black bile and therefore strengthened the imagination, fostering in particular religious inspiration and literary genius'.[23] This interaction between climate and melancholic humour also served to explain why Italy should have been so highly productive of artists of genius, in that artists were thought to be endowed with a form of melancholic disposition.[24]

Montesquieu reports that, the day after his arrival in Rome, no sooner had he presented himself to the French Minister to the Holy See, cardinal de Polignac, than he found himself part of a conversation on 'Rome's inclementness' ('l'intempérie de Rome'), and its complex causes.[25] Other interlocutors present opined that Rome's 'inclementness' only had an effect after having slept (the 'malignant parts' entering more easily when bodily fibres were relaxed),[26] or after some form of excess ('débauche'), and that the 'inclementness' was spreading in the Roman *campagna* but not in the city. Three causes were cited. First, that water no longer flowed effectively; second, in the summer, the drying of water-containing hollows by the seaside produced insects and 'vapeurs mauvaises'; third, the presence of mines for alum and other minerals, from which vapours escaped. Montesquieu adds another cause: in the winter, water filled the hollows left by disintegrated buildings.[27] Shackleton notes that Montesquieu owned Giovanni Maria Lancisi's *Dissertatio de nativis deque adventitiis Romani caeli qualitatibus* (1718),[28] in which the inherent healthiness of Roman air was asserted. Lancisi had argued that it was the combination of various deposits, such as vitriol, nitre, sulphur and alum, with stagnant water which resulted in noxious contamination of the air.

Like Dubos, Montesquieu pondered the physical and cultural differences between modern Romans and their forebears. He found the answer to changes in the physical constitution of modern Romans in their diet and a regime of self-protective health-consciousness. In the prevailing competitive environment fuelled by papal patronage, ambition was focused on achieving preferment, and this often required a lengthy wait, thus: 'everyone protects their hopes by continually looking after their health, Rome is a people of convalescants'[29] – a metaphor, too, for its artistic stagnation. Moreover, he drily noted that the propensity to do nothing was encouraged by the abundant provision of charitable institutions and hospitals; these 'mean that everyone is at their ease, except those who work, except those who engage in industry, except those who cultivate the arts, except those who have land, except those who engage in business'.[30]

In terms of changes in the theorising of the causes of artistic decline and revival, an important role is usually ascribed to Winckelmann's innovative conception of the causes of the peerless achievements of Greek art. He should be mentioned here in order to highlight the degree to which his ideas depend on the powerful role of climate and environment, elements in his ideas which are more usually seen as somewhat backward-looking or outmoded. This is not to deny the role played by socio-political context in his thinking. Indeed, Winckelmann himself, rather in the manner of Montesquieu (whom he had read), sees law and political system as being fundamentally shaped by prevailing climatic conditions. He summarises the causes for the superiority of Greek art thus:

> The superiority that art achieved among the Greeks is to be attributed in part to the influence of their climate, in part to their constitution and form of government and the way of thinking induced by it, yet no less to the respect accorded to artists and to the use and application of art among the Greeks....The influence of climate must invigorate the seed from which art is to germinate, and Greece was the preferred soil for this seed; the flair for philosophy that Epicurus wanted to attribute solely to the Greeks could with greater justification have been claimed for art. Much that we might imagine as ideal was natural for them.[31]

That Greece, more specifically Athens, had an exceptional climate, and that this had had a profound effect on the nature of its civilisation, had been asserted by Dubos, citing Fénelon as his guide: 'It seems that nature has a force in Greece that it does not have in other countries.'[32] Ultimately this depended on retrospective inference, supported by the same kinds of descriptions extracted from ancient texts adduced for Rome. However, as David Bindman notes, Winckelmann 'appears to have been the first in the eighteenth century to privilege the Greek climate over all others'.[33] But Rome was not without defenders of its organicist supremacy. Carlo Fea cited Winckelmann in his defence of Rome's claims to continued artistic splendour since the Renaissance, and explicitly compared the Roman climate to that of Greece.[34] Moreover, he made a virtue out of the otherwise problematic aspects of Rome's climate by claiming that the difficulty in pursuing industry or agriculture was in fact an advantage since this allowed more time for the cultivation of the arts.[35]

Further evidence that attitudes to the role of climate were a matter of dispute, with particular regard to what this meant in terms of the experience of artists, is to be found in the views expressed at length by Paillot de Montabert in his *Traité complet de la peinture* (published from 1829). Although not published until the second quarter of the nineteenth century, they reflect opinions formed as a pupil of Jacques-Louis David at the turn of the century. By virtue of the comprehensive vision of art in all its theoretical, technical and moral aspects which he sought to elaborate, Paillot's comments on the role of climate provide a particularly revealing justification of the need, as viewed from the perspective of practising artists, to resist and restrict the degree to which climate should be acknowledged as a powerful, if not irresistible, force.[36]

While acknowledging the primacy of Greek art, Paillot rejected many of the arguments, familiar from Winckelmann, which sought to explain its causes. In this respect his comments on Greek climate accurately reflect his point of view on climate in general. Paillot reacted against Winckelmann's claim that Greek climate was crucial to the creation of its supreme artworks. As an example of the modern influence of these ideas, he quotes Chateaubriand: 'In Greece...everything is softened, everything is full of calmness in nature, as in the writings of the ancients....In this homeland of the Muses, nature does not encourage deviation; on the contrary it tends to steer the spirit to love of harmonious and uniform things.'[37] In response to these eloquent but unsubstantiated views, Paillot asks if Greece's climate was, in fact, uniformly 'delicious'.[38] He admits that he has no evidence, but uses this admission to expose the fact that neither did Winckelmann, nor those who echo his extremely influential views.

Surveying the modern age, Paillot asserts that the argument in favour of good climate causing good art cannot be sustained, because it is easy to find examples of places with good climate which do not produce good art. However, perhaps most seriously for Paillot, the idea of climate as an inescapable factor in determining levels of creativity which varied according to local conditions was anathema, because it denied the possibility of artistic independence. He proceeds to demolish the basic set of Winckelmann's ideas by addressing the influence of institutions and *mœurs*. Varied forms of art have appeared while *mœurs* have remained the same: 'David changed art because at the age of thirty he changed his doctrine: it is not that he was influenced by the *mœurs* of his country, for it was in Italy and Rome that he perfected his art, but it was because he had recourse to other ideas and another theory.'

When Paillot addresses climate and its influence on art, he wastes no time in clearing the ground of unnecessary, and in his view false, generalisations: 'Everything which can be said on the influence of climate seems to be reducible to two or three very simple ideas suggested naturally by good sense, thus that in a country where the climate is extreme, this must be an obstacle to works of the imagination; that in genuinely temperate countries, this obstacle does not apply; and that in countries favoured by a pure climate, [and] a benign sky, not only does the spirit of men not have such obstacles to overcome, but their imagination is indeed excited by this beauty of the sky, [a] beauty which extends to all of nature.'[39] 'We should thus recognise only that the beauty of climate favours all dispositions for the arts, and no-one would wish to deny this. In effect, the gentleness of the sky and the fine aspect of nature not only sustain ideas, but they enliven and renew them. A pure sky seems to purify us....The pleasures of fine climates are for all, and it is only because of this that one should say that the sun shines for everybody.'[40] Sunlight was both an aesthetic stimulus and a political blessing.

Despite this enthusiasm, presumably derived from his own experience, he is absolutely clear about the distinction between potential and realisation: providing a favourable context was not the same as a direct cause.[41] Equally, the obstacle of a difficult climate does not prevent artistic progress; but the results are not proportionate to the degree of climatic comfort: rather, men are formed fundamentally by institutions.[42] Moreover, artists who live in good climates with plenty of resources do not automatically make good art. (In passing, we may note that Paillot dismisses Vasari as a reliable historian of the Renaissance on the basis of climate, or rather a belief in its effects and impact, arguing that Vasari's essentially Tuscan roots and sensibility blind him to the true variety of Italian art engendered by the other local climates.) Once again, it is the artist's 'models' (that is, the content of their training) which determine the results. If an ignorant, badly trained artist were to be transported to Rome (or Greece) 'under the most beautiful sky on earth', he would only reproduce the distorted academic models he had already absorbed.[43] More specifically, a weaker student who was capable neither of focusing on correct principles, nor of purging himself of bad habits, once arrived in Rome was bound to be unable to find his way in this new artistic environment, with the redundant result: 'Then, in Rome all he sees is Paris.'[44]

Paillot's lengthy rebuttal might seem to be comprehensive and progressive, but I would argue rather that it should be taken as clear evidence that climate was in fact still felt to play a significant role in shaping artists and their art. Jean Ehrard argued that the 'decisive contribution' of the eighteenth century's philosophy of climate to the progress of Enlightenment was not so much in respect of substantive scientific enquiries as to have encouraged a liberating reassessment of an 'old myth'.[45] And, indeed, throughout the eighteenth century, widespread willingness to believe in the preponderant influence of climate had also been consistently challenged.[46] Yet according to Cabanis, writing during the aftermath of the French Revolution, opinions on climate's importance were 'still a topic of debate amongst very well-informed men', amongst whom one would include Cabanis himself, since climate plays a key role in his *Rapports du physique et du moral de l'homme* (1802).[47] His example provided an intellectual model for Stendhal, who applied Cabanis's theory of humours, including the role ascribed to climate, to Italy.[48] In Michel Crouzet's view, the theory of climates survived from Montesquieu to Taine with little essential change, albeit that it might be variously adapted to the priorities of political, 'sentimental' or existential geography.[49] Yet Crouzet's brilliant account of Stendhal and 'Italianness' ('italianité') makes abundantly clear how compelling and persistent assumptions about the profound role of climate in stamping a local, yet transcendant, identity on artistic sensibility could be, even in the case of someone who was as familiar with Rome as he was. Stendhal, of course, did not hesitate to plagiarise from Cabanis in order to lend his convictions scientific credibility.[50]

The writings of the Swiss traveller and naturalist Charles Victor Bonstetten are further evidence of the way climate was given a renewed authority in the early nineteenth century, coinciding with a time of transition from one general 'state of morals' ('état moral') to another – a euphemism for the unsettled predicament of post-revolutionary Europe. To this extent, we can see his observations as a reassertion of faith in deep natural laws, which endure despite the turbulence of contemporary political and social shifts. He positions difference according to a north–south polarity, within which the Midi emerges as unquestionably superior in regard to fine art: 'The sun', he writes, 'so strongly requires everything which belongs to beauty, that the artists of the North have always felt the need of a different climate; all those who distinguished themselves in the career of art were formed in Italy; or at least, they have felt as if by instinct the need to live there.'[51] Clearly, the theory of climate and its influence on cultural phenomena was a matter which generated both affirmative fine-tuning and repudiation in equal measure. The 'old myth' seems indeed to have had more life in it than has usually been assumed to be the case. It remained a deep-seated and compelling explanatory framework, which also found expression in less empirical, more associative and metaphorical terms.

ATMOSPHERIC AURA

In France, one of the most interesting – and contentious – sequels to the kinds of environmental theory of cultural formation articulated by Winckelmann is to be found in the writing of Quatremère de Quincy, sculptor turned academic theorist and administrator. However, Quatremère's importance here is to demonstrate the continued presence of a belief in climate as an essential, defining feature of Rome's artistic identity in the aftermath of the French Revolution.

The Revolution had a powerful impact on attitudes to the nature and mechanisms of artistic influence, and towards Italy as a cultural environment – both for the making and viewing of art. It also saw the promotion of an institutional museum culture which was to transform and polarise arguments on environmental theories of cultural efflorescence. The creation of a national museum in the Louvre and the expansion of its collections – in part as a result of a policy of appropriating works of art from the victims of the French armies' successful campaigns in the later 1790s – were justified in revolutionary rhetoric by claiming that the masterpieces taken from Rome had been languishing in a state of neglect and, moreover, soiled by unwholesome papal despotism.

In 1796, Quatremère de Quincy published a letter challenging the legitimacy and advisability of this policy.[52] Beyond the specific political context for the ensuing debate, Quatremère's text is interesting because it reworks ideas about Rome's artistic potency, relating this to the determining role of local circumstances in giving a distinctive identity to indigenous forms of art, society and culture. For Quatremère, the essence of Rome's unique environment was 'this concert of things and ideas, of forms and feelings, public admiration, affections, sympathy, which form as it were an atmosphere of models of beauty'. Here he pointedly avoids any mention of the context provided by the now defunct Académie de France in Rome, a royal institution which would have to wait until the eve of the Napoleonic Empire to be reincarnated. Fundamental to this 'atmosphere' was the organic bond of 'monuments' (meaning artworks of all media) to the soil. If uprooted and removed to an alien location, this bond would be broken, and the works' aura would be drained from them, cut off from the sustaining ambience which had contributed to their creation and continued vitality. This was much more than a matter of meteorological propriety:

> Apart from Rome, there is no European city which can provide a refuge worthy of them, nor a temple suitable for the calm reflection which their study requires. It is neither in the midst of the fog and smoke of London, nor the rain and mud of Paris, the ice and snow of Petersburg; it is not in the middle of the tumult of Europe's great cities, nor surrounded by the chaos of distractions created by a people obliged to look after their mercantile needs, that there can develop this deep sensibility for beautiful things, this sixth sense that contemplation and study of the beautiful gives to the students of the arts. Whatever one does, it is always necessary that those who dedicate themselves are able to breathe an air free from all these vapours which obscure from our eyes the images of the beautiful and the true.[53]

Quatremère's ideas serve as a prelude to an intense sense of contestation surrounding the status of Rome's artworks as being inextricable from their historic matrix. Louis-Pierre Deseine employed similar ideas to those of Quatremère as part of his Paris-focused attack on Alexandre Lenoir's Musée des monuments français, and its wanton *bricolage* and consequent effect of aesthetic alienation. In Deseine's opinion, the monuments of Egypt, Greece and Rome were exemplary in the respect that their 'impressiveness' and 'charm', and their embodiment of 'everything which belongs to history, the world, politics', depended on their connectedness to their original environment, even if they were in ruins: 'Monuments inseparable from history, what would you become if we ripped you out of the place which had witnessed your antique splendour?'[54] Interestingly, Deseine exempts paintings and sculptures from his stricture, since they only required sufficient light and appropriate space, and so could be displayed effectively in other locations. Indeed, at the beginning of the eighteenth century, Jonathan Richardson (senior) had argued that there was no need for an Italian trip, since excellent Italian works could be viewed better in England.[55]

Chateaubriand spoke approvingly of the melancholy sight of 'masterpieces by great artists thus sown in the desert', as in the case of a head of Christ by Michelangelo which 'guarded' the almost abandoned convent of Sant'Agnese: 'I lament that the pictures from Rome have been gathered together in a museum.'[56] Schiller shared Quatremère's anti-Napoleonic opinions and aggressively echoed the argument against the illegitimacy of museums' dislocating effects on artworks.[57] However, the debate was not one-sided. An official report argued that the Italian works now in Paris would in fact only heighten artists' desire to go to Italy itself in order to study 'these remains of monuments which belong to the soil of ancient Rome'.[58] If the admittedly pro-Napoleonic A.V. Arnault was sceptical about the petition against the removal of artworks from Rome and noted that

Italians themselves had not been especially bothered,[59] Édouard Pommier has shown that there was disquiet in Rome when faced with the prospect of a systematic denuding of the city of its celebrated artworks. Indeed, the argument that French liberty would provide a proper home for art was appropriated by Romans sympathetic with the Revolution: works of art would be better 'liberated' from the Pope and aristocratic families, so that they could be redisplayed as the property of a new 'nationalised' state.[60] The creation and later partial dispersal of the museum collection in the Louvre also meant that there was a generation of artists and tourists who first encountered many of the canonical great works of European art in a museum, only to rediscover them subsequently once they had been restored to their original setting. In an epithet symptomatic of this reorientation, Girodet referred to Rome as 'the Central Museum of Europe' (Musée Central being the name for the Louvre in the later 1790s).[61] Etienne-Jean Delécluze later reflected that enriching the Louvre's collection might help to form artists' taste, but this was distinct from nourishing the 'fire of genius'. Moreover, he recalled J.L. David's opinion that works seen in museums were treated as 'curious treasures' whose charm had been lost with their removal from their original sites; such institutionalised collections were prone to create critics, not 'true artists'.[62]

Quatremère claimed for Rome not merely that its atmosphere was free from natural vapours or industrial pollution, but that the clarity of vision it was capable of fostering was tantamount to a higher sensory dimension. These ideas may seem to rely more on metaphysics than contextual empiricism, but they nonetheless reiterate a willingness to seek an explanation for Rome's special effects on creativity in some empirically definable combination of its environmental conditions.

At root, the superlative artistic achievements to which the city had been host were believed to have been caused by the all-pervasive qualities and properties of Roman air, which had impregnated the city's fabric and atmosphere, and still had an almost magical effect on travellers. Such claims might well be polemical, as in the case of the anti-academic Swedish sculptor Johan Tobias Sergel, who claimed that 'the air of Rome is unique' in terms of the creative stimulation it engendered: 'All the Nordic countries are graves to artistic genius.'[63] In more celebratory mode, for Alphonse de Lamartine Rome was an aesthetic continuum: 'There is no prose in this air, everything is music, melody, ecstasy or poem!'[64] Indeed, Creuzé de Lesser observed that even sceptical or dispassionate newcomers found themselves transformed as the result of inhaling the special air of Rome: 'What is remarkable is that one breathes the taste of the arts in this city, and the man who arrives here with the greatest lack of interest for them ends quite quickly by becoming very enthusiastic.'[65] Joseph Forsyth's conviction that Roman air and associated physical phenomena were crucial to stimulating the artists who came to the city was based on his observation that they became dependent on this effect: 'Canova, Kauffman [sic], Benvenuti, Mengs, Thorwalden [sic], all the principal artists of Rome are foreign to it. They came hither to form or to perfect their style. Here they meet congenial society, they catch inspirations from the sight of great works, they contract a dependance on such helps, and at last they can do nothing well out of Rome. Poussin ascribed it to the air: I have heard Angelica say that the waters of Rome revived her powers, and gave her ideas.'[66] As the landscape painter Théodore Gudin put it, in Rome respiration and inspiration were almost identical: 'We came here to breath the same air which had so powerfully inspired the great Italian painters.'[67]

In celebrating Rome's air, the mysteries of creativity were connected to a primordial form of natural cause. Moreover, this was something which established an intimate link between the individual body and the larger environment. Stendhal made this explicit when he stated: 'Through every pore, I feel that this country is the country of the arts.'[68] By this means, something quintessentially Roman literally entered into the body's inner workings, and thereby infused the mind with its exceptional qualities. Indeed, so strong was the effect of the local environment that it almost seemed to render the agency of the individual artist redundant: 'Here the climate is the greatest artist.'[69] Although Paillot de Montabert censured such loss of artistic autonomy, for Stendhal this was a liberating form of surrender.

As testimony to the longevity of the idea of atmospheric causality, we may note the reflection of Eugène Viollet-le-Duc, one of the most thoughtful analysts of the experience of Rome in the early nineteenth century. In 1837, he puzzled over what the fundamental cause which underlay Rome's inspirational effect might be, as manifest in the glories of past achievements, yet still palpable in the present: 'I ask myself, I search for the spirit which has been able to inspire in ancient artists this beauty of proportion, this purity of form, this vigour of execution which informs all their works, and I do not know where to find the source. The air (if I can speak thus) has in Rome retained something of the artistic perfume of the happy times of its prosperity.'[70] His invocation of Roman air has the feeling of a perfectly plausible suggestion, qualified by a self-consciously metaphorical understatement. Air still had a piquant ambiguity: a powerful environmental factor, yet something fundamentally as inscrutable as it was invisible in terms of how such effects were produced.

Roman air was a potent bearer of meanings, uniting the palpable and the mythic. For Hazlitt, this tantalising yet poignant ambiguity was a hallmark of the experience of Rome: 'An air breathes round her stately avenues, serene, blissful, like the mingled breath of spring and winter, betwixt life and death, betwixt hope and despair.'[71] The rise and fall of civilisation found its equivalent in the intimations of mortality which might insinuate themselves into the minds of modern visitors (as in the tomb imagery used by visitors to evoke a sense of decrepitude). Others were less equivocal and, indeed, more wholeheartedly gustatory in their savouring of the Roman atmosphere. Henry Matthews, in *The Diary of an Invalid* (London, 1820), compared 'the genial air of Rome' to deliciously sweet cowslip wine.[72] Writing of the Pontine marshes no less, with reference to its reputation as a seat of disease, William Wetmore Story claimed that 'this infected air is sweet to breathe as if it had the very elixir of Hygieia in it.'[73] His friend Henry James shared this view of Roman air as a kind of narcotic: 'Life on just these terms seems so easy, so monotonously sweet, that you feel it would be unwise, would be really unsafe, to change. The Roman air is charged with an elixir, the Roman cup seasoned with some insidious drop of which the action is fatally, yet none the less agreeably, "lowering".'[74]

Ideas about the powerful potential of Rome's air, both as a dimension to the city's identity as a site of cultural imagination, and also in terms of a vocabulary for making sense of the way it impinged on the senses and sensibility, are vividly expressed in Gustave Flaubert's letters preceding and accompanying his visit to Rome in 1851.[75] For Flaubert, Roman air was first and foremost a metaphor for an imaginary realm of invigorating artistic stimulation, untested as yet by direct experience, but nonetheless eliciting a powerful sense of excited physical contact. On reading Michelet's *Histoire romaine* he declared to Maxime Du Camp that antiquity made him feel giddy: 'I lived in Rome, it's certain, in the time of Caesar or Nero.... It's there one should live, do you see. We only have air from there and we have enough of it, of poetical air, to fill our lungs as on a high mountain, so much that your heart is thumping.'[76] Even if it only existed in the imagination, Roman air was a potent life force, whose power was an indication of the supreme reality of art. Art was another country, another dimension, access to which could be gained through the body by means of a kind of transcendant involution: 'The homeland [of art], it's the earth, it's the universe, it's the stars, it's the air. It is thought itself, that's to say the infinite in our chests.'[77] In Rome, this otherness was palpable, indeed almost commonplace, yet nevertheless intoxicating: 'It is indeed the city of artists. One can exist in a completely ideal atmosphere, outside of the world, above [it].'[78]

Flaubert's way of expressing his distaste for Catholicism's choking the spirit of antiquity, and the degree to which this had spoilt his pleasure in finding himself in Rome, also relies on a metaphor of atmospheric disease: 'So then, old fellow, I'm angry to have to admit it: my first impression was unfavourable. Like a bourgeois, I was disillusioned. I looked for the Rome of Nero and I only found that of Sixtus V. Priestly air hangs like a stultifying miasma over the Rome of the Caesars.'[79] The poetic atmosphere was vitiated by the inescapably intrusive presence of modern religion and its institutions that had settled like a stifling vapour on the eternal city.

The way Flaubert's ambivalent response to Rome is registered through his use of atmospheric metaphors illustrates a deep-seated problem inherent in the city's identity. On the one hand, air is given a powerful catalytic role. On the other, it is capable of having damaging effects on body and mind. Writing home about his first impressions of Rome after three months, Ingres expresses precisely this ambivalence: 'One would have to be blind or in bad faith not to admit that it is a climate and a city inexhaustible in beauties of all kinds, in picturesque architecture and above all in fine effects. It is a Babylon.'[80] In 1843, the painter Isidore Pils despondently acknowledged the dangerous contradiction he was living: 'I am weary of my sojourn in Italy; it seems to me that the climate is killing me; and yet it is so beautiful!'[81]

In a sense the enthusiasm for ideas as to the presence of an 'antique perfume' can be seen as a compensation for, or the displacement of, the recognition of other, insidiously deleterious qualities. Just as Rome's climate was ambiguous and 'inconstant', so opinions oscillate as to whether its salient characteristics were benign or harmful. The problem for commentators was that relying on Hippocratic ideas left them with a contradiction: the same set of physical conditions produced both a remarkable artistic propensity but also recurrent insalubriousness. In the next chapter, we will consider Roman air in more detail, and especially the search to understand the causes of 'bad air' and the range of effects it produced.

FACING PAGE: Ippolito Caffi, *Ballon Ascent over Campagna Romana*, detail of fig. 19.

4

CONFRONTING *MAL'ARIA*

Bad air, *mal'aria*, *aria cattiva*, *aria malsana*, miasma, Roman fever – from antiquity to the Risorgimento, Rome's reputation was marred by the persistent accusation that the local atmosphere was fatally tainted. The array of names used to refer to what medical research at the end of the nineteenth century would identify as malarial fever signals an enduring reliance on varieties of classical disease theory; at the heart of such ideas was a belief in the powerful, pervasive effects of air, be they salutary or damaging. Despite the tenacious survival of such ideas, they failed to provide a means to counter the awful effects of this environmental affliction. Bad air, a contemporary hazard whose effects were harrowingly obvious in the ravaged state of the local population, the ubiquity of corpses in the *campagna*, and the overflowing wards of Santo Spirito, the hospital which received the hundreds of fever victims every autumn, was also endowed with a historic heritage as ambiguous as it seemed to be deep-seated. In the eighteenth and nineteenth centuries, historians of ancient Rome puzzled over the role of 'bad air' in the rise and the decline of a great civilisation. Was it a further aspect of the arduous conditions out of which the indomitable temperament of early Roman society had been forged, or was it rather a noxious symptom of political decadence, social breakdown and the abandonment of agricultural cultivation, leading to environmental degeneration? Such reflections in fact only seemed to encourage the fatalistic view that these public health problems were, in some ineradicable way, inherently Roman.

Certainly, the association of bad air with Rome was in its turn reinforced by the large body of medical literature on the subject. Even those who sought to discredit the idea that Rome's bad air was a peculiarly toxic local phenomenon nonetheless admitted that it was widespread and a seemingly inescapable aspect of the city's atmosphere. Most commonly, explanations of its essential nature were sought in terms of its topographical distribution across the *campagna*, and more finely tuned location in the city, as well as geological and meteorological causes. However, before we look more closely at ideas about the special characteristics and properties of Roman air and its pathological effects, we need to get the measure of prevailing eighteenth-century attitudes to air, which provide a framework for this localised problem.

FACING PAGE: Ernest Hébert, *Malaria*, 1848–9, detail of fig. 62.

EMPIRE OF THE AIR

As a matter of scientific enquiry, air had been treated as of primal importance for health in antiquity, notably in Hippocratic texts, and these ideas had a remarkably durable legacy. However, the nature of Enlightenment science and its language was such that it was possible for appraisals of air to rely on antique precedent as well as be informed by novel chemical and physical theory and analysis. In the case of Rome, medical and scientific enquiries sought verification of this amalgam of old and new ideas through empirical observations which were tailored to the particular spaces and contours of the city and its landscape.

For the abbé Richard, author of a mammoth natural history of the air and its 'meteors', air was the most profound and essential component in nature: 'Air is the most universal and powerful agent that there is in Nature, it is its principal instrument in all its workings on the earth's surface and its interior, nothing can be produced, live or grow without air.'[1] The late eighteenth century saw numerous attempts to understand the essential nature of air. On the one hand, it was the object of extensive empirical investigation; on the other hand, it continued to embody an accumulated array of metaphorical, and indeed metaphysical, meanings and capacities.[2] Yet the very enthusiasm with which Enlightenment science sought to debunk old ideas, while seeking to forge new alternatives through indefatigable measuring and analysis, ensured that there was considerable scope for speculation and imaginative projection. In the view of the chemist Pierre Thouvenel, this was at once fascinating and challenging: 'We should not believe that the action of climates on those who inhabit them is only caused by the sensible qualities of the atmosphere, its temperature, aquosity, its meteors etc.; it is also caused by occult or imperceptible qualities, mixtures of other invisible elements, undetectable by any instrument.'[3] Indeed, rather than identifying any pathogenic elements, the chemical analysis of air in different places using the eudiometer merely served to demonstrate that air's constitution was exactly the same everywhere.[4]

Seen from a slightly later and more sceptical perspective, it was precisely the eclectic and evasive range of language which exposed the shortcomings of earlier ideas based on traditional humoural theory. For L.D.A. Bouffey, writing in 1813, such authors:

> have only imagined these effects [of air on the human body] in terms of physical relationship, or according to the the principles agreed by those who believe in the theory of the humours....When attention has been turned to the qualities communicated to the body by the heterogeneous bodies distributed throughout this vast sea of electrical fluids, hypotheses and abstract ideas or vague expressions have taken the place of more exact knowledge and more precise language. Saline, nitrous, sulphurous molecules and deleterious miasmas have been held to be responsible for most of the phenomena which could only be explained by analogy with various approximate experiences or in terms of ideas about the effects of substances whose existence was often no more than imaginary.[5]

One consequence of this lack of securely established knowledge was to reinforce belief in the existence of air's benign – indeed life-enhancing – aspects, or what is sometimes known as the 'intelligence of the air'. In 1718, the influential Roman doctor G. M. Lancisi, himself a methodical empiricist, adapted this Hippocratic premise to a physiological model of behaviour: 'Knowledge comes to the brain from the air.'[6] To this extent, ancient ideas, such as those espoused by the Roman physician Galen, 'that heavenly bodies endowed air in its upper reaches with a kind of "intelligence"',[7] were reinforced rather than dislodged by the new science of chemistry.[8] Reminiscing about his time as chief of Rome's police in the Napoleonic administration, the Baron de Norvins employed the language of Galen to highlight the presence of an especially invigorating kind of air in certain elevated regions of the *campagna*: 'From the Saturnian walls of the former citadel which crown Monte Circeo, to Poniatowski palace and gardens and the village of San Felice, a pure, light, vital, embalmed air exhaled the ether of the tropics; in breathing it after the air of the Maremma, one felt that it had its origin in the sky's high region, where the heavy and mephitic vapours of the earth could not reach.'[9]

The ambiguities surrounding air and its properties and effects on health were highly charged; being in contact with good air was a potent stimulus to physical well-being, mental clarity and equilibrium. According to William Falconer: 'A pure air…was esteemed favourable to the functions of the mind, which are so intimately connected with those of the body.…everyone must be satisfied from experience of the effect of a fresh and pure air upon the mental powers, and how much they are elevated and improved by it.'[10] Such ideas were surely behind the poetic and olfactory celebrations of Rome's supposed possession of a uniquely inspiring local atmosphere, and survived through the eighteenth and into the nineteenth century.[11]

Yet it is not difficult to find contradictory reports on the qualities of Roman air. Such divergences of opinion illustrate the way individual experience of Roman air worked on different levels of analysis and impression. When Stendhal asked himself what the pleasures of a journey in Italy were, the first one he named was 'to breathe a sweet and pure air'.[12] Lamartine claimed that he was intoxicated by Italian air from the first breath.[13] For the painter Léopold Robert, the artistically absorbing prospect of Rome was experienced within a sensory continuum in which the city's benign air played a key role. Writing to his fellow artist Schnetz in 1830: 'I am in an empassioned calm which charms me: I philosophise on my own quite peacably, while contemplating our beautiful Roman plain, the horizon and the sky, and it is with a real exhilaration that I breathe the excellent air we have here.'[14] The excellence of Roman air as understood from a medical perspective was no less readily translated into palpable qualities. In his review of early nineteenth-century European medical conditions, James Clark bore witness to the fact that 'the air [of Rome] has a softness that I never felt in the south of France, or at Nice.'[15] In 1774, a visitor such as Joseph Wright of Derby, who was particularly preoccupied with his health, attended carefully to the question of the air and how it impinged on him: 'The air here is not so cold as in England but it is thin and searching.'[16] Others were set against the local climate. Joseph Joubert tried to dissuade Mme de Beaumont, already suffering from the advanced consumption that was to kill her, from travelling to Rome: 'I have never heard it said that Rome's air was good for anything.'[17] After his attendance on the dying Keats, James Clark was convinced of the pointlessness of consumptives seeking respite in Rome, despite its atmosphere's therapeutic prestige.[18] Yet, such was the variable understanding of both consumption and fever that different medical opinions can be found asserting that Rome's bad air could in fact be beneficial for the former (Armstrong) or that 'malarious effluvia' made it worse (Burgess).[19]

INVISIBILITY

In thinking about the nature of Roman air and its effects, the wealth of historic and artistic expectations weighing on the city and the puzzle of its inspiring and dangerous atmosphere could not disguise the fact that the central object of enquiry was invisible, and to all intents and purposes out of reach, as mysterious as it was malignant. Invisibility had been one of the characteristics of miasma, the Greek term which referred to generic causes of disease. In the *Encyclopédie*, Menuret de Chambaud noted the Greek etymology for the term, 'souiller' (soil), 'corrompre' (corrupt): 'By miasma we understand extremely subtle bodies, which we believe to be the propagators of contagious illnesses.' Although there were recognised to be different modes of transmission – proximity, direct contact, as well as air – 'the nature, properties and the mode of action of these contagious particles or miasmas are completely unknown.' These particles were conceived of as being not merely invisible, but so small as to push them towards the boundaries of the material world: 'on the threshold which separates abstract beings' from matter.[20] Propelled by faith in empirical observation, such resolute scrutinising found itself struggling to engage with the imperceptible.[21] The paradox of an intensified visual enquiry confronting an invisible entity was precisely the case in Rome. Here, too, the strategy for seeking an elusive adversary was to approach it through its tangible traces, whether on the bodies of its inhabitants, in the streets and spaces of the city, or in its surrounding landscape.

This predicament was sharply felt by contemporary analysts. John Macculloch's book *On Malaria* (1827) reviews existing opinion regarding the causes, incidence and location of 'malaria' (bad air) throughout the world, treating the problem as one of global extent, explicitly connected to the wide reach of British military activity. Yet Rome recurs throughout the book as one of the most notorious sites of malarial blight – one, moreover, with a long history of this endemic condition. Although Macculloch insisted that any progress in identifying the essential nature of the phenomenon would only emerge out of a synthesis of empirical observations, he willingly drew attention to incompatible findings in different locales. Indeed, he repeatedly emphasises that the provisional and fragmentary conclusions he was able to offer were an accurate reflection of the lack of reliable information available. The fruits of his endeavours were expressed in the form of a call for more systematic keeping of medical records, but this did nothing to conceal his sense of frustration at the as yet unfathomable logic of malaria's distribution and incidence. Little concerning mal'aria was certain beyond the enormous extent and devasting nature of its effects. At the outset of his book, in order to characterise Rome's predicament, he did not flinch from a grim candour: 'This must suffice for the pure, the bright, the fragrant, the classical air of Italy, the Paradise of Europe. To such a pest-house are its blue skies the canopy – and where its brightness holds out the promise of life and joy, it is but to inflict misery, and death.' Nor, in his conclusion, could he offer any more comfort: 'To him who knows what this land is, the sweetest breeze of summer is attended by an unavoidable sense of fear – and he who, in the language of the poets, wooes the balmy Zephyr of the evening, finds death in its blandishments.'[22]

Macculloch claimed to hold no partisan prejudice against Rome and its climate, but his description was no less damning. It was precisely the invisible nature of the problem – the ambient, deadly malaria – that disturbed and shocked him: 'It is impossible to express the horror which one experiences on discovering that this is all deception; that [the traveller] is in the midst of dangers of which no indication exists; and that, with the soft air that he is breathing, he may be inhaling a poison destructive of life.'[23] Yet his final conclusion was resolutely empirical: 'It is plain that we have no mode of examining this subject but by the road of effects, unless any analogy derivable from contagion can also be drawn into this service.'[24]

Macculloch wrote as a doctor, but his remarks are, in fact, typical of the general tenor of the language employed in commentaries on Rome in order to characterise its problematic climate and the specific phenomenon of 'malaria' or bad air. Such rhetorical circumlocutions were justified – and necessitated – by the general admission that medical understanding of the problem was extremely limited. Where medical knowledge ended, the language of the poets began. Indeed, a writer like William Falconer drew on a prestigious array of literary sources – Milton, Virgil, Shakespeare, Ovid, the Bible and Ariosto – as a means to substantiate his claims about the role of air in climate's effects.[25]

The consequences of this invisibility were to add an ambiguous frisson to the experience, at once intimate and expansive, of being surrounded by an environment which was as deceptive as it was delightful. In the rueful words of Corinne's beloved Oswald, Lord Nelvil: 'The malignant influence does not make itself felt by any exterior sign: you breath an air which seems pure and which is very agreeable; the land is cheerful and fertile; a delicious freshness restores you in the evening after the burning heat of the day!: and all that, it is death!'[26]

It was precisely this kind of self-indulgent delectation in the mysterious malignity in Rome's air which prompted medical writers such as Louis Valentin to ignore literary sources and their emotive obfuscations: 'everything which tends too much towards enthusiasm or the marvellous, and above all judgements dependent on other travellers – *multum mentitue* who *multum vidit* – for most people only saw what others had seen.' Rather, he resolved to adopt a rigorous stance of empirical scepticism based on his observation of local conditions.[27]

But such resolve continually came up against a recognition of the limits of knowledge. At the beginning of the nineteenth century, Bonstetten concluded: 'There is in the air of Rome's *campagna* a cause of illness of which no one has yet calculated the real force.'[28] For all his desire to undermine the view that malaria was something inherently Roman, and therefore at odds with the city's role as modern capital, especially for the audience to the 1878 Paris Exposition universelle, Guido Baccelli was forced to conclude: 'The malaria is a poisonous power which is more a matter of experience than it is understood.'[29]

MALARIAL BODIES

This disagreement over the presence and effects of malaria in Rome was also played out in terms of highly aestheticised descriptions of local people. It was widely assumed that human physiognomy and stature were a readily graspable and expressive index of the presence or absence of bad air. To the author of the inherently partisan *A Comparative Sketch of England and Italy, with Disquisitions on National Advantages*, 'the content, and rosy health glowing in the cheeks of [England's] rustic inhabitants, form a splendid contrast to the meagre, livid, and dispirited peasants of ITALY.'[30] This was at once a political and aesthetic judgement, based on the premise that bodily consitution was a direct expression of ambient social and environmental conditions, and therefore a symptom of the state of good (English) or bad (Italian) government. For Dr Maihows, that there was something profoundly amiss in Rome's countryside was demonstrated by the state of its inhabitants: 'They are all pale, and even something worse, for they have the look of patients in a hospital.'[31]

In his 1822 treatise on the project to drain and thereby purge the Pontine marshes of 'bad air', conceived as part of a programme of improvements under the Napoleonic administration, Gaspard de Prony mentions in passing the dreadful sight of the region's benighted inhabitants, as described by a respected but unnamed medical colleague. Referring to Pius VI's earlier initiative: 'one part of the inhabitants of the centre [of the marshes] had such œdematic skin across the entire surface of their bodies, and muscular systems so lacking in elasticity, that the impression left by pressing a finger on the skin only disappeared after some time; such an effect is caused by a general atonic state, a weakness of [bodily] organisation, which makes the living state very close to that of death.'[32] At the time Prony was writing nothing had changed. Giovanni Battista Brocchi, in his neo-Hippocratic study on Roman geology, emphasised the state of mind associated with the effects of bad air as it spread through victims' blood: 'This anger and desire to harm which overcomes those in whose veins breeds the seed of marsh fevers,

this inclination to lose oneself in dark thoughts, these sinister and troubled physiog-
nomies convince us of this truth.'[33]

Foreigners who were intent on enjoying Italy as the home of art could scoff at what
they took to be no more than travellers' exaggerated tales by reference to superficial
generalisations regarding appearances: 'Malaria, or bad air, in Rome is all humbug as I
never saw a finer or more healthy people.'[34] Such positive assertions took on a different
political significance in the context of Rome's new role as national capital after 1871. In
order to appreciate 'the true hygienic condition of Romanness', Baccelli explained that
all that was needed was to look at the spectacle of Rome's contemporary citizens: 'Ultimately, a single glance at *our* city is enough to deal summary justice to all the accusations
that were made against it.'[35] Similar rhetoric was to be repeated early in the fascist era,
as proof of a liberation from the ancient curse of malaria thanks to modern improvements instigated by the new regime. In 1925, Dr Pecori proclaimed: 'A stay in Rome, for
the healthiness of its climate, is now acclaimed by all. And the Romans manifest this
health by their robustness, their colour, the vigour of the youth, the pride of the
people.'[36] Such comments rely on an assumed awareness of the commonplace that
Italian natives seemed to have retained a timeless beauty which had inspired earlier
generations of great artists. However, the realm of appearances was contested ground.
On the one hand, insistence on simple visual facts was a way to prevent evasive equivocation. Thus, in 1840, Gaspare Colizzi, member of the Deputazione Sanitaria of Castel-
nuovo, confronted the local governor with a bowl of foul local water, and the challenge:
'One only has to look at it to assess its limpidity…without resorting to chemical observations and experiments.'[37] On the other hand, progressive medical writers like Cabanis
had realized that while the specificity of symptoms required meticulous observation,
this was not on its own enough to get at the true nature of many diseases: 'How can
one grasp the true nature of these illnesses which are concealed beneath the appearance of moral affectations, or of the moral alterations which have the appearance of
certain illnesses?'[38]

THE LANGUAGE OF AIR

One revealing aspect of the desire to categorise air and its different aspects was the
spectrum of vocabulary employed. It is an irony of history that modern medicine continues to employ malaria, a word attached to a set of ideas which had been discredited
by medical discoveries at the end of the nineteenth century.[39] That Italian words are
adopted is consistent with the idea that local lore might be as reliable a guide to dis-
cerning Roman malaria's particular identity as more professional medical analysis. Thus,
in 1698, reporting on the precarious state of health of the artist Pierre de St-Yves, the
director of the Académie de France in Rome, La Teulière, laid great stress on the interaction between the artist's constitution and the local environment, and cited a Roman

saying to explain the predicament he and his *pensionnaires* found themselves in: 'He is of a rather delicate constitution and I do not believe that the air here suits him; as it is quite thick and very variable it doesn't suit everybody. The local people have a nice expression, that one must give it due respect: *si deve portare rispetto a l'arria* [sic], probably meaning that one needs to take care so as not to suffer ill effects.'[40] J.B. Michel, chief medical officer to the French garrison during the Napoleonic occupation of Rome, notes the existence of what in his opinion was a pseudo-scientific local vocabulary for different kinds of air: 'bad', 'heavy', 'fine' and 'subtle', 'that the common people have imagined in order to distinguish the air of the plain, low places near the marshes, and the coast with those areas situated on the summit of a mountain'.[41] The comte de Tournon noted a slightly larger range, preferring to retain their Italian form: 'aria pessima, aria cattiva, sospettta, sufficiente, aria buona, aria fina, aria ottima' (worst, bad, suspect, adequate, good, fine, best).[42]

Comparative studies of diseases in different places tended to weaken the assumption that they were as particular as their locations. For example, James Clark was of the opinion that the fevers experienced in Rome were precisely the same as those found in the Lincolnshire fens or Holland.[43] Yet although the idea that there was a specific condition known as 'Roman fever' ceased to be medically respectable by the mid-nineteenth century, the term clung on, and remained current in terminology and the popular imagination (interestingly, seeming to enter French in this form from English).[44] To that extent it may seem less remarkable that the term Roman fever was still used, if argued against, as late as 1896 in a book with this very title. William North dismissed the term as manifestly too imprecise – it covered a range of conditions, and was misleadingly tied to the specific location of Rome.[45] Nonetheless, in later nineteenth-century usage, it lodged itself in the vocabulary and imaginations of visitors alike, surviving until perhaps its most famous occurrence as the title of a story by Edith Wharton.[46] It is surely significant that Macculloch acquiesced in taking 'malaria' as the key title word for his book, even though he acknowledged the perfectly valid claim of the more venerable Greek miasma to fulfil his diagnostic purpose.[47] Indeed, miasma was still current in the 1870s both in Britain and France.[48] A variant on this, applied to London, was the term 'Disease-Mist' as used by the Registrar General in the later 1830s.[49] At this time malaria referred as much to the cause as to a form of disease itself, and, as already noted, this was to carry on beyond the scientific discoveries of the later nineteenth century.[50]

Writing in 1875, Pietro Balestra noted the varied forms current in Roman usage – 'malaria', 'aria cattiva', 'aria contaminata' – as synonymous, implicitly reinforcing the idea that this was an indigenous condition.[51] Those like Léon Colin who argued against the term and in favour of 'telluric intoxication', on the basis that its causes were to be identified as emanating from the ground, were in a minority, albeit one with a certain legitimacy in so far as the non-specificity of *mal'aria* in Rome was concerned, recognising rather that identical kinds of fever were experienced in a variety of countries, and, indeed, continents.[52] Yet, in the mid-twentieth century, the Romanness of malaria still informed outsiders' expectations. Giovanni Berlinguer recalled that, coming to the capital from Sardinia after the Second World War, he was forced to realise that malaria was neither inherently Roman nor a scourge of malevolent nature, but rather that widespread health problems were fundamentally social in origin, responsibility for which lay with a small clique of greedy and negligent landlords.[53]

HISTORY IN THE AIR

In the later nineteenth century, an awareness of the historical dimension of bad air was an integral part of medical research. For example, the pioneering malariologists W. H. S. Jones and Ronald Ross approvingly note the way William North assimilated a survey of remarks on 'malaria' and related diseases in ancient sources into his account.[54] Following his scientific research, Angelo Celli and his wife, Anna Fraentzel, assembled a history of malaria in the Roman *campagna*.[55] By the time of Arcangelo Ilvento's 1936 study, tracing the history of malaria was a way of throwing into triumphalist relief the achievements of both modern science and also the fascist regime.[56] Robert Sallares has provided a remarkable updating of this convergence between science and medical history as applied to ancient Rome.[57]

For those preoccupied with Rome's ancient history, the city's air was a continuum at once metaphorical and tangible. Indeed, for Montaigne, visiting in 1580–1, given the ruined state of the ancient city, the only aspect of Rome which could be said to have survived was the canopy of its sky and the outline of its situation: 'He said "that one saw nothing of Rome but the sky beneath which it had been settled and the layout of its site;...that those who said that at least one saw Rome's ruins were saying too much; for the ruins of such a forbidding entity would bestow more honour and reverence on its memory; it was no more than its sepulchre".'[58] Montaigne was also aware of Rome's reputation for having ambiguous air, something of particular relevance to him as his travels had a therapeutic motive; manifesting a candid self-interest while clearly responding to reports that Roman air had proved disagreeable, he reported: 'I don't know how others find the air of Rome: myself, I found it very pleasing and healthy.'[59]

As Montaigne's remarks illustrate, history could be evoked through the perception of similarity and contrast. Against the grain of a prevailing thematics of ruination in which Rome was shrunken, fragmented, pulverised, decomposed, the modern climate acquired a paradoxical pathos for being more hospitable than that endured by ancient forebears. In his history of ancient Rome J.J. Ampère played up this contrast in order to celebrate republican fortitude: 'This sky, beneath which one comes to breathe a sweet and salutary air for weak chests, was an inclement sky; today's mild winters were [then] severe.'[60] It was, however, precisely such challenging conditions which brought out the best in this people, and prepared them for their historic destiny: before they had to combat intimidating neighbours, they had to overcome other enemies: 'even the ground they worked, the air they breathed into their lungs. They overcame this as they had to triumph over everything; fate had dealt them a harsh destiny; that is why they were great.'[61] But Ampère recognised that something of the fortitude of Romans' ancient forebears continued to be needed in modern times because of the persistence of *mal'aria*: 'A characteristic of the Roman climate, which time has unfortunately not eliminated, is malaria; it is this fatal influence which, during several months of the year, hovers on the city and above all the Roman *campagna*; it is this Roman fever, which one can avoid with the right precautions, but which the slightest imprudence risks your succumbing to, which strikes the inhabitants, drives away foreigners, ensures that the plain which surrounds Rome is a desert and endows it with a form of intimidating poetry.'[62] In his *Économie politique des romains* (1840), Dureau de La Malle came to a somewhat different conclusion; since *aria cattiva* was clearly widespread through Rome's history, in order to flourish as they had done, he argued that the ancients must have had prophylactic methods and hygienic recipes, as well as remedies proven from experience to protect them, or at the least offset its pernicious effects. Dureau also agreed with Brocchi's argument that the major preventative measure in times both ancient and modern was the wearing of wool, whose oily thickness stimulated the 'exhalation of the skin' which was favourable to circulation and transpiration.[63]

The most well-documented account of the long-standing interest in the problem of Rome's bad air is an essay on this subject published in Rome in 1817 by the historian Francesco Cancellieri, addressed to the German doctor Joachim Salomon Koreff.[64] Primarily concerned with modern rather than ancient history, Cancellieri noted that he had not found references to bad air until the eleventh century. Medieval popes chose to avoid Rome in the summer, which doubled as a way to avoid political factions. Conclaves had a history of high mortality, and to that extent bad air could take on a momentous significance as something which disrupted a key European political event.[65] While he cites a number of texts on 'l'aria di Roma' from the seventeenth century,[66] they increase through the eighteenth century. Indeed, Cancellieri's text appeared at a time when a considerable body of writing on Rome was being produced, in part a by-product of the Napoleonic occupation, and, as far as non-French travellers were concerned, its demise in 1814. This included commentary both general and specialist on air and associated health problems. The need to deal with military casualties of fever was to be a recurrent French medical predicament, renewed when Napoleon III shored up the papacy by installing a large garrison in Rome in 1849.

MAPPING

In considering the relation between ideas about the presence in Rome of an ambient poison, and how this impinged on the experience of the city as a cultural spectacle, location provides a useful way to understand prevailing beliefs about the specificity of the city's identity. It is also a complement to more familiar antiquarian and historical itineraries, by means of which the city was rendered navigable.

Location had always been central to explanations of the nature and causes of the specificity of the city's identity because of a reliance on essentially Hippocratic principles according to which particular aspects of environment and climate were primordial factors in determining a place's degree of salubrity. Thus, Giorgio Baglivi (1668–1707), physician to Innocent XII and Clement XI, was renowned for the cautious specificity of his observations, which he consistently qualified by stating: 'Vivo et scribo in aere romano' (I live and write in Roman air), a salutary means to avoid extravagant claims, and one approvingly noted at the end of the eighteenth century by Cabanis.[67]

During the eighteenth century, these beliefs were translated into detailed studies of the physical and pathological characteristics of specific locations.[68] Enquiries into the particularities of the Italian climate in general, and that of Rome in particular, are examples of the deployment across Europe of the type of essentially empirical and statistical study that constituted medical topography.[69] One characteristic outcome of this approach was maps. In the case of *mal'aria*, graphic specification was a highly promising way of trying to pin down and get hold of what was a notoriously elusive phenomenon.

The process of mapping was also closely associated with an investigative outlook which involved not relying on secondhand information, as so many did when addressing Rome. The comte de Tournon, justifying his *Études statistiques*, based on information gathered during his tenure as prefect of Rome, asserted that 'my constant intention has been only to tread where I could find no previous footprint.'[70] Tournon's peripatetic approach was both metaphorical and literal, and conceived as a resolute antidote to years of accumulated clichés.

In his *De Romani aeris salubritate* (On the Salubrity of Roman Air) (Rome, 1599), Marsilio Cagnati includes two quintessentially Hippocratic maps, one locating Rome in terms of longitude and latitude, another showing a city bounded by its historic hills and the city walls, framed by personifications of the prevailing winds, as much an expressive image as an empirical description (figs 8, 9).[71] The earliest cartographic essays in medical topography addressed to the problem of bad air were published in a text by Giovanni Maria Lancisi at the beginning of the eighteenth century. Lancisi is also significant in so far as his opinions continued to be respectfully referred to well into the nineteenth century.[72] Indeed, his views were to remain something of a benchmark for the later evolution of ideas on the endemic nature of Roman *mal'aria* and its relation to environment. Giovanni Maria Lancisi (1654–1720) was a prominent Roman medical figure, for 30 years professor of 'practical medicine' at La Sapienza, and doctor to three popes, Innocent XI, Clement XI and Innocent XII. He relied on a broad environmental framework allied to extensive empirical observation to account for both general conditions of salubrity and outbreaks of particular diseases.[73] In his study of Roman marshes

16.

Capo dell'armi) & excurrat vlterius versus solis ortum; quantum vltra Leucopetram porrigitur lapygium promontorium (hodie vocatur capo di S. Maria) & ex altera parte ducatur idē latus ad alterum Italiæ extremum, qua scilicet amnis Varus, Italiam ipsam à Prouincia Narbonensi seiungit, sitq; lineæ AB cuius longitudo sit partium quindecim

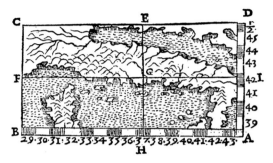

cuiusmodi trecentum sexaginta partiū est totius terræ ambitus, scilicet à gradu vigesimo nono, ad quadragesimum tertium, vt numerantur ducto ab Insulis fortunatis initio, vt ante dixi, huicq; parallela ducatur altera lineæ per extremos Italiæ fines ad septentrionem (nam prior spectat ad meridiem) putà per Tridentum; sitque eiusdem figuræ latus, CD, Deinde iunganuúr hæc latera duabus item parallelis lineis, quæ sint in eadem figura duo latera BC, AD, quæ singula sint partium similium septem, & semissis, scilicet à gradu trigesimo nono, vt à Ptolomeo proditum est,

8 *Map of Rome, Latitude and Longitude*, in Marsilii Cagnati, *De Romani aeris salubritate* (On the Salubrity of Roman Air) (Rome, 1599). British Library, London.

and their relation to the incidence of disease, he acknowledged the crucial role of winds, and the way that their course had been altered by the felling of ancient woods. At the same time, he ascribed great importance to telluric influence. One of the maps he produced as part of his investigations identified areas of 'black' and 'red' soil as influential in determining the salubrity of particular locations (fig. 10).[74] This reflected his belief that Roman air itself was not inherently unhealthy; only 'accidental' causes were responsible, that is, airborne pathogenic matter emanating from the Pontine marshes. For Lancisi, it was the mixture of 'coarse' and 'subtle' air which created a versatile environment for old and young, 'bilious' and 'pituitary' alike. Having to respond to atmospheric

72

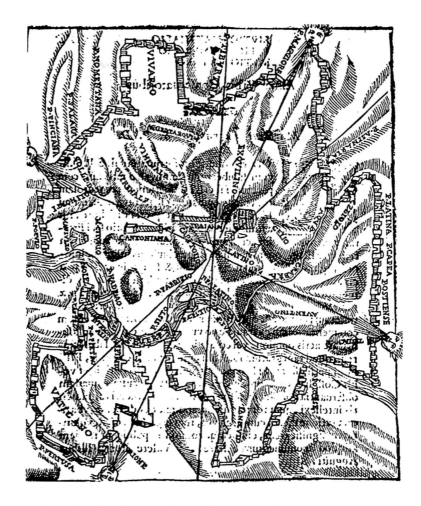

9 *Rome: Prevailing Winds and Seven Hills*, in Marsilii Cagnati, *De Romani aeris salubritate* (On the Salubrity of Roman Air) (Rome, 1599). British Library, London.

fluctuations prevented temperamental torpor and kept constitutions in trim. Moreover, the presence of many fountains and the constant toing and froing of the city's inhabitants ensured that the air was continually refreshed.[75]

Lancisi's analysis of the 'noxious effluvium' which he held to be responsible for the seasonal problem of fevers and other epidemics was essentially Hippocratic, as understood through *De aere aquis et locis* (Of Airs, Waters and Places).[76] The explanation for the presence of particular diseases was to be found through an examination of the situation of a place, and its exposure to different winds, sunlight, available water and its qualities, the nature of the soil, its elevation, and the distribution of vegetation and

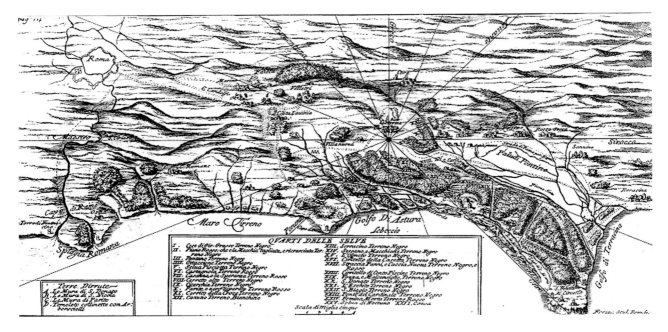

10 *Map of Pontine Marshes, with Prevailing Winds and Wooded Areas*, in Giovanni Maria Lancisi, *De noxiis paludum effluviis, eorumque remediis: Libri duo* (Rome, 1717). Wellcome Collection, London.

trees, and resulting dryness or moistness. In his discussion of marshes and their effluvia, he argued that marsh water itself only became harmful once it had absorbed poisonous particles and been concentrated by evaporation caused by hot wind. He noted the variety of types of fevers and their seasonality. His interest in the life cycle of mosquitoes, and their potential role as vectors of an organic pathogen, has been predictably highlighted. However, it is mistaken to see this as an anticipation of the later discovery of the real nature of malaria in its modern sense. Mosquitoes were merely an ingenious and suggestive variation on the general idea that miasma and its mobility was the cause of disease. Indeed, Lancisi was at pains to repudiate the idea that Rome's bad air was caused by a deep-seated pathogenic essence.[77] For Lancisi, miasma was inorganic – though its effects could be significantly increased by virtue of combination with organic matter or vapour.[78] Ultimately, he had no answer as to the essential identity of the pathogen, but his study illustrates the way he methodically considered – and rejected – various claims.

Two of the most influential aspects of Lancisi's analysis which are of especial relevance to a consideration of ideas on Roman air are the south wind or *sirocco* and its detrimental effects, and the prophylactic role of trees. The two were intimately connected as regards his understanding of Rome's health problems. It was because of the strong fermenting power of the south wind that particularly noxious exhalations were drawn out of the marshes.[79] This wind was unimpeded in its passage towards the city following extensive (and misguided) deforestation. Trees had previously 'absorbed, separated, as if by a screen', impurities held in suspension in the air, which, following its passage across sea and marshes, had become 'humid, thick and glutinous'; cavities between trees trapped these wind currents 'as if in a labyrinth', where they were 'broken down and dispersed'.[80]

These issues were made part of a more public discourse when Lancisi was involved in a celebrated dispute between Michelangelo Caetani and the papacy concerning the proposal to fell extensive woods near Sermoneta and Cisterna, to the south-east of Rome. In 1714, family debts prompted Caetani to offer for sale the felling rights over a period of 18 years to 74,000 hectares of woodland near these two towns. Pope Clement XI set up a *congregazione* to consider this proposal, and Lancisi was deputed to report on its public health aspects. After inspecting the area, mapping the woods,[81] and noting local wind patterns, he concluded that it would be dangerous to allow the felling as proposed, because this would leave the city unprotected from the harmful south wind heavily laden with noxious effluvia after its scorching passage over the Pontine marshes. Following initial rejection and an appeal by Caetani, partial approval was granted with conditions. The woods which protected Cisterna and Sermoneta were to be retained in the form of a high cordon; any roads created by felling should be aligned obliquely with the southern marshes; no felling was allowed in marshy areas; young trees were to be left; 1,500 mature trees were exempted for use in shipbuilding; the area was divided into 18 annual parcels.[82] Exemption from limitations on tree felling had earlier only been allowed as part of attempts to curtail brigandage, clearing areas around roads which had facilitated concealment and ambush.[83]

Lancisi's belief in the harmful effects of the south wind (combined with the problem of the Pontine marshes), and the role of trees as a purifying barrier, were old ideas which retained modern currency (added to this was the memory of woods as homes to sacred sites).[84] Although the papacy's attempt to prevent rampant profiteering, with its harmful consequences for the city and the inhabitants of the southern *campagna*, was based on medical reasons and also a certain political prudence, it could not save the *campagna* from progressive deforestation. By the beginning of the nineteenth century, when a similar but much smaller request was made in 1808 to fell trees from the woods at Sermoneta and Cisterna (4,000 rather than 115,000 in 1714), it could not be fulfilled because there were not enough trees.[85]

Joseph Jérôme le Français de Lalande acknowledged the antiquity of the problem of the 'Scirocco' or 'Chiroque' being the same wind known as Euronotus or Vulturnus by ancient Romans. Its presence was connected to astrological theory, arriving on 22 July, one month after the summer solstice, at the moment the sun entered into the sign of Leo. In Rome, he reported, the *sirocco* was considered as the cause of 'the crushing heat that one experiences on some days, when it seems that one's legs and arms are incapacitated, with discomfort of the nerves, lassitude and a universal sense of collapse'. In extreme cases it sent people and horses mad.[86] For Arthur Young, the physical evidence for the harmful nature of this wind was the corrosion of south-facing walls; he also claimed it caused suicide amongst the common people who lived in low areas.[87] To outsiders, notably English travellers, who were thought of as coming from a country with a national predisposition to suicide, the *sirocco* was part of a cult of morbid melancholy.[88] For Ménageot, director of the French Académie at the end of the eighteenth century, 'the continual sirocco which affects all the faculties and which causes the numerous illnesses that there are in Rome' meant a collective cessation of work.[89]

As noted earlier, trees were thought to purify the air by absorbing noxious particles.[90] Nicola Maria Nicolai, an important early nineteenth-century Presidente delle Strade, echoed the belief that this effect required the presence of sunlight (dense dark woods would not work); leaves also absorbed humidity and carbonated hydrogen gas.[91] At this period, olive and mulberry trees were proposed as especially effective;[92] later in the century the new vogue for eucalyptus attracted much attention as an economically advantageous potential cure for bad air.[93] Such proposals extended the idea that plants were able to absorb and neutralise noxious emanations. Observing the matted surface of the *campagna*, 'embossed with spontaneous shrubs', Lady Morgan opined 'that which is fatal to man, gives vigour to vegetation'.[94] A variation of this type of organic cleansing was the idea that grain fields were capable of counteracting miasma by 'feeding' on it, drawing it out of the ground and breaking it down as a source of generative energy.[95]

Unfortunately, the idea that cultivation was a form of decontamination failed to encourage agricultural activity in the *campagna* to a degree which could reverse the process of deterioration of the land and its inhabitants. This notion of a kind of organic antidote was consistent with the claim that different types of disease-causing particle could cancel each other out. John Charles Atkinson observed that consumptives in fact benefited from Rome's bad air: 'Antagonist action is what is wanted in that fatal malady, not pure air....as Milton says, "Evil, be thou my good"';[96] and the beneficial effect of being vaccinated against smallpox on a fever victim.[97]

Lancisi was treated as a modern medical authority who studied local conditions closely, and moreover was identified with the institutional authority of the papacy. This may in part have encouraged the idea that he was adopting a defensive position, attributing Rome's health problems to 'accidental' causes, as opposed to something inherent in the air or climate.[98] Louis Valentin was more forthright, wondering why Lancisi contrived to locate the origin of Rome's unhealthiness in a region some distance from the city – that is, the Pontine marshes, arriving via the south wind and no longer impeded by woods. He blamed a combination of 'the absence of public and private hygiene, the neglect of the government for matters of medical administration, and the physical and moral education of its inhabitants'.[99]

A century later, Jean-Baptiste Michel's *Recherches médico-topographiques sur Rome et l'Agro Romano* (Rome, 1813) provides a focused update to Lancisi's survey. Like Lancisi,

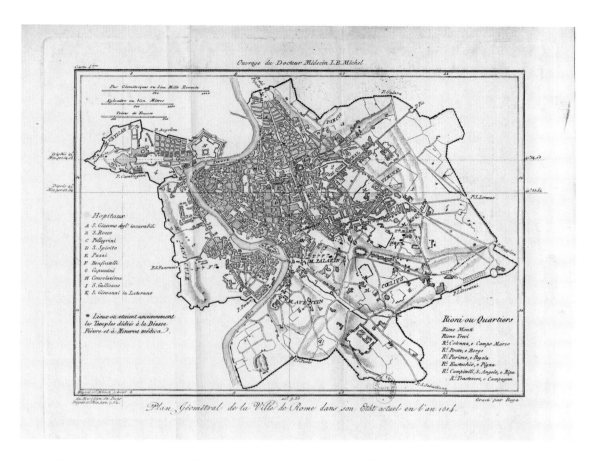

11 *Geometrical map of the city of Rome in its present state in 1814*, in Michel Jean-Baptiste Michel, *Recherches médico-topographiques sur Rome et l'Agro Romano* (Rome, 1813). Bibliothèque Nationale de France, Paris.

there was a contingent agenda behind his study. Michel was 'médecin en chef de l'Hôpital militaire à Rome', the doctor in charge of the French military garrison. His study was primarily intended for the expatriate French audience, but also contains opinions on the state of the local population's health. Like Lancisi, he produced two maps relating to the distribution of disease across the city. One map serves as a frontispiece to his book, 'Plan géométral de la ville de Rome dans son état actuel en l'an 1814' (fig. 11). This combines hospitals and local topography in the form of *rioni* with a historic dimension, for he also notes the sites of ancient Roman temples to the goddess of Fever and to Minerva Medica, thus reinforcing the recognition that the city's health problems had a long-term history. In this latter respect his approach was entirely consistent with the mind set of Giuseppe De Matthaeis, physician at the hospital of Santo Spirito and a key figure in Roman treatment of fever, who had researched the ancient Roman cult of the goddess of Fever and their hospitals.[100]

Michel's other map was more extensive, taking in the environs of Rome, including the Agro Romano, and identifying three types of location in the area surrounding Rome: healthy, unhealthy, very unhealthy ('endroits sains', 'endroits malsains', 'endroits très malsains') (fig. 12). In his text, he characterised places' healthiness according to a combination of their physical situation and population. Like Lancisi, he clearly regarded the empirical conditions of the general environmental context as the fundamental determining factor in this differentiation. This understanding was complemented in the text by detailed judgements on the degree of salubrity of different parts of the city itself, creating a perplexingly variegated jigsaw.[101] Such an uneven distribution necessitated explanations of why two places close together might fall into different categories. Indeed, Michel was one of many to observe that *mal'aria* was unevenly localised, to the extent that it might strike not just in a particular street, but even a particular house within a street that was otherwise free from the problem.[102] Such observations go back as far as Montaigne in the sixteenth century.[103] Others compiled instances of local peculiarities. As Joseph Forsyth recorded: 'Only a narrow road separates the two villas of Lodovisi and Medici; yet the former is subject to malaria, and the other a refuge from

12 Topographical map of Rome and Environs inclusing the Agro Romano, 1814, in Jean-Baptiste Michel, *Recherches médico-topographiques sur Rome et l'Agro Romano* (Rome, 1813). Bibliothèque Nationale de France, Paris.

it. At St Calixtus, the cells next to the country are unhealthy in summer, while the opposite side of the convent is safe.'[104] Montesquieu had earlier been perplexed by the same observation: 'What I find astonishing is that the bad air is so close to the good air. You see a house where the air is good. Twenty or thirty paces away, there is another with bad air. This is because one is high, the other low.' He found an explanation in exposure to the south wind; it only needed a small hill to provide protection.[105]

This was a tangible and perhaps predictable result of what J.B. Michel proposed as the dominant feature of Rome's climate – its inconstancy. This in turn rendered medical advice highly unreliable.[106] Rome's longitude suggested that its climate should not be so extreme; however, frequent variations of temperature, the nature of the air and the quality of winds gave Rome a climate *sui generis*.[107] He asserts that the miasma which was believed to be in Roman air and responsible for 'endemic intermittent fevers' was merely a fiction or hypothesis which lack of research allowed to hold sway; 'simple and pernicious fevers develop wherever there is no marsh provided the nervous system acquires this predisposing diathesis which suits them and is specific to them.' Michel was convinced that wind itself, without marsh emanations, had 'different contractilities' which caused 'its loosening and debilitating influence on our organs whose action it seems to paralyse. It numbs the living system, and causes an extreme prostration of energy, a tendency to sleep, and thus becomes a powerful predisposing cause of all nervous illnesses.'[108]

The way maps express a form of knowledge which exists in both two and three dimensions, and the persuasiveness of medico-topographical ways of thinking, generally ensured they would continue to be made throughout the nineteenth century. In his *Promenades dans Rome* (1829), Stendhal refers to a map by 'M. Metaxa, I believe, famous doctor and wit', of places 'attacked by fever': 'nothing is more baroque than the contours of contagion on this map. A fine subject to go into, but reasonably, and not with vague elegant, pretty phrases.'[109] Stendhal's comments signal the difficulty in making sense of the distribution of fever sites, whose 'baroque' character hinted at the insufficiency of location as an explanation.

Two of Michel's successors as French medical practitioners in Rome held contrasting views on the causes of *mal'aria*. François Balley, writing in 1863, insisted that meteorological factors had not been properly studied and sought answers through extensive statistical analysis.[110] Balley's work also highlights the ambiguity as to whether *mal'aria* in Rome was the same as that found elsewhere, and draws on French experiences in another foreign site of military occupation, Algeria.[111] In contrast, in his treatise on intermittent fevers (1870), Léon Colin believed the source of *mal'aria* was to be found in the earth, and proposed that the term 'telluric infection' be used instead. Colin's views tend to reinforce the association of *mal'aria* with location in so far as he rejects the idea of wind as a cause. He argued that winds had remained the same, but the disease's distribution had changed; if wind played a role it was because it was 'a low wind, hugging the ground'. His assertion of the prime importance of 'telluric infection' is consistent with an essentially topographical logic to its distribution.[112] Indeed, both refer to maps as part of their basic conceptualisation of the problem.[113]

We have already seen that one of the distinctive features of bad air was the sometimes perplexing unpredictability of its locations. This was rendered potentially even more frustrating for those who aspired to fix some kind of correlation between certain physical conditions and the presence or absence of bad air by the fact that it was recognised to be changing. Focusing on the precise locations where bad air's effects were evident brought to the fore the alarming fact that it was on the move. Lancisi himself noted this. Since Petronius's account of areas of bad air, *De victu Romanorum et de sanitate tuenda* (Rome, 1581), prevailing winds had stayed the same, but some areas had improved. Léon Colin pointed out that the area around the Trevi fountain, which had been surrounded by stagnant water, had improved following repairs under Gregory XIII connected to the building of the College of Propaganda Fide.[114]

Forsyth noted the problem of mobility in typically xenophobic fashion when in Rome in 1802–3: 'This mal'aria is an evil more active than the Romans, and continues to increase.'[115] 'Last autumn four thousand persons died victims to it in the Roman hospitals. It is a battle renewed every spring, and lost every fall….it is advancing on the suburbs, and the city of Rome, while the checks opposed to its progress are either defective or absurd.'[116] Returning to Rome in 1802 27 years after his first visit, Charles Bonstetten was shocked to find that 'the map of bad air has completely changed. In 1775, the heights of Trinità dei Monti were reputed to be safe from bad air, and in 1802, they no longer are.'[117]

In 1813, J.B. Michel pointed out that Doni's list of places drawn up in the late seventeenth century as being more or less salubrious was out of date: 'good' places had become 'bad' and vice versa.[118] In 1817, Frédéric Lullin de Châteauvieux found that 'Malaria…appears to be investing the city on every side. The hills and elevated grounds within the walls of the city, where this insalubrity in former times was never felt, nor even suspected, are now affected by it in summer.' Rome was 'about to fall prey to an invisible enemy, which a vigilant and wise administration would have enabled it to resist'. Areas newly infected include the relatively elevated areas of the Quirinal, the Perician, the Palatine, the area surrounding the Villa Borghese, the Monte Mario and the surroundings of the Villa Pamfili.[119] William Gell recorded in 1846 that at Frascati 'most of the villas have fallen into neglect and desertion.' Albano and Castel Gandolfo had superseded its former status as the fashionable and salubrious retreat of choice.[120]

Madame de Staël made the spread of *mal'aria* part of *Corinne*'s *mise-en-scène*: 'This bad air is so to speak laying siege to Rome; each year it advances a few paces more, and we are forced to abandon the most charming dwellings to its empire.' Bad air threatened the city and encouraged depopulation but added to the appealing effect of extensive gardens within the city walls.[121] James Clark reported the French view of 'malaria', 'which of late years has excited so much attention', that 'the metropolis of the world' would soon 'become a desert'. He observed wearily: 'The Romans themselves smile at these exaggerated prospects.'[122] Lady Morgan, who was all too aware of the threat of *mal'aria*, found it difficult to get any clear information on its progress: 'The natives being used to the evil, treat it with great comparative disregard; and jealousy for the honour of the city prevents their speaking freely on the subject.'[123]

The seasonal impact of Roman fever had led to well-established habits of relocation. A.V. Arnault was puzzled and disturbed to encounter Rome as an all but deserted city.[124] However, Rome had long had a reputation as a dead city. James Johnson considered the empty palaces which were everywhere to be found in the centre of Rome as so many 'gloomy' but entirely empty 'prisons'.[125] Tournon thought that population increase had in the past helped to stem the tide of bad air, but this had remained stagnant (indeed, the arrival of the French had in fact initially caused something of an exodus).[126]

ADAPTATION

Complementary to the deployment of medical topographical research from the later eighteenth century was the evolving literature on climatology.[127] This was primarily oriented towards recommending therapeutic places rather than identifying causes of disease in unhealthy places. Progressively, particular locations were identified as beneficial for the treatment of certain types of conditions. However, nationalism, local partisan feeling and xenophobia, fuelled by the economic benefits of popularity amongst health tourists, played a significant role. Yet in the case of Rome, the recognition that its climate was only suitable for the treatment or relief of some ailments, and then only at certain times of the year (for example, that consumptives should make Rome their residence in winter only), was slow to become accepted.[128] Visitors to Rome were drawn by the general myth of the Warm South, what T.H. Burgess sceptically referred to as the 'talismanic efficacy of foreign climes';[129] Emile Decaisne more enthusiastically termed Italy 'the promised land of invalids', where they would be delivered from their afflictions.[130] This informed the deep-seated belief that the city was, in ways that were intimately connected, a source of health and also cultural and artistic stimulation. However, observation and experience demonstrated that, in both respects, Rome was in fact a much more unpredictable environment.

Irrespective of the inconstancy of Rome's climate, travellers and visitors had to deal with a change of atmosphere, and commentaries on reactions to Rome pay particular attention to the question of physical and psychological adaptation. In addition to the threat of bad air, a further aspect of Rome's climate which could destabilise and discommode travellers was the heat of the summer; this changed how they conducted themselves and where they chose to live. On the one hand, heat could have beneficial effects. Even the author of the staunchly pro-English *Comparative Sketch* conceded: 'Profuse perspiration, which the heat of their climate necessarily promotes, may be considered as the reason that so few chronic complaints are known among them. The excessive thirst which this excites, is quickly allayed by the refreshing juices of acid fruits so admirably adapted by Providence to their soil; and they afford no small preservative against those putrid disorders which are so destructive in warm climates.'[131] Moreover, it was possible to imagine nocturnal heat and the sleeplessness it caused as a spur to creativity. In his 1789 sculpture, Pierre Julien created an image of the long-term Roman resident Nicolas Poussin 'in the hot season'; preoccupied by the composition for the *Testament d'Eudamidas*, he has got up to 'fix' 'a felicitous idea' (une idée heureuse) (here using a tablet) draped only in his conveniently sculptural cloak, as if the sleeplessness caused by the heat of the night had been responsible for this insight.[132] But adapting to advice on where to live in relation to bad air could have disagreeable consequences in the summer. Joseph Wright moved to 'the most healthful part of the city. This house stands upon the highest ground, and we have 109 stairs to ascend,' which was unbearable in the heat.[133] However, for David Wilkie, whose primary motive in travelling was to restore his health through a 'change of air and cessation of work', the benefits of southern climes were decidedly ambiguous. His biographer Allan Cunningham records that, as Wilkie waited in Paris and listened to contradictory medical advice as to the desirability of travelling south, his own feeling was that 'travel had never done him any harm': 'the heat is the only thing I dread'.[134] The terminology employed is revealing: 'He only waited until the fever-heat of the sun [in Rome] should lessen, to be gone [from Paris].'[135] Indeed, Wilkie's prevarication was based on the fear of too much sun, and the contrasts of heat and cold 'which I think do more mischief in Rome than the malaria'.[136]

The unfamiliar and for many uncongenial extremes of heat are an example of the more complex question of adaptation to the Roman environment. In the eighteenth century, there was a general, and ultimately Hippocratic, belief that bodies were indelibly stamped by their original environment and climate. As was the case for all places with a pronounced local atmosphere, this created a particular set of problems for foreigners or outsiders who entered an alien atmosphere. The awkwardness of such a transition had been made a feature of Rome's reputation in the Renaissance – admittedly by the Tuscan Vasari. As André Chastel has noted, Vasari's belief that some outsiders might find Rome's air difficult, if not intolerable, was intertwined with the idea that the city had an intimidating array of art. His explanation for the strange incident of Rosso painting what was considered to be his worst ever picture was based on this predicament:

I cannot imagine where this came from other than in a reaction which he is not the only one to have experienced. This is what happens: it seems an astonishing and mysterious aspect of nature, but the fact is that to change country or location is like changing nature, the way of living and personal habits, such that sometimes one is not oneself; one becomes another person; one becomes bewildered and dazed. This is what must have happened to Rosso in Rome's air, because of the remarkable works of architecture and sculpture that he could see there and the painted and sculpted works by Michelangelo which perhaps made him not be himself. The same troubles caused Bartolommeo di S. Marco and Andrea del Sarto to leave Rome, without them being able to achieve anything worthwhile.[137]

Michelangelo himself, to Vasari's embarrassment, thrived on Roman air, because it evidently suited his temperament, hence his decision to reside there from 1534: 'If he stayed far from Florence for a long time, it was exclusively because of the quality of the air, for experience had taught him that Florentine air, however keen and subtle, was very harmful to his temperament, and that of Rome, sweeter and more temperate, had kept him in perfect health to the age of ninety years, remaining fully active and vigorous which, despite his age, allowed him to keep working until his last day.'[138] It is symptomatic of modern scepticism regarding the effects of air that Chastel translates 'aria di Roma' as 'milieu', somewhat misleadingly insisting on the social and cultural context rather than on Vasari's elemental conception of artists' susceptibilities.

In the early eighteenth century, Giacomo Baglivi recommended that sobriety needed to be adopted by foreigners when in Rome because of the slowing of blood circulation they would experience.[139] The abbé Dubos claimed that Rome's air could only be borne by those who had accustomed themselves to it little by little. Each year this process had to be repeated as soon as its seasonal 'corruption' set in. Indeed, without such preparation, the impact could be fatal: 'One is as little surprised to see someone die who, arriving from the countryside, lodges in a place where the air is corrupted, and even those who, at these times, come to settle in a place in the city where air has remained healthy, as to see the death of someone struck by a cannon ball.'[140] In a way which seemed to argue for a cessation of travel (but also anticipated aspects of the more elaborate later specialism of climatology), Dubos claimed that 'native air is a remedy for all of us'.[141] Indeed, as already noted, Lancisi had argued that Romans were in fact all the more resilient because of the atmospheric variety of their native environment – an echo of Baglivi's observation on the Athenians' constitutional vigour.[142]

Yet change of air was also a medical formula persistently associated with therapeutic benefits. As in the case of Johnson and Wilkie, however, the debate within British literature was far from consistent with respect to the advantages of travelling over the merits of a sedentary policy. Johnson himself produced a cannily complementary pair of volumes on the relative merits of foreign and home itineraries.[143] Most opinion argued that change could be harmful because of the tension it created between a constitution which had been shaped by one climate having to cope with quite different air and weather. Francesco Cancellieri noted the advice that illness could be caused by moving from an area of bad air (aria cattiva), to which one had become accustomed, to an area of 'good air'.[144] This was invoked by Montesquieu as a qualified possibility: 'Even freedom appeared unbearable to peoples who were not accustomed to enjoy it. It is thus that a pure air is sometimes harmful to those who have lived in marshy country.'[145] This was a variation on the theme that the prevalence of bad air was implicitly political in so far as it was a symptom of maladministration.

Whereas earlier settlers had originally come from inhospitable areas, which had led to them becoming congenitally accustomed to bad conditions, and therefore enabled them to cope with even the worst that Rome could offer, modern travellers were thought less likely to have a sturdy and adaptable disposition.[146] Indeed, J.B. Michel observed that, after a few years in Rome, foreigners ended up contracting 'nervous maladies' and 'complain of hysterical effects'.[147] 'It is thus that the unstable climate and always humid atmosphere of Rome develops nervous temperaments, and at the same time reduces the tonicity of organs and muscular force.'[148] Consistent with the dependence of bodily state on ambient conditions, he was inclined like Dubos to the view that often only 'native air' could effect a recovery from a state of ill health developed in Rome.[149] Yet, there was also an alternative discourse around the idea of mastering nature, both necessary for and fostered by greater cosmopolitan travel (new technologies, notably the train, bringing their own hazards).[150] By contrast, opinions on Rome and what it meant to visit the city are very much coloured by the desire to be receptive to the unique array of art and architecture on view – a state of mind somewhat at odds with the recognition that the local climate and all-enveloping atmosphere might be hostile.

According to Edward Trelawny, there was a more irreversible aspect to the insidious effects of local climate, as in the case of succumbing to fever: 'There is this peculiarity in malaria fevers, that if you have once had them, you are ever after peculiarly susceptible to a renewal of their attacks if within their reach, and Byron was hardly ever out of it.'[151] For the climatologist Carrière, although 'the habit of displacement and the activity of intellectual work produced in organisms a new kind of temperament', the corollary to this was the judgement that resistance to the effects of different climates was likely to be overcome when in a state of exhaustion or illness, with the result that 'far from escaping meteorological agents, they become the puppets of them prior to becoming their victims.'[152]

The explorer and polymath Charles Marie de La Condamine recorded the received wisdom regarding how best to conduct oneself current in mid-eighteenth-century Rome. It was not safe to depart from the city in summer after any stay in it, nor to return thither having once left it; nor to sleep there, even in the daytime, in any home but one's own: 'At this present time a lodger in Rome cannot be compelled to quit during the summer season, even for deficiency of payment,' but he added that 'these old simples are now pretty well worn away.' Moreover, he witnessed 'experiments made on purpose to prove air really wholesome, which has long been acknowledged pestiferous', a performance which 'savours much of novelty'.[153] While he begins by noting that, as he had set out on his travels 'chiefly for the recovery of my health, I did not choose to encumber myself with an apparatus of instruments', he ends by noting that he had 'pretty well recovered my health during my long residence at Rome'.[154] Hester Piozzi remarked that the 'air of this city is unwholesome to foreigners' but conceded that 'if they pass the first year, the remainder goes well'.[155] However, the example of Lauchlan Aitken, who lived in Rome for fourteen years and spoke up for the local climate, was exceptional.[156]

Nonetheless, for those who wished to spend time in the Eternal City, the advice purveyed by Giacomo Barzellotti was to try to follow Italians' example – a kind of behaviourist style of adaptation.[157] Later, Baedeker recommended that most travellers must in some degree alter their mode of living whilst in Italy, without, however, wholly adopting the Italian style.[158] Other Roman sayings included: 'None but Englishmen and dogs walk on the sunny side of the street, Christians walk in the shade';[159] on location of residence: 'Where the sun does not enter, there the physician invariably must.'[160] In *Daisy Miller*, Henry James nicely expresses equivocation as to the reliability of such local advice by putting the claim that 'if we get in [home] by midnight we are quite safe' into the mouth of the untrustworthy Gianelli.[161]

Opinion as to whether mal'aria was contagious was divided. Armstrong, in a study of typhus fever, inclined to doubt this mode of transmission; nonetheless, we find an experienced traveller such as Mary Shelley in 1818 worrying about her husband having spent time in a carriage with a feverish German.[162] Prosper Mérimée, discussing the death of the archaeologist Charles Lenormant from fever, recalled how in Greece as in Italy 'one flees with a kind of superstitious terror contact with the dying'.[163] This area of uncertainty linked malaria with other diseases, notably consumption. In Rome, the persistence of popular beliefs about, for example, the contagious nature of consumption, which in institutional medical terms led to separate wards being set aside for its victims, was condemned as cruel and out of date by commentators who regarded northern European medical practices as more enlightened and modern.[164] In Britain, fever wards were instituted at the end of the eighteenth century, linked to the idea of contagion; but at Santo Spirito, the main destination for Roman seasonal fever victims, their ailments and causes of death were in fact usually multiple.[165]

Foreign opinion on doctors in Rome also reflects this ambivalence. Baedeker advises consulting English and German doctors, with the proviso that local maladies might respond better to 'native' skill.[166] Similarly, the entry on health in Murray's guide to Rome was written by a 'local authority', but one who had trained abroad.[167] Such scepticism fitted in with the expectation that local advice might be disingenuously designed to reassure foreign visitors and, in the case of invalids travelling in pursuit of health, encourage trade. Examples of this can certainly be found in medical writing as far back as the mid-eighteenth-century text by Giovanni Girolamo Lapi, *Ragionamento contro la volgare opinione di non poter venire a Roma nell'estate* (Argument against the Common Opinion that one should not come to Rome in the Summer) (Rome, 1749).[168] More generally, as has already been noted, nineteenth-century climatology was inherently, and often explicitly, partisan, resulting in the most extreme form of sceptical recommendation that it was safer to stay at home. In so far as cultural and also therapeutic travellers constituted one of Rome's crucial economic resources, obviously it was in the interests of Roman inhabitants and authorities to promote understanding of the causes of 'bad air', and to play down the notion that it was ineradicably rooted in the Roman environment. In this retrospective light, even an erudite authority like Lancisi was liable to be undermined. If anything, Rome's nomination as capital provoked further polemical accusations against its climate and bad air from disappointed Florentine rivals for this privilege.[169]

PREVENTION

Recipes and devices which promised prevention are a fascinating *mélange* of folk custom and the scientifically plausible, but also have a long history. Laura Lane has described the array of medical and magical objects and practices current in ancient Rome.[170] The eclectic range of modern advice gives a good sense that the scourge of bad air was at once so threatening, and so elusive, that all potential aids were legitimate. It is remarkable that the list of preventatives given at the end of Lancisi's *De noxiis* was to remain accepted wisdom well into the nineteenth century.[171] Some seem plausible approaches to cleansing the air, others more superstitious: houses should be perfumed with resinous woods and sulphur; a moderate diet observed; use of acidic and strong condiments – ground up quince, orange, lemon, vinegar – was encouraged; going out on an empty stomach was discouraged; Brocchi recommended fire, chlorine and fumigation with aromatics;[172] one should eat before opening windows; wine should be this year's, being careful to avoid the lees; if diluting, care needed taking with the source of the water; ice from snow was recommended to cool wine – this was a kind of antidote; Valentin noted the continued belief in the protective effects of mixing ice from melted snow with wine at mealtime against 'emanations', as had been prescribed by Galen, based on the idea that snow could not absorb contagion;[173] morning and evening air should be avoided; saliva should not be swallowed; a sponge soaked in 'thieves' vinegar' (a mixture of vinegar, herbs and spices) should be carried. Stendhal took no half measures: 'I soaked myself with thieves' vinegar when crossing the Pontine marshes.'[174] In her *Travels*, Mariana Starke gives an unacknowledged digest of Lancisi's list, to which she adds that 'quicksilver put into a quill, and fastened round the neck, so as to touch the bosom, is likewise deemed an excellent preservative against every kind of infection.'[175] Lancisi is very sceptical of Helmont's amulets – which he refers to as having 'ridiculous inscriptions', and being in the form of idols, yet accepts that these have an effect in so far as they boost confidence.[176] His unscientific but prudent conclusion was to invoke divine assistance. Already at the beginning of the eighteenth century, in listing preventative measures against disease in general and bad air in particular, Lancisi included 'calmness of the soul' ('Tranquillità dell'anima'), on the basis that low spirits leave the body in a weakened state and therefore unable to resist 'miasmatic air' ('aria miasmatica'); whereas 'the steady and strong soul, and the hope of good things despite adversity, has the effect of exciting the villi of the brain and the heart into a state of lively contraction, which is their natural state; whereby the juice of the nerves is gently stirred, and the material flows in the praecordia. The blood, with its force and vitality, absorbs a greater part of the noxious effluvia, which insistently spread in the viscera. And we do not praise laughter as an antidote to pestilential diseases from reasoning, but because we are impressed by experience.' He cites A. Quirino Rivinos (1652–1723), Professor of Physiology at Bologna, 'who had never seen anyone ill with the plague…who had not contracted it because they were afraid of it'.[177]

J.J. Ampère had singled out the harsh conditions in which the early Roman Republic had been forged, arguing that this had been an ideal preparation for later military achievements. James Johnson made a more disease-specific point, claiming that the ancient Romans had warded off bad air by means of a psychology of active resistance. Thus, he encouraged the view that 'power and pride, leaving all the comforts of wealth out of the question, are amongst [the] most potent antidotes to external agents of morbific nature, and especially to the impressions of malaria.'[178] An aristocratic version of such an attitude may lie behind Byron's reference to 'a sharp gentlemanly fever that went away in a few days', rather than 'the low vulgar typhus, which is at present Decimating Venice'.[179] In 1817, William Stewart Rose referred to his 'short but sharp attack of ague' as having 'paid my footing', reducing a bout of fever to a disagreable rite of passage associated with the descent into Italy.[180]

Certainly some travellers took this view, though it is not evident that it was informed by awareness of such attitudes to Roman history. Thus, Edward Trelawny, eager to satisfy his desire for exercise so as to re-establish a 'just equilibrium' between body and brain, 'determined to pass the coming winter in the wildest part of Italy, the Maremma, in the midst of marshes and malaria'.[181] Horace Vernet's pair of paintings showing hunting scenes in the Pontine marshes (1831 Salon) (see figs. 41, 42) seem to exemplify this kind of recreational bravura.[182]

The adage that one must not sleep crossing the *campagna* is consistent with this linkage of physical and mental state. Sleep meant one's defences were down, even if in an agitated state of apprehension. Despite breaking one of the cardinal rules of *campagna*-crossing by keeping the window open, Etienne de Jouy believed his restless state and convulsive movements had protected him against the bad air.[183] A comparable idea was that there was safety in numbers, as if the bustle of a group could ward off bad air, as Léopold Robert and his brother sought to explain to his worried patron Marcotte regarding travelling in the *campagna*: 'Last year my brother and I had already made a reconnaissance in the places little known to foreigners, but as we were only two, we were too few to be entirely free from the danger, or to put it better, the fear of danger.'[184]

The disaffected Romantic stereotype enshrined in the person of Oswald, Lord Nelvil, relished this kind of risk: 'I love', said Oswald to Corinne, 'this mysterious, invisible danger, this danger beneath the form of the sweetest impressions. If death, as I believe, is only a summons to a happier existence, why should not the perfume of flowers, the shade of fine trees, the refreshing breeze of the evening, be charged with bringing us this news?…I easily understand that the inhabitants and foreigners do not find themselves sated by Rome because of the type of peril that they run during the best seasons of the year.'[185]

As Carl Thompson has noted, the generation of early nineteenth-century English travellers in Italy played up to their devil-may-care reputation; according to Leigh Hunt: 'Englishmen are called the mad English from the hazards they run. They like to astonish the natives by a little superfluous peril.'[186] Charles Eastlake recalled how he 'drew in the open air in August without an umbrella whence the painters call me "the Salamander"'.[187] In the view of Norvins, after the fall of Napoleon, Rome became 'the plague-house needed for the illness which torments in different ways spirits and souls'; neither the threat of brigands nor malaria put off the fashionable Europe of the *salons*, impatient to travel and enjoy themselves after an era of war: '[the] bad air of the Pontine marshes is no more than a quarter of an hour to endure; they close their windows, stay awake, and unconcerned by the scourge, go to and fro between Rome and Naples, Naples and Rome....Rome benefits from this general malaise on the part of a Europe impatient to come to breathe the perfume of its altars, its glory, its climate.'[188]

Such attitudes seem either artificial or a kind of defence mechanism, given Rome's established reputation as a city of death – whether on the scale of past imperial extinction or individual fate.[189] At the beginning of the seventeenth century, Annibale Carracci had viewed a return to Rome as a death sentence: 'He recently went, almost as if tired of life, to seek death in Naples, and, not finding it there, came back to face it in Rome, in this dreadful season which is the most dangerous for such a change of air.'[190] As James Johnson reflected when visiting the Protestant cemetery, many for whom Rome proved to be their last resting place had come with precisely the opposite hope that 'azure skies' would restore their health and prolong their lives. Mary Shelley, who had lost one child to fever in Rome, was understandably reluctant to return there: 'But for my child, I would take up my abode at Rome. Rome is a good nurse, and soon rocks to a quiet grave those who seek death.'[191]

THE PERILOUS PURSUIT OF CULTURE

One aspect of medical uncertainties about Rome was the question of whether the pursuit of culture was likely to be more injurious than therapeutic. While the inspirational effects of Roman landscape, its light, and the atmosphere which created such effects were recognised not only to lift the spirit but also to have a restorative effect on ailing constitutions, pursuing cultural itineraries was, nonetheless, not without its problems and dangers. On the one hand, Jean-François Dancel, in his study of travel and illness, viewed Rome's art treasures as a beneficial array of 'distractions' which could enhance the salutary effects of travel by providing a stimulating psychological boost.[192] James Whiteside found that the 'delightful confusion' of sightseeing allowed him to forget that he was meant to be in Rome as an invalid dedicated to recuperation.[193] On the other hand, James Clark spelt out the dangerous aspects of cultural tourism, particularly the extreme contrast of temperature and humidity experienced in moving from sundrenched exterior spaces to shady ruins and dark, dank churches, whose chilled marble floors were especially dangerous for lightly shod women.[194] Indeed, T. H. Burgess extended this observation and argued that, when talking of 'the climate of Italy', a distinction should be made between external conditions and those found within churches and galleries.[195] Simond warned of the nocturnal torchlight visit to the Vatican because of the risk of fever, not to mention the cold marble floor, exacerbated by the cooling effect of the fountain.[196] By contrast, Pucinotti warned that the interior of the mausoleum of Augustus, where performances were put on in the hot season from 6 o'clock until just after sunset, was perfectly designed to encourage the contraction of fever.[197] Mariana Starke provided a whole catalogue of advice for those travellers who sought to combine tourism with the promotion or preservation of their health:

> There are cloth shoes sold in the streets of Rome for about three or four pauls the pair, which Invalids should always put on over their shoes, or boots, when they visit churches, palaces, and villas. It is likewise prudent to put on an extra coat, or cloak, on going in to most of the just-named edifices, and to pull it off on coming out; in short, too many precautions cannot be taken, in order to mitigate that dangerous chill which is the inevitable consequence of remaining long in large, damp, and uninhabited apartments, with marble or brick floors; and Persons afflicted with weak lungs should, on no consideration, venture into the coldest churches, palaces &c. During the months of May and October, however, the contrast between the external and internal air is less great than at other periods.[198]

One of the best known, if not unavoidable, of these problematic sites was the Colosseum at midnight, preferably illuminated by moonlight. Since the later eighteenth century, a moonlit visit to it had become one of the obligatory ports of call for tourists to Rome, predating Staël's *Corinne* (1807) but undoubtedly amplified by that example.[199] However, it has not been noticed that this ritual intersects with still resonant ideas as to the psychologically disturbing effects of moonlight.[200] In a sense this was reinvented in the form of the horror and disgust provoked by the thought of slaughtered Christian martyrs and exotic beasts. That is to say, for all the well-rehearsed expectations which such a visit required, the experience could activate deep levels of subjective disorientation, or its simulation. Anna Jameson includes the following vignette in her *Diary of an Ennuyée*, describing the spectacle of a young French artist she came upon in the Colosseum: 'who, as if transported out of his senses by delight and admiration, was making the most extraordinary antics and gestures: sometimes he clasped his hands, then extended his arms, then stood with them folded as if in deep thought; now he snatched up his portfolio as if to draw what so much enchanted him, then threw it down and kicked it from him as if in despair'.[201]

It should be added that the Colosseum was recognised to be a 'focus of malaria, in a very insalubrious district', characterised by 'moist and stagnant air', exacerbated by the extensive vegetation – all combined to create a noxious atmosphere. In this case, asked Thomas Burgess, why was it so popular with the ill? Echoing Byron he suggested: 'It may be, perhaps, that ruins console each other.'[202] But by the later nineteenth century, it had become known as what Henry James, in *Daisy Miller*, termed a 'nest of malaria'. Hence, nocturnal meditations there were, as James put it, 'recommended by the poets, but deprecated by the doctors'.[203]

The pursuit of culture in Rome was all the more dangerous because it was irresistible. For one thing, in medical terms, James Johnson suggested that the 'excitement of novelty and the exhilaration of travelling' disguised the initial effects of disease, thus delaying remedial action.[204] The city's riches induced over-exertion and excitement which frequently resulted in a state of serious debilitation. This was itself sometimes classified as a pathological condition, what Burgess called 'the inveterate sight-seeing mania'.[205] As we saw in chapter 2, for artists and architects, this could also lead to – or perhaps be confused with – a psychological crisis, in so far as the long-awaited rush of inspiration and the sense of a state of creative regeneration associated with the encounter with Rome might fail to materialise, leaving a dangerous vacuum.

Classical archaeology required on-site investigation, and therefore confrontation with ambient conditions and especially with the unpredictable distribution of 'bad air'. In addition to his vivid, closely observed accounts of Roman sites, William Gell's *The Topography of Rome and its vicinity* (1846) is a veritable guide to the irregular, mosaic-like presence of 'aria cattiva' in the *campagna*; indeed, he also includes the quintessential medical topographical evidence of demographic statistics in his notes on specific places.[206] Archaeologists were likely to expose themselves to risks because excavations removed the barrier that had existed between the modern atmosphere and potentially noxious archaic miasmas trapped beneath layers of stone and rubble.[207] As we saw in discussing Rome's climate, the presence of bad air was in part attributed by Dubos and Montesquieu to underground cavities within ruins. Indeed, one explanation for the surprising salubrity of parts of central Rome was precisely the insulation provided by several layers of masonry accumulated over centuries of demolition and the collapse of monuments.[208]

Gaspard de Prony, supervising work on a new bridge over the via Appia as part of an ambitious scheme to drain the Pontine marshes and finally to rid them of bad air, had to deal with a variation on this problem. They found they were breaking into 'a source of deleterious air'. Many workers fell ill; three died later. The *chef d'atelier*, who had never been ill at Terracina, notoriously noxious, where he worked every year, never really recovered. Prony, too, had not flinched from first-hand extensive reconnaissance, and duly paid for it: 'Last year, I myself was attacked twice by the fever, having stayed two or three times close to the excavations.' He sought an explanation for the concentrated bad air released by these excavations in 'the exhalations from the peat which comes into contact with air, exhalations whose abundance is indicated by the shrinkage of the dried peat'.[209] Digging down into Rome's ancient layers merely seemed to expose further degrees of stench and harmful emanations. Noting that the Cloaca maxima was 'in very bad order', Keysler warned of the dangers for 'those who dig deep in the earth, and happen to light upon an aperture of such an obstructed sink or shore', and thus expose themselves to 'putrid effluvia', which had been the cause of several deaths.[210]

Established in 1666, the Académie de France in Rome had a long history of interaction not only with the Paris art world and French state on which it depended and of which it was a part, but also with local conditions. What has not previously been taken into account is the unrelenting chronicle of *pensionnaires*' ill health and the continual sense of fraught negotiation with the threat Rome's climate posed to artists' well-being if not survival. No less than three directors died in post in the eighteenth century.[211] The memorials and tombs which crowd the interior of San Luigi dei Francesi are witness to the high mortality rate of France's artistic élite.

One of the early directors of the Académie, Nicolas Vleughels, encouraged his superior in Paris, the duc d'Antin, to think of the institution as ideally placed to foster artistic activity: 'Rome is a country of study and our home, by all that one finds there of the beautiful and the good combined.'[212] Nonetheless, he recognised that such aspirations were in tension with a tendency to be lulled into a state of enjoyable inertia by the local environment, and succumb to 'the idleness that the young people contract easily in this country'.[213] D'Antin had ceased to be surprised by reports from Vleughels's predecessor Poerson of students' illness, almost coming to expect this as an unpleasant but avoidable phase of acclimatisation.[214]

In 1724, the Académie's relocation had been considered, with the Villa Farnesina on the west bank of the Tiber a candidate as a new home, but this was advised against because the site was reputedly 'cursed' by bad air.[215] Lalande reported that, whatever the environment in the city of Rome, within the Palazzo Mancini living conditions were harsh; students' rooms were under the roof, behind the cornice, where 'heat and cold are felt in turn in an inconvenient way'.[216] In 1790, when the artist-émigrée Elizabeth Vigée-Lebrun was accommodated there, she found conditions intolerable and left as soon as possible.[217] If further disincentive to nostalgia was needed, the institution was forced to close in 1793 by an anti-revolutionary mob. In 1804, the new director, Suvée, played up this reputation for being in the noisiest part of Rome, which could also be suffocatingly hot, when praising the new, more tranquil and better ventilated site of the re-established Académie in the Villa Medici on the Pincio.[218]

Having to deal with the various ways in which the health of *pensionnaires* responded to Rome's climate, and the impact of bad air, was an essential aspect of directors' responsibilities. For example, deciding whether to follow local advice and use *quinquina*, a popular local remedy for fever, preoccupied Ménageot. In the case of Gauffier, who had a delicate chest, he was reluctant to administer *quinquina* because it might be too powerful for his constitution, but gave in to medical advice. Indeed, he was concerned as to whether Gauffier could cope with local conditions in the long term. When he had been ill the previous year, only a stay outside the city had allowed him to recover and put some weight back on. But the day after he returned to Rome he fell ill once again; Ménageot was forced to conclude that 'Roman air is at odds with Gauffier.'[219] However, the Académie's *pensionnaires* were constrained from leaving Rome by virtue of their official status, even when the local climate and prevailing unhealthiness encouraged such evasive action. In May 1790, Ménageot reported that the comte de Vaudreuil, the duc de Polignac and his family had fled the unseasonable heat and 'the inclementness of Rome' for Venice; as far as his students were concerned, they were bearing up surprisingly well.[220] But overall, Ménageot was pessimistic about the Académie's artists' high casualty rate, so much so that he warned: 'The cradle of the arts will end up becoming the tomb of artists.'[221]

Thus, in the course of somewhat prolonged negotiations over the acquisition by the French state of the Villa Medici as a proposed new home for the Académie (which it became in 1803), one of the distinct advantages of its location was the healthiness of the air, which, as Letourneux pointed out to Talleyrand in 1798, 'is something to be considered in Rome'.[222] Moreover, in the proposed 'Règlement' of the Académie, a place was to be set aside – somewhere 'suitable, clean and quiet' – where ailing students could be cared for, anticipating the need for such a facility based on previous experience.[223] Angelo Celli had lauded the Villa Medici as part of a 'garland of green' around the city in the sixteenth century, ornamented by such architectural features and sustained by excellent air, but by the eighteenth and early nineteenth centuries opinion on the character of the air on the Pincio was divided.[224]

According to James Clark, the best-placed residences were 'somewhere about the Piazza di Spagna, which is well-sheltered, and has the advantage of being close to the Pincian Mount, which affords the best protected and most delightful walk at Rome....via Babuina is a bad situation.'[225] Writers such as Hazlitt strongly recommended visitors to seek their lodgings in the hotels found in this area. However, the Pincio later succumbed to malarial presence.[226] Caroline Carson denounced the Hotel de Russie 'just under the Pincian Hill, wh[ich] we Romans look upon as stepping into a fever trap'.[227] Berlioz reported that Romans disappeared from their promenade on the Pincio 'like a cloud of gnats' at 7 p.m. in the evening.[228]

But already in the early eighteenth century, the abbé Dubos had remarked on the generally unhealthy atmosphere of Trinità dei Monti and the Villa Medici.[229] In 1804, Augustus von Kotzebue had insisted on the unhealthiness of the Villa's situation which threatened to snuff out the promise of young French artists: 'Every one of them has given proofs of his genius and they will not disappoint the great hopes of their country, unless they are snatched away by a premature death; the frequent consequence of the situation of the villa, which in summer receives the pernicious exhalations of the Campagna romana in full force.'[230] As already noted, in 1802, 27 years after his first visit, Charles Bonstetten was dismayed to find that Trinità dei Monti was now infected.[231] The salubrity of the adjacent Borghese gardens had already been called into question by Germaine de Staël.[232]

J. B. Michel described the complex microclimate of the Académie created by its being subject to different winds, and the way its internal spaces were variably responsive to the external climate. The main cause of fevers amongst *pensionnaires* was the sudden transition from hot to cold. The entrance hall was as cold as a cellar in summer. The interior first floor was dark, with no circulation of air. The south façade received the full brunt of the *sirocco*. The adjacent Trinità dei Monti was considered unhealthy. The Borghese gardens created 'columns of humidity', which meant that in the afternoon the air was cool. By virtue of being isolated, the gardens were also subject to winds directly from the north. His advice was to approach the Académie slowly and to cover up before entering. Windows on the north should only be opened during the day, those facing south between 9 and 10 a.m.; all must be closed at sunset.[233]

According to Simond, the new location gave students 'annual fevers': 'Last year, out of twenty-two students, seventeen were ill; the air of this Villa Medici was healthy before the nearby Villa Borghese created a lake, and it will get worse unless these waters are removed.'[234] For Etienne-Martin Bailly, the explanation that at least half of the *pensionnaires* contracted fever seemed more likely to be to do with a problem of maladaptation; yet he pointed out that such localised problems also affected Romans. He therefore held to the view that the 'the influence of the causes of illness…derives from Rome's soil.'[235] Writing of his encounters with French artists in Rome, Joseph Guislain, another medical traveller, shared the sense that those who had not yet had fever were troubled by its threat.[236]

As in the case of the French Académie's students, living in Rome could be as much a matter of survival as it was a routine process of working through a prescribed series of artistic and architectural studies. Staying alive, let alone elaborate and sustained artistic engagement with the city, could be a complex, uncertain and hazardous business. Despite its reputation as a universal haven for artists, the reactions of individual physical consititutions interfered with the achievement of an undisturbed state of viewing and studying. In the next chapter, we will reconsider the making of landscape imagery in and of Rome and its *campagna*. Rather than offering unimpeded escape from the city's insalubrious vicissitudes into the seductive realms of historical imagination and idealised nature, the *campagna* was often seen as the prime source of contamination. Bad air's essential nature might remain a mystery, but it could be given a tangible identity through the association with specific places, of which the most notorious was the sinister void of the *campagna*.

5

FATAL PROSPECTS: VISIONS OF THE *CAMPAGNA*

Whether en route to Rome for the first time or making an excursion from the city as a seasoned resident, all who traversed the *campagna* did so in a state of heightened emotion and imaginative engagement. In 1818, Léopold Robert was 'prodigiously aston-ished' by the final stages of his journey to 'the world's mother-city' since he found the *campagna* to be more arresting than the city itself, which for him was spoilt by the inescapable presence of priests. By contrast, he revelled in the way the empty 'desert' of the *campagna* allowed his mind uninhibited scope to picture 'the great Romans'.[1] A century later, Thomas Ashby, director of the British School (1906–25), a veteran of the *campagna*, wrote of his undimmed sense of euphoria and veneration whenever he entered this mysterious and inexhaustible space. He confessed 'that every fine day spent indoors, with the Campagna so close, is in a sense wasted'.[2] Ashby wrote with added urgency because he anticipated an imminent invasion by new building and modern agriculture with its destructive motorised ploughs. He relished the *campagna*'s unrivalled wildness and extraordinary wealth of Roman remains precisely because they were precariously contained within an envelope of timelessness. In *Some Italian Scenes and Festivals* (1929), as a corollary to antiquarian surveying of ruins and topography, he sought to record disappearing local rituals and customs; the Roman *campagna* in particular was precious because of the way it seemed to be inhabited by people who were living vestiges of classical civilisation. This sense of a tangible continuum between past and present continues to be found in the work of more recent scholars, manifest in their use of nineteenth-century and modern photographs to illustrate historic settings.[3]

Prior familiarity with prestigious classical texts combined with ideal landscape imagery of the seventeenth century to establish an expectation that the *campagna* would reveal itself to be a suitably picturesque and poetic setting for the historic scenes which had been enacted there. Encountering the contemporary reality of a bleak expanse of land-scape provoked various kinds of response – consternation, bewilderment, denial. Recol-lection of descriptions of the area in its heyday prompted musing on the decline of great empires, and questions as to how and why this drastic transformation had occurred. As we have already seen, one compelling explanation sought the key in the impact of

FACING PAGE: Johann von Rohden, *Roman Campagna*, detail of fig. 26.

'bad air'. Indeed, in describing their arrival on the threshold of the *campagna*, it is unusual for travellers not to mention that they were about to pass through a zone notorious for its 'bad air'. Of all the locations which were associated with 'bad air', the *campagna* and especially the Pontine marshes were the most consistently accused of being the cause of Rome's ills. In this sense there was recognised to be a deleterious connection between the city and its surrounding countryside which was as unwelcome as it was undeniable.

However, this aspect of Rome's physical situation has played no part in the complex of ideas and images associated with the *campagna*'s special place in the history of art as the site of the creation of a new form of landscape painting in the later eighteenth and nineteenth centuries. In the seventeenth century, the *campagna* had became endowed with a further form of cultural prestige through the belief that it was here that Claude Lorrain and Nicolas Poussin discovered the inspiring raw material out of which they created ideal landscape painting. This association was based on an idea of Claude in particular inhabiting the landscape, savouring and absorbing its beauties, and translating them into pictorial form. As will be suggested below, this mythologisation of the process of the *campagna*'s transcription into paintings was to be tenaciously influential. Indeed, approaching the *campagna* primarily as a resource for landscape painting's pursuit of an ideal level of representation is in fact a very effective way of steering historical understanding away from problems which were recognised as intractable and disturbing – a landscape which was thought to produce deadly miasma, devastating what remained of its indigenous population, and threatening the health and lives of those who were obliged to pass through it.

At first sight, this heritage would seem to be in poignant contrast to the neglected and diseased condition of the physical terrain of the *campagna* throughout the period with which we are concerned. Yet there is in fact much common ground between the various initiatives to investigate the root causes of this pervasive but mysterious disease-producing agent and the excursions of artists in search of sites which would illustrate Rome's mythic beauty. Both were premised on the importance of what could be learnt from studying the distinctive visual appearance of the land and its inhabitants. Such scrutiny focused closely on topography and the less tangible matter of air, factors at once aesthetic and medical which were assumed to have shaped the physical constitution and appearance of local people.

Artists were predisposed to seek out locations which matched their expectations of a terrain defined by its purported abundance of beautiful motifs. Equally, cognate qualities were assumed to have been inherited by the inhabitants of this landscape from their ancient forebears. Such well-established and widespread expectations might either block out the recognition of disturbing signs of chronic ill health, or else lead to jarringly discordant observations on modern deterioration. The tension between these contrasting models for Roman bodies can be explained in terms of an interplay between a belief in the topographical determinants of health and a biological notion of cultural inheritance. However, accounts of the *campagna*'s appearance are often curiously uninformative precisely because of the burden of expectation weighing on the moment of travellers' encounter, and the overwhelming sense of a discrepancy between the anticipated spectacle and the impoverished reality revealed from first-hand inspection. In both respects, the attention given to visual characteristics in the early nineteenth century was a change from more established literary conceptions of the *campagna*. Charles Bonstetten, himself undertaking a tour of Latium in search of Virgil's sites and settings, justified his project by claiming that previous scholars had neglected empirical observation in favour of predominantly poetic concerns – they had not looked around them but remained fixated on texts. Having taken the trouble to do this, he found that the image of nature given by Virgil, 'although disfigured, still survives in the landscape'.[4]

COUNTRY AND CITY

The *campagna* played a fundamental role in ideas and images of Rome because the city was viewed and understood to be coextensive with the surrounding landscape. This was a connection that had been politically and economically sustained over time by virtue of the entrenched ownership of land by a symbiotic combination of papal state and Rome's élite families. As was repeatedly observed, the whole Agro Romano was owned by a small number of families, who in turn paid *mercanti di campagna* to manage their property. Land was valued as a sign of status more than as a source of income. Indeed, the conservatism of landowners towards any improvement in agricultural exploitation of the *campagna* was usually pointed out as the crucially obstructive factor in its almost unrelieved stagnation.[5] Thus, as with atmospheric contamination, and in a way which was fundamentally connected, the city was tied by deeply entrenched bonds of ownership and privilege to its hinterland.[6]

The question of definition extended to the interrelation of eternal city and country, or more precisely involved recognising that this distinction did not apply in any familiar or simple way. For all its density of monuments ancient and modern, the city of Rome was a patchwork of archaic and majestic townscape juxtaposed with parcels of cultivation, the *disabitato*, which filled the spaces left vacant as the city had shrunk within its ancient walls. Indeed, as Silvio Negro pointed out, this sense of an inert continuum was to remain a notable feature of Rome's appearance until the latter part of the nineteenth century.[7] This unusual configuration of urban and rural spaces gave to Rome an identity that fed into perceptions of the city in a way which was just as distinctive as the specific effects produced by individual ruins and monuments. In 1804, for Wilhelm von Humboldt, it was indeed impossible to compare Rome and its surroundings with any other place; the incomparable physical presence of the city – its 'loveliness of forms', the 'grandeur and simplicity of its figures, the richness of the vegetation…, the definition of outlines in the translucent medium, and the beauty of the colours' – engendered a sense of 'pure aesthetic pleasure without a trace of desire'. So compelling was this level of experience that Humboldt condemned the excavation of half-buried buildings and viewed the idea of cultivating the *campagna* as a calamity.[8] By contrast, in the view of the comte de Tournon, prefect of Napoleonic Rome, the fact that city and country were indistinguishable was the result of a local attitude of blasé neglect: 'No nation could care less about the charms of the countryside than the Romans.'[9] However, this aesthetically productive equilibrium has important consequences for our understanding of the place of landscape painting in Rome. Jerome McGann's otherwise compelling idea that Rome was unusual in being the city of Romantic significance par excellence (whereas Romantics usually sought identification with nature) fails to take account of this ambiguous situation.[10]

Images such as Jakob Philipp Hackert's *View of Rome* (c.1780) (fig. 13) and Giovanni Battista Lusieri's *Extensive Landscape* (1781) (fig. 14) emphasise an interlocking view of buildings, cultivation and open countryside, in which these different types of structure and terrain are elided together. Hackert shows neat, cultivated fields in the foreground overshadowed by the Aventine to the right, with St Peter's in the distance. In both cases

13   Jakob Philipp Hackert, *View of Rome*, c.1780, watercolour on paper, 49 × 72 cm. Kupferstichkabinett, Staatliche Museen zu Berlin.

foreground figures seem to be local not outside viewers. In Lusieri's watercolour a bourgeois couple are looking at a seated peasant; the harmoniously complementary unit of difference embodied by this group echoes the similar disposition of agriculture framed by a river valley in the view which extends behind them.[11] Similarly, less sophisticated scenes such as John Izard Middleton's *View of an Ancient Tomb near the Scite [sic] of Bovillæ* (1809) (fig. 15) encapsulate an emblematic vision of the *campagna* as both fertile, under active cultivation, and strewn with majestic ruins. Moreover, its authenticity is underpinned by the inclusion of topographical details in the caption ('Monte Cavo', 'Castle Gandolfo', 'Ancient Tomb').[12] Such benign conventions for showing the *campagna* continued through the nineteenth century almost unchanged in their ingredients. For example, Caruelle d'Aligny's 1844 print (fig. 16) shows a remarkably intact aquaduct running across the *campagna*, in the midst of which a group of peasants are placed before a solid wall of corn, with a fig sprouting vigorously from a ruin.[13] Precisely the same juxtaposition of monument and cultivation is found in photographic views of Rome from the mid-nineteenth century. Representing such contiguity as natural acts to hold at bay not only anxieties about the *campagna* as barren and poisoned, but also the unwelcome spectre of modernity.[14]

14 Giovanni Battista Lusieri, *An Extensive Landscape on a Road above the Tiber Valley, North of Rome*, 1781, pen and grey ink, watercolour, 28.3 × 45.8 cm. British Museum, London, 1980, 1213.7.

15 John Izard Middleton, *View of an Ancient Tomb near the Scite [sic] of Bovillœ*, 1809, in *Grecian Remains in Italy: A Description of Cyclopian Walls, and of Roman Antiquities; With Topographical and Picturesque Views of Ancient Latium* (London, 1812), plate 2. pp. 18–19. British Library, London.

In saluting Rome as 'that garden of the world, that great temple of the arts', James Northcote gave an Edenic dimension to the harmonious symbiosis of city and country-side.[15] However, the disconcerting absence of suburbs was more prosaically construed as a sign of contraction – in modern times, Noel Humphreys claimed in 1840, the city had been reduced to a tenth of its former population, thereby risking the loss of its cultural identity: 'so shrunk is the city within the cincture that once with difficulty compressed it within its circuit. The deserted *campagna* itself, sweeping up itself in many places close under its walls, a few half cultivated gardens and vineyards, with here and there a noble but half-ruined villa, of some Roman prince, or a few roadside inns, or osteria, more wretched than the nearest beershop in England, form the only suburbs of Rome.'[16] Emptiness could be read as a stark sign of depopulation and decline, or treated as a pleasing form of stripped down picturesqueness. Walking near Pratica, Charles Bonstetten seemed to discover a new aesthetic dimension to this sense of absence: 'Little by little the trees disappeared, and in the immense plain which we had before us, one saw neither buildings, inhabitants, travellers, water, nor any trace of life. In this universal silence, one could hear the sound of one's own footsteps, and my eyes focused involuntarily on some clouds moving in the wind, as the only object which still manifested movement and life.'[17]

For Chateaubriand, this human vacuum was a disturbing challenge to his sense of identity: 'If you see this great solitude of the Roman countryside, the Tiber which flows almost invisibly between its abandoned banks, you would be struck as I was by the only idea which follows me everywhere, the nothingness of human affairs.'[18] Such an extreme state of affairs was redeemed for him by a religious destiny as great as the former empire had been. Indeed, the *campagna* could be envisaged as a sanctifying frame, residually aesthetic but primarily providing a way of imagining the city as exclusively dedicated to prayer and meditation. Like Chateaubriand, Philippe Olympe Gerbet was scandalised by the prospect of any introduction of modern industry into the *campagna*, which threatened to create an 'arena of factories'. Rather, Rome was and should remain 'pre-eminently the city of the soul', surrounded by 'a serene suburb, which has the majesty of the desert without its harshness', a space which was 'melan-

16   Théodore Caruelle d' Aligny, *Roman Campagna: View from the Ancient Avenue of Tombs V*, 1844, etching, 24.7 × 37.9 cm. Private collection.

choly and bare,…muffling the noise of the world around the holy city' like a 'great cloister for Christendom'.[19]

It was precisely the empty and arid aspect of the *campagna* – 'barren, empty, blighted, like the desert, with its great pieces of aquaduct and its herds of massive oxen' – which stirred Flaubert's imagination. 'Antiquity survives in the campagna' rather than the city: 'It is there you find true beauty, and the Antique beauty one dreamt of.'[20] The appeal of emptiness also applied to ruined, abandoned buildings. However, in many such cases, emptiness was more a matter of an outsider's presumption than based on a fuller, more contextually informed understanding. In the eighteenth century, emptiness was more likely to be recuperable through a picturesque reading of the expanse of the *campagna* and its incidents. However, pictorial effect might become secondary to the less savoury appropriation of ruins and abandoned buildings by brigands. In this light, the landscape's physical desolation was only accentuated for Lady Morgan by 'one of those terrible ruins called by the natives "Cassaccia de'Assassini"'.[21] For Morgan, this physical threat was amplified by the 'fearful succession' of grim, lifeless sights. As Antoine Jean-Baptiste Thomas had done in one of his numerous gruesome images of Rome (fig. 17), she begins with the everyday sight of dismembered limbs: 'A gibbet hung with human limbs; the ruinous inn of Fossaccio (so called from its neighbourhood to a putrid ditch); the solitary post-house of La Storta; the mouldering, isolated Villa Giustiniani, and the rude tomb, called Nero's, follow in fearful succession, till the walls of suburban villas, now uninhabited and cheerless ruins, shut out the desolate view from the narrowing road.'[22] After describing a den encountered in caves adjacent to the Ponte Mammolo as being so covered in moss, verdure and lichen as to form an 'enchanting picture', Antonio Nibby pointed out that this was only spoiled by the unwelcome revelation that such a delicious spot was in fact the primitive home of a 'dirty peasant'.[23] Bonstetten remarked that some of the tombs on the Appian Way had become cabarets or stables 'where filthy animals abide with the ashes of the masters of the earth'.[24] In the early nineteenth century, with the Napoleonic dissolution of religious communities, a new generation of vacated buildings was created. Church property, too, became a 'desert'.[25] Léon Cogniet made one of these uninhabited buildings the subject of an almost allegorical study of desolation and neglect, placing it in a dramatic pool of light beneath a dark storm cloud (fig. 18).[26] In the city itself, the historical shrinkage of its population, and the widespread availability of apartments to rent as studios, accentuated the degree to which Rome was an artists' city.

Consonant with the trope of coming across ruined and abandoned villas and buildings is the larger sense that the *campagna* was considered to be uncharted territory. There is a parallel here between historians of Rome and medical investigators, the former aiming to identify and map the sites of ancient history, the latter, as we saw in the last chapter, to discover and plot a topographical answer to the causes of bad air as a means to improve public health.[27] More general scientific investigation was also undertaken in the form of natural history and the cataloguing of flora and fauna.[28] A century

17   Antoine Jean-Baptiste Thomas, *Labourage*, coloured lithograph by Villain, 24.9 × 18.2 cm, in *Un An à Rome et dans ses environs: Recueil de dessins lithographiés, représentant les costumes, les usages et les cérémonies civiles et religieuses des états romains, et généralement tout ce qu'on y voit de remarquable pendant de cours d'une année, dessiné et publié par Thomas* (Paris, 1823), plate 38. Private collection.

later, Thomas Ashby emphasised the 'infinite variety' of the terrain, and the way that the first impression of flatness and vastness yet contained a more unpredictable undulation, 'furrowed in all directions', and the continued relevance of the remark by Elphinstone, writing to Sir William Gell in 1835, that the *campagna* was home to innumerable 'lost and mislaid cities of Latium'.[29]

A sense of emptiness could also prompt a desire to isolate artistic characteristics which then have the effect of standing in for the lack of other features. Eugène Pelletan's claim that the popes had deliberately maintained the desolation of the Agro Romano so as to increase the drama of visitors' sense of encounter with a beautiful and sanctified city was vigorously rebuffed by the more pragmatically minded Roman medical authority Corrado Tommasi-Crudeli.[30] The painter David Wilkie commented: 'In approaching [Rome], we had to pass an immense plain, uncultivated, unwholesome, and yet beautiful.'[31] Such beauty could be substantiated, and indeed aggrandized, by calling to mind artists' names. Wilkie's description shifts into recollection: 'In the blue

18 (DETAIL) Léon Cogniet, *Group of Buildings abandoned since the Occupation of the French, Environs of Rome*, 1817–22, oil on canvas, 24.5 × 33 cm. Musée des beaux-arts, Orléans, inv. 217.

distance [we saw] some of those mountains one is familiar with in the pictures of Claude. From Albano to this place [Velletri] we passed through scenes that realise all that Salvator Rosa conceived or Poussin drew.'[32] 'The first bit of Claude', noted J.M.W. Turner on his way to Rome in 1819;[33] and 'Wilson-brown Campagna' once he had arrived.[34] The invocation of artists' names is a way to distance the viewer from any sense of discomfort, but yet also to identify with and lay claim to the prospect. It is as if the gaze needs to be focused on distant mountains, which occupy a realm above the more sordid, increasingly empty conditions immediately underfoot. Ippolito Caffi's 1847 views of the *campagna* from a balloon seem to work in the same way, celebrating the aesthetic pleasures to be had by rising above the glowing but sinister evening mists (figs 19, 20).[35]

The tension involved in recognising which mode of viewing to adopt when confronting the *campagna* is inherent in the way the zone was named. Bonstetten bluntly challenged the accuracy of the name: 'The campagna of Rome, which is probably called countryside out of politeness, is nothing but a poisoned and often sterile plain on all sides.'[36] In doing so he hints at the way Rome was bound to its surroundings by the immaterial but inescapable presence of bad air. The sense of intervisibility between the city and its *campagna* was also reinforced by an all too seamless atmospheric connectedness. The harrowing contrast of the *campagna* with the prospect of the great city was rendered not merely a dramatic anti-climax, but was potentially life-threatening. This was poetically alluded to by William Hazlitt, when he asked why artists would want to remain in Rome at all: he conceded that the entrancing experience of being able to watch 'the morning mist rise from the Marshes of the Campagna and circle round the Dome of St Peter's' might persuade some that this was enough to offset the city's squalor and disease which the reference to marsh mist might otherwise seem to reinforce.[37] Lady Morgan was a connoisseur of such symbolic conflicts: 'St Paul's and St John Lateran rise on the dreary frontiers of the infected deserts they dominate, like temples dedicated to the genius of the *mal-aria*.'[38] Later in the century, it was precisely the bareness of the ground which was blamed by Léon Colin for giving unimpeded access to the city to marsh vapours coming from far and near:

> The surface of this campagna is almost wholly lacking in habitations and elevated vegetation; one sees nothing more than a very occasional oasis, and some wretched houses; solitude begins at the very gates of the city, and, as a modern writer rightly observed, Rome is the only great city with no suburbs. This complete barrenness of the soil, this absence of natural or artificial barriers, seems to allow the atmosphere of Rome to be penetrated by marshy exhalations whose origins are a certain distance from the city, whether beyond the campagna, or in the Agro Romano itself.[39]

Whether the collapse of the Roman Empire had led to the *campagna*'s physical degradation, or rather indigenous bad air was to blame for the destruction of a wealthy and sophisticated culture, was a moot point. However, the problem was certainly recognised as having existed in antiquity. Robert Sallares has recently provided an authoritative account of awareness of and attitudes to this in classical texts, informed by a modern understanding of malaria. By virtue of this literary evidence, later commentators were able to carry on an extended debate on the changing condition of the ancient and modern Roman landscape. J.J. Ampère, for example, sought to establish a physical context for the evolution of early Roman history. Indeed, as we saw in the last chapter, that Roman culture was successful in its struggle with an inhospitable climate and environment was for him further evidence of the indomitable spirit of these early generations of Romans.[40]

The *campagna* was thus the antithesis of conventional ideas of rural retreat where, in Arthur Young's words, 'the peaceable man has retired from the tumult of cities and the home of intrigue, to give himself over to the cultivation of land.'[41] It was a space seen as empty and forbidding: even to antiquarians it was little known. Rather it was

19   Ippolito Caffi, *Ballon Ascent over Campagna Romana*, 1847, oil on paper laid on canvas, 17.9 × 29.2 cm. Musei Civici, Galleria Comunale d'Arte Moderna, Treviso, inv. P292.

a territory which predominantly encouraged quick traversal, cautious if not distant inspection, accompanied by melancholy reflections perhaps alleviated by scientific curiosity. This sense of circumspection can be linked to the way drawn and painted views of the *campagna* are often constructed as if looking out from a protective screen of buildings or vegetation – a way of reading such imagery which could be applied to the studies of P.H. Valenciennes, more usually celebrated as paving the way for full-blown *plein air* painting.[42] Seen in this perspective, these studies retain their sense of being products of a desire to explore Rome as a source of landscape imagery, but express that engagement precisely through setting the motif at one remove from the space occupied by the artist. Although Valenciennes himself does not address the problem of the *campagna*'s bad air in his comments on Rome as a place for the education of landscape artists, the use of screening elements may have a function beyond that of compositional equilibrium. We can compare this pictorial device to the quintessential Claudeian motif of trees framing a vista: as well as modulating the intensity of light effects, eighteenth-century enthusiasm for this aspect of Claude's *campagna*

20   Ippolito Caffi, *Rome: Balloon Ascent*, 1847, oil on paper laid on canvas, 27 × 43 cm. Galleria Internazionale d'Arte Moderna di Ca' Pesaro, Venice, inv. 1700.

imagery might also have been informed by the idea that trees acted as a cleansing filter, thereby counteracting the threat of poisoned air. Valenciennes' *View of Rome*, by contrast, seems to present the city as at once submerged and dematerialised by a forbidding vapour (fig. 21).

REGENERATION

During the eighteenth century, proposals to realise the economic potential of the *campagna* were more idealistic than effective. Thus, in 1785, Giuseppe Francesco Maria Cacherano di Bricherasio, governor of the province of Marittima e Campagna, published *De'mezzi per introdurre a* [*sic*] *assicurare stabilmente la coltivazione e la popolazione dell'Agro romano* (Of the means for introducing and ensuring the cultivation and population of the Agro Romano). He envisaged new 'colonies' which would be agricultural and social centres. These would be free of the hitherto stifling control of land and its economic

21   Pierre-Henri de Valenciennes, *View of Rome*, c.1782–4, oil on paper laid on board, 18 × 25 cm. Louvre, Paris, inv. 23675.

yield maintained by the small cadre of landowners. Land would be transferred to the peasants, who would in consequence be free to take advantage of modern agricultural techniques and improve productivity. Such initiatives were given new political impetus by the *repubblica romana* of 1798–9. Silvia Bordini notes that proponents of such schemes were often outsiders, with the implication that they were therefore prone to uninformed optimism as to the *campagna*'s potential.[43] In 1797, for example, in his treatise on the Italian climate, the chemist Pierre Thouvenel saw the *campagna* as a promising site for the establishment of a colony formed by people seeking refuge from 'nations in revolution' and in search of solitude and celibacy. Such a colony would reinvigorate the *campagna* and cleanse it of bad air, as if the renewal of its atmosphere would be a direct expression of a state of libertarian rectitude.[44] It is perhaps a measure of the implausibility of the idea of returning the *campagna* to its former vigour that this became associated with fraudulent speculation. As Tommasi-Crudeli wearily observed, 'The "redeemer of the Agro Romano" became a type of philanthropic swindler, well-known throughout Europe, and has already found a place in modern literature.'[45]

Such progressive proposals were not without their opponents. Chateaubriand argued that the *campagna*'s beauties – which he claimed to have discovered – risked being compromised by modern agricultural development, however well intentioned. Indeed, in order to parry assertions of reactionary callousness, he cited Tournon's economic analysis of the agricultural exploitation of the *campagna* which proved it to be far more effective than usually asserted; assertions it was not fulfilling its potential were based on misleading impressions.[46] Chateaubriand thus accepted his compatriot's positive assessment of the *campagna*'s relative agricultural effectiveness in order to discourage any intrusive disturbance into a space he cherished because of its rich capacity for imaginative and spiritual projection, predicated on resistance to change. Such an affirmative statement of the *campagna*'s productivity allowed him to leave its indigenous peasants, their living conditions and appalling mortality rates, out of account. As Carlo Travaglini has shown, of the numerous projects to cultivate the *campagna* proposed during the early nineteenth century, all failed because of decimation from malarial fevers. Schemes often sought to put beggars and orphans to work, thus clearing the city's streets and reforming these unfortunates, but illness led to their abandonment. The papacy, which had a history of being disinclined to pursue any innovative policies in the *campagna*, especially ones which might be uncongenial to the landlords, was circumspect in contemplating such schemes, for example refusing a French company in 1828 on the grounds that the rates of return were disadvantageous.[47] The political underpinning to such debates became explicit in 1848 when the Roman people were rightly defended against any responsibility for the neglect and deterioration of the *campagna*.[48]

The *campagna* was considered to be a space which was trapped in the past, a vast showcase for ruins of a former age; that the terrain was impressively desolate merely threw into starker relief the grandeur of the antique remains strewn across it. In so far as they were acknowledged, the diseased bodies of the few local people visible acted as a rebarbative *repoussoir*. If Feuillet de Conches, Léopold Robert's biographer, could celebrate the 'magnificent frame...for these great bones of the past' provided by 'these Pontine Marshes, this solemn infinity of the Roman *campagna*',[49] such a viewpoint was criticised in France for its self-indulgent pursuit of art for art's sake and disregard of social realities. An article in *Le Globe* objected that: 'One strolls in this country as in a vast public Salon exhibition where the masterpieces of great masters of the time of Leo X and the monuments of antiquity have been gathered: as for the people, no one thinks of them. Under the French sword, or the Austrian baton, of what importance is the unfortunate slave – however full of genius? What does that matter to an artist, a poet, a dreamer?'[50]

Such attitudes to the *campagna* were shaped and reinforced by the visual aide-memoire of landscape imagery. The aestheticisation of the *campagna* was emblematically expressed in a pictorial modus operandi premised on the idea that the artists concerned were drawing on some form of first-hand observation or contact. But this was understood to be subordinate to the need to yield an essentially ideal image which would therefore stand as a true record of the region's immutable beauties. Although this formula evolved through the eighteenth and nineteenth centuries, it remained consistently dependent on a belief that the Roman landscape itself offered unrivalled opportunities to store up a rich fund of unique visual experiences. Moreover, this had the effect of placing painters in close proximity to seventeenth-century masters: literally treading the same ground in search of the same motifs, trying to read back into the landscape the pristine poetic views created by Claude and Poussin. A review of Claude's reputation illuminates the ways in which both landscape painters and theorists and modern commentators dealt with the mixture of rare beauty and sinister threat at large in the *campagna*. Addressing these questions offers a different context within which to understand the making and the expressive and representational status of Roman landscape imagery from that provided by narratives which primarily see the protocols of ideal landscape as being inherited and reinvented in the form of progressive *plein air* painting.

CLAUDE'S *CAMPAGNA*

If Claude's name has been indelibly imprinted on the *campagna*, how we should understand his images of it remains a contested matter, whether played out through biographical accounts from the seventeenth century onwards or in contemporary art-historical studies. Mirka Beneš's work on early modern villas and gardens has provided the framework for an original interpretation of Claude's image of the *campagna*. When Claude shows the *campagna* in his paintings, she argues that he is in fact providing a faithful version of how it appeared in the seventeenth century, rather than – or perhaps as well as – conjuring up an elaborate but artificial idyll. She proposes a direct correlation between the mixed nature of agricultural practices found there (arable and pastorage) and their depiction in his paintings and drawings. The crucial link in this argument is provided by the expectations of certain of his patrons who were also important landowners with interests in agriculture and art, and for whom ownership of large tracts of the *campagna* provided a powerful symbolic measure of status. Indeed, her argument relies on the idea that Claude was responding to an ideological imperative: his patrons required images which legitimized not only their ownership but also the way their estates were managed.[51] In this reading, Claude's images mediated between two worlds: the day-to-day activities of the *campagna* and the cultural self-representations of those who owned it. Yet, for all the elaborate historical analysis of farming and landownership patterns amongst the seventeenth-century Roman élite underpinning this argument, it remains an extension of the idea that Claude painted what he saw irrespective of his complementary ability to create poetic visions. The problem with Beneš's argument is that while it convincingly suggests a specific correlation between elements of Claude's imagery and the cultivated estates of some of his patrons, it fails to address the fact that the *campagna* was more generally synonymous with neglect and sterility. It also assumes the audience she invokes were in the habit of observing or surveying the *campagna* and its agriculture, and that they were prone to evaluate paintings in terms of such direct comparison. A similar equivalence is invoked by Helen Langdon, who suggests that a Latin poem by Maffeo Barberini, one of Claude's patrons, expresses an empirically grounded appreciation of the beauties of the Roman landscape. But composing such a poem is more a matter of rehearsing a literary genre and its in-built generic conventions than it is a spontaneous response to observed experience; indeed, Langdon goes on to note that this is an example of a well-worn formula by means of which to read Italy as a microcosm of earthly beauty.[52] That landowners employed *mercanti di campagna* to run their estates and were more likely to view the *campagna* from the terrace of a villa or the windows of a coach, if indeed they were interested at all, also seems to work against this line of argument. Both as economic beneficiaries and as viewers, they were at one remove from the land they owned. Sabrina Norlander Eliasson's study of eighteenth-century aristocratic and papal Roman portraiture highlights the way landscape functions as an essentially symbolic setting for changing claims of status rather than as a form of empirical representation.[53]

Successive generations of commentators admired Claude's images of Rome and the *campagna* above all others precisely because of the way they were believed to have translated the artist's direct experience into a peerless poetic vision: here the notion of direct experience was more in the nature of being enveloped rather than a simple form of empirical transcription. By the same token, in the early nineteenth century, his paintings were repudiated because they came across as stylised recreations which failed to convince as faithful images. Claude's *campagna* is anchored in the imagined realm of antiquity, whether mythological or historical, but always employing a visual idiom designed to create a sense of the ideal, and to that extent not merely remote from the particularities of agricultural practices but occupying a quite distinct dimension of culturally coded experience. Moreover, if Claude is assumed to be pictorially faithful, how do we deal with the complete absence of any sign of the *campagna*'s reputation as an unhealthy, desolate space?

Lisa Beaven has suggested that we see Claude's Roman landscapes as a decorous equivalent for the *campagna*, so as to provide a satisfying and sophisticated visual substitute for a disagreable and unhealthy terrain. The instance she explores in detail is that of the Villa La Crescenza and its estate.[54] Otherwise, almost the only commentator on Claude to acknowledge the *campagna*'s diseased aspect was Pierre de Nolhac, drawing on the opinion of Ugo Fleres, who claimed that artists in general, and more especially

Claude and Poussin, in fact failed to penetrate into the interior of the Roman *campagna* because of fear of fever.[55]

Claude's art and its changing reputation was crucial to shaping eighteenth- and nineteenth-century ideas about the *campagna* as a place for making art, and for what was involved in converting a somewhat amorphous location into a coherently defined painted view. His ideal, stylised images acquired the status of truth: in 1777 Richard Earlom treated them as 'information', equivalent to the 'writings of faithful travellers'.[56] But subsequently they came to be condemned as little more than self-contained clichés. Although the belief that the Roman landscape, irradiated by a special light and endowed with ineffable pictorial qualities, was itself already ideal encouraged the expectation

22   Jean-Baptiste Lallemand, *Landscape of the Roman Campagna*, oil on canvas, 63 x 75 cm. Musée de Tessé, Le Mans, inv. 10.218.

that it could be readily converted into art, this was more often a recipe for the rehearsal of convention and artificiality. A typical example of the pictorial form this took is Jean-Baptiste Lallemand's *Landscape of the Roman Campagna* (fig. 22). The view includes a temple, sheep, and laundry in the foreground with aquaducts in the vista beyond. It entirely lacks topographical specificity, but relies on a generic evocative ethos expressed within a faithful Claudean idiom.[57] Indeed, it was none other than P.H. Valenciennes who complained that those artists who were concerned with 'types of antiquities, ruins and landscapes' too faithfully followed 'in the footsteps of the predecessors, and only focus on the views and sites which have already been painted'; they literally walked in the footsteps of their artistic predecessors, as well as remaining within established conventions of looking and representing.[58] Although Claude and Poussin were often bracketed together as exemplary exponents of Roman landscape, the latter is more associated with place than with method. His closeness to the landscape is expressed through the revered 'promenade de Poussin' on the banks of the Tiber to the north of the city painted by Corot and others (fig. 23).[59] There is a sense in which Poussin's walks were assumed to be as much a time for reflection as for observation.[60] Images which depict Poussin's 'promenade' are themselves relatively banal, but allow the viewer to savour an essentially empty landscape site which resonated with the presence of a great artist of the past. Indeed, the fascination with the building known since the seventeenth

23 Jean-Baptiste-Camille Corot, *Poussin's Walk (Roman Campagna)*, 1826–8, oil on paper, 33 × 51 cm. Louvre, Paris, inv. RF 1941–6.

24   Claude Lorrain, *View of La Crescenza*, 1677, pen and brown ink, 19.6 × 25.7 cm. British Museum, London, 1957, 1214.124.

25   Edward Lear, *La Crescenza*, watercolour dated 17 March 1867, 29.2 × 49.9 cm., British Museum, London, 1929, 0611.6.

century as the 'Fabrique du Poussin' (figs 24, 25), hallowed because it had been chosen as a pictorial motif by Poussin, highlights the fact that this is the only Roman topographical motif with a specific connection to his art.[61]

The early years of the nineteenth century saw a particularly intense reconsideration of Claude's status as a model for contemporary landscape artists, with special reference to his focus on the *campagna*. The idea that Claude's art is special because of its fusion of observation and ideal is mobilised polemically in an essay by Quatremère de Quincy in 1806. Quatremère observes that Claude is by common agreement 'at the head of all landscape artists': 'The qualities whose synthesis would achieve the perhaps chimerical perfection of landscape are very numerous, and perhaps there are some which are mutually incompatible....He alone, in this art, was able to make nature yield up the secret of that calm movement, those magical effects of air and light, which are the life of landscape....We do not see his pictures; we are in them, we breathe their air, we are enveloped by their atmosphere.'[62] Claude's magic is that of nature, the artist having achieved the incomparable feat of capturing the maximum number of physical beauties transposed – in the case of air and atmosphere, one might almost say made safe – into the realm of art. However, Quatremère's hyperbolic accolade is in fact a means to censure Claude's successors. Although landscape painting retained a certain 'purity' during the general corruption of taste in the seventeenth century, by the end of the eighteenth century this had been compromised by a 'mean and cramped pretension' which had caused subsequent landscapists 'faithfully [to] represent given sites, and to make what one would call portraits of nature,...one would have to say that nothing has contributed more to the extinction of genius and poetic invention in landscape.' When Claude copied nature faithfully this was only as an 'étude', to be used as a guide for his 'genuine works', not a 'servile imitation of any point of view'.[63] In his *Histoire du paysage*, Jean-Baptiste Deperthes makes the same point about close study of the *campagna* being a means to an end. He explains Claude's choice of 'moments of calm', because this was when nature revealed its true nature, and was therefore more moving to behold.[64]

As Quatremère's remarks illustrate, one of the central features of Claude's Roman imagery and its interpretation is the role of atmosphere. Chateaubriand claimed to be the first to have explained in his 'Lettre à M. Fontanes' (1804) that the mesmerising beauty of Claude's painting was the result of the artist having captured the unique qualities of Roman light, and more specifically its atmosphere. He puts special emphasis on 'a particular vapour, visible in the distance, [which] rounds off objects and disguises whatever they might have of the hard or harsh in their forms'.[65] Chateaubriand sets up a highly aestheticised account of the *campagna*'s visual character, and then ascribes to Claude the role of peerless pioneer in translating its distinctive light qualities into paint: 'You have probably admired in Claude Lorrain's landscapes this light which seems ideal and more beautiful than nature? Well, this is the light of Rome!'[66] Yet despite his emphasis on a central criterion of empirical fidelity, Chateaubriand's invocation of atmosphere as a quintessential aspect of Rome's visual character excludes any historical or topographical considerations.[67]

In supporting the claim that exposure to Rome and its 'environs' had been crucial in endowing the art of Claude, Poussin, Gaspard Dughet and Salvator Rosa with unique qualities, amongst the unrivalled advantages for the pursuit of landscape painting which Adrien Pâris singled out in 1807 was the way that 'the air always charged with vapours produces emphatic and resolved effects of aerial perspective'.[68] Thomas Lawrence also pointed to a particular atmospheric effect as constituting a quintessentially Roman quality: 'The exceeding beauty of the hues and tints, and corresponding harmony of the sky, give a charm to the whole effect that divests it of every gloomy or depressing feeling, and fixes the mind in a state of the *purest admiration* that it is possible for it to enjoy.'[69] Here Lawrence strikes a note entirely in tune with the perception that French landscape artists had proliferated in the uniquely propitious conditions of Rome, by asserting: 'Only Turner could render the subtle harmony of this atmosphere, that wraps everything in its own milky sweetness.'[70] In doing so he echoes Turner's own self-conscious rivalry with Claude as the acknowledged master of Italianate light. William Gell, who had exhaustively explored the *campagna* in search of its antique sites, was also responsive to its distinctive visual effects and singled out: 'An almost constant haziness (producing beautiful and varied effects for the painter) is rarely without one or more murky squalls sweeping across the plain....the whole plain is subject to most remarkable and frequent changes of aspect and temperature, deriving from them some of its most striking beauties and picturesque effects.'[71] Looking north from the Villa Albani, Lady Morgan described how 'a distant blue mist veiled the intervening wastes of the Campagna,' thus simultaneously concealing the disagreeable surface of this blighted zone and endowing it with an appealing visual aura.[72] Johann von Rohden's studies capture these atmospheric effects with uncanny precision (figs 26, 27).

Implicit in these remarks is an idea of the *campagna* as a space dedicated to the viewing of different kinds of light effects – atmospheric haziness or fluctuating chiaroscuro projected across the terrain. Specific evidence of the contemporary moment is irrelevant and invisible, as if studying landscape, and channelling such experiences into painted or graphic form, was essentially a problem of abstraction or distancing. This sense of abstraction was inherent in the celebration of the vapour-laden atmosphere's pictorial effects. This acts like an aestheticising prism, viewed through which Roman vistas were rendered into a seamless picturesque expanse. In so doing, the threatening ambient presence of bad air or miasma is euphemistically acknowledged and neutralised. Something of this seems to be behind Hazlitt's observation that it was precisely Claude's rendition of the atmosphere which exposed his shortcomings: 'He saw atmosphere, but he did not feel it.'[73]

This conception of landscape – or Rome-as-landscape – was expressed in part through descriptions of artists' sense of visual confinement, at once metaphorical and

26   Johann von Rohden, *Roman Campagna*, c. 1806, paper laid on canvas, 36.5 × 63.5 cm. Museumslandschaft Hessen Kassel, inv. 599.

27   Johann von Rohden, *Subiaco*, c. 1805, cardboard, 37 × 50 cm. Museumslandschaft Hessen, Kassel, inv. 600.

28   Léon Cogniet, *The Artist in his Room in the Villa Medici*, 1817, oil on canvas, 44.5 × 37 cm. Cleveland Museum of Art, Mr and Mrs William H. Marlatt Fund, inv. CMA 1978.51.

29   Achille-Etna Michallon, *View of the Villa Medici and Santa Trinità dei Monti from Ingres's Studio in the Pavillon San Gaetano, Rome*, 1819, graphite on ivory laid paper, 28.6 × 27.5 cm. Art Institute of Chicago, Regenstein Endowment.

spatial, within their Roman working environments. This was especially so for the artists of the Académie de France in its new home in the Villa Medici. In 1804, Suvée, director of the re-established institution, sang the praises of the new locale and explained: 'The studios of the painters are arranged so as to be able to enjoy successively the city of Rome and the *campagna*, as varied in its forms as its effects.'[74] Thus, they could study landscape without leaving their studios. In an image like Cogniet's, the room seems an elaborate frame for the view (fig. 28); a drawing by Michallon from the 'atelier d'Ingres' turns this logic back on itself, making the villa itself the focus for a view (fig. 29). Suvée was clearly not proposing this as a self-sufficient approach to landscape painting, but his characterisation of the *campagna* as a pictorial resource visible from within the Académie's studios is a corrective to assumptions about the inevitability and irresistibility of direct engagement with a surfeit of motifs. For Bonstetten, within their studios artists were aware of light to the exclusion of all else: 'See at Rome the solitary life of the artist; there he lives so shut up in his studio that one would take him for a holy hermit. His windows, closed to exclude the ground, only allow him to see an almost constantly serene sky, or else varied by luminous or stormy clouds.'[75] How far this could be thought of as a means to achieve a more intense engagement with Rome rather than being in the landscape itself with all its distractions and practical inconveniences, or whether we might sense an element of evasion and a preference for this kind of distanced scrutiny, is a moot point. Whereas Peter Galassi sees the motif of the view framed by a window as an allusion to 'the repertory of outdoor painting', it could also be read as a recognition of the fact that such views were just as likely to be generated and reinvented within the studio as they might be tokens of an immediate impression.[76]

Claire Pace has shown how the earlier eighteenth-century celebration of Claude's intimate and faithful translation of the *campagna*, based on the tradition that he was a careful observer and transcriber of his Roman surroundings, was succeeded by a preference to see his art as evocative of an Arcadian past. In terms of the way this shaped experience of the paintings themselves, they were applauded as a captivating means to envisage the classical world. This kind of reading was in turn repudiated as being exclusively poetic. When compared to the experience of the Roman landscape, Claude's art was found to fall short.[77] In 1820, Henry Matthews objected that 'the pictures of Claude represent nature rather as she might be than as she is. His pictures are poetic nature; nature abstracted from all local defects.'[78]

Nonetheless, by the 1840s, so entrenched was a certain view of Claude's Roman landscapes as ineffably, or rather blandly, poetic that this provided John Ruskin with the point of departure for *Modern Painters*, in which he championed the cause of landscape painting's reform. His withering demolition of Claude's facile artificiality begins with a description of the *campagna*. Ruskin uses his own ambivalence about the experience of the *campagna* to expose Claude's lack of a grasp of the laws of nature. His specific target was Claude's *Marriage of Isaac and Rebecca* (fig. 30).[79] First, Ruskin creates his own image:

Perhaps there is no more impressive scene on earth than the solitary extent of the Campagna of Rome under evening light. Let the reader imagine himself for a moment withdrawn from the sounds and motion of the living world, and sent forth alone into this wild and wasted plain. The earth yields and crumbles beneath his foot, tread he ever so lightly, for its substance is white, hollow, carious, like the dusty wreck of the bones of men. (The vegetable soil of the Campagna is chiefly formed by decomposed lavas, and under it lies a bed of white pumice, exactly resembling remnants of bones.) The long knotted grass waves and tosses feebly in the evening wind, and the shadows of its motion shake feverishly along the banks of ruin that lift themselves to the sunlight. Hillocks of mouldering earth heave around him, as if the dead beneath him were struggling in their sleep; scattered blocks of black stone, four-square, remnants of mighty edifices, not one left upon the other, lie upon them to keep them down. A dull purple poisonous haze stretches level along the desert, veiling its spectral wrecks of massy ruins, on whose rents the red light rests, like a dying fire on defiled altars. The blue ridge of the Alban Mount lifts itself against a solemn space of green, clear, quiet sky. Watch-towers of dark clouds stand steadfastly along the promontories of the Apennines. From the plain to the mountains, the shattered aqueducts, pier beyond

30   Claude Lorrain, *Marriage of Isaac and Rebecca*, 1648, oil on canvas, 152.3 × 200.6 cm. National Gallery, London, NG 12.

pier, melt into the darkness, like shadowy and countless troops of funeral mourners, passing from a nation's grave.[80]

For Ruskin, Claude's decorous and dainty imagery was too feeble to confront the *campagna*'s bitter truths, and was therefore deemed to be morally vacuous and artistically risible. Whether Ruskin is implying that Claude recognised the desolate condition of the *campagna* but preferred to reinvent it as an idyllic vision, rather than simply being incapable of registering its funereal decrepitude, is not clear. If Claude has expunged the 'poisonous haze' from his image, Ruskin disperses its sombre presence across his own purple passage, accentuating the landscape's forbidding, deathly aspects. In his description, it is as if the 'solemn space of green, clear, quiet sky' offers a consolatory respite from the diseased panorama beneath. This was a feature which was strongly associated with the *campagna* for Ruskin. Recognising Richard Wilson as a 'connecting link between [the English school] and the Italians', Ruskin criticised him for having been 'corrupted by study of the Poussins, and gathering his materials chiefly in the field, the district about Rome – a district especially unfavourable, as exhibiting no pure or healthy nature, but a diseased and overgrown flora'.[81] To this extent, Ruskin's remarks perhaps reveal more about his pathological rapport with Rome and its landscape than they do about Claude's process of representation.

COROT *IN EXTREMIS*

The unravelling of Claude's mythic reputation as the painter of the *campagna* par excellence has played an important role in defining the terms in which landscape painting's progress in the nineteenth century has been understood. A crucial episode in this history is the idea that there was a need to be liberated from the artistic authority of Italian sites and the belief that they alone could reveal true natural beauty.[82] The key to achieving this was to shift the emphasis from finished work to sketch, such that the talismanic significance of painting out of doors which had been acknowledged since the pioneering sorties of Claude was, so to speak, withdrawn into the act of painting itself. The Roman *campagna* as a source of motifs thus became a space for achieving what was both a form of technical mastery and a liberation from the confines of tradition. In various ways, the most exemplary protagonist in this transition is Jean-Baptiste-Camille Corot, whose sojourn in Rome during 1826–7 unquestionably produced a number of remarkable painted studies of the city and its landscape. However, Corot will be considered here in a different light, drawing attention to the way his response to Rome was as much characterised by ambivalent recoil as by virtuoso mastery of the oil sketch.

Arguments over the degree to which he remained loyal to pictorial templates firmly rooted in the landscape tradition while yet experimenting radically in his oil sketches have dominated acounts of this phase of his career. What has not been properly acknowledged is the degree to which he felt himself to be uncomfortably dependent on and vulnerable to local environmental conditions, and that this can be recognised in the unresolved nature of some of his Roman work. Indeed, his recourse to established compositional formats could be considered a palliative reaction to the arduous conditions he had to contend with.

Interpretations of Corot's first Roman years have struggled to escape from the assumption that this was a decisive chapter in his development of a successful method of painting in oil out of doors, in a way which secured the qualities of the sketch, such as to resist the refining and smoothening process required in the making of works worthy of the Salon, and its exigent audience, schooled to apply precisely this type of criterion. This argument is loosely but inextricably attached to a larger narrative which leads to Impressionism as a great modernist leap forward. To this extent, it is hardly surprising that this episode has been stripped of any sense of contextual connectedness and has remained within the limits of an account of painting which assumes its historical destiny to consist of the pursuit of certain inherent aesthetic qualities. Thus, Vincent Pomarède approvingly invokes Prosper Dorbec's paean of praise to the otherworldly ethos of mid-nineteenth-century Italian art-making, and its profound significance for the future: 'Returning from Italy, where, far from the combative fever of Parisian studios, far from any provocative preoccupations, they experienced days of reflection and gratification, [landscape painters] took from this an artistic gravity and serenity whose imminent role they were were not yet aware of.'[83] Similarly, Anna Ottani Cavina cites 'the cathartic experience of *plein air* with its crucial legacy for the nineteenth century'.[84] Sarah Faunce argues that artists were drawn to the sites of Nemi and Olevano in search of 'pure landscape values, of light and space and terrain', and sees Johann Martin von Rohden as an early instance of responding 'to the character of the deserted landscape around Rome…in terms of the pure elements of landscape painting'.[85] The purity here invoked projects an aesthetic value onto physical aspects of the landscape, or rather substitutes one for the other. For Michael Pantazzi, Corot's painting had captured the essence of Rome, almost relieving subsequent French artists of the need to look for themselves.[86]

Paradoxically, the argument of Anna Ottani Cavina in *Paysages d'Italie* is that a commitment to record sites faithfully gave way to Romantic visions 'heavy with unreality, which no longer expressed geographical locations'.[87] The implication here is that there was first a progressive move towards topographical authenticity and accuracy, and then a further liberating move away from this. What this reading leaves out of account is the way landscape painting can focus on atmosphere, a pictorial component with both physical and visual dimensions, as something local, what we might plausibly call a Hippocratic approach. Moreover, in the case of the *campagna*, describing it as an empty space in which artists revelled in the freedom to create a pure form of landscape is misleading: this was a space not only saturated with history, myth and fantasy, but also – as will be discussed below – widely recognised to be disfigured by chronic social and medical problems. The study of *plein air* painting has almost become an end in itself (notably in the hands of certain collectors), and been given a more historically rooted (but perhaps also diluted) status by embracing an ever larger range of artists. Recent exhibitions have sought to internationalise this type of painting in Rome, and especially to reveal the considerable contribution of Italian artists. But this has not altered the status of such studies within the established narrative of the history of landscape painting, which has celebrated their directness and atmospheric fidelity as evidence of aesthetic modernity.[88]

One influential account which goes against the modernist grain is Peter Galassi's *Corot in Italy*. Galassi claims Corot as a traditionalist, and thereby adds further force to the idea that he worked within conventional conceptions of the *campagna* as a source of ideal beauty. Inherent in this reading is the assumption that what Rome offered to landscape artists had remained constant: a rich array of sites and, above all, a unique atmosphere which endowed everything viewed within it with a remarkable aura. Moreover, the idea of following literally in the footsteps of revered forebears gave to the topography of Rome a sense of august predictability. In Corot's Roman studies, Galassi writes, 'light is often dramatic, but its principal role is to reveal the timeless splendour of the motif.'[89] However, Galassi's terms of reference remain wholly within a conception of nineteenth-century art's history as being essentially made up of a stylistic transition from Neoclassicism to Impressionism.

We might read Corot in Rome rather differently if we attend to how he reacted to the intractable nature of local conditions. Corot describes what he encountered as beyond the range of his experience and his painterly competence. Rome's climate and light overpowered him:

> You can have no idea of the weather we have in Rome. For a month now each morning I am awoken by the brightness of the light which strikes the wall of my room. It is just that it is always fine. But then, on the other hand, the sun shines with a light which is impossible for me. I feel the complete impotence of my palette. Send consolations to your poor friend, who is so tormented to see his painting so awful, so pathetic by the side of this dazzling nature which he has before his eyes. In truth there are some days when I would abandon everything.[90]

Indeed, Corot's description of being about to 'depart to conduct a campaign' has the ring of a military enterprise, as if engaging with a threatening adversary; moreover, in a play on words which may be unconscious, he here designates the *campagne / campagna* as a battlefield.[91] The sense of being engaged in a struggle with the landscape, whatever its historic aura and reputation as a source of the beautiful, echoes that vividly described by Ampère in his celebration of the indomitable efforts of the early Romans to overcome their environment: 'But before having to struggle with their formidable neighbours, they had to combat other enemies, the very soil they worked on, the air which they breathed in their lungs. In this they triumphed, as they triumphed in everything; the climate had given them an arduous destiny. This was the source of their greatness.'[92]

Corot's contemporaries recognised the way the powerful action of Rome's sun on the artist played an instrumental role in consolidating his sensibility. As characterised by Théophile Silvestre in 1855: 'Italy struck him greatly because of its dazzling climate, its vigorous contrasts of light and shade, and the grandiose manner in which masses define themselves beneath its beautiful sky.' Indeed, this was a kind of painterly endurance test, after which he was more than capable of dealing with 'the countries which have a veiled aspect'. Without the 'the violence of the Italian climate' and its 'implacable sun', he might have succumbed to an easygoing softness; yet his sensitive nature preserved him from the dryness such bright light tended to produce. Silvestre applauded the way Corot seemed to paint as if he was assembling a mosaic because it was a means to achieve a 'rightness'. For Silvestre, and later Galassi and Emmanuel Pernoud, this corresponds to a pragmatic means by which to transcribe what he saw before him, breaking it down into manageable, paintable sections, and therefore ushering in a new pictorial vocabulary and idiom. Yet one could also interpret this as a consequence of the way Rome's light disabled his painting technique, such that he found himself forced to resort to assembling his images out of separate patches (figs 31, 32).[93] In a sense, Corot's response to Rome in 1826 can be thought of as equivalent to Valenciennes's evocation of something close to incoherence in the array of different elements which painters

31   Jean-Baptiste-Camille Corot, *Aqueduct in the Roman Campagna*, oil on canvas, 24.1 × 43.8 cm. Philadelphia Museum of Art, the Henry P. McIlhenny Collection in memory of Frances P. McIlhenny, 1986, 1986-26-5.

32   Jean-Baptiste-Camille Corot, *The Roman Campagna with the Claudian Aqueduct*, oil on paper laid on canvas, 22.8 × 34 cm. National Gallery, London, NG 3285.

found themselves confronted by: 'This mixture of the antique and the modern, this assemblage of irregularity and symmetry, of incoherence and harmony, of madness and reason, creates an original whole which we only find in Italy and above all in Rome.'[94] If an artist responded to this challenging spectacle by concentrating on painting what he saw before him, then the result might well be a mosaic which lacked overall coherence – a jumble of fragments.

J.W. Schirmer's studies of the *campagna* offer a useful companion to certain of Corot's, in so far as they also accentuate the arid terrain and its expanses of bleached, scorched rock and earth (fig. 33).[95] However, unlike Corot, Schirmer explained his enthusiasm for such apparently intimidating sites in terms of their affective solace. In his journal (10 November 1839), he bore witness to the therapeutic potential of this unpromising environment, finding it 'much more salutary than formerly…the great sympathy of solitary nature fosters and at the same time satisfies a desire which…can very easily become burdensome.'[96]

33   J.W. Schirmer, *In the Roman Campagna*, 1840, oil on canvas, 35 × 51 cm. Staatliche Kunsthalle, Karlsruhe, inv. 1349.

This sense of a degree of extremity of temperature and intensity of light capable of rendering painting impossible recurs in responses to Rome. According to *L'Artiste*, one of the distinctive reasons for the success of Léopold Robert's *Arrival of the Harvesters in the Pontine marshes* (see fig. 48) was the way the picture captured 'a strong, powerful nature, where life, light and heat are everywhere overflowing'.[97] In Rome, Guinan Laoureins was struck by 'this learned tint which is so pleasing to painters, while at the same time being their despair. This sky is unrelentingly beautiful.'[98] Writing home in 1843, the painter Isidore Pils acknowledged how debilitating the pursuit of his art in Rome was: however beautiful the surrounding environment, he found the climate unbearable.[99]

Similar problems of excess and intensity were encountered by early photographers in Rome in the 1850s. Roman light, which was a central element in the city's artistic aura, threatened to overwhelm the medium. As the chemist Richard Thomas reported in 1852, 'the state of the atmosphere [was] so rare, and the effulgent light of a southern

34 M. Dubourg after J. I. Middleton, *Ruins of the Town of Nympha*, engraving, in *Grecian Remains in Italy: A Description of Cyclopian Walls, and of Roman Antiquities; With Topographical and Picturesque Views of Ancient Latium* (London, 1812), pp. 35–6, plate 15. British Library, London.

sky so intense', that it had required prolonged experimentation to succeed in establishing a stable procedure for the production of photographs.[100] Nonetheless, despite this technical struggle, the results seemed to achieve a new representational dimension that somehow got beneath the surface of things. In the words of a review in the *Art Journal*: 'It has been left to photography to picture Rome in such detail as it is not the province of painting to attempt....In the light and shade of these ruins there is a sentiment which, with the stern truth of the photograph, affects the mind more deeply than a qualified essay in painting.'[101] The sense that Roman sunlight had a dark side to it, so to speak, is also evident in medical observations. For Léon Colin, a proponent of miasmatic theory, it was precisely the relentless baking of the ground, especially in marshy areas, which released deadly 'telluric exhalations'.[102] The tradition of endowing Rome's light with the character of a violent catalyst survived in Italian art language of the twentieth century. Enrico Prampolini characterised the novel work Picasso produced in Rome in 1917 as having been provoked by the irresistible qualities – at once challenging and inspirational – of the local climate: 'Picasso, overwhelmed by Raphael's visions, showed me in his room at the Albergo di Russia in the via del Babuino the first classicist drawings he had made in the serene, imposing, admonitory climate of Rome.'[103]

STUDIES IN TIME AND PLACE

That both tourists and landscape painters were aware of the threat of 'bad air', and adapted their itineraries and movements accordingly, there is no doubt. Despite being lost in introspective reverie, Stendhal records that he left his vantage point on the Gianicolo, a site well known for its bad air, in order to avoid the harmful effects of evening mist.[104] In his memoir of Ingres's studio, Amaury-Duval recalled his time spent with Édouard Bertin, whom he accompanied in the *campagna* until the end of the spring, when it became too hot, and 'the *malaria* threatened to arrive soon with its cortege of fevers, and Bertin, not daring to carry on working in the *campagna* of Rome, one day announced to me that he was going to install himself in Ariccia.'[105] Theodore Gudin chose 1832, when he was recovering from cholera, to make his Italian trip; despite his convalescent state, he 'risked himself' in the Pontine marshes. As the sun set, 'the most dangerous moment for this fever which never leaves you', he was sufficiently overcome by the beauty of the scene, recalling Byron's comparison of sunset over the sea to the rainbow which accompanied the death of a dolphin, that he resisted his coachman's entreaties to return. He was nonetheless able to come away with 'a precious sketch made out of dabs of paint, for night had made it hard to see my paintbrushes', a picture which indeed made his name, being acquired by the emperor of Russia.[106] Although employing a different technique, J.I. Middleton experienced a similar situation at Ninfa, notorious for its bad air. 'The place itself has a most melancholy appearance, and we were told that it had been abandoned on account of the bad air which prevails on the plain during the summer. We had not time to enter this deserted village, but made use of the light afforded by the last rays of a setting sun to take the sketch I have given here' (fig.34).[107] Adding this dimension to accounts of the making of landscape imagery in Rome encourages us to reconsider certain aspects of the procedure and the formats given to *plein air* paintings and drawings. Expeditiousness was encouraged as much by risk of infection as by a desire to abbreviate landscape painting's technical elaboration. This gives a different slant to the sequence of stages recommended in the production of landscape painting by Cozens or Valenciennes whereby drawing and painting after nature was only a provisional, perhaps necessarily hasty, step in the elaboration of a landscape image.[108]

35   Aleksandr Ivanov, *Appian Way at Sunset*, 1845, oil on canvas 44 × 61 cm. Tretyakov Gallery, Moscow.

36   Aleksandr Ivanov, *Christ appearing to the People*, 1837–57, oil on canvas, 750 × 340 cm. Tretyakov Gallery, Moscow.

37   Aleksandr Ivanov, *Pontine Marshes*, oil on paper, 45 × 31.4 cm. Tretyakov Gallery, Moscow.

One artist who adopted an approach which is an antithesis to both Claudeian poetic truth and Corot's overexposed if carefully composed topographical studies was Aleksandr Ivanov (1806–1858). Ivanov's images of the Roman landscape accentuate its sombre overtones of historical degeneration (fig. 35). More specifically, his studies of the Pontine marshes are exceptional in so far as they embrace the poisoned atmosphere and its visual character and harness it to specific iconographical ends. Ivanov recognised in the marshes a site whose desolate aspect perfectly suited the background he sought for *Christ appearing to the People*, the monumental painting he laboured on for twenty years in Rome (figs 36, 37, 38). For Ivanov, the Pontine marshes were the desert from which Christ reappeared having fasted and resisted the Devil's temptations. This substitution of Pontine marshes for biblical desert or wilderness is less implausible than it at first appears, for the term desert is habitually used to describe the *campagna*.[109] We see Christ emerging unexpectedly towards the figures gathered around John the Baptist in the foreground. Christ's body links the arid mid-ground, the thin slice of flat marsh, and the pale mist rising against the backdrop of mountains. His purple cloak binds him to the hazy background. Two mounted soldiers, and one on foot holding a spear, remind us that both the Holy Land and Pontine marshes were Roman territory. What is remarkable is the way Ivanov adapted his rather heavy painting technique to create delicate atmospheric effects, so as to achieve an accurate and therefore chilling

38 (DETAIL) Aleksandr Ivanov, *Pontine Marshes*, c.1840, oil on canvas, 28 × 92 cm. State Russian Museum, St Petersburg, inv. 25298.

image of the miasmatic vapours rising from the marshes. As they rise they become more translucent and take on a pearly glistening light, which does nothing to lessen their sinister presence. This is a counter-example to the idea of Claude's poetic authenticity. In Claude's images the view is veiled, shifting it into the realm of delectable but distanced prospect. Ivanov focuses on the immaterial in order to intensify its forbidding effect.

To capture these pictorial effects, Ivanov equipped himself so as to cope with the discomforts of the environment into which he embarked, wearing sunglasses and straw hat, a long cape and galoshes.[110] He exemplifies the idea of the landscape artist as intrepid and determined, prepared to pursue his motifs into extreme situations. We might also see his outfit as carefully designed to protect him from the bad air, perhaps further reinforced by his resolute state of mind. Indeed, he criticised English, French and German artists who worked up their studies of particular locations in their studios over the winter; for Ivanov, it was nothing less than a sin not to work after nature in order to achieve truth.[111] In inserting his subject into a setting which includes the Pontine marshes, whose noxious exhalations he meticulously depicts, Ivanov sought to transform particular localised atmospheric effects into a transcendent biblical narrative. This reference would have been immediately recognisable while the painting was visible in Rome during the course of its protracted production.[112] Such a degree of specificity had only previously been sought in images which commemorated papal attempts to drain the marshes.[113] In 1784–5 Ducros was commissioned to paint Pius VI visiting the Pontine marshes; since 1777 Pius had initiated a scheme to create a canal, the Linea Pio, parallel to the Via Appia Antica, joining the sea by Terracina (fig. 39).[114] An anonymous painting celebrated the blessing by Pius on 14 May 1795 (fig. 40).

39   Raphael Morghen after Louis Ducros, *Pontine Marshes*, 1784, etching, 27.2 × 36.8 cm. British Museum, London, 1843, 0513.638.

A review the currency of *campagna* imagery will help to recontextualise the respective status of Claude as the norm and Ivanov as a remarkable exception. The *campagna*'s ambiguous reputation emerges clearly if we trace the frequency and format of its depiction in the landscape and genre imagery exhibited at the Paris Salon (which included studies and finished paintings). The terminology used in landscape imagery to identify Italian sites in general and Roman ones in particular is inconsistent. Classical sites are predictably common; and landscapes may pick out certain favoured locations, such as Tivoli or Albano.[115] Yet often they remain within the general terminology of the landscape study (Bertin, 'Vue d'Italie, au bord d'un lac', 1814 Salon, no. 82), or the emphasis can be on a view from a particular site (Lethière, 'Vue des plaines de Rome et de la petite Eglise succursale des Dominicains, prise de la villa Meline sur le Monte-Mario', 1817 Salon, no. 537).

The marshes are rarely specified before the example of Léopold Robert's *Arrival of the Harvesters in the Pontine Marshes* (1829–1831) (discussed at length below).[116] However, given their sinister reputation as the prime source of Rome's bad air, and consequent unsuitability for conventional landscape imagery, it is perhaps surprising that they

40   Anonymous, *Pius VI blessing Pontine Marsh Drainage Scheme at Terracina*, 14 May 1795, *oil on canvas*, 170 × 235 cm. Kunsthistorisches Museum, Vienna, GG2393.

41   Bartolomeo Pinelli, *Marius discovered hiding in the Pontine Marshes*, 1818, 42 × 34 cm, engraving. Private collection.

appear at all. One means by which their forbidding reputation could be referred to was through the story of Marius, who sought refuge from Sulla there in 88 BC.[117] In a Roman example not included in the Salon, Pinelli's print shows Marius being pulled out of the boggy reeds, his body half-submerged in the mire (fig. 41). In situating this Roman story in the marshes, Pinelli treats ancient history as if, like Marius, it too might emerge dramatically, still living from the environment. More positive images of the marshes are to be found as a place for hunting: that is, the antithesis of agriculture, for example painted by Adolphe Roger (*La Chasse au buffle dans les marais Pontins*, 1831 Salon, no. 1817), and Horace Vernet (figs 42, 43).[118] Yet the recognition that such images consciously ignore the marshes' impoverishment and insalubriousness is suggested by remarks such as those by James Skene, who decried the 'machinations of private interest' which preferred to maintain the area as a place to hunt and fish.[119]

The visibility of illness, or the identification of the *campagna* as a place of illness, is channelled through images of prayer for the dying or scenes of burial: for example, Leblanc, 'A Woman and her Feverstruck Child consulting a Hermit' (1822 Salon, no. 808).[120] Schnetz's monumental altarpiece, *Vow to the Madonna* or 'Unfortunates imploring the Help of the Virgin' ('Des malheureux implorant le secours de la Vierge') as it was titled at the 1831 Salon, gave Roman fever victims a high profile (fig. 44).[121] One of the most explicit references to harvest and the *campagna*'s dangers from fever, including the role of confraternities in recovering corpses, is a lost painting by Schnetz from the 1845 Salon: *Young Woman weeping by her Husband*. The harvest of Rome's *campagna*, which is uninhabited, is carried out by peasants who come from the mountains, who camp during the time needed for their work. Fever takes many victims amongst the unfortunates who do not have time to be transported to Rome's hospitals. In the background we see the Fratelli della morte, who come to take the body away.'[122] The association of death with Rome was part of the pictorial mythology of the early nineteenth century: Géricault was fascinated by Roman executions; Haudebourg-Lescot painted a brigand's widow recovering her husband's severed head at night after his execution; Thomas showed the cemetery of the hospital of Santo Spirito, where cadavers were used to compose 'tableaux morts' on All Souls' Day (fig. 45).[123]

One should include here the unusual case of Félix Boisselier's *A Shepherd weeping at the Tomb which he erected in Memory of a Gnat* (fig. 46). Based on a text attributed to Virgil ('Culex'), the picture shows a shepherd weeping at the tomb of a gnat (whose image is incised in outline on the tomb). The gnat had bitten the sleeping shepherd, thereby waking him; having swotted it, he then saw a snake about to bite him, which he also killed. The ghost of the gnat rebuked him, such that he constructed a tomb in memory of the unlucky insect. If we take this as an image prompted by an association between the risks of outdoor life in the *campagna*, it is doubly oblique, being projected back into classical times and reversing roles: it is the gnat which dies.[124]

~

42 Horace Vernet, *Hunting in the Pontine Marshes*, 1833, oil on canvas, 100 × 137 cm. National Gallery of Art, Washington, D.C. Chester Dale Fund, 1989.3.1.

43 Horace Vernet, *Departure for the Hunt in the Pontine Marshes*, 1833, oil on canvas, 100 × 150.7 cm. National Gallery of Art, Washington, D.C. Chester Dale Fund, 2004.38.1.

44 Jean-Victor Schnetz, *Vow to the Madonna*, 1831, oil on canvas, 282.5 × 490 cm. Louvre, Paris, RF 2410.

45 Antoine Jean-Baptiste Thomas, *All Souls' Day*, coloured lithograph, 26.8 × 18.8 cm, in *Un An à Rome et dans ses environs: Recueil de dessins lithographiés, représentant les costumes, les usages et les cérémonies civiles et religieuses des états romains, et généralement tout ce qu'on y voit de remarquable pendant de cours d'une année, dessiné et publié par Thomas* (Paris, 1823), plate 64. Private collection.

46   Félix Boisselier, *A Shepherd weeping at the Tomb he erected in Memory of a Gnat*, 1808, oil on canvas, 178.4 × 146.7 cm. Lee Mulder Collection, Palm Beach, Florida.

LÉOPOLD ROBERT'S *ARRIVAL OF THE HARVESTERS IN THE PONTINE MARSHES*

Léopold Robert's career and reputation is defined by his years in Rome and the work he made there, which was directly concerned with aspects of the lives of local people as set within their respective landscapes. Robert's subjects were predominantly drawn from Rome and the *campagna*, extending, as in his first major painting, *Return from the Festival of the Madonna dell'Arco* (fig. 47),[125] down towards Naples, until he embarked on what was to be his last painting, *Fishermen of the Adriatic*, which he worked on during an extended stay in Venice. From the outset of his Roman experience, he was drawn to 'the serious and melancholic character' of the inhabitants of the mountains in the Papal States.[126] This included very specific social and medical phenomena. Thus, in a picture for his patron Marcotte, he showed a woman and child from one of the mountains near Lake Fucino on a pilgrimage, but forced to halt because of 'a serious illness which frequently afflicts the inhabitants of the *campagna*; her child has a bout of pernicious fever, she is on the point of losing her.'[127] To some extent, the same is true of the work we will be considering here, *Arrival of the Harvesters in the Pontine Marshes* (fig. 48). Indeed, it is precisely the way in which his painting's title articulates a particular relation to its setting which requires careful scrutiny.

47 Léopold Robert, *Return from the Festival of the Madonna dell'Arco*, 1827, oil on canvas, 142 × 212.5 cm. Louvre, Paris, inv. 7664.

Return from the Festival of the Madonna dell'Arco was envisaged as one of a series of four pictures which would take his work onto a more ambitious level. Previously he had remained within the well-established genre of scenes of brigands, nuns, and studies of picturesque Italian women. Indeed, it was the very demand for such scenes which impeded his ability to devote himself to more ambitious projects. In 1829, he explained that the *Return from the Festival* was part of a series of 'the four seasons of Italy....The first will be the representation of the surviving festivals of Flora in Naples, the second those of Ceres in the Roman States, the third, which will be the last executed, those of Bacchus in Tuscany and the last the Saturnalia in Venice.'[128] While the subjects he produced were to take on quite different form, his reference to 'restes' (that is, remains, or surviving examples) signals a sense of archaic survival that is especially relevant to the *Arrival of the Harvesters*.

Like many other travellers and artists, he had been delighted by the spectacle of harvesters with their musical accompaniment and their buffaloes in the Roman countryside.[129] Writing to his friend Brandt, he repeatedly speaks of the 'wild' (*sauvage*), whether of the people, 'their picturesque and wild clothes', or the 'most wild mountains' that were their home, where he made excursions. For Robert, this seems to be a guarantee of 'this simplicity and nobility', which he presumed to be 'a characteristic inherited from their ancestors'.[130]

In 1819 he had seen brigands close up when they were gathered in the prisons at Termini in a form of amnesty-cum-imprisonment. However thrilling this was, it presented brigands and their families as models in captivity, detached from their natural habitat. It is clear that, once over the initial frisson of proximity, Robert found this unsatisfactory, and was committed to pursuing such native curiosities into their proper environment, thereby adding a dimension of what he considered to be authentic sombreness to the resulting imagery. Such a quest was further motivated by the sense that the distinctive physical appearance of the Roman people who inhabited the city was steadily disappearing.[131]

Writing to his patron Marcotte about his plans for a picture on the same dimensions as what he referred to as 'The Festival of Naples', he declared: 'The Pontine marshes have given me the subject: it will be of quite severe character, although it will have some connection to the first [picture]. I find the land of Naples is entirely poetic and its inhabitants recall unmistakably the Greeks, their festivals and habits. The Papal States seem to me to have a different aspect: the Romans have something more serious which relates to the idea that one generally has of their ancestors. I hope to make visible, if it is possible, the difference which I find between these two peoples, and for that, more or less similar subjects are needed.'[132] Thus, in a form of anthropological retrospection, Robert sees through the contemporary lives of the inhabitants of the *campagna* to a deeper layer of identity, in search of their archaic forebears, as he had done for the Neapolitans.

Another kind of seriousness applied to the environment in which the artist sought to work in pursuit of his subject. He envisaged a journey dedicated to immersion so as to locate and assemble 'the materials necessary to make my painting....To give a more positive, special quality to what I am going to undertake, I would really like to install myself in the *campagna* and this is what I will do if I can find somewhere to be able to work. It is in the Pontine marshes that we are going; although I don't dread the fever, it would perhaps be unwise to commit to spending the months known as unhealthy there.'[133] One thinks here of the contemporaneous images of hunting in the *campagna* by Horace Vernet which seem to treat the area as a playground for gentlemanly sport.

Robert's willing self-exposure to arduous, if inspiring, conditions parallels the slightly earlier form of investigation conducted by Gaspard de Prony when researching the state of the Pontine marshes in 1812, with a view to devising the best method of draining them. Norvins, prefect of Rome at the time, saluted 'the courage to live the life and eat the food of these shepherds, to study the sanitation works he had planned, and that he would have had the glory of achieving without the fall of the French Empire'.[134] This kind of investigative travel should be distinguished from the more general notion of rediscovering vestiges of antique customs, a phenomenon which attracted considerable antiquarian interest in the later eighteenth century, as in the case of Richard Payne Knight's study of the cult of Priapus. Robert, of course, acknowledged the alleged status of the peasants of the Roman hills as bearers of a classical inheritance, but he was primarily concerned with the way their social and physical identity was bonded to the landscape, its remoteness and austerity.[135]

Certainly, Robert's enthusiastic pursuit of his motif led him to what he recognised were hazardous sites. 'Hoping to go harvesting while watching the harvesters,' he stayed four days at Cisterna, a location with a reputation for bad air: 'I rapidly explored the area and have been to find the harvesters even in their tents.' He spent two days in a small buffalo farm, 'which had nearly three thousand beasts'. There he studied close up 'one of the vast waggons,...it is almost the motif of my picture, or rather it is the most substantial detail'. This ambiguity between central motif and detail perfectly expresses the artist's uncertain attitude to the status of his painting and its narrative impact. He immediately claimed the artistic benefits of this close-quarters inspection: 'I saw extremely picturesque things and I am certain that my picture will require a quarter of the time the other took and perhaps (at least I hope so) it will be much better, because I feel it better. I have drawn a painted sketch since my return and I have drawn the whole picture and I am going to make the *ébauche*.'[136] Thus, the key foundational steps in constructing the image were stated as having been crystallised when his encounter was fresh in his mind.

Robert refers specifically to the way the body, and especially faces, express health as a complement to their primitive beauty. The abatement of fever he observed in the towns of Cisterna, Norma, Sermoneta and Sezze in 1829 was visible in the way the inhabitants 'bear the sign of perfect health on their faces, when formerly one only saw yellow and livid complexions'.[137] As he emphasised to his sister Adele, Cisterna and

Nettuno were places which no one went to. Yet he enthused about these visits: 'I am crazy about the Pontine marshes; I believe I want to pass my life there';[138] 'I am happy in these almost uninhabited places, and I find their character has a quite different kind of purity [*en est bien autrement vierge*] than in the environs of Rome.'[139]

Nonetheless, as he acknowledged, that year had been unremittingly bad, 'indeed deadly for all individuals who habitually work in the surrounding countryside. Mortality has been greater than in preceding years; the hospitals, which are numerous here, are full; and with that, the number of foreigners being fewer than during the last winters, misery will be felt more than usual.' Yet he considered the poorest were not so badly off as in the north, as demonstrated by their lack of desire to escape this state: 'A pure sky and southern sun gives them a gaiety and an appetite for life which is hardly conceivable for we who always bring into beautiful places a principle of death....Yet it seems that for the most part they always have something to live on, and the usual result is the achievement of a genuine earthly happiness, even in their afflictions.'[140]

Nature provided salvation from hardship created by ingrained social problems. For himself, he stressed that the climate suited him, unlike many.[141] And he found warnings

48   Léopold Robert, *Arrival of the Harvesters in the Pontine Marshes*, 1829-31, oil on canvas, 141.5 × 212 cm. Louvre, Paris inv. 7663.

Detail of fig. 48.

about bad air exaggerated, as he repeatedly had to reassure the apprehensive Marcotte.[142] The artist's suicide has led some commentators to overdetermine how we read Robert's attitude to his environment. In fact, rather than being an echo chamber for his melancholy, Robert's reading of the Roman *esprit public* is essentially upbeat, influenced by his tendency to aestheticise what he saw, even if with a fatalistic undercurrent.

The finished painting was shown at the Rome Capitol in January 1831, and then from March to August at the 1831 Salon in Paris. The *livret* entry is as follows: 'Arrival of Harvesters in the Pontine marshes. A waggon, pulled by buffalo, has stopped in the place chosen by the master to set up tents' ('Arrivée de Moissonneurs dans les marais Pontins. Un char, traîné par des buffles, est arrêtés dans l'endroit que le maître a fixé pour dresser les tentes', no. 2836). In Paris, the painting was bought by Louis-Philippe, who displayed it in the *galerie particulière* of the Palais-Royal; only after the artist's death in 1835 was it given to the Louvre in exchange for a painting by Granet. Before analysing the picture's reception at the Salon, and situating it in contemporary discourses on primitivism, let us pause to consider its structure and the components it offers to potential narratives.

The women at the front of the group to the left have a strong early Renaissance flavour – ingeniously linked to Warburg's *ninfa moderna* and the *nachleben* of the antique

49 Léopold Robert, *Pifferari before a Madonna*, 1829, oil on canvas, 86 × 75 cm. Musée des beaux-arts, Vevey.

by Stephen Bann.[143] Certainly, reviewers were not slow to find Raphaelesque passages in the female figures,[144] although as in the case of Lamartine, this was oriented towards a biblical reading of the picture's subject.[145] But as well as constituting an art-historical echo, the way one female figure bears an impressive sheaf of corn also suggests the coming together of a team of workers, some of whom have already got underway with the harvest, rather than this being exclusively a scene of collective arrival. It is tempting to read the presence of the artist, who had identified himself as another kind of harvester, as also being part of the picture's sense of 'arrival' in the Pontine marshes.

The women in the left foreground are complemented to the right by two men, a dancer and a bagpipe player wielding the raucous *zampogna*. Centrally, a massive cart, drawn by

50   Jules-Elie Delaunay, *Harvesters in the Roman Campagna*, 1857–61. Musée Bonnat, Bayonne.

two equally massive buffaloes, dominates the picture. This supports what is in effect a tableau of the ages of man – from *père de famille* to swaddled baby held by a dainty Madonna figure – a group which echoes Robert's earlier *Pifferari before a Madonna* (fig. 49), painted at the same time he was working on the *Arrival of the Harvesters* in 1829. But here a group of peasants are displayed in a moment of provisional celebration, as they arrive in the evening before work begins. The Pontine marshes themselves are barely visible. This marshy, irregular terrain did not fit easily with conventions of the *pittoresque*. Robert discreetly signals something of the marshes' forbidding status in the exhausted, troubled features of the seated woman who appears between the men on the right: that we recognise an echo of Poussin in her dark features does not mask the hint of sombre

51   Jean-Baptiste-Camille Corot, *The Roman Campagna, Cervara*, 1826–7, oil on canvas, 68 × 95 cm. Kunsthaus, Zurich.

dissonance in an otherwise limpidly celebratory image. This art-historical echo has an added biblical layer, for Poussin's *Summer* or *Ruth and Boaz* (1660–4, Louvre) also includes a *zampogna* player. Such archaism is consistent with Robert's desire to see the *campagna*'s inhabitants as flesh and blood descendants of their ancient forebears. However, it is also a further means to ennoble the image and distance it from ideas of the gruelling and hazardous circumstances of harvest in the *campagna*. The decorous compromise which Robert effects is thrown into relief by two other representations of related subjects: a later painting by Jules-Elie Delaunay, which shows harvest as a scene of work, but incongruously uses two unapologetically academic and antique-oriented naked male figures (fig. 50); and Balze's sentimental painting which, despite the artist's Ingriste credentials, belongs more in the repertoire of *imagerie populaire*.[146]

While a connection to antiquity lies behind the ideal beauty of Robert's figures, a perhaps stronger link is that of the oxen. Unlike their masters, they seem to be indomitably powerful and to be immune to the 'pestilential' atmosphere, at once a force of nature and another kind of biological survival from former ages, which had the further merit of being monumentally sculptural. Such animal vigour seems to enshrine the

52   Jules Didier, *Ploughing on the Ruins of Ostia*, c.1866, oil on canvas, 116 × 170 cm. Musée d'art et d'histoire, Strasbourg, Lux. 85.

belief that, despite the degraded condition into which the *campagna* had been allowed to fall and beneath the miasmatic haze, the region yet retained a tremendous natural energy.[147] Corot, who hardly shows figures in his Roman landscapes studies, includes a pair of oxen pulling a cart of hay in *The Roman Campagna* (fig. 51), a sign of cultivation surrounded by dust cloud, storm, dry rocks, and the sombre, hazy plain beyond. Artists such as Charles Coleman made the herds of oxen and their *cavalcatore* a productive theme for the representation of the *campagna*, in so doing avoiding the problems of genre and decorum associated with depicting peasants as latter-day Romans or pathetic victims of *mal'aria*.[148] A work such as Jules Didier's *Ploughing on the Ruins of Ostia* (fig. 52), in which teams of powerful oxen drive ploughs beneath a horizon interrupted by ruins, almost seems like an emblem for the idea that cultivation could render healthy a place cursed by bad air.[149] In 1859, a large painting by Rudolf Lehmann entitled *Pontine Marshes* showed buffaloes clearing a canal meeting a barge full of maize, thus combining ideas of regeneration and productivity.[150]

There are two aspects to the *Arrival of the Harvesters* which define the limits of Robert's conceptual and representational vocabulary as brought to bear in the making of a picturesque, *antiquisant* image of the *campagna* and its inhabitants. First, Robert shows the harvesters arriving in the evening, which was understood to be the most dangerous moment in the day for bad air to strike, as it was concentrated by condensation on the surface of the skin. Second, it is not accidental that Robert selects the moment of arrival, before these workers were exposed to the rigours of harvest in the Pontine marshes, for this was recognised to be a time of high levels of casualties to bad air, or fever and general debilitation. To this extent, his composition is an implicit concession to or evasion of well-known harsh realities. However, the image contains a contradiction. Robert's harvesters seem to correspond to those inhabitants of hill villages who descended to the plain for harvest, but these workers usually returned home in the evening precisely to avoid the ravages of bad air, a claim made in the picture's critical reception discussed below. However, the majority of those who worked in the plain were hired labour, brought from Umbria, the Marche and Abruzzo.[151] Hanns Gross notes that the ratio between indigenous population and temporary workers was at least 1:3, for some areas 1:7, and the worst, such as Ostia, as high as 1:10.[152] Such bleak conditions were sustained by an unchanging structure of landownership and economic exploitation. The Agro Romano contained the greatest concentration of privileged landholders in Italy, and from the late seventeenth century through the nineteenth, this continued to shrink. Between 1690 and 1803, proprietors fell from 443 to 362; by 1870 there were only 70 (by 1910, only 21 owned 75 per cent of the Agro).[153] Indeed, as Giorgio Rossi has shown in his classic study of living and working conditions in the Agro Romano from the sixteenth to the nineteenth centuries, the combination of coercion, which created gangs out of a mixture of beggars, artisans, prisoners as well as a few voluntary labourers to work in the summer, their appalling conditions, mostly being left to sleep out at night, and high mortality were observed at the end of the nineteenth century not to have improved.[154] Such an arrangement discouraged adoption of modern agricultural techniques, and therefore productivity remained low, with the result that using the *campagna* as pastorage continued to be the preferred mode of exploitation.[155]

It is striking that, at a time when the backwardness and neglect of Roman peasants was a topic of routine dismay, Robert insists on the unalterable virtues and physical distinction of figures who inhabit his vision of the Pontine marshes. They are made to seem as if immune to the austerities of their living conditions by virtue of being beneficiaries of the 'pure sky' and 'meridional sun', which despite everything endowed them with a 'gaity' and appetite for life. In his turn Robert seems to have thought of himself as either lucky or somehow protected from the vicissitudes of the environment by his euphoric response to close contact with a form of pristine artistic source. Robert's painting depends on the idea of antiquity as a living presence. However, this commonplace idea was given a sharper, more intense visual presence by his preference for models from the most remote and inhospitable locations, where he found a 'sauvage' and 'vierge' character which inspired him.

If we consider contemporary responses to the *campagna*, and in particular its rebarbative aspects, in tandem with the picture's reception at the Salon, we get some sense of the discrepancy or tension between the wealth of readily proffered outspoken social and political perspectives, and the kinds of pictorial vocabulary brought into play by Robert.[156] What does this tell us about the limits of early nineteenth-century imagery's capacity to acknowledge and make visible bodies and landscapes which had fallen victim to disease and degeneration?

PRIMITIVISM

A measure of the strangeness and discomfort caused by confronting the *campagna* is the way it repeatedly called forth comparisons with 'primitive' non-European cultures. In 1723, having left Rome to the north, and arriving in Otricoli at 3.30 p.m., Montesquieu described 'a heat which burns the earth....This part of the Papal States is awful. The air is very unhealthy. One would believe oneself in Arabia.'[157] When visiting the Ponte Mammolo and finding it harmoniously rendered into a state of nature by a luxuriant covering of vegetation, Nibby baulked at the repulsiveness of a peasant who intruded into this idyllic scene, whom he described as resembling more a 'spectre from Tartary' than a man who had been born in the most beautiful part of Europe.[158]

In his chapter on the *campagna* in *Italie pittoresque*, Ernest Legouvé recalled two scenes of hunting in the forest of Nettuno shown at the 1831 Salon by Horace Vernet and compared this 'strange, wild, sombre' terrain to the 'virgin forests of America': 'Nothing could be more beautiful, more poetic, more primitive, than this forest.'[159] In the same volume, Norvins described how, from Nettuno to Astura, an immense forest was only interrupted by lakes and marshes. These 'terrifying solitudes' were only inhabited by buffalo, bora, semi-naked sun-blackened spear-carrying cowherds: 'One is really in Africa; one sees the kraals of the Hottentots. Filthy reptiles and myriads of insects gorged on blood complete this hideous resemblance.'[160] He used this comparison to evoke the distance between this hellish world and that of ordinary social life:

> These forests have all the majesty and all the horror of a primitive nature, of which they retain the wild independence. Night and day they echo to the sound of winds and tempests, mixed with the roaring of animals and the raucous cries of the shepherds, as well as the sweet and lively melodies of the birds, who, safe from men, under impenetrable foliage, celebrate the peace and delights of such a sanctuary; but, as in the woods dedicated to the divinities of Styx, the echoes of these forests have never included songs of joy, of poetry and of love.[161]

Yet primitivism could nevertheless be aligned with an august genealogy of Roman identity. Jean-Jacques Ampère saw in the *campagna*'s inhabitants the characteristics of the race who had founded Rome:

The race who took possession of this diseased soil was a strong, rustic race; like today's shepherds of the *campagna* they covered themselves with wool from their flocks; they lit fires in its forests, where wood was not lacking: they settled on high places from where each day they descended to cultivate the places thay had cleared, as do the inhabitants of the small towns of the Roman state, who one sees every morning going several miles to their work in the *campagna* and returning in the evening with their sickle and mattock.[162]

Similarly, amongst his equivocal remarks on contemporary agriculture, Tournon lauded the unchanged use of a type of plough which, under its Latin name of *aratrum*, had been employed by Cincinnatus.[163] It is not clear if he regarded it as unbettered in its technical efficacy or merely possessing an antiquarian charm.

The corollary to this sense of an alien people, at odds with ideas of art, beauty and the sacred attached to Rome, was a scientific type of curiosity and investigation, usually associated with an attempt to gather information with which to understand the scourge of bad air. Thus, A.J.C.A. Dureau de La Malle, author of *Économie politique des romains*, included reference to his journey from Rome to Naples, on 22 July 1811, when, like Robert and Prony, he entered locals' houses, only to find a complete absence of precautions and a torpid sense of fatalism. He also compares the *campagna* towards Naples to 'the wild aspect of the marshy steppes of Asia or the plains of the Orinoco'.[164]

If external appearance could be called on as evidence of health by defenders of Rome's reputation, the opposite could also apply. Alfred von Reumont set up his critique of the *campagna romana* by pointing accusingly at the state of the *basso popolo*. In his view, no artist's eye could redeem their 'sloth, squalor, filthiness, indecent, nauseating beggary'; to provide work to alleviate this fate was ultimately a political problem. Although this argument is not in itself original, it mirrors the celebratory representation of Roman peasants as noble savages by Léopold Robert, in that Reumont takes the *basso popolo* to be a revelatory index of the more general state of Rome as a city, a culture, a population.[165]

As we saw in the previous chapter, the Napoleonic occupation of Rome left a considerable legacy in terms of scientific studies of the city's problematic public health. Indeed, awareness of the topography and its pathological aspects have become part of the contemporary French political vocabulary. A pseudo-Orientalist poem published in the Parisian oppositional journal *La Pandore* drew on an aqueous Roman metaphor (which ought surely to be understood as a more topographically specific adaptation of the use of the term *marais* to ridicule the moderates in the Convention). If the empire could be lauded as a fast-flowing torrent, leaving 'seeds of abundance and fecundity' behind it, the Restoration was likened to stagnant water which had seeped through a dyke, corrupting the atmosphere:

> Corrupted seeds in the earth's bosom
> Exhale a deleterious vapour towards the heavens;...
> Impure miasmas condensed in clouds,

Like a jealous veil, cover the earth,
And conceal the fire of evenings and mornings;
Thus politics has its Pontine marshes.[166]

The two texts already cited by Tournon and Norvins were the fruit of the Napoleonic occupation.[167] They give detailed reflections and observations on the *campagna's* indigenous population and its condition, and provide revealing contexts for the abundant imagery of Rome produced in the early nineteeth century. The *Études statistiques sur Rome et la partie occidentale des états romains* (1831) published by Camille comte de Tournon, formerly prefect of Rome (1809–14), is a meticulously documented statement of unfinished business; he gives a detailed analysis of the economic and social world he had been responsible for, keenly aware of its shortcomings and the frustration of having had to abandon a series of projects and interventions before they could take full effect. Norvins, former police chief, edited *L'Italie pittoresque* (1836), containing major texts by him, which are a literary paraphrase of his more factual bureaucratic reports.[168] Both texts are fascinating in the way they draw on cultural and historical references to illustrate and sustain their arguments and aperçus. Norvins in particular provides a vivid evocation of preparations for harvest – which offers a revealing contrast to Robert's composition.

Tournon gives an unusually detailed description of the physical appearance of the different types he associated with specific locations. This, he points out, was based on the experience of reviewing over 20,000 potential conscripts.[169] He defined four distinct types. In the mountains of Albano and their foothills, one found people with tall, supple, regular physiques, with singularly proud and soft features: 'One would take them for the type of Apollos and Bacchuses.' The harsh mountains of Alatri and Veroli were inhabited by people with shorter, stronger limbs, and 'something wild which harmonises perfectly with the sheep and goat skins with which they dress themselves': 'One would believe that the blood of the awful Hernicans flowed in their veins.' The environs of Corneto and the northern slopes of the Cimino also had a race remarkable for their height, elegant forms, regularity and sweet expresson of their physiognomy: 'It is there that one finds, though in small numbers, the most beautiful men of the province, and one likes to consider them the representatives of noble Etruria.' Finally, a fourth race seemed to have survived in the Sabine hills: of average stature but having agile limbs and regular features, the beauty of a straight profile, large eyes and an abundance of curly hair: 'Surely these are the sons of the companions of Tatius and Numa?'[170]

These descriptions are most unusual in their topographical specificity (including the observation that he could find no evidence to support the myth of Trasteverines' resemblance to ancient Romans).[171] Tournon's qualified praise then becomes a yardstick for the shortcomings of the majority of the population, living in less fortunate locations. Although many Roman women were judged to have a serious and imposing beauty, 'goddesses descended from their pedestals', the male population was mostly ugly.[172] The inhabitants of the southern basin were a mixture of ill and handsome; those of the central basin were small, thin and feeble.[173] The worst condition was that of the 'Pontine marsh basin'. Here the 'bastardisation and impoverishment of the species' was appallingly obvious: 'The ugliness of the rare inhabitants of this plain is extreme, their debility even more so. Ringworm, hernias, rickets is so bad that several unfortunates hardly attain the height of a metre, and then obstructed viscera and ulcerated limbs afflict and destroy this population.'[174] Tournon concludes by turning to the status of 'bad air' and the alleged scope of its effects: 'Such is the physical state of a people who mostly live beneath a very pure sky, perfumed by the sweetest emanations. Can bad air explain all these phenomena?'[175] Resolute and comprehensive compilation of information and observations in Rome and the *campagna* thus seemed to challenge the widely held assumption that bad air was the root of general insalubriousness.

In his discussion of agriculture, Tournon deals with the organisation of harvest. His evocation of 'long columns of harvesters who descend singing from their healthy rocks, to confront a death without glory on an awful battlefield' nonetheless insists on the shocking casualties which were a matter of annual misery.[176] Yet, in his concluding remarks on the *campagna*'s agricultural yield, he calculates that it had roughly the same level of productivity and revenue as the department of the Gironde. This, he asserts, was proof that the shortcomings of Roman agriculture were not the result of simple laziness.[177]

Norvins's text has more the flavour of a worked-up literary piece, reinventing the administrator as *littérateur*, but his account of harvest preparations intersects with Tournon's in its classical references and the ultimately sombre appreciation of the brutal conditions. His writing has the sense of a voyeuristic combination of 'fascination and repulsion'. Such a stance is announced at the outset of his essay, where he stresses the alien character of the Papal States: 'The form of dress, faces, manners, even life's needs, everything is foreign to you.... No more verdure, no more arts, no more flowers, no more marbles, no more gaiety, and no well-being.' Moreover, he reiterates an Orientalised condemnation of papal callousness: 'The rags of the filthiest misery, which belong to the pope's beggars and those of the Grand Turk, have replaced the gracious costumes of Etruria.'[178] This sceptical predisposition is in tension with the classical elements and echoes he refers to. The harvest is preceded by the descent of 'great herds of oxen, linen grey, with long horns, from the antique race of bulls of Clitumnus'. The workers gathered before the 'custodian' of the 'rustic manor', who was 'like an ancient Sabine king'. Like Tournon, he employs a military metaphor: seen from a distance Norvins thought he was looking at an artillery column 'with its cannon and ammunition boxes', but once it approached closer he made out 'the most stunning, most beautiful rural paraphernalia I ever saw in my life. Everything is grandiose, gigantic, almost sublime in this Roman country.' Peasants, ploughs and oxen were decorated with madonnas and flowers. In the Agro Romano, Romans laboured, Neapolitans harvested; together in their thousands, they formed 'troupes of savages from the Abruzzi or Calabrians, born slaves of the Roman land' (perhaps alluding to the idea that the *cam-*

pagna had fallen into neglect because, as the empire expanded, slaves were used for farm work; with the empire's collapse, both they and their masters abandoned the land). 'These canicular men, almost naked, bronzed by the sun, of a huge stature, manifestations of a race mixed between savages and brigands, carry sickles and forks, a veritable rural pandemonium.'[179] At the end of his tour of rural inspection he arrived at Genzano, thereby setting up an extreme contrast, for this was one of the few places which had a reputation as a picturesque site with appropriately beautiful inhabitants: 'I saw myself really transported from hell to paradise. I thirsted for shade and freshness, and also to see once again beings who were wholly human. The fever victims of Ostia and Terracina, the brigands of Fondi, the spectral riders of the Pontine marshes, the buffalo, boar, Calabrians of Princess Caetani, and the dogdays of the harvest and the Mass [in the fields], pursued me like unbearable vampires, and held me, wide awake as I was, within the torture of a genuine nightmare.'[180] Indeed, it is not too far-fetched to think of Robert's *Arrival of the Harvesters* as applying the ideal beauty of Genzano to the degraded primitivism of the Pontine marshes. The dainty local colour of which his painting is made up stands in for the hazardous conditions and fateful outcome of harvest. Such representational displacement forms an important element in the critical response to the picture.

RECEPTION

The interplay between a certain model of faithful naturalism and the survival of antiquity were central themes in the picture's reception. Each aspect involves reflections on how close Robert was to his subject, or rather how he had expressed his closeness, and how the subject might contain layers of significance beneath the surface. The ambiguity inherent in the picture acts as a revealing test of critics' preconceived ideas about the Roman *campagna*. Although clearly related, this perspective is quite different from the more familiar debate both amongst contemporary critics and in later historiography around the status of the *Arrival of the Harvesters* as being either a genre scene or a history painting, or a hybrid of the two.[181]

Horace de Viel Castel invoked the banal, automatic, effortless process behind the making of the picture: he had 'taken his picture ready made, on a beautiful summer's day, in the Roman *campagna* where everything is a subject for painters'.[182] More interesting is Auguste Jal's hyperbolic response. His comments are based on the idea that Robert's picture achieved a sympathetic synthesis of the popular – showing people who are physically adapted to work in an inhospitable environment – with the antique, indeed to such a degree as to surpass their model: 'The characters are peasants; they have their own beauty: vigour, energetic elegance, dark skin, fine proportion of forms; one sees that they are capable of the arduous work they have to accomplish; one sees that they are the natural inhabitants of this roasting countryside which is covered by a sky so hot that it would destroy whoever was not fit to endure it, as a mortal entering Vulcan's forge would instantly have been consumed [by fire].' This is another world – alien certainly, but undeniably impressive precisely because of certain correspondances with antique ideals: 'There is perhaps no figure in all that has survived from Greek and Roman antiquity with more beautiful movement, pose, contour, naturalness and style than the herdsman who rests between his sweating oxen.'[183] Moreover, for Jal the picture itself takes on the status of an antique: 'Seen close up, the *Harvesters* is a picture which makes one think, like those precious survivals which the ground delivers up to us sometimes.'[184] Jal employs a powerful literalism to align this ambitious genre picture with the august standards of the antique. For him, the picture has literally grown out of the soil and atmosphere of the *campagna*. He invokes extreme heat rather than bad air as the life-threatening aspect of the depicted landscape, but deflects this reference by invoking Vulcan's forges.

A more detailed explanation of what Robert had achieved, in which the picture's narrative is related to specific sites in the *campagna*, is given by the archaeologist and historian Charles Lenormant, who had known the artist in Rome in the 1820s.[185] Initially, he describes the picture as if he was dealing with real people, and moreover privy to the artist's intentions: 'The father of the family, who lives in one of those picturesquely situated towns perched on the majestic chain of mountains which border the Pontine marshes to the east, has departed from Piperno, Cora and Sezze for the fields which he possesses in the plain; when he arrives in the evening in the midst of his harvesting, the sun, which sets behind the peak of the island of Circeo, only gilds those figures who are still relatively raised up, and already shadows mark the features of the harvesters and the folds of their clothes.'[186] That the evening twilight is celebrated here is striking – this was believed to be the most dangerous moment for bad air to make its mark, yet Lenormant shifts his account towards the enhanced aestheticisation of contour and expression: 'and above all, drawing of a resolved correction, expressive heads that no one finds anymore, a characterisation strong like Poussin and ingenuous like Holbein'.[187] Robert is seen as a successor to previous artists who had continued the tradition of the antique – Michelangelo, Puget, Lesueur, Géricault ('who sketched with a palette knife on the walls of his studio motifs worthy of the Parthenon frieze').[188] However, Lenormant claims that Robert is quite exceptional in his successful reanimation of the spirit of antiquity:

We have sublime imitations such as those achieved by Poussin and dreamt of by David, we have the *Psyché* of M. Gérard and the *Endymion* of Girodet, but only Robert enters into antique feeling without recourse to statues. To achieve this, he lived with these men in their native world;…he found nothing more than reminders of the primitive state, or reversions to ancient life, in this class of men whose life in the fields and mountains has protected them from social revolutions;…in their build, their features, their habits, he recognised the imprint of a strong and simple nature, which we other degenerated races, out of a sense of self-regard, take to be the dreams of an exalted imagination, when we find it in works of art.[189]

Reviewing Delécluze's 1838 monograph, written in homage to Robert after the artist's premature death, Lenormant recalled their time spent together. He compared his own archaeological endeavours, searching for 'the idea of antiquity' amongst fragmentary debris, with Robert's more effective pictorial realisation of 'what the old populations of Italy had retained of antique physiognomy', an aesthetic achievement in harmony with the century's penchant for historical recreations.[190]

Delécluze himself also saluted Robert's assimilation of antique sculptural qualities, and the way he had achieved a fusion of this with a contemporary immediacy, such that the viewer's sense of time was undermined: 'To see the *naïveté* which informs the gestures of all the characters in the *Harvesters*, and when one feels oneself held by this air of power, by this elevated beauty and this grandeur, imprinted on the calm features of these peasants, one really does not know from what time the picture comes, in which one finds all the gravity of antique statuary, combined with this immediacy which is only found in works inspired by nature, and copied in some manner from it.'[191]

Ambroise Tardieu gives a confused reading of the painting, in that he acknowledges Italy's pre-eminence when it came to the nobility of its human stock – a result of the implantation of the classical heritage through immigration – yet he asserts Robert could have achieved an 'ideal' beauty just as well by painting the harvesters of the Beauce region.[192] For him, the subject is wholly pastoral, therefore inadmissable to the category of history painting. On the other hand, he judges the picture by means of a literal verisimilitude: he finds the picture implausible, since the figures seem too poised, rather than actively preparing to set up camp. Reference to the *campagna* is absent.[193]

The tension between Italian and French provincial subjects was later to be invoked by Théophile Gautier in his discussion of Courbet's 1851 Salon exhibits, in which he encouraged the artist to do what Léopold Robert had done for 'the rustic types of Italy, whose beauty he idealised by his elegant and pure style'. The French provinces were capable of providing comparable motifs with which to create truly popular works, a preferable alternative to the aesthetically indigestible and politically unpalatable works Courbet had exhibited. As we have seen, Robert's popularity was a matter of polemical assertion not consensual cliché, but Gautier makes it seem as if he is speaking of an established opinion so as to reinforce his censure of Courbet as a recalcitrant socialist and iconoclast.[194]

That the celebration of working peasants need not be subordinate to the authority of the antique is also borne out by Saint-Simonian critics such as Decamps or Blanc, who applauded the 'profoundly plebeian idea' and their 'majesty, grace, [and] energy'.[195] In a later article Théophile Thoré was to reiterate this theme, claiming that it was, indeed, the prime cause for the popularity of Robert's work: 'It is that he has poeticised human nature in the people, through telling of work and its perils, its joys and suffering, as part of the hazards of communal existence. It is that he has rehabilitated inferiors, by endowing them with beauty, intelligence and virtue. And he has not only given beauty and noble passions to the people but he has idealised nature.'[196]

The paradox of Thoré's advocacy is that, in championing the political and aesthetic status of the people, he detaches them from their indigenous environment. To this extent, aestheticisation undermines the persuasiveness of his political engagement. For Thoré, Robert's peasants are an ideal form of 'le peuple', but living in the present and independent of any substitution for antiquity. Yet for an unsympathetic critic such as Gustave Planche, 'the passion for the natural, too much exploited in detail, has seduced the artist's imagination so as to produce nothing more than a more or less ingenious mosaic,' with the result that the painting appeared dry and hard. 'There is, if you will pardon the expression, abuse of nature.'[197] In trying to push his painting towards an ideal idiom, Robert had ended up with a distorted naturalism. However, Planche focuses exclusively on the figures and ignores what might be at issue in the representation of the site at the moment of harvest.

Imaginations nourished on antique history were readily able to populate the *campagna*'s desolate emptiness with characters and narrative incident. Robert presents an image in which the figures are loosely arranged as if in a frieze – they not so much inhabit the *campagna* as take on the role of a collective personification of its historical and temporal double identity. In enacting the seasonal work of harvest, they are made part of a natural, inexhaustible cycle, which reinforces their plausibility as descendants of antique forebears. Yet this presents us with a paradox: in order to find materials with which to construct an ambitious multi-figure picture which would exemplify a new form of pictorial authenticity, Robert delved into remote parts of the Roman *campagna*. To this extent, the *Arrival of the Harvesters* is an image predicated on different forms of dislocation: that of the artist through his exploratory travels; that of the audience vis-à-vis the unfamiliar subject; and that of the indigenous Romans whose seasonal displacement provided the inspiring picturesque spectacle for the artist. The commonplace identification of the *campagna* and its surrounding hills with brigands, an imagery Robert himself had done much to sustain, was complemented by offering an idyllic scene of communal agriculture. Finally, it shifts the image of the Pontine marshes into a realm of untarnished antique beauty, thereby neutralising memories or anxieties regarding the poisoned landscape, which Robert in fact keeps all but out of sight.

By harnessing ideas of antiquity to a genre scene, Robert sought to raise his professional status. To this extent, we should read Robert's celebratory pictorial rhetoric as a calculated alternative to the dominant conception of the Pontine marshes as a blighted region. However, it is surprising how rare challenges to the picture's plausibility are. The anonymous review in *Le Voleur* illustrates precisely an awareness of the way the subject was dependent on competing conventions. The painting worked as a scene of agriculture, albeit referred to as a 'fête'; its site was the problem: 'But in the Pontine

53 Guillaume Bodinier, *Evening Prayer: Shepherds of the Roman Campagna*, 1835 (1836 Salon), oil on canvas, 128 × 176 cm. Musée des beaux-arts, Angers, inv. MBA 215 (J.1881).

54 Rudolf Lehmann, *Pope Sixtus V blessing the Pontine Marshes*, 1846 Salon, oil on canvas, 262 × 353 cm. Musée des beaux-arts, Lille, P 560.

55 August Kopisch, *Pontine Marshes: Sunset*, 1848, oil on canvas, 62 × 111 cm. Alte Nationalgalerie, Berlin, WS 118.

marshes, that's what destroys the whole painting for me. Why? You ask? Ah! Why? Where is the fever? – What is that? – I need fever, the fever of the Pontine marshes which kills travellers, and makes the miserable inhabitants of the place feeble and pale. The rags of an Italian, the knife with which he bleeds himself in the morning, a haggard face, a stupefied look, skinny bulls, and I am in the Pontine marshes: so get rid of the Pontine marshes and I would find the picture ravishing.'[198] Later, more plausibly, Louise Viardot was to claim that the festive appearance made sense because these people were enthusiastically returning home, leaving the risk of *mal'aria* behind.[199]

The Pontine marshes had an ambiguous identity in terms of the types of genre in which it appeared. As we have seen with Corot and Ivanov, in the early nineteenth century, the marshes themselves and the bleak, empty areas of the *campagna* were relatively neglected as a *mise-en-scène* for subject pictures, and indeed for landscape studies. It offered a challenge, in terms of both the experience of making work there and how such views were to be orchestrated. Perhaps, indeed, it was in part by virtue of the exceptional choice of his site that Theodore Gudin made his reputation with a Pontine marshes landscape in 1832, exhibiting the same traits of bravura in his painting as he was to do in his heroic maritime subjects.[200] In his *Evening Prayer: Shepherds of the*

56   Pierre-François-Eugène Giraud, *Fever Victim in the Roman Campagna*, 1845, oil on canvas, 130 × 161 cm. Musée d'Art Roger-Quilliot, Clermont-Ferrand.

Campagna of Rome (fig. 53), Guillaume Bodinier achieved a pictorial equilibrium between sinister landscape setting (endowing the instense strip of orange horizon with an ominous glow) and timeless actions by depicting the moment of evening prayer, when work was suspended, a state of being affecting peasants and animals alike.[201] Indeed, Robert's *Arrival of the Harvesters* was also taken to show 'the hour of the Ave Maria', endowing the scene with a protective aura of sanctification.[202] In 1846, Rudolf Lehmann (1819–1905) invoked the marshes' poisoned reputation through a historical subject, *Pope Sixtus V blessing the Pontine Marshes* (fig. 54), showing the initiation of a programme of drainage, which had the added benefit of encouraging local brigands, who represented another form of infestation, to seek papal forgiveness.[203] Equally, from the 1830s, it was possible to use the flattened landscape format associated with Barbizon, in which trees are sandwiched between sky and water, to give the Roman marshes a distinctly French character.[204] However, a work by August Kopisch, not bound by French landscape conventions, shifts the crepuscular, not to say apocalyptic, spectacle of the Pontine marshes into what must be called the miasmatic sublime (fig. 55).

Subsequent Pontine imagery either focused on an ethnographic and medicalised type of representation or retreated into the evocative imprecision of landscape. Pierre-

57   Edward Lear, *Ostia*, lithograph, 25 × 15.7 cm frontispiece in *Views of Rome and its Environs*, (London, 1841). Private collection.

58   Edward Lear, *Norba*, lithograph, 36.3 × 21 cm, in *Views of Rome and its Environs* (London, 1841). Private collection.

59   Edward Lear, *Ninfa*, 30.3 × 15.9 cm,   in *Illustrated Excursions in Italy*, 2 vols (London, 1846), vol. 2, pp. 20–1, plate 11. British Library, London.

60   J. Bastin after Edward Lear, *Ninfa*, wood engraving, 19 × 7.5 cm, in *Illustrated Excursions in Italy*, 2 vols (London, 1846), vol. 2, p. 21 (vignette). Captioned: 'The Lake and ruined Town of Ninfa form one of the most romantic and striking scenes in Italy'. British Library, London.

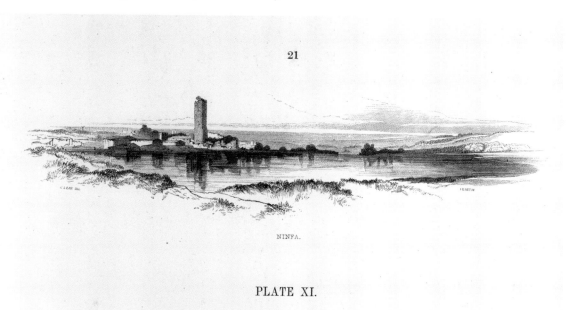

21

NINFA.

PLATE XI.

NINFA.

François-Eugène Giraud's *Fever Victim in the Roman Campagna* (fig. 56) makes a simple but compelling equation between the suffering peasant and the lowering landscape which frames his debilitated body, and where he seems destined to expire.[205] As in earlier theories of climate and its effects, we are here shown a causal connection made flesh – it is this landscape which has reduced the fever victim to a state of physical collapse. This is a Realist *académie* on a substantial scale – an individual if anonymous subversion of the idea of local colour by means of the pathologisation of expression. Giraud's painting is exceptional in his own work, and within French painting of the second quarter of the nineteenth century, in depicting the victim of a specific disease.[206] Yet even here the wasted body retains a physical coherence and residual decorum – quite unlike the damaged and enfeebled inhabitants of the Pontine marshes described by Tournon.

Edward Lear's engagement with Roman landscape sites is striking for his willingness to include a number of sites strongly associated with bad air, as represented in his *Views of Rome and its Environs* (1841) and the sequel, the *Illustrated Excursions in Italy* (1846).[207] Indeed, a view of Ostia serves as the frontispiece to *Views* (fig. 57), a site with a fearsome reputation for the appalling quality of its air and being inhabited by spectral beggars and criminals. He also included a view of Norba above the lake and abandoned village

61 (DETAIL) Robert Macpherson, *Deserted City of Ninfa in the Pontine Marshes*, 1860s, albumen print from dry collodian negative, 19.7 × 40.1 cm. Victoria and Albert Museum, London, PH.28–1983.

of Ninfa, long associated with endemic bad air (fig. 58).[208] However, his pictures in *Views of Rome* make no reference in style or character to the insalubrious reputation of the sites. And only the text accompanying a view of the 'Palace of the Chigi, Ariccia' (no. 9) mentions the 'salubrity of its serene air'. *Illustrated Excursions*, however, includes a view of Sermoneta (vol. 2, plates 9 and 10) with the comment: 'Sermoneta is but thinly inhabited, owing to the insalubrity of its atmosphere'. Ninfa reappears as a full-page plate (fig. 59), 'a town as well-known for having been destroyed by Barbarossa in the twelfth century as its subsequent abandonment because of bad air', as well as a vignette (fig. 60), captioned: 'The Lake and ruined Town of Ninfa form one of the most romantic and striking scenes in Italy.'[209] Of Pratica (plate 24), site of ancient Lavinium, Lear notes: 'As is the case of the neighbouring city of Ardea, the devastations of war and the badness of the air gradually caused the decay of Lavinium; [which was] nearly deserted by the middle of the sixth [century].' As made explicit by the texts accompanying each image, Lear thus inscribes into his views reflections on the role of environmental factors in historical transformation. His precedent at Ninfa could well have been the model for Robert Macpherson's sombre image of the same site (fig. 61), although Middleton had also produced a picturesque version of the same view in 1812.[210]

However, the picture that came to dominate ideas of the Pontine marshes, even more than Robert's *Arrival of the Harvesters*, was Ernest Hébert's *Malaria* (fig. 62). Both acquired a quasi-official iconographic status: the former entered the Louvre in 1835, the latter the Musée du Luxembourg.[211] As J.J. Ampère observed in the early 1860s: 'One cannot write this word [malaria] without immediately thinking of the beautiful and moving picture by M. Hébert.'[212] Larousse's entry for 'mal'aria ou malaria' is followed by one on Hébert's painting.[213] Moreover, this has built into it commentary from *Les Beaux-Arts en Europe en 1855* by Théophile Gautier, which had also achieved the status of a kind of orthodoxy (amplified by the inclusion of a poem on the painting in his canonical collection, *Émaux et camées*). Gautier places the picture in a French pictorial tradition: 'After Schnetz, after Léopold Robert, he presented Italy under a true and original aspect; to the picturesque he added feeling. This was no longer bronzed types, clearly delineated in a crude light, but an ailing grace, a languishing charm, an enervated melancholy, a sad poetry, which touched you to the heart.' But ultimately this was a painting which spoke more about the artist than the subject. For Gautier: 'The painter's dreamy soul is all there.'[214]

Indeed, in 1851, Gautier had already used Robert's *Arrival of the Harvesters* as a yardstick by means of which to judge Hébert's painting,[215] and the rapport between the pictures was again brought into play by Gautier when Hébert's painting was re-exhibited in the Exposition universelle of 1855.[216] Hébert's biographer, Joseph Péladan, celebrated the way the picture successfully evoked the diseased Roman locale: 'If *Malaria* is a beautiful work, it is because fever emanates from the canvas and one feels the weight of the sky, the water, the air, one feels oppressed by the pestilential atmosphere; the artist has literally painted bad air.'[217]

Yet, Gautier's too readily quotable comments need to be set aside in order to assess the work in terms of its title, *Malaria*, and consider what kind of a representation of the Pontine marshes it is.[218] Hébert conceived the picture in Rome, but executed it in Paris. This was to be the main item for his Salon debut, and thus the culmination of his Prix de Rome: *La Malaria: Famille italienne fuyant la contagion* (Malaria: Italian family fleeing the contagion (1850 Salon, no. 1436).[219] The initial landscape studies made by Hébert in the *campagna* create vistas framed by rocky hills, almost abstract in their bareness.[220] However, in the final painting, we are given no view beyond the boat and its occupants. While this might seem designed to emphasise the subject's inescapability, it fails to provide a context in any topographical sense. As the single word of the title implies, this is an evocation of the relentless effects of an endemic insalubriousness. Indeed, the family's supposed flight seems entirely arrested. Rather than Giraud's pathologised close-up, Hébert takes a step backwards and creates a claustrophobic space around the boatful of victims of the marshes' bad air. The landscape such as it

62 Ernest Hébert, *Malaria*, 1848–9, oil on canvas, 135 × 193 cm. Musée d'Orsay, Paris, inv. 5299, RF 2260.

 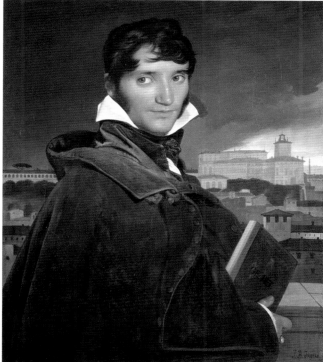

63 François-Marius Granet, *Self-portrait*, 1802–11, oil on canvas, 38 × 29.2 cm. Musée Granet, Aix-en-Provence.

64 J.A.D. Ingres, *F. M. Granet*, 1807, oil on canvas, 72 × 61 cm. Musée Granet, Aix-en-Provence.

is seems indeterminate, lacking any clues to the Roman setting, in a way which could be read as a sign that Hébert sought to give his painting a more general evocative character, consistent with its terse title. Indeed, it is the absence of precise reference which allowed the picture to have greater currency. For Albert de la Fizelière, it was the image of an Italy that was 'living, sick and poetic'; it was an emblem of the country's misfortunes.[221]

Perhaps the most poignant and explicit pictorial outcome of the impact of Rome's bad air on artists and the making of art is not a landscape but a self-portrait (fig. 63).[222] François-Marius Granet spent twenty-two years in Rome, where he specialised in church interiors and subject paintings primarily in the genre of historical scenes. Although he produced an enormous quantity of landscape views of Rome and its environs, none were included in his Salon exhibits.[223] While some studies fed into subject pictures, most seem to be part of that productive culture of nature studies which was particularly identified with Rome as a place of inspiration and documentation. Yet Granet was to become a victim of his commitment to close inspection of the

65 François-Marius Granet, *Interior of Subterranean Church of San Martino ai Monti*, 1803, oil on canvas, 125 ×
158 cm. Musée Fabre, Montpellier.

motif, and the belief that he was inhabiting an environment where art took precedence
over all other considerations; however, he did succeed in making art out of this
experience.

When in 1803 he set out to work in the vaults of San Martino ai Monti, formerly part
of the Baths of Titus, he was alerted by monks there to its 'deadly' atmosphere. Granet's
guide similarly urged him to make haste because of the danger of bad air.[224] As he ruefully records in his memoirs, he spurned this chorus of local advice and duly succumbed
to a prolonged bout of fever. On the one hand, Granet's pursuit of certain Roman motifs
exemplifies a reckless determination to capture Romantic picturesqueness regardless
of the consequences. On the other hand, his experiences illustrate the ambiguities

involved in following or ignoring local advice about a problem whose intangibility encouraged a certain blasé nonchalance. In his case, he was specifically warned by his guide that working in cold and damp crypts and other subterranean spaces was almost certain to damage his health. He describes the ambient dangers which artists who worked on Roman sites risked: the *aria cattiva* 'was waiting for me concealed among the splendid ruins, shaded by garlands of ivy, surrounded by a thousand flowers'.[225]

Although Granet's studies of San Martino ai Monti do not include figures, his finished painting has a shrouded corpse as its centrepiece (fig. 64). While Granet evidently recovered from this illness, he nonetheless received a reminder of his own mortality. Although, as noted above, Roman imagery of the early nineteenth century included plentiful and often gruesome variations on the theme of death, the final form of this painting may not be unconnected to Granet's own sobering experience.[226]

His self-portrait while in the grip of fever appears at first sight to be an example of the Romantic convention whereby extreme physical states were cultivated in order to gain access to new kinds of inspiration.[227] Granet, however, avoids self-heroisation, and even introspection. Indeed, it might rather be seen as a kind of forensic self-reproach, capturing his unhealthy pallor and documenting the wasted state which his illness had reduced him to, leaving him housebound and obliged to use himself as a model, although it is likely that this is at least in part a retrospective image. This self-portrait takes on a further degree of pathos when compared to Ingres's portrait of Granet (fig. 65), a veritable icon of the self-possessed Romantic artist, standing imperiously against a Roman backdrop made up of a lowering sky above the Quirinal Palace.

Granet's *Self-portrait* reminds us that exploration of Rome and its unique landscape might lead an artist to become imprisoned by illness. Rather than the animation engendered by excitation of sensibility, responding to a superabundance of great art and awe-inspiring ruins, Granet's self-image shows a different kind of destabilisation. To make a self-portrait at all was an unsatisfactory substitute for being out in the city and its landscape. In recording his state of physical incapacitation, he reproaches himself for having compromised his artistic endeavours.

Treating Rome as an array of motifs and sites to be absorbed and transcribed left artists vulnerable to dangers which respected none of the cultural hierarchies or qualities assumed to be embedded in the fabric of the eternal city. Rome and its *campagna* was far from being the idyllic promised land of artists' dreams. The sight of ruins strewn across a poisoned landscape was testimony not only to the vicissitudes of history, but also to the vulnerability of a sophisticated and prosperous civilisation to insidious environmental conditions of devastating potency. 'Bad air' was dangerously ubiquitous, but also unsettlingly enigmatic and elusive. Yet the history of landscape painting in Rome suggests that cosmetic compromise was so ingrained a habit as to insulate ideal visions from the threat of miasmatic interference.

6

'IT WAS DIRTY, BUT IT WAS ROME'

Writing in 1763 of the disappointing impression made on him by Rome's buildings, Tobias Smollett observed: 'Here, all is engaged,'[1] regretting the way that palaces were given no space to breathe, and thus were difficult to view as independent architectural entities. Smollett's remark is primarily aesthetic, but it carries the clear implication that this unsatisfactory aspect of urban design was symptomatic of wider political and social shortcomings. In early nineteenth-century observations, such a connection became more explicit, as expressed by James Johnson: 'between the palace and the hovel there is no intermedium'.[2] For Charles Dickens, Rome's spaces were incongruously compressed together: 'The narrow streets, devoid of footways, and choked, in every obscure corner, by heaps of dunghill-rubbish, contrast so strongly, in their cramped dimensions, and their filth, and darkness, with the broad square before some haughty church.'[3] All of these visitors to Rome share the perception that these problems had a long pedigree. Their predecessors in the sixteenth and seventeenth centuries would not have demurred.[4]

As Richard Krautheimer has shown, awareness of the unsavoury condition and rebarbative aspect of Roman space was already acute in the seventeenth century. Krautheimer analyses Lorenzo Pizzati's recommendations for cleaning up the city and implementing a coherent policy of social housing.[5] This provided a complementary perspective to Alexander VII's transformation of the Roman cityscape by the insertion of a series of spectacular architectural set-pieces. Although Krautheimer saw Pizzati as a self-promoting pen-pusher, he nonetheless gave him credit for being three centuries ahead of his time in his (unrealised) vision of a reformed urbanism.[6] However, the assumption that it was not until the fascist *ventennio* that effective policies for improving hygienic conditions were implemented is misleading, for initiatives to clean up the eternal city were already a well-established preoccupation by the end of the eighteenth century, in theory if not in practice.[7]

Nonetheless, Pizzatti's proposals point to a distinctive feature of the way monuments were situated within the space of the city. Rather than existing as pristine theatricalised showpieces, according to the spectacular architectural rhetoric of 'Roma Alessandrina', Rome's monuments struggled to escape from a congested and messy urban environment. The juxtaposition of ancient and modern was a well-worn formula in observations on the aspect of the city. At first sight this was assumed to be a simple matter of chronological difference and succession. In practice such viewing in historically distinct terms was subject to interference and obstruction. Until effective initiatives to clear away rubbish and detritus got underway in the early nineteenth century, Rome's grand buildings were characteristically obscured by the deposits of centuries, constantly renewed layers of modern waste, and the revered ancient remains themselves were also likely to be smothered by vegetation.

Whatever the ambition of Alexander's redesigns and other monumental interventions, the city appeared to Smollett, Dickens and their contemporaries as a connected – not to say congested – spectacle, in which monuments were not only embedded within a continuous urban fabric but inextricable from the surrounding dross. Conceived in this way, architectural set pieces become absorbed into a more troublesome space, in which their interstices and edges are places for indecorous opportunism – erecting lean-tos, begging, fly-tipping, and as impromptu latrines. Architectural display and hygienic propriety were indeed closely related. As Renato Sansa has shown, the papal politics of show was complemented by local resistance to and manipulation of legislation designed to maintain clean streets.[8]

Attending to the presence and status of dirt in Rome is a way of reconsidering the familiar notion of the urban fabric perceived as a series of superimposed art-historical layers.[9] Rather than seeing the city as being made up exclusively of ancient and modern architecture, ruins and subsequent accretions, if we take into account short- and long-term accumulations of quotidian detritus (an extreme instance of this from classical times being the Monte Testaccio, a 'prominence' created from discarded pottery), our sense of the city's form and structure takes on a different character.

Indeed, perceptions of historic structures being made up of a series of layers are complicated by the recognition that some more recent additions compromised their predecessors. Giulio Carlo Argan, writing in 1979 as mayor of Rome, gave a deprecating twist to the idea of Rome's layered historic inheritance: '[Rome] is a city which lived on its spoils, then on its ruins, and today on its refuse.'[10] Decay and economic stagnation created a setting in which the city's antique remains and rubbish were somehow equivalent. Such reflections enshrined the idea that Rome's cultural riches were encased in a matrix of filth. In terms of viewing the city, intrusive matter provided a physical barrier to spectatorial mobility, discouraging proximity, and thus creating a challenge to artistic contemplation.

In this chapter, I will suggest that we should understand the experience of the assembled set pieces and itineraries of Rome's antiquities, art and architecture as being intimately connected, both physically and conceptually, to problems of cleanliness and hygiene and the threat of disease. As we will see, dirt and rubbish occupy a peculiarly pivotal position at the intersection of aesthetic and medical commentaries on Rome. Moreover, the importance of corrupted matter and the surfaces of things – the ground on which Rome sat, made up of an aggregate of historic fragments and latterday deposits, the result of both natural decay and incontinent social laissez-faire – was closely associated with perceptions of a pathologically inhospitable environment and responsible for the city's compromised atmosphere. In all of these perspectives, ample consideration is given to dirt as a problem which needed to be solved if the visibility of artistic treasures and the well-being of the city's inhabitants were to be protected. Dirt, in the words of Mary Douglas, is matter out of place.[11] In the case of Rome, dirt is a problem which, it might be said, gets everywhere – under the feet and into the mindsets of Romans and visitors alike.

The question of salubriousness is a vivid example of the way that viewing the modern city inevitably involved making a comparison with its ancient 'double'.[12] There can be no doubt that by modern standards Rome in the early nineteenth century, like most other cities of the time, was dirty. Dirt, however, is a relative concept, and it is striking how frequently it was asserted that Rome was probably pre-eminent in this respect. The most obvious comparison was between an imagined magnificent past and contemporary filth. Writing of his visit in 1802–3, Joseph Forsyth warned: 'Whichever road you take, your attention will be divided between magnificence and filth. The inscription "Immondezzaio" [rubbish dump] on the walls of palaces is only an invitation to befoul them. The objects which detain you longest, such as Trajan's column, the Fountain of Trevi, &c., are inaccessible from ordure. Ancient Rome contained one hundred and forty-four public necessaries, besides *Sellae Patroclianae*. The modern city draws part of its infection from the want of such conveniences.'[13] Lady Morgan compressed her opinion of Rome's current condition into that of 'the *immondezzaio* of that world, of which she was once the mistress'.[14]

Louis Simond was serious when he reflected that, following an exploration of the area around the Jewish ghetto, 'of all Rome's antiquities, it is its filth which is the most antique; for it seems as if it has never been removed.'[15] The Roman administrator Nicola Maria Nicolai regarded a proper investigation of ancient sewers and drains as a necessary first step towards improving such matters in modern Rome.[16] That the ancients were believed to have had a more effective approach to sewage was a further aspect of their superiority over the moderns. In his comparison of ancient and modern Rome, Dureau de la Malle saluted the policy of having a tax on sewage conduits and their contents, which he believed to have promoted salubriousness.[17]

After remarking on the relative of quietness of Rome after Naples, Augustus von Kotzebue also claimed it was cleaner:

> Many of my readers may perhaps laugh at me when I speak of cleanliness at Rome: but it is indeed clean when compared to Naples; and without having been in the latter city, it is impossible to conceive how far the love of filth may be carried. It must be owned, that on many walls in Rome, we find the word *immondezzaio* inscribed; signifying a place where everyone may throw all manner of dirt – a privilege which is

but too frequently made use of; but these are only particular places; and however near they may be to each other, the intervals are clean. At Naples, on the contrary, *immondezzaio* should be written over the gates, for the whole city is a temple of Cloacina.[18]

In fact, Kotzebue's benchmark of urban propriety was St Petersburg, an altogether cleaner, cooler and therefore more hygienic city, whose pre-eminence emerged all the more unquestionably from his observations abroad. Moreover, the prime register of Kotzebue's engagement with Rome, as for many travellers, was as the site of former classical splendour, which he engaged with in terms of euphoric reverie, devoting far less space to its contemporary physical aspect.[19] British visitors judged London to be much closer to rivalling the salubriousness of ancient Rome than the squalor of the modern city.[20] James Johnson, however, was not impressed by the majestic but rudimentary Cloaca Maxima (fig. 66); in his view, London, 'modern Babylon', had far surpassed Rome's

66   Robert Macpherson, *Cloaca Maxima*, 1857–8, albumen print, 31.5 × 38.5 cm. W. Bruce and Delaney H. Lundberg Collection.

cult of Cloacina in the sense of having a more efficient sewerage system.[21] Others sought an explanation for this offensive aspect to Rome's assault on the senses in southern Italy's pagan heritage. For Thomas Uwins, having been shocked by the Madonna dell'Arco festival near Naples in 1826: 'Such a mixture of filth and piety, drunkenness and devotion, must have had its origin in the ancient Bacchanalian orgies, of which it is a most lively and animated illustration.'[22] James Whiteside recoiled from the 'inconceivable filth' – literally something he found hard to understand – wherever he turned, whether attending to antique remains or the 'City of churches', which perhaps even more jarringly he judged to be 'defiled', as also the 'fine squares' delineated on his map, which resembled 'waste ground reserved for rubbish or the refuse of a great city'.[23]

According to Mary Douglas, nineteenth-century thinkers viewed primitive religions as being 'separated from the great religions of the world' because they were 'inspired by fear' and 'inextricably confused with defilement and hygiene' – fear inhibiting reason, hence this propensity to confusion. (Douglas herself uses a metaphor of Roman impropriety to describe the anthropologist, 'expecting to see rituals performed with reverence…finding himself [*sic*] in the role of agnostic sightseer in St Peter's, shocked at the disrespectful clatter of the adults and the children playing Roman shovepenny on the floor stones'.)[24] Defilement was certainly an issue for some visitors to Rome, as will be discussed later in this chapter, but this was as much entangled with aesthetic matters as with more conventional censure of Catholicism and the failings of the papal administration.

DIRTY AND DISEASED

The medical writer James Johnson, in his *Change of Air, or the Pursuit of Health* (1831), wrote that Rome was the 'dirtiest city of Europe – with the exception of Lisbon'.[25] Since he was seeking to advise invalids and travellers interested in staying healthy, this judgement sounded an unequivocal warning, for at this period dirt was considered to be synonymous with disease. Johnson's censorious attitude to the city corresponds to what the medical historian Owsei Temkin, in his study of Galenism, has called the aesthetic theory of disease: the idea that dirtiness, based on displeasing appearance or smell, is directly equated with unhealthiness, this at a time before the germ theory of contagion was established.[26] An example of this view, in which Rome's dirtiness is causally linked to its unhealthiness, is the comment of George Augustus Sala in 1869: 'The streets of Rome, the houses of Rome – to the very palaces and museums – reek with such horrible odours that you are very soon led to conjecture that the ever-quoted mal'aria from the Pontine Marshes has been made responsible for a great deal of which it is quite innocent, and that one of the chief predisposing causes of the Roman fever is the inconceivable filthiness of the people and their dwellings.'[27] Disease in the countryside was also blamed on dirt and general, if not extreme, insalubriousness.[28]

However, when considered from an artistic point of view dirt could be redeemed. As William Wetmore Story pointed out, the indefensibly insalubrious state of Rome's streets was almost necessary to the creation of certain kinds of picturesque effect: 'It was dirty, but it was Rome; and to any one who has long lived in Rome even its very dirt has a charm which the neatness of no other place ever had. All depends, of course, on what we call dirt. No one would defend the condition of some of the streets or some of the habits of the people. But the soil and stain which many call dirt I call colour, and the cleanliness of Amsterdam would ruin Rome for the artist. Thrift and exceeding cleanliness are sadly at war with the picturesque.'[29] Henry James, writing after Rome had become the new capital and was at last being cleaned up, took the aestheticisation of dirt to a new level of euphemism and subtlety. He invoked the advice of Story, 'an old sojourner' in Rome, that 'you don't really like [Rome] till you like the dirt'. James admitted that he had previously seen 'the nameless uncleanness with which all Roman things are oversmeared' as a 'damning token of moral vileness'. To a friend who could not stand squalor, he explained that 'the love of Rome is, in its last analysis, simply that perfectly honorable and legitimate instinct, the love of the status quo – the preference of contemplative and slow-moving minds for the visible, palpable, measurable present – touched here and there with the warm lights and shadows of the past.[30]

Though he never succumbed to reverie in the face of antique remains, John Ruskin had similarly outspoken views on Rome's exceptional filthiness. He recalled that he had 'never been hindered from drawing street subjects by pure human stench, but in two cities: Edinburgh and Rome' – an unexpected and uncongenial comparison which also came to the mind of Lady Eastlake. This he links directly to religion: 'Strange, too, how these two great pardoning religions ['Evangelical and Papal sects'] agree in the accompaniment of physical filth.'[31] Significantly, he parries any accusation of routine anti-Catholicism by the pairing with Evangelicalism. Others were more direct in justifying their dislike of Catholicism by pointing to its unsavoury olfactory consequences. Thus, George Augusus Sala, who found Rome especially dirty, asked sarcastically: 'Would you tell me, if you please, why it is that the most orthodox Catholic cities always stink so intolerably? It is the odour of sanctity, I suppose.'[32]

Flaubert found the smell of manure, which had a reputation for healthfulness, a relief from what he considered the stench of incense: 'It takes time to get a grip on ancient Rome, caked with incense as it from all the churches. Yet, there are some quarters, on the banks of the Tiber, some old corners full of manure, where one can breathe a little.'[33] Indeed, olfactory ambiguity – between fragrance and stink – was the keynote to Rome's identity. For the Goncourt brothers: 'Things and people: everything here is a little like the odour of the streets of Rome, where one doesn't exactly know if what one smells is shit or orange flower.'[34]

To Hazlitt's nose, the 'odour of antiquity' struggled to make itself smelt through the prevailing stink of garlic.[35] Stendhal lamented that the 'sublime' Corso was poisoned by the stench of rotting cabbage,[36] and his disgust acquired a more sinister edge having seen burials occurring at San Lorenzo in Lucina at a time when the insidious sirocco was blowing.[37] He claimed that ladies of quality never went out on fine days without a bunch of marjoram or chamomile ready to inhale so as to mask unpleasant odours.[38]

PERFUME

Problems associated with a vitiated sense of smell were another reason that modern Romans' living conditions were compared to their ancient predecessors. More specifically, numerous writers observed that the city's prevailing stench had rendered the wearing of perfume problematic. In 1764, on a visit to the Princess Palestrina at the Barberini palace, Dr J. Parkinson was startled to find fumigation with brown paper in progress. This, he hastened to explain, was not because of the presence of British guests, but rather the expected arrival of a French officer, who would without fail be wearing perfume. 'There was an instance a few days ago', he writes, 'of a lady fainting away at the sight of an artificial violet. She mistook it for a real one' – although he was inclined to think this was more the result of affectation than physical aversion.[39] Hester Lynch Piozzi's discovery that 'the Roman women cannot endure perfumes, and faint away even at an artificial rose' stemmed from her own experience; she recorded that she was perplexed 'when I perceived all the company shrink from me very oddly, and stop their noses with rue, which a servant brought to their assistance on open salvers'. Her 'kind protector, Memmo, the Venetian ambassador informed me of the cause; [he] said I had some grains of maréchale powder in my hair perhaps, and led me out of the assembly.' Piozzi recognised that this problem had a historical dimension. Reflecting that the Romans' ancient predecessors 'liked perfumes well enough', she asked: 'Are the modern inhabitants still more refined than they in their researches after pleasure? And are the present race of ladies capable of increasing, beyond that of their ancestors, the keenness of any corporeal sense? I should think not.'[40] Parkinson noted the social consequences of this sensitivity: 'I may take this opportunity of mentioning that the Roman ladies have a particular aversion to Perfumes.' Lady Warren was not aware of this and wore perfume as usual, and 'so spread general alarm. The ladies by whom she sat down quitted their seats, as if she had been an infectious person.'[41]

Indeed, according to Thomas Watkins, this problem had spread across the whole of Italy. He writes of his visit in 1787 to the convent of San Marco in Florence in order to buy perfume produced by the Dominican friars. 'But the use of perfumes is interdicted in the softer climate of Italy, because ladies would faint at a scented headdress or handkerchief. I should have considered this an affectation, if it were not so universally proscribed. Indeed, the French who are of all people the most partial to perfumes, find them intolerable after some years residence in this country.'[42]

Commentaries on the problem of perfume, as Piozzi noted, unite the medical with the historical. The historian Luigi Martorelli, in his *Dissertazione sugli odori usati degli antichi romani* (Rome, 1812), asked whether susceptibility to odours was greater now than in antiquity, and if so why this was the case. If one accepted that the climate was unchanged, then this would also apply to the southern winds, which were considered to be a source of disease. However, following Lancisi, he argued that the loss of protective trees and a diminished population had left Rome more exposed to these winds, and its inhabitants had suffered accordingly, although Martorelli acknowledged that there been no plague there since the seventeenth century.[43] Increased vulnerability to variation of climate caused by exposure to southern winds may have worsened the effect of smells, leading to 'a permanent feebleness of the nervous system of the moderns'. The ancients, he presumes, had been more resilient. But in the end, he doubted any general rule; reacting badly to smells probably came from unfamiliarity, and to that extent was no more than a self-perpetuating convention of fashion.[44]

It is significant that the English medical writer James Johnson came up with what we might call a more contextual, indeed specifically urban, explanation for the 'inordinate sensitiveness of the Roman ladies to perfume', shifting consideration from the rather elusive question of whether ancient nostrils had been more or less sensitive than modern ones. He suggested that the tendency to nervous afflictions found amongst Romans and long-term residents was caused by the perversion of the olfactory nerves wrought by the stink of Rome's deplorably filthy streets.[45] For Jean-Baptiste Michel, such symptoms were rather to be blamed on Rome's climate, one which was *sui generis*, and more specifically its dominant feature – inconstancy (an idea dependent on the view that sudden changes of temperature, wind direction and humidity were always harmful because of the way they too rapidly altered the body's condition – especially as regards nervous, rheumatic, and lymphatic maladies).[46] Such an unstable climate and perpetually humid atmosphere accentuated nervous temperaments while at the same time reducing organs' 'tonicity' and depleting muscular strength.[47] This meant that inhabitants of Rome were almost always 'in a state of pathological predisposition'.[48] After a few years in Rome, foreigners ended up by contracting 'nervous illnesses', and 'complained of hysterical effects and avoid even odours whose refined perfume had so often flattered our sense of smell'.[49] However, he suggested that abreaction was a recent phenomenon, since Lancisi had said nothing of it in the early eighteenth century, and Domenico Panaroli, in his *Aërologia, cioè discorso dell'aria, trattato utile per la sanità* (Rome, 1642), had encouraged the use of flowers and 'odiferous substances', such as rose, orange flower, hyacinth, rosemary, musk, amber and storax, in order to purify fetid air in apartments, which would not be possible in the early nineteenth century. Indeed, Michel notes, this would be discouraged because it was recognised that 'these odours mask unhealthy vapours; and far from purifying the air they vitiate it.' However, rather than conforming to the tree-felling theory or conceding that climate was the sole source of explanation, Michel preferred to look to human actions and how best to adapt oneself to a given climate through 'physical and moral education'.[50]

RUBBISH AND ITS RATIONALE

In the same way that Kotzebue had only drawn attention to rubbish plaques to ridicule their inefficacy, many commentators used their dismay at Rome's dirt not merely to highlight the city's underlying administrative problems, but to suggest the existence of a peculiar indigenous mindset. Having been puzzled to discover a sign inside a palace's staircase forbidding its use as a latrine, Simond recounted the riposte of someone caught *in flagrante*: 'What are you complaining about! Isn't this a palace?' On another occasion he came away from visiting a palace which, despite its impressive fine art collection on the *piano nobile*, was similarly soiled at ground level, almost admiring this fatalistic *laisser-allez*: 'there is a grain of the *grandioso* concealed beneath the foul encrustations of a Roman palace,' which he dubbed 'The grandiosity of filth'.[51] It is interesting to compare this relativist respect with Smollett's quasi-medical repugnance: 'The corridors, arcades, even the staircases belonging to the most elegant palaces, are depositories of nastiness, and indeed in summer smell as strong as spirit of hartshorn.'[52]

Montesquieu noted the franchise granted for clearing away 'the city's filth. They put it in a place where the Tiber runs. It leaves things of value which are in the rubbish, like pieces of silver, lost jewels, antique items, and carries away the muck.'[53] As if aspiring to parody the association of dirt with Jews (see below), the *Encyclopédie* stated that Rome's Jews had offered to clean the clogged riverbed of the Tiber if they were allowed to keep any antiquities found in the process, an offer unwisely refused.[54] The Tiber was another instance of Rome's capacity to elicit uncomfortable ambivalence. On the one hand, as Mariana Starke declared, the forbidding sight of the '[Tiber's] bed is choaked up by filth and rubbish thrown from the houses situated on its banks', yet her imagination thrilled to the idea of the 'immense riches' that it would yield if it were ever dredged: 'What a harvest for the Antiquarians might its present bed afford!'[55] Alternatively, the lost opportunity to convert this waste to manure which could have fertilised the sterile *campagna* was regretted.[56] Pierre-Jean Grosley's account of Roman administration offers an antidote to the idea of wanton neglect and the widely shared belief that Rome's streets were a repository for civic incontinence: 'Report is made to the health-office of every creature dying at Rome, men, women, and beasts down to the very dogs and cats,' whose burial was then seen to, with the exception of undiseased horses, whose flesh was fed to cats.[57]

Yet policies designed to remedy the undeniable problem of the accumulation of dirt and rubbish were more evident on paper than in practice. Through the seventeenth century, the annual number of bans on leaving rubbish in specified locations increases more than threefold between 1605–23 and 1667–76.[58] In the early and mid-eighteenth century, there was evidently a spate of plaques produced, attached to street corners and inviting niches, which warned would-be fly-tippers that the dumping of rubbish at these sites would incur a fine (figs 67-70), the authority of the Presidente delle Strade. Francesco Palermo has counted 67 such plaques between 1700 and 1790 (two from the seventeenth century: 1646, 1690s).[59] Approximately a third are associated with churches and a third with palaces. The most active *rione* were Campo Marzio (10), Sant'Eustachio (10), Regola (9), followed by Colonna (7), Parione and Ponte (6), Pigna and Trevi (4), Trastevere and Campitelli (3), and Monti (2); thus, broadly speaking the historic centre, which housed the most palaces and churches. The busiest decades are between 1730 and 1769: 12 (1730–9); 20 (1740–9); 14 (1750–9); 11 (1760–9). Benedict XIV (1740–58) presided over the peak period. Presidente delle Strade responsible for the bans during this period were Giovanni Girolamo D'Afflitto (1730–4), Giovanni Battista Mesmeri (1734–9) and Nicola Casoni (1739–51). They nonetheless constituted a merely piecemeal response to an endemic problem.

For the early nineteenth century, the relevant legislation is gathered together in the volumes published in 1829 by Nicola Maria Nicolai to commemorate his administrative achievements as Presidente delle Strade.[60] Nicolai argues that cleaning the streets was necessary for the specific reason of making the city a more healthy place to live in, because this would improve air quality and therefore the well-being of citizens. Air quality was both the key element in judging the degree of salubriousness and, in the form of the notorious *mal'aria* or *aria cattiva* of Rome, the cause of disease, especially the fevers of summer. Clean – or cleaner – streets, he argued, also accorded with maintaining the decorum necessary to encourage the numerous foreign visitors, who came to Rome for religious, cultural and touristic reasons. Rubbish was to be put out between 11 o'clock and midnight, when collection began, from specified points. However, as we have seen, the signs which identified these points tend to be read by foreign visitors less as evidence of an organised policy for dealing with rubbish collection than as highlighting the city's insalubriousness.[61]

Complementary to the clearing away of rubbish was the tree-planting programme Nicolai oversaw. Again, this had a practical, aesthetic and medical logic. Trees provided shade; they added to the pleasing picturesqueness of the streets' appearance; and they were believed to assist in cleaning the air by means of a process of filtration. Moreover, as discussed in the previous chapter, in the case of trees around the city, notably woods to the south, they created a barrier preventing southerly winds, which were believed to bring noxious exhalations from the Pontine marshes, from infiltrating the city's interior.[62] To some extent, pressure on the city's administration to improve street cleaning was reduced because of the weight given to the influence of bad air coming from outside the city. Indeed, according to Anna Lia Bonella, the introduction of more effective public health measures in Rome was only precipitated by the threat of cholera in the 1830s.[63]

DI ORDINE DI MONSIG·ILLMO E RMO
PRESIDENTE DELLE STRADE
SI PROIBISCE A QVALVNQVE PERSONA
DI QVALSIVOGLIA GRADO DI GETTARE
E FAR GETTARE IN QVESTO SITO
IMMONDEZZE DI OGNI SORTE
E MOLTO PIV FARVI IL MONDEZZARO
SOTTO PENA DI SCVDI VENTICINQVE
PER QVALVNQVE VOLTA OLTRE LALTRE PENE
AD ARBITRIO DI SVA SIG·ILLMA
COMINATE NELL EDDITTO PVBLICATO
LI IV·GIVGNIO MDCCLXIV·AL QVALE

67   Rubbish plaque (4 June 1764), via delle Coppelle, Rome. Photo © David Marshall.

68   Rubbish plaque (no date), Vicolo de Maroniti, Rome. Photo © David Marshall.

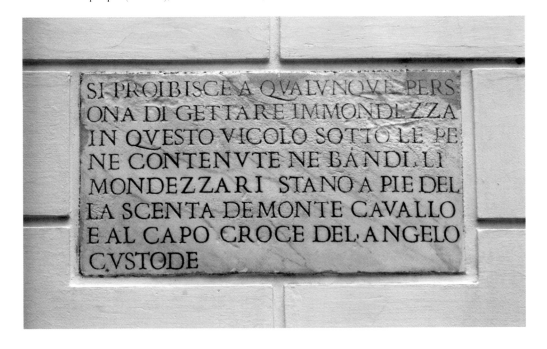

SI PROIBISCE A QVALVNQVE PERS
ONA DI GETTARE IMMONDEZZA
IN QVESTO VICOLO SOTTO LE PE
NE CONTENVTE NE BANDI·LI
MONDEZZARI STANO A PIE DEL
LA SCENTA DE MONTE CAVALLO
E AL CAPO CROCE DEL ANGELO
CVSTODE

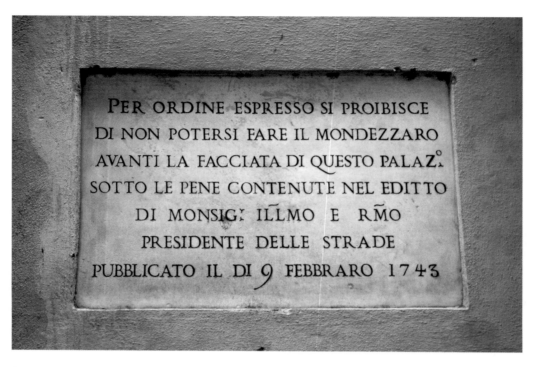

PER ORDINE ESPRESSO SI PROIBISCE
DI NON POTERSI FARE IL MONDEZZARO
AVANTI LA FACCIATA DI QUESTO PALAZ.°
SOTTO LE PENE CONTENUTE NEL EDITTO
DI MONSIG: ILLMO E RM̃O
PRESIDENTE DELLE STRADE
PUBBLICATO IL DI 9 FEBBRARO 1743

69   Rubbish plaque (9 February 1743), via Seminario, Rome. Photo © David Marshall.

70   Rubbish plaque (6 August 1748), via Lata, Rome. Photo © David Marshall.

D·ORDINE DI MONS·ILL E REV·
PRESID DELLE STRADE
SI PROIBISCE A TVTTE E SINGOLE
PERSONE DI NON FARE
IL MONDEZZARO IN QVESTO
SITO SOTTO LE PENE ESPRESSE
NELL EDITTO EMANATO
IL DI 6 AGTO 1748

71 (DETAIL) Antoine Jean-Baptiste Thomas, *Galley Convicts*, coloured lithograph, 22.6 × 10.7 cm, in *Un An à Rome et dans ses environs: Recueil de dessins lithographiés, représentant les costumes, les usages et les cérémonies civiles et religieuses des états romains, et généralement tout ce qu'on y voit de remarquable pendant de cours d'une année, dessiné et publié par Thomas* (Paris, 1823), plate 40, no. 1. Private collection.

Nicolai's initiative to clean up the city was part of a long-term ambition to improve public health by regenerating the city's physical conditions, notably, of course, draining the Pontine marshes and reintroducing agriculture to the notoriously desert-like and unhealthy *campagna* with a view to normalising its atmospheric conditions. He saluted Pius VII's personal intervention to ensure the clearing away of the fish-market in front of the Pantheon – cause of many travellers' outraged comments. Rubbish was offloaded into parts of the Tiber which were not bordered by houses (a sensitive point given the persistent flooding problem).[64] He also proudly recorded that he had made a profit by recycling rubbish as fertiliser for vineyards and market gardens.[65] Earth transported from the Tabulario in the Foro Romano was deposited in an abandoned garden near San Gregorio, which reportedly had the result of improving the air.[66] The degree to which such enlightened environmental policies failed to elicit a more widespread application is illustrated by the need to use prisoners as labour: it was not unusual to find shackled convicts gardening on the Pincio;[67] similarly, during the French occupation, convicts were put to work in archaeological digs (fig. 71).[68]

THE PARADOX OF FERTILITY

This sense of a holistic approach to the city's rubbish problem, which aspired to recycle waste and contribute to agricultural regeneration, can also be related to how the special relationship ascribed to antique remains and modern artworks and the Roman environment in which they were embedded was construed. Implicit in such remarks is a sense of crossover between notions of organic fertility and a belief that artworks in Italy were literally and metaphorically rooted in their environment, one which had nurtured their production and endowed them with a special aura. Within British Romantic writing, the *locus classicus* for fusing vegetation and ruin in a picturesque vision is Shelley's preface to *Prometheus Unbound* (1820), where he recalls the idyllic circumstances of the poem's composition: 'This Poem was chiefly written upon the mountainous ruins of the Baths of Caracalla, among the flowery glades, and thickets of odoriferous blossoming trees, which are extended in ever winding labyrinths upon its immense platforms and dizzy arches suspended in the air. The bright blue sky of Rome, and the effect of the vigorous awakening spring in that divinest climate, and the new life with which it drenches the spirits even to intoxication, were the inspiration of this drama.'[69] We might see this celebration of prolific natural growth as being informed by an ecological dualism: the belief that antique remains had a tangible charge or aura emanating from their constituent materials was linked to a process of organic generation in which antique debris was reassimilated by nature. In Byron's poetic terms: 'Thy very weeds are beautiful, thy waste / More rich than other climes' fertility.'[70]

More prosaically, Bonstetten remarked on the strange nature of the modern city's commercial activity:

> There is nothing more singular than the commerce of this old capital of the Christian world. The vessels which bring provisions to Rome only have rags as their return cargo, but their destiny is remarkable: for the Genoese put them around the base of orange trees, where they encourage flowers, fruits and delicious perfume. Pozzolana, this volcanic earth which makes mortar almost indestructible, constitutes, with rags and antiquities, Rome's only export. The present time is the only one which gives nothing to the city, half of whose inhabitants only live off the ruins of past centuries, while the other half engages in the commerce of a future life.[71]

Echoing Bonstetten, Michelet created an aphorism: 'Rome's only export is the ground itself, rags, and antiquities'. In a note he added an organicist observation as regards antiquities, which were sold like agricultural produce by peasants who brought the finds they had dug up to market: 'Medals, figurines, etc. are sold like fruits, vegetables and other products of the soil.'[72]

For Germaine de Staël, the *campagna*'s vegetation was enacting a kind of decorative homage to Rome's ancient forebears:

Parasitical plants insinuate themselves into tombs, decorate ruins, and seem to be there only to honour the dead. One might say that proud nature has overcome all the works of man, since Cincinnatus and his kind no longer guided the plough which made furrows in its breast: it produces plants at random, without letting the living take advantage of its riches. The barren plains must displease agriculturalists, administrators, all those who speculate on the earth, and want to exploit it for the needs of men; but dreamy souls, who are as much concerned with death as with life, please themselves in contemplating Rome's *campagna*, where present times have left no trace; this land which cherishes its dead, and lovingly covers them with useless flowers, useless plants which cover the ground, and never grow tall enough to separate themselves from the ashes which they have the air of caressing.[73]

The vicomte de Sennones added a fascinating further dimension to this idea by claiming that ancient dust had a life force, a power all the more remarkable because it expressed itself in a poisoned environment: 'Rome's *campagna*, everywhere broken up by enormous cracks, often by [the remains of] aqueducts as far as the eye can see, bereft of vegetation, a desert, arid, barren, resembles a vast sepulchre. The bad air, which, during part of the summer, ravages a third of the city, has cast a deathly pall over its vast territory: fear of it has driven away all those who survived fever…on this life-giving dust of antiquity, some artistic debris and of the opulence of modern times still attract travellers, and present a spectacle worthy of their whole imagination.'[74]

Such inconsistencies seemed to be an ingrained feature of the Roman environment. Nicolai noted the perplexing fact that the Porta San Paolo has 'the most unhealthy air', which may well have been exacerbated by the frequent flooding of the area; however, the surrounding vineyards benefited from silt deposited by the flood waters and were highly productive.[75] Writing on the biological basis for the generation of disease and organic fertility as observed in Rome, Léon Colin drew an analogy from his experience in the Algerian Sahel: 'It seems that this ground has a latent energy, which, released by the slightest cultivation, would be as propitious for the development of plants as deadly to man.' If, on the one hand, such remarkable land only needed to be scraped and watered in order for crops to grow abundantly, on the other, this risked releasing a 'toxic power'.[76] Tommasi-Crudeli shared the idea that the 'morbific agent' which was responsible for bad air emanated from the soil, while admitting the lack of preventative measures.[77]

'STRIPPED, SCRAPED AND SWEPT'

As we saw earlier, the removal of many artworks from Rome in the 1790s by the French provoked a debate around the legitimacy of this policy and the notion of artworks' rootedness.[78] The disconnection of artworks from their native environment was closely paralleled in Napoleonic Rome (1809–1814) by the programme of freeing monuments from their encrusted accumulations of detritus.[79] The comte de Tournon, prefect of Rome under the occupying French imperial administration, celebrated this liberation of major Roman monuments from their surrounding accretions as part of the comprehensive programme of economic reform and renewal which was set in train – though interrupted by the Empire's abrupt fall. Significantly, he referred to the Forum as having been treated as a vast 'immondezzaio', having served as a dump for construction debris

72 Capitol and Temple of Vespasian and Titus in 1809 before French archaeological clearance, in Camille, comte de Tournon, *Études statistiques sur Rome,* vol. 2, (Paris, 1855), plate 18. British Library, London.

73 Capitol and Temple of Vaspasian and Titus in 1813 after French archaeological clearance, in Camille, comte de Tournon, *Études statistiques sur Rome,* vol. 2, (Paris, 1855), plate 20. British Library, London.

(figs 72, 73).[80] Such a process of monumental reclamation substituted a protocol of quasi-scientific museological conservation for an earlier aesthetic, which valued the picturesque intertwining of plants over and around partially ruined and buried monuments.

The process of clearing vegetation from antique monuments continued in the 1820s; when the French painter François-Marius Granet returned to Rome in 1829 after four years absence in Paris, he was shocked by what he regarded as the profanation of the Colosseum by the removal of its covering of profuse vegtation.[81] Rembrandt Peale cited the opinion of an 'old artist friend' who regretted the change, 'for he remembers seeing the Colosseum a beautiful wilderness of ruins, vines and shrubbery. But though the total amount is reduced, the variety, in its exposed points, and warm nooks and corners, is not less than it was; for Sebastiani, a Roman botanist, in his *Flora Colossea*, describes two hundred and sixty plants which grow there; and the number has since been found to reach three hundred.'[82] Yet in 1852 Burgess could still complain that one of the factors making the Colosseum and the surrounding area a 'focus of malaria, in a very insalubrious district' was the presence of vegetation.[83] In the 1860s C.E. Hallé recalled that the Colosseum was 'still half overgrown with trees'.[84]

Indeed, it is probably no coincidence that Antonio Sebastiani's survey of the flora growing in and on the Colosseum, *Romanorum plantarum* (1815), was produced just after the end of the French occupation and the discontinued programme of monumental restoration, some two and a half centuries after Domenico Panaroli's *Jatrologismi sive medicae observationes quibus additus est in fine Plantarum Amphitheatralium Catalogus* (Rome, 1643). Sebastiani's book is little more than a list, but its sequel, produced in 1855 by the Revd. Richard Deakin, *Flora of the Colosseum of Rome; or, Illustrations and Descriptions of Four Hundred and Twenty Plants growing spontaneously upon the Ruins of the Colosseum of Rome*, attributes special significance to plants' interaction with their historic habitat. He spoke of flowers as forming 'a link in the memory, [they] teach us hopeful and soothing lessons, amid the sadness of bygone ages ... for, though without speech, they tell of that regenerating power which reanimates the dust of mouldering greatness, and clothes their sad and fallen grandeur with graceful forms,...and perfume the air with their exquisite odours'.[85] Of course, the Colosseum's status as a shrine to Christian martyrdom underpins the redemptive message. Deakin's book is a celebration of the symbolic symbiosis whereby plants were imagined to be nourished by their proximity to the still animate remnants of past grandeur.[86]

Such a sensibility may not have always fully informed the souvenir hunting of visitors, but by the mid-nineteenth century collecting plants from the Collosseum became a compulsive habit, as if driven by a recognition of the arena as a site of martyrdom. Joseph Severn climbed up the Collosseum to bring back a wallflower for the dying Keats; Michelet made a point of sending dried flowers home.[87] Other sites elicited similar reactions: Florence Nightingale took away a fern leaf from Michelangelo's house, having also drunk from the fountain, like some ritual of communion.[88] By the 1860s, as noted by William Wetmore Story of visitors to Rome, this insistent botanical acquisitiveness had become a matter of banal collectability: 'Everybody has an herbarium of dried flowers from all the celebrated sites.'[89] The spectacle of monuments covered with vegetation apppealed to sensibilities accustomed to the conventions of picturesque viewing. Nature was seen to embrace man-made relics, and thus create a satisfying unity. In this sense, rather than acting as a framing device, as Chloe Chard has argued, such foliage and floral adornment in fact had the opposite effect – to blur the boundary between architecture and nature, and to absorb masonry into a continuum of animate natural activity.[90]

In the early nineteenth century, the systematic scraping of Rome so as to reveal more authentically its many-layered monumental fabric began to make it a modern museum city in a double sense. Not only did it house a museum-like wealth of art, but the historic fabric of the city was being consolidated as a spectacle for the pedestrian, and horse-drawn, inspection of tourists. Superseded by Paris, London and Berlin in terms of museums per se, Rome capitalised on its inherited monumental riches – riches which were increasing as excavations continued.[91] This institutionalisation of the city's identity as a place where the contemporary had atrophied is usually linked to the policy consolidated by Pius IX to cease adding new layers, and rather to develop an adminstrative aesthetic of conservation, exemplified by the decision to reconstruct the church of San Paolo fuori le mura following its destruction by fire on 15 July 1823 rather than creating a new building.[92]

The process of archaeological reclamation systematically initated under the French occupation continued after their departure.[93] In 1846, Hans Christian Andersen lamented that Rome 'is not the same Rome it was thirteen years ago when I was first here'.[94] The process of cleaning and clearing was to be comprehensively accelerated after Rome assumed the role of capital in 1870. In that year, Henrik Ibsen drew an aesthetically pessimistic conclusion from the prospect of the city being sanitised: 'So they have finally taken Rome away from human beings like us and handed her over to the politicians….everything we loved, the spontaneity, the dirt, will now disappear; for every politician that springs up in that city there will be one artist the fewer.' By contrast, his compatriot, Victor Rydberg, was more sympathetic to such reforms, observing approvingly: 'It is no longer the capital of ignorance and filth.'[95] When editing a letter from the young Ruskin in 1841 in which he mused that his early visits to Rome had tempted him to take up botany as a response to the profuse local flora, his editors Cook and Wedderburn nostalgically noted that this would not be possible in modern Rome, which had been 'stripped, scraped, and swept,…to the joy of the archaeologist, to the sorrow of the aesthetic'.[96]

Scraping and stripping also had a highly charged, directly medical, rationale in more domestic, corporeal circumstances. As had been the case for plague, in cases of consumption, which in Italy at this period was believed to be contagious, not only were victims' clothes and effects burnt, but the rooms where they had died were scoured and ventilated, their wallpaper stripped, walls replastered and floors relaid.[97] The micro-environment within which people had been confined was assumed to have been impregnated by the dangerous exhalations of the victim. It was because of this that (as noted earlier) consumption victims were isolated in Italian hospitals, in a way which British commentators such as James Clark, who did not share the belief in the disease's contagiousness, found inhumane.[98] Equally, the idea that malarial fever could be directly transmitted from one person to another can be found amongst English observers. Thus, albeit sceptical about 'such species of contagion', Shelley obeyed his wife's entreaties not to share a carriage with a German who had just come from Rome, and was recovering from 'a malaria fever' contracted in the Pontine Marshes.[99]

THE ENIGMA OF THE JEWISH GHETTO

One of the areas which remained untouched by archaeological reclamation until the end of the nineteenth century was the Jewish ghetto on the east bank of the Tiber above the Isola Tiburtina. The ghetto had a paradoxical reputation. On the one hand, this was agreed to be the dirtiest part of central Rome; on the other hand, it was acknowledged that it was not afflicted with 'bad air'.[100] Exceptions to this are Montesquieu, who thought it a source of contagious diseases, and Louis Valentin, who in the 1820s claimed that he had found the effects of *mal'aria*.[101] Nonetheless – perhaps, indeed, because of these conflicting views – the area raises important questions. Considering attitudes to the ghetto also allows us to observe how ideas about ambient dirt and endemic disease inform attitudes to exploring Rome. Moreover, this rebarbative aspect can also be seen to be at work in images of the ghetto, or at least of some of its edges and access points. Perhaps nowhere better exemplifies the quintessentially Roman effect of eliciting visual and historical fascination and tactile repulsion in tandem.

The paradox of the ghetto's unexpected atmospheric salubrity was explained in the same manner adduced by Lancisi in the link he made between the course of winds being altered by the presence of woodland. In the case of the ghetto, it was argued that it was its very congestion which obstructed the influx of tainted air. This example challenged the relevance of the common sense aesthetic criterion for associating the presence of disease with dirt, and further exposed the shortcomings of medical understanding of *mal'aria*. To the Very Revd. Jeremiah Donovan, being exempt from bad air was divine compensation for horrid living conditions: 'Notwithstanding its narrow lanes, crowded inhabitants and accumulated filth, the ghetto, by a merciful dispensation of Providence, is one of the healthiest quarters of Rome, its dense population being its best security against the scourge of malaria.' Attilio Milano has noted that informal estimates of its population always exaggerate numbers, consistent with this belief in overcrowding.[102]

George Augustus Sala, who was inclined to think of disease as caused by dirt, nevertheless acknowledged the peculiar prevailing situation: 'Whenever a large number of people have been crowded into a confined space in Rome, as in the Ghetto and the densely thronged quarter about the Capitoline Hill, the salubrity of the situation has been apparent, in spite of the dirty habits of the people.'[103] In recounting his 'peripatetic rambles in Rome', James Johnson highlighted the benefits of narrow streets which protected one from the sun and helped to keep bad air out of the ghetto.[104] Macculloch suggested that 'malaria' was a chemical compound which may be destroyed by 'the unknown mixture which forms the atmosphere of crowded streets or habitations'.[105] The notion of movement and its effect on air links the ghetto with Rome more generally. The abbé Richard had earlier recommended that, to cope with Rome's thick, heavy air, especially during summer, it was necessary to keep moving, 'to allow the humours to retain their fluidity, and the limbs their normal suppleness', which would be an antidote to the 'the inclementness of the air' exacerbated by the scarce population and therefore too much left in a kind of stagnant state.[106] The ghetto's reputation in this respect was so notorious that it found its way into a description in Balzac's novel *Cousin Pons* of the life-giving effects of air breathed by crowds on Parisian boulevards: 'Having reached the boulevard Poissonnière, Pons regained his colour, from breathing the atmosphere of the boulevards where the air has such power; for where there is a crowd, the fluid is so vital, such that at Rome the absence of *mala aria* has been observed in the foul ghetto where the Jews swarm.'[107]

Alternative explanations were offered by Augustus Hare, who reckoned the ghetto benefited from the requirement to apply a coat of lime to walls on religious festivals, a practice noticed by Florence Nightingale, who also observed that when this was done in wet weather, 'all the smells come out like ramping lions to enjoy themselves abroad'.[108] She reported her visit: 'Then we went through the Ghetto, in order to gratify our love of dirty places.'[109] For Dickens the miserable conditions were redeemed by the industriousness and 'money-getting' activities of the inhabitants – a surprisingly benign view of Jewish connections to money. 'In the day-time, you make your way along the narrow streets, you see them all at work: upon the pavement, oftener in their dark and frouzy shops: furbishing old clothes, and driving bargains.'[110] Dickens omits to mention that selling old clothes was one of the few commercial activities which Jews were allowed. Simond also ignored this constraint, and accused them of trickery: 'The Jews who crowd into the Palazzo Orsini have monopolised this hillock to a singular branch of commerce, that of transforming old clothes into new ones. Stretched out in the sun, the old garment is carefully scraped with a fuller's card, so as to give to the wornout cloth a false youthful down which fools the ignorant purchaser.'[111] Grosley claimed to have encountered Jews selling 'filthy rags spread out for sale' in the Piazza Navona twice a week, noting this was their only trade.[112]

Another association of trade with the ghetto, or more precisely its threshold, is the fish-market held in the Portico of Octavia until it was moved in 1868, outside the east entrance to the ghetto.[113] As we will see in discussing its imagery, this monument – its surroundings and interior – represents an intersection of decrepit antiquity and unhygienic modern life, with the added complication of its contiguity with the ghetto. The portico exemplifies Smollett's point about monuments being 'engaged', in this case messily absorbed into the urban fabric. In addition, the portico had also been co-opted by the Catholic Church to serve as the entrance to Sant'Angelo in Pescheria.[114] Like the gate in Piazza Giudea, which we will encounter below, the portico was a transitional space in more ways than one.

For some observers, it was a disappointing site, and one which, to Augustus von Kotzebue, was not worth suffering the unpleasantness of the market's smell: 'Nothing remains of the portico of Octavia, dedicated by Augustus to his noble sister, but the entrance; where we cannot stay without disgust, on account of the modern market for meat [sic] kept here, which fills the air with a pestilential stench.'[115] Mariana Starke was more approbatory, claiming to have found 'considerable remains', but this was compromised by the damp situation, which put it off-limits for invalids.[116] Charlotte Eaton may have succumbed to hyperbole when she announced that the Pescheria was the 'filthiest spot upon the whole face of the globe'.[117] The dangers of trying to approach the cornice more closely were recounted by Louis Simond. Having gained entry to the upper floor of an adjacent building, he found himself in a dark, bare interior inhabited by a large semi-naked family sleeping on a mattress on the floor; repelled by the 'foul air of this haunt of poverty', he withdrew rapidly, covered in fleas.[118]

It is as if the ghetto's reputation for filthiness has been displaced onto the combined spectacle of portico and fish-market, a phenomenon which can also be read into the images. In fact, the ghetto itself is hardly present in the visual imagery of Rome. Earlier imagery is no more than fragmentary and indirect in its inclusion of references to the ghetto. That said, the ghetto or its edges in the first half of the nineteenth century seems to have become a fairly stable feature in the itineraries of picturesque motif-seeking artists.

The most commonly reproduced images postdate the moment of its abolition in 1870, and the ensuing process of demolition and clearance to make way for modern housing and a new synagogue. Ettore Roesler Franz's photographs and the watercolours he worked up from them between 1884 and 1887 are part of a wider European genre, familiar from Thomas Annan's photographs of the tenements of Glasgow or photographs of 'Vieux Paris' by Atget, Marville and others.[119] Images are produced both officially and independently either to justify demolition and modernisation or to record for posterity forms of architecture and design which have fallen victim to modernisation. Roesler Franz's images from 1884–7 in a sense fill a vacuum in the historical imagination created by the prior absence of imagery.[120]

From the time of its creation in 1555, the Jewish ghetto in Rome was primarily represented by means of interdiction and confinement. Without going into religious aspects of their control and ritual attempts at conversion, Jews were both prohibited from any trade other than that of used iron work and old clothes and also expected to pay onerous taxes.[121] The complement to visitors' comments on dirt and disease is protest at the harsh, inhumane treatment of the Jews by the papacy. While not being visual in any simple sense, comments on oppressive living conditions and the degrading enclosure of the community deal with space in a way which, for outsiders, was both imaginary and uncomfortably tangible.[122]

The evidence of maps raises a question of terminology. Lafréry's 1577 map shows 'La Iudea' inscribed in what is an artificially broadened via della Fiumara. The extent of the ghetto is indicated by the clearly visible gates, closed at night, which too have been expanded, and aligned towards the viewer, to assure their visibility. Equally, the 'piazza Iudea' is labelled. This piazza extended both sides of the gate on its south-east corner – a point spelt out in later images. In Jacopo de la Feuille's map, the term 'Delle Hebr[e]I' is used, which Christopher Browne's 'A new map of Rome shewing its antient and present scituation [*sic*]' anglicises into 'The Jewry'. In 1748 G.B. Nolli spells out 'Ghetto degli Ebrei' in the index to his map.

The term ghetto is a version of the Hebrew word 'get'. While a ghetto is rightly understood as an imposed condition of existence, nonetheless, as Kenneth Stow has shown, its occupants possessed a well-established and positive sense of identity, defining themselves as the Jews of Rome, talking of 'nostro get'; that is, they saw themselves as Romans *and* Jews, not separating the two – indeed, resisting such a separation – despite the harsh burden of legal and economic obligations and interdictions.[123] The ghetto was thus in more than one sense in and of Rome, yet at one remove from the city. We might say that it was a marginal space embedded in the centre of the old city.

Viewed from the outside, so to speak, the ghetto became visible, if only peripherally, in images of monuments which were adjacent to entry points or gates. Rose Marie San Juan has discussed the earlier example of Corduba's 1618 image of the fountain in the Piazza Giudea as bearing witness to a kind of extrapolated image of Jews as traders in second-hand objects and clothes – the ghetto itself is literally outside the picture.[124] Vasi's later image of the piazza creates a sense of rather artificial urban space, including the guardhouse and gallows, and clearly showing the massive gate on the right, marking and sealing access to and egress from the ghetto. The central feature is Giacomo della Porta's 1591 fountain,[125] a metonymic reference to Rome's provision of drinking water, and implicitly to the city's potential for conditions of healthiness and cleanliness. The fountain's proximity to the ghetto is highly charged: this was a way of implying that the city's unresolved problems of rubbish, sanitation and the threat of disease might be projected or siphoned off into this lost space excluded from view.

In Piranesi's pair of prints (figs 74, 75), the Portico of Octavia characteristically provides an archaic framework inhabited by quotidian Rome, but also a space of transition. The portico stood adjacent to the north-east corner of the ghetto. Piranesi shows us the walls inserted within the arch, which reinforce a sense of enclosure and which mark the extended limits of the ghetto. As with Piazza Giudea, here it is commerce, in the form of the fish-market within the portico, which obscures, and stands in for, the nature of Jewish life; fishmongering was not one of the trades permitted for Jews, but it is being carried on at the very edge of the ghetto.

74 Giovanni Battista Piranesi, *Portico of Octavia*, exterior view, engraving 60 × 38 cm. Private collection.

75 Giovanni Battista Piranesi, *Portico of Octavia*, interior view, engraving 54.6 × 39.3 cm. Private collection.

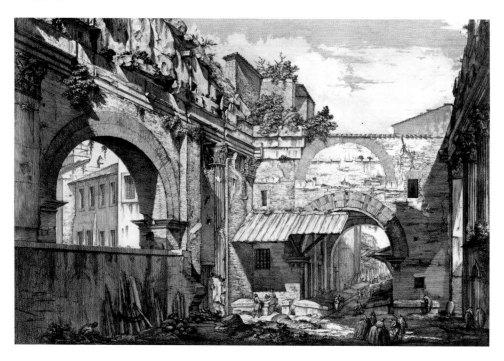

76   Luigi Rossini, View from the side of the *Portico of Octavia*, today *Sant'Angelo in Pescheria*, 1819, lithograph 35.3 × 44.3 cm. Private collection.

In the exterior view, Piranesi made visible a piquant conjunction of a rubbish plaque on the portico and the presence of 'modern painters' ('Pitture moderne', coded '4' in the caption), as if the viewing of the portico as an antique monument was associated with a sense of propriety. His *View of St Peter's and Castel St Angelo* had also drawn the viewer's attention to the major 'outlet for the city's rubbish'; given its pictorial position in between the spectator and St Peter's and Castel Sant'Angelo, it is hard not to read this as an admonitory allusion to a contrast between past architectural splendour and present administrative failure. Indeed, he also devoted a print to the Cloaca Maxima, as if it were an ever-present reproach to modern neglect of sanitation.[126]

Giuseppe Vasi, as with his print of the Piazza Giudea, increases the sense of viewing distance from the portico, including the dome of Santa Maria in Campitelli, making the portico more of a backdrop and the fish-market more part of the city's commercial activity.[127] The same is true of the plate in *Italian Scenery* (1806), which makes the further

77 (DETAIL) Nicolas-Didier Boguet, *View of the Ponte Quattro Capi*, pencil and grey washes, 23 × 42 cm., fol. 46 of sketchbook, inscribed 'Ponte Fabricio' 'disegnato del ghetto'. British School at Rome.

historical claim that 'the ancient forum piscatorium et olitorium or fish and vegetable markets, were on this spot, or near it'.[128] Like Piranesi, Luigi Rossini produced two views of the portico in 1819. One reminds us of the ghetto as a place of confinement, pointedly showing the walls that close off the main, south-western aperture of the portico, and the wall with closed gate across the south-eastern arch that blocks visual access to via della Pescheria and the fish-market.[129] The other has a closer viewpoint from within the gated wall, but interferes with visual access to via della Pescheria by having a line of figures receiving a blessing on the steps of Sant'Angelo in Pescheria (fig. 76). Not surprisingly, there seem to be very few images of the ghetto from within before those of Roesler Franz.[130] Nicolas-Didier Boguet's drawing seems to be the only view from the ghetto, using its southern bank as a place from which to draw the ancient Ponte Fabricio crossing to the Isola Tiburtina (fig. 77).[131] In *A New Collection of Views of the Ancient City of Rome* (Rome, c.1816–30), Antonio Aquaroni includes an atmospheric

78   Antonio Aquaroni, *Portico of Octavia*, 1816–30, etching, 17.8 × 23.5 cm, in *Nuova raccolta di vedute antiche della città di Roma* (A New Collection of Views of the Ancient City of Rome), Rome, *c*.1816–30). British Museum, London.

shady view looking into the portico from via della Pescheria, showing the fish-market slabs and also the gate topped by a cross (fig. 78). A. De Bonis created a dramatic view down via Rua, with only the soffit of the arch visible in the upper corners of the image (fig.79). More generally, the portico was well established within the early photographic repertoire of Rome.[132]

Albert Bierstadt's *Arch of Octavia (Roman Fish-Market)* (1858) is the most elaborate representation of the portico in oil from this period (fig. 80).[133] He shows a view from the south-east, placing the stone tables outside. Bierstadt turns the portico and market into a sunny entertaining genre scene,[134] moralised so as to poke fun at the couple who enter stage right, clasping Murray's reassuring *Handbook*, the man's nose in the air, perhaps looking at the architecture of the portico, the woman's gaze – and as many senses as possible – averted. They are surrounded by a gallery of local types – fisher-men, women wearing distinctive head-dresses; recumbent figures in the foreground personify indigenous *dolce far niente* (and the thriving Roman subculture of modelling for artists), indeed are almost a parody of the idea that local Romans resembled figures in paintings. Yet dirt and filth are referred to by means of the inactive broom as well as the fish strewn on the ground.[135]

79   A. De Bonis, *Portico of Octavia*, 1855–60, albumen print from glass negative, 23.6 × 19.2 cm. W. Bruce and Delaney H. Lundberg Collection.

80   Albert Bierstadt, *Arch of Octavius (Roman Fish-Market)*, 1858, oil on canvas, 70.2 × 94.9 cm. Fine Arts Museums of San Francisco. Gift of Mr and Mrs John D. Rockefeller III, 1979.7.12.

Perhaps the most familiar image of the portico is that by Samuel Prout, first produced as a watercolour, and subsequently as a print widely circulated in *Sketches in France, Italy and Switzerland* (1839) (fig. 81). Of this image, Ruskin wrote: 'All the life and death of Rome is in this quite invaluable drawing.'[136] Prout raises the viewpoint to emphasise fish as commodity and as still life, displayed in a dainty, if oddly out of scale, basket in the foreground, with a scattering of local colour. He also includes a belfry attached to Sant'Angelo in Pescheria – an accommodating gesture which, like Rossini's print, brings the scene under the purview of the Church. Prout's watercolour exemplifies an early nineteenth-century mode of topographical imagery, ideally suited to the representation of Rome in terms of speckled, crumbly surface and fragments, decaying gracefully, returning to a state of nature. Yet he illuminates most of the scene with bright sunlight, making the columns and architrave the primary, decoratively archaeological focus.[137]

Prout's self-confessed student, the young John Ruskin, writes in his correspondence of visiting the ghetto (in 1840), and how he found it to be a rich source of picturesque

81   Samuel Prout, *Fish Market, Rome*, engraving, 14.8 × 9.7 cm. Private collection.

motifs, also producing a watercolour of the Piazza Santa Maria del Pianto, now Piazza Giudea (fig. 82).[138] His drawing allows us to look more closely at the place of dirt in relation to notions of the picturesque, in the sense of motifs construed as being readily translatable into pictorial form, and to digression as an aspect of travellers' approaches to the experience of Rome which may yield a more authentic, because less hackneyed, contact. This will lead to consideration of another form of contagion: the gesture of touching the city – its soil, pulverised remains and fabric – a highly charged form of active contact; and finally the equally emotive act of walking, in the sense of being literally in touch with a surface which was resonant with history, indeed was history in tangible form.

In his diary of 1 December 1840, Ruskin reflects on how artists might apprehend Rome's fabric:

> Found throughout long walk not one subject which, if sketched carelessly or in a hurry, would have been fit for anything; and not a single corner of a street which, if studied closely and well, would not be beautiful. So completely is this place picturesque, down to its door-knockers, and so entirely does that picturesqueness depend, not on any important lines or real beauty of object, but upon little bits of contrasted feeling – the old clothes hanging out of a marble architrave, – that architrave smashed at one side and built into a patch of broken brickwork – projecting over a mouldering wooden window, supported in its turn on a bit of grey entablature with a vestige of inscription; but all to be studied closely, before it can be felt or even seen, and, I am persuaded, quite lost to the eyes of all but a few artists.[139]

Ruskin's enthusiastic description of the quotidian sights of Rome seems like an illustration of Gilpin's formula for 'Picturesque Travel', 'primed, above all, to enjoy ruins, relics, and other architectural remains, because of their equivalence to works of nature': 'Thus universal are the objects of picturesque travel. We pursue beauty in every shape; through nature, through art; and all its various arrangements in form, and colour; admiring it in the grandest objects, and not rejecting it in the humblest.'[140] In so far as Rome turned out to be less of a city properly speaking than an array of sites which had become integrated into the landscape, it was all the more prone to be considered within the conventions of the picturesque. Like England's ruined cathedrals, Rome's ruins were elaborately embedded in nature (even if this was compromised by the sobering aspect of the *campagna*'s desolation). Rome's neglect, manifest in its uninhibited dirtiness, in fact enhanced its picturesqueness, but left the problem of how to reconcile visual appeal, olfactory recoil and hygienic alarm.[141]

Two days later, Ruskin made a drawing as if to illustrate the characteristics he describes. This shows the Piazza Santa Maria del Pianto (now known as Piazza Giudea).[142] In their different media and vocabularies, drawing and diary together raise certain general points about picturesque and anti-picturesque protocols for representing Rome and its streets. Ruskin's view shows a space which borders the Jewish ghetto; we see

82   John Ruskin, *Piazza Santa Maria del Pianto*, now *Piazza Giudea*, 1840, pencil with heightening, 46 × 34 cm.. Museo di Roma, Rome, MR 706.

one of its gates to the right (in the later lithographic version (fig. 83), this has been made taller and broader so that it frames a further view of a street, and has figures entering). Although outside the ghetto proper, the piazza was a place where, as we have seen, Jews were allowed to sell old clothes, and was therefore associated with the very limited public presence of this community. This was much less common than views of the fish-market adjacent to the Portico of Octavia.

Ruskin structures the drawing within a monumental framework – the Renaissance fountain and the façade of the house of Lorenzo Manilio. Clothes hang in swags across the upper storey. The inscription across the architrave is legible, but partly obscured by the bowl of the fountain; the intersection of the fountain's stem and bowl with the vertical alignment of windows and the horizontal band of the architrave has the effect of integrating these features with the play of relief across the window frames and skeins of sheets and clothing. In the print, a cart pulled by two white oxen has appeared to the left of the fountain, as if to signal the underlying connection to and compatibility with rural life, despite being in the heart of the old city. Colour has only been introduced in the clothing of the figures around the fountain, the hanging fabric and the wall surface on the upper left. It would seem reasonable to imagine Ruskin thinking of this motif as a picturesque digression from the prescribed sites of the city. Indeed, in his memoir

83   John Ruskin, *Piazza Santa Maria del Pianto*, now *Piazza Giudea*, lithograph. From John Ruskin, *The Works of John Ruskin*, ed. E.T. Cook and A. Wedderburn, 39 vols (London, 1903–12), vol. 1, p. 382.

Praeterita, he claimed that this was a calculated act of defiance: having rejected Raphael and the Vatican sculpture galleries: 'I took the bit between my teeth, and proceeded to sketch what I could find in Rome to represent in my own way, bringing in primarily, – by way of defiance to Raphael, Titian, and the Apollo Belvedere all in one, – a careful study of the old clothes hanging out of old windows in the Jews' quarter.'[143]

The sense of the location as being apart from the city is signalled by the presence of one of the ghetto's entrance gateways to the right of the image. As a draughtsman, he has not gone beyond a Proutian attention to unevenness of surface and busy, gently jagged linearity. He includes no direct reference to the Jewish identity of the locale, except perhaps in the presence of the hanging clothes. As noted above, the old clothes which Jews were permitted to sell double as laundry in the sense that they were cleaned to enhance, or disguise, their condition.

Yet in some images, the array of old clothes on the periphery of the ghetto seems like a provocative form of anti-drapery, so unappetising do they appear.[144] To this extent, laundry and old clothes effect a double reversal. Jews selling old clothes was permitted (even if this was a sign of their almost non-existent rights), whereas hanging laundry to dry in public places was illegal. As Katherine Rinne has shown in her compelling research into Roman waters and their uses in the sixteenth century, to intrude into public space in this way was forbidden and severely punished.[145] If we were to read the hanging laundry visible in Roman streets as corresponding to a social presence, then it would be a sign of illicit, opportunistic appropriation.

However, when laundry appears in landscape views of Rome and its monuments and sites, it seems more plausible to treat most of these images as aestheticised fantasies rather than documentary statements. In paintings and drawings by Hubert Robert and Fragonard from the later eighteenth century, such an association became almost obsessive or commonplace. Their images situate scenes of laundry in different contexts, both in terms of setting and according to varying degrees of invention and particularity.[146] Images which seem to show actual washing are unusual.[147] The theme can form part of a loosely topographical view: thus, Robert and Fragonard add a group of women gathered around a basin below a cascade at Ronciglione.[148] More common is the addition of this motif to monumental settings, for example showing the Villa Madama.[149] Washing can be shown as part of domestic life, in which it takes on the role of quotidian equivalent to drapery.[150] Laundry can be a central motif in an invented architectural scene,[151] or be included in capriccios with Roman monuments, ancient and modern, for example where the Pantheon and the Porta di Ripetta are combined.[152] Precedents for this motif in images of Rome can be found in seventeenth-century Dutch art. Cornelis van Poelenburch's *Ruins of Ancient Rome* (c.1620) and *View of the Campo Vaccino in Rome* (fig. 84) show laundry in progress at a large basin, fed by a fountain, whose pictorial centrality expresses the emblematic plausibility of what is topographically inaccurate.[153] In the eighteenth and nineteenth centuries, this leitmotif was widely employed (figs 85–87). Boucher makes cascading water and laundry an active part of his fluid pictorial structure; Hubert Robert enlivens the picture's narrative focus through the animation of washing as a collective activity, providing a counterpoint to the tombs to the right. A more topographically focused artist, such as Turpin de Crissé, integrates the hanging sheets almost as an extension of the architectural structure of the Temple of Vesta at Tivoli.

In these images, the city is treated like an antique sculpture, disarticulated and picturesquely reconstituted within the format of a landscape view or study. The public activity of washing clothes seems a displaced reference to the nude, as if such imagery stands in for the pictorial theme of bathers (the nude in the open air), which, perhaps out of a sense of propriety or plausibility, seems to be absent from Roman works.[154] In the case of Robert this is not suprising given his landscape-centred imagery; with Fragonard, there never seems to have been a fusion of nude study with Roman setting. Yet Robert's imagery repeatedly associates a sculptural figure presiding over a fountain and basin where women work at laundry. Water spurts from spouts either directly beneath the monumental figure or sometimes from a lion's head, in a way which seems to humanise this motif, and to that extent inviting a reading which sees cascading pure water as a witty and purgative substitution for the urine which liberally befouled Roman spaces.

The imagery of Roman laundry survives into the nineteenth century, and is taken up in early photographs which, if anything, make more emphatic the sense of continuity

84 Cornelis van Poelenburch, *View of the Campo Vaccino in Rome*, 1620, oil on copper, 40 × 54.5 cm. Louvre, Paris.

85 François Boucher, *Washerwomen*, *c.*1730, oil on canvas, 95 × 78 cm. Musée d'Art Roger-Quilliot, Clermont Ferrand.

86   Hubert Robert, *Fountain of Minerva in Rome*, 1772, oil on canvas, 48 × 67 cm. Musée des beaux-arts, Angers.

between architectural framework and draped fabric, and intensify the connotation of an archaic corporeality (figs 88, 89). The railings around the excavated areas of the Forum were a favourite site for draping sheets to dry, such a display of public cleansing complementing the archaeological recuperation below.[155] Edmond About acutely observed that the widespread visibility of laundry misled visitors: 'The extensive sheets which are hung out to dry all along the fronts of houses and palaces lead foreigners to believe that they have entered the capital of laundry.'[156] Rather, this was quite distinct from the more sordid conditions which prevailed beyond the spectacle of freshly laundered fabric. Adding expanses of drapery to representations of monuments reinforces the primary status of Rome as antique terrain. Moreover, the preoccupation with laundry provides a means to show local people as active in a way which is at once social and symbolic. Thus, drying laundry invites the recognition of a harmonious inheritance of the past by its modern inhabitants. In Tivoli as elsewhere, Edward Lear found the spectacle of 'all sorts of clothes' hanging from 'all their windows' made 'the towns always so gay' – an example of the Italian people's innate inclination to artistic expression.[157] Clothes detached from their owners become a form of quintessential local colour – both decorative and aestheticised. They also embody an ambiguity which is at the heart of

87   Lancelot-Théodore Turpin de Crissé, *View of the Temple of Vesta in Tivoli*, 1831, oil on canvas, 90 × 74 cm. Musée des beaux-arts, Angers.

88   Unknown photographer, *The Roman Forum*, 1857, coated salt print from a glass negative, 36.5 × 29.7 cm. Private collection. Courtesy of Hans P. Kraus, Jr, New York, inv. 102802.0.

89 Giacomo Caneva, *Temple of Vesta at Tivoli*, c.1850, salt print from paper negative, 20.9 × 27.2 cm. Dietmar Siegert Collection, Munich.

viewing Rome: clothing pertains to the contemporary world, drapery belongs to the timeless sphere of art. Moreover, the visibility of laundry activates the discourse on Rome's excellent water supply, thus effecting a double assertion of cleanliness and health. In this sense, Rome's fountains could be applauded not just for their architectural ambition, but as a means to cleanse the city of its encrustation of rubbish – or at least provide some relief from a sense of ambient filth.

In Ruskin's drawing, the fountain is curiously dry, which may be the result of a decision to avoid dealing with a tricky matter of draughtsmanship rather than being emblematically significant. In a letter of the same date as the drawing, Ruskin reformulated his original remarks quoted above, amplifying and editing them: 'In the city, if you take a carriage and drive to express points of lionisation, I believe most people of good taste would expect little and find less. The Capitol is a melancholy rubbishy square of average Palladian-modern; the forum a good group of smashed columns, just what, if it were got up, as it very easily might be, at Virginia Water, we should call a piece of humbug – the kind of thing that one is sick to death of in "compositions";…As for ancient Rome, it is a nasty, rubbishy, dirty hole – I hate it.'[158]

Such sentiments were expressed in more measured language by Arthur Clough: 'Rome disappoints me much; I hardly as yet understand, but / Rubbishy seems the word that most exactly would suit it.'[159] Antiquity takes on the role of rubbish – antiquity *is* rubbish. Ruskin's language is that of the first volume of *Modern Painters*, damning the artificial and bankrupt conventions of landscape painting and their concomitant touristic redundancies. He continues by explaining the benefits of casting off such a formulaic mode of attention:

> But, if, instead of driving, with excited expectations, to particular points, you saunter leisurely up one street and down another, yielding to every impulse, peeping into every corner, and keeping your observation active, the impression is exceedingly changed. There is not a fragment, a stone, or a chimney, ancient or modern, that is not in itself a study, not an inch of ground that can be passed over without its claim of admiration and offer of instruction, and you return home in hopeless conviction that were you to substitute years for the days of your appointed stay, they would not be enough for the estimation or examination of Rome.[160]

The ghetto was evidently a 'corner' into which Ruskin 'peeped' repeatedly, undeterred by its forbidding unhygienic character. In April he was still at it: 'in afternoon explored some bits behind the theatre of Marcellus, new to me, passing the vicolo di Madama Lucrezia, the dirtiest place in Rome'.[161] It seemed to offer an abundance of such fragments and details, despite the filth, at once inconvenient and compelling.

ROMAN *FLÂNERIE*

Walter Benjamin asked why the *flâneur* had not originated in Rome: 'Paris created the type of the *flâneur*. What is remarkable is that it wasn't Rome. And the reason? Does not [even] dreaming follow well trodden paths? And isn't that city too full of temples, enclosed squares, national shrines, to be able to enter "toute entière" – with every cobblestone, every shop sign, every step, and every gateway – into the passerby's dream?'[162] The delightful profusion of things to inspect which ought to have sustained extensive *flânerie* had been compromised by generations of tourists and their well-worn itineraries. However, some visitors pointedly claimed to prefer Rome's archaic byways precisely as a relief from other cities' new forms of visual spectacle and consumption. At almost the same moment as Ruskin, Florence Nightingale and her companion deliberately sought to avoid the Corso in their walks through Rome, because of its abhorrent modernity.[163] In fact, Ruskin's conception of a certain kind of visual attention experienced by someone who 'saunt[ers] leisurely' corresponds more closely to the original sense given to the persona of the *flâneur* as urban witness in Restoration Paris; that is, one who, as if by accident, comes across unsavoury or controversial sights and incidents, thereby licensing apparently innocent, but in reality deliberately provocative, remarks designed to challenge the status quo.[164]

While Ruskin's formula of sauntering, yielding and peeping seems as much a way of avoiding being confined within the boredom of prescribed itineraries, and thereby maintaining a sense of alert individuality, it should also be related to the physical structure of Rome, whose streets, once off the beaten track, were notoriously labyrinthine; getting lost in Rome was a staple of travel narratives.[165] Indeed, wilful travellers like William Beckford relished precisely the prospect of viewing 'nothing at all in a scientific way' but rather intended to 'straggle and wander about, just as the spirit chuses'.[166] The possibility of taking a wrong turning down what might reveal itself to be a filthy street added an element of risk. Such unexpected and unpalatable conditions fuelled a willingness to play up the discrepancy between exalted expectations and the banal, if not disagreable, physical reality of the city. 'This', wrote Hazlitt, 'is not the Rome I expected to see'; instead, he found himself 'for the most part lost in a mass of tawdry, fulsome commonplaces.'[167] A little over twenty years later, George Augustus Sala characterised Rome 'as a city of no streets at all';[168] the Corso was 'simply a very long, narrow, and dirty lane'.[169] 'Do you remember those long dreary drives through by-lanes full of hovels and pigsties, full of dirt and beggars and foul smells? Surely you would not call those slums streets!'[170] Significantly, as a traveller not an artist, he was not faced with the choice of having to enter a dirty lane to appraise a pictorial motif, and could afford to remain fastidiously in his carriage. As regards being a destination for off-piste rambling, the ghetto remained fascinating until the later nineteenth century when Julia Cartwright, in a spirit of art-historical conscientiousness, 'explored its narrow streets thoroughly'.[171]

A HANDFUL OF DUST

Ruskin's enthusiastic impression of a profusion of picturesque details, gratefully embraced as an escape route from preordained touristic itineraries, was not to last. His more considered reflections on his experience of the city were dominated by a much darker, dispirited outlook. Striking a note of shrill Huysmanian disgust, he confessed that his initial revelling in Rome as inexhaustible had given way to a darker vision of Rome as unbearable:

Yet the impression of this perpetual beauty is more painful than pleasing, for there is a strange horror lying over the whole city, which I can neither describe nor account for; it is a shadow of death, possessing and penetrating all things. The sunlight is lurid and ghastly, though so intense that neither the eye nor the body can bear it long; the shadows are cold and sepulchral; you feel like an artist in a fever, haunted by every dream of beauty that his imagination ever dwelt upon, but all mixed up with the fever fear. I am certain this is not imagination, for I am not given to such nonsense, and, even in illness, never remember feeling anything approaching the horror with which some objects here can affect me. It is all like a vast churchyard, with a diseased and dying population living in the shadow of its tombstones. And in fact all the soil round is black, heavy and moist; the dew lies on it like sweat. Wherever there is a tuft of grass to shade it, if you take it up in your hand, it will not dry, it seems one mass of accumulated human corruption.[172]

We recall Ruskin's later remarks on being prevented from continuing his drawing by 'pure human stench'. Ruskin was in a sense the victim of his own aesthetic appetite for 'yielding to every impulse' and his desire to engage with the tangible presence of the city, archetypally manifest in the gesture of picking up and taking possession of a sample of the city's matter.[173]

His remarks here are at once a projection of his uncertain inner state and a literary exercise whose self-contained formulas provided an illusion of immunity from the sickly realities of Rome's degraded fabric and its repulsive interstices: 'The air is sulphurous; the water is bilge; the sun is pestiferous; and the very plaster of the house looks as if it had got all the plagues of Leviticus.'[174] Here, albeit in the form of rhetorical hyperbole, Ruskin articulates a perception of the city as having succumbed to a kind of ambient corruption; the picturesque rewards of digression have been tarnished by the recognition that these are, rather, symptoms of a sinister pathological environment, fundamentally at odds with the pursuit of aesthetic pleasure.

Unlike many such reported gestures, which are merely rhetorical, Ruskin's reaching for a handful of grass seems to be describing a compulsive action, which elicited an ambivalent shudder. At root, the gesture expresses a desire for close physical contact with the dispersed remains of antiquity. However, close contact became an ambiguous matter in so far as Rome's fabric was compromised by its reputation for filth, and moreover in a way which was continuous with anxieties about the rising up of poisonous vapours from its ground. Indeed, touching Rome at all could be discouraged if its coating of dirt was assumed to carry the threat of contagion. Thus, Hugh William Williams noted the disagreeable experience of entering churches whose entrances were lined with large stuffed mats to keep out the external air, but which had become soiled by contact with the local 'squalid looking wretches': 'It does not seem safe to touch them without a glove.'[175]

Having arrived in Rome, it was indeed impossible to move without finding oneself in contact with its remains. As Joseph Wright explained when describing his encounter with 'the amazing and stupendous remains of antiquity;…so numerous are they, that one can scarce move a foot but the relics of some stupendous works present themselves'.[176] An aspect of ruins which emphasises their materiality rather than their role as literary prompt is their dispersed form as dust or pulverised debris. Dust figures as an interface between the viewer and the physical presence of the city, but it is an interface which is as unstable as it is alluring.

Nicolas Poussin's seventeenth-century biographer, Bellori, reports that, visiting ruins with a foreigner who wanted to take home a sample of rare antiquity, the artist replied that he would give him the finest antique he could wish for. Bending down, he scooped up a handful of Roman soil and gravel with small pieces of pulverised porphyry and marble, and said: 'Here take this for your museum, and say this is antique Rome.'[177] Poussin was doubtless familiar with the primacy given by collectors and *curieux* to handling the precious objects, as if coins, medals and sculptures were an extension of the body, and could best be appreciated within its compass. Despite its tersely ironical comment, Poussin's gesture expresses a tactile literalism, implying his own close contact with the fabric of Rome in all its aspects. Moreover, by offering a handful of Roman dust in place of one of his pictures, Poussin deftly made the point that he considered his own art as subordinate to the example of antiquity.

Stooping to pick up a handful of Rome signals both the ubiquity and the fragility of the antique past. A typical remark is that of Bonstetten: 'It is not without shuddering that, approaching them, the hand touches so to speak the century of Nero, or that of Constantine.'[178] In his poem 'L'Homme', Lamartine expressed his disdain for ancient heroes by weighing in his hand their insubstantial remains:

> In her sacred tombs Rome saw me descend;
> Disturbing the cold repose of the most holy shades,
> In my hands I weighed the ashes of heroes.
> I asked of their vain dust
> The immortality which every mortal hopes for![179]

For George Keate, as apprehended within Rome's ruin-strewn landscape, Time teaches 'an awful moral in the Dust': that individuals and states will be subject to dissolution, arriving ineluctably at the same humbled final state.[180] But by the mid-nineteenth century, it could be a mere matter of accumulation: 'My table is already loaded', wrote Charles Eliot Norton in 1855, 'with bits of marble, pieces of inscriptions, fragments of broken ornament, and parcels of mosaic, that I have picked up in the fields, on my walks during this month.'[181] In the opinion of Joseph Péladan, Rome's dust was without equal: it 'contained more of the purest gold, and the noblest blood than all of the dusts of the West.[182]

However, one should not forget the essentially agricultural connotations of picking up a handful of soil to sample its texture. En route to Rome, Hazlitt asked his *vetturino* if the 'dreary aspect of the country' was the fault of the soil or just neglect: 'He pulled a handful of earth from the hedge-side, and showed a rich black loam, capable of every improvement.'[183] This idea was given an existential dimension by Kierkegaard: 'Just as one discovers which land one is in by sticking a finger into the soil and smelling it: I stick my finger into life – it smells of nothing. Where am I? "The world".'[184] That such an investigative gesture could be endowed with a larger epistemological purpose can be compared to the perception that Rome's soil was not only a home for antique remains, in which they were literally rooted – all the more so as their degradation led to the dispersal and assimilation of their fabric into ambient detritus – but also, in theory at least, an economic and social resource which had been allowed to become degraded.

TREADING ON TIME

In an alternative figure, which had been current since the Renaissance, the past is experienced literally as classic ground, as something disconcertingly close to hand, or rather foot, which one walks upon. Unlike the distancing normally inherent in viewing a monument, by contrast, pedestrian participation engenders physical contact, perhaps even a sense of intimacy – if not embarassment at indecorously or presumptuously standing upon the remains of past grandeur. It was precisely the contrast between Rome's 'mean and disgusting' appearance, 'while one literally often walks upon granite, and tramples red porphyry under one's feet', which disconcerted Hester Piozzi.[185] In the *campagna* the ground beneath one's feet contained an emotive historic dimension. On the one hand, there was the release of miasmas, rising up to corrupt the air; on the other hand, a common motif in landscape imagery is the inclusion in the foreground of features which resemble caverns, grottoes or trenches, revealing a rough-hewn section of this historic ground (figs 90, 91).

As an idea, treading Roman ground, and thereby being in contact with venerated forebears, had a talismanic force. Indeed, for Jeremiah Donovan, the idea of pedestrian contact in Rome was so compelling that he misquoted Samuel Johnson, substituting Rome for Iona: 'Far from me, and from my friends, be such frigid philosophy, as may conduct us unmoved over any ground which has been dignified by wisdom, bravery, or virtue. That man is little to be envied, whose patriotism would not gain force upon the plain of Marathon, or whose piety would not grow warmer on the sacred soil of Rome.'[186] Through Johnson's words, Donovan evokes not just an imagined state of being when actually in such hallowed sites, but an effect of intensification when experienced through the sense of touch.

The act of walking literally in the footsteps of the ancients could elicit immensely powerful emotions. For Middleton, arriving in Rome on the road from Palestrina, he was thrillingly conscious of walking on a road 'which has been worn by the steps of thousands of Romans. – He treads the ground which was once the site of a populous city, and sees nothing around him but a rutless plain....here once stood palaces and temples, which the hand of time has crumbled into dust....Such are the ideas which crowd upon the mind on approaching Rome, and I awoke as from a dream of the past, as I entered the "Porta Maggiore".'[187] It could be argued that the same effect was experienced by artists who traversed the *campagna* in search of sites and views.[188]

Such intimate contact with the past endowed pedestrian exploration of Rome with an inescapable pathos. In Byron's reproachful words:

90   Jean Charles Joseph Rémond, *A View of the Roman Campagna: Landscape with Caves in the Foreground and Figure with Goats(?), Hills in the Distance*, watercolour strengthened with gum, 22.0 × 38.4 cm. British Museum, London.

91   Paul Chevandier de Valdrôme, *Landscape, Roman Campagna*, c.1846 (1846 Salon), oil on canvas, 90 × 195 cm. Louvre, Paris, RF 1987-4.

> What are our woes and sufferance? Come and see
> The cypress, hear the owl, and plod your way
> Oe'r the steps of broke thrones and temples, Ye!
> Whose agonies are evils of a day –
> A world is at our feet as fragile as our clay.[189]

Byron insists on the inevitable transition from human clay to the dust of ages past. This is more than a reminder of mortality, and maps the sense of self onto, but also against, the dissolution of Empire. That some entity, at once physical and symbolic, should be located underfoot has an iconographical link to the representation of subjugation. But here the hierarchy of significance is inverted, humbling the latter-day tourist. Byron famously 'kicked the dust' of his native country from his feet, as satirized by Max Beerbohm, before striding forth on his Continental tour. However, in the forensically analytical opinion of Carrière, he was unlikely to have eradicated all trace of his origins: 'The émigré may well try to shake off the dust of his native soil from his feet, some will always remain, and this residue is petrified within the substance of his organism.'[190]

In his poem *Italy*, Samuel Rogers brings out this emphasis on the physical and tactile:

> Let us descend [to the Forum] slowly.
> At every step much may be lost.
> The very dust we tread, stirs with life;
> And not a breath but from the ground sends up
> Something of human grandeur.'[191]

Others such as Lamartine, with a different, more pessimistic political agenda, judged that the virtues of Italy's ancient civilisation had been compromised by contemporary efforts to ignite a nationalist consciousness. As Carolyn Springer has shown, Lamartine's poetry was a disillusioned riposte to what he found to be intrusive evidence of political organising:

> Crumbled monument, inhabited by an echo!
> Dust of the past, stirred only by a sterile wind!
> Land, where the sons no longer have their ancestors' blood,
> Where on the agèd soil men are born old,...
>
> I will seek elsewhere (pardon, Roman shade)
> Men, and not human dust![192]
>
> Rome! So there you are! Shade of the Caesars!
> I like to crush beneath my feet your disintegrated monuments.[193]

It is important to remember that this sense of physical continuity was lost by virtue of the archaeological excavations of the early nineteenth century, so as to create cordoned off objects more exclusively to be considered as visual spectacle. To this extent, there was an accentuated physical separation of monument and spectator. As monuments, whole or fragmented, were cleared of accumulated dust, rubble and rubbish, so the tourists and artists who had been able to inspect them in an unimpeded fashion were disengaged from such palpable proximity. However, a further dimension to walking upon antique remains is the idea that such debris, or the foundations of monuments, create an insulating barrier against the residue of corrupted, stagnant water which periodically saturated much of Rome's substrata. In the sixteenth century Sixtus V had forbidden the use of flint for new paving since it absorbed moisture and would thus be no more than a conduit for such harmful vapours.[194]

A focus on surface can also be reworked as evidence to support scepticism regarding the value of Roman antiquities. Lady Morgan's prose followed Byron's poetic scepticism. Byron's verse reads:

> Cypress and ivy, weed and wallflower grown
> Matted and mass'd together, hillocks heap'd
> On what were chambers, arch crush'd, columns strown
> In fragments, choked up vaults, and frescoes steep'd
> In subterranean damps, where the owl peep'd,
> Deeming it midnight: – Temples, baths, or halls?
> Pronounce who can; for all that Learning reap'd
> From her research hath been, that these are walls – .[195]

Morgan's commentary on this text places Byron's cynicism about archaeological speculation within the context of the experience of exploring Rome, and illustrates the way pedestrian progress was a balancing act between following learned guidance and maintaining a sense of empirical integrity: 'The indisputable remnants of antiquity bearing any tangible evidence of their original destination, are in Rome few and precious. But there are *sites* innumerable, consecrated by classic research, and "Hillocks heap'ed o'er what were chambers". Cells of mystery and dens of darkness, deep buried under mountainous fragments of their own ruins, present themselves on every side. Into these subterranean labyrinths, all who visit Rome descend; and, tottering over mounds of earth or tessellated pavements, by the murky light of flaring flambeaux, the votarists of virtù follow the high-priests of their religion through the suites of mouldering vaults.'[196] Here Morgan equates antiquarian investigation with visiting catacombs. Historical knowledge comes from such descents through time and space. However, the flickering illumination and musty atmosphere of this subterranean spectacle rendered such encounters highly impressionistic and trepidatious, allowing the imagination full rein.

In this reading antiquity was in fact elusive – if not illusory – in terms of its material presentness. She concludes: 'The great majority of nameless, formless piles, dignified with the epithet of "remains", are in fact the ruins of ruins – the remnants of repeated desolations and incessant injury.'[197] This enhanced sense of tangibility, of the broken up state of things, shifted attention to the contemporary environment. To a sceptical, unforgiving visitor, the poetics of pulverisation was nothing more than an inflated myth, readily exploited by profiteering cicerone and their successors. Antiquarian inspection seemed to have become perverted into a form of religious veneration, sharing a reliance on blind faith.

Such resentment at the misappropriation of authentic remains is consistent with the attitudes which sustained a policy of cleaning and revealing as previously mentioned. Morgan objects, precisely, to a willingness to resort to a generic celebration of sites and materials which by her standards were indecipherable, and therefore liable to be exploited in an unscrupulous way so as to reinforce a coarsened version of the cult of ruins. It was a necessary consequence of the application of serious study to Roman remains that accumulated misunderstandings had to be disposed of. For Morgan, walking on, and thus being in contact with, ancient remains was not a sufficient means to identify and understand them; rather, this required proper visual scrutiny. The tactile ambiguities which flowed from the threat of contagion and similar uncertainties as regards air, odour and incrustations of dirt could be said to have the consequence of giving priority to the sense of sight.[198] While Flaubert might embrace the medicalised notion of manure as health-giving, and a way to alleviate the oppressively priestly milieu, most travellers baulked at the disagreeable obligation in Rome of enduring unpleasant smells as part of the activity of viewing sites and monuments. In a sense this had the effect of promoting – or reiterating – an idea of Rome as a series of visual sights, a succession of views. As we saw in relation to Rome as a subject for landscape imagery, a similar process of aestheticisation was imposed on the distinctive character of the local atmosphere, whereby its toxic threat was neutralised. The tendency to intensify and isolate visual attention had the effect of decontextualising objects, images and monuments.

Rome's reinvention as the national capital was to encourage the tendency to aestheticise its reprehensible state. Modernising initiatives to clean and renew the city sharpened nostalgia for the unsavoury but decoratively gratifying patina which had become synonymous with the decrepid urban fabric. Celebrating the city's picturesque qualities was, however, also a way of offsetting and legitimizing former neglect; an attitude which involved ignoring the competing claims of public health and hygiene. This could be said to involve detaching perceptions of the city as an array of art and architecture from the social envelope which surrounded them. Rather than promoting the virtues of synaesthetic wholeness, the experience of Rome seems to have exacerbated the dissociation of the senses.

CONCLUSION

INFLUENCE RECLAIMED, OR THE PREDICAMENT OF ROME

This book reconsiders the idea of artistic influence through the eighteenth and nineteenth centuries by approaching the familiar terrain of Rome as a place of artistic pilgrimage from an unaccustomed angle – but one which would have immediately been recognisable to all visitors and residents of the city in this period. By taking account of Rome's challenging climate and more specifically the endemic problem of 'bad air', which had contaminated the city and its *campagna*, we are forced to acknowledge the degree to which the business of viewing, studying and making art should be thought of as being vulnerable to, if not dependent on the combined physical and psychological impact of the local environment. For most of the period considered, influence was thought of as a primordial dimension of cultural experience whereby artistic sensibility was imposed on by art understood as being embedded in a charismatic alien environment – even if a degree of resistance was exhibited in individual cases. By the late nineteenth century, the idea of influence emerged as a much more academicised and codified conception of the ways in which artists engaged with the art of the past. In part, this can be understood as a form of distancing or abstraction: the evident physical and psychological difficulties that artists underwent as part of the journey to and sojourn in Rome disrupted and undermined expectations that it would be a place of both professional consolidation and unalloyed exhilaration. The older holistic notion of influence was shifted towards a more formalised emphasis on the assimilation of purely visual models.

In the early part of the eighteenth century, influence had functioned as an instrumental concept: a rite of passage by means of which to be granted a sight of past art's true grandeur and thereby to be inspired to emulate such exceptional creative achievements. Rome had a mythic status as the privileged place for this to be enacted. Viewed in this light, Rome's whole environment was considered to have contributed to the inspiring and edifying effects that artists and their patrons and mentors expected to enjoy having made the pilgrimage. However, it rapidly became apparent that visitors were liable to fall victim to various aspects of the city's insalubrious and infected state, in a way that was as destabilising of artists' expectations and morale as it was of their physical constitution. Engaging with Rome enthusiastically, and treating the city and its landscape as a site for the garnering of precious observations, turned out to be constrained by certain inhospitable aspects of the climate, and the disagreeable consequences of the neglect and decline of the surrounding *campagna*.

In so far as the invisible and insidious presence of 'bad air' percolated through the streets and spaces of the city, this added a pathological dimension to the drama of a Roman artistic pilgrimage. The imaginative geography of Rome as a place of pleasure and discovery, where it was possible to experience a temporal and cultural union of present and past, was revealed to have a dark and threatening dimension, all the more so as this could be perceived as inescapable. Intrepid or blasé visitors might derive a frisson of excitement from what they trivialised as an exaggerated problem.

Once this aspect of the Roman environment is acknowledged, the idea of enthusiastically taking possession metaphorically and tangibly of the city's artistic materials and resources acquires a troublingly ambiguous character. Enthusiasm might indeed be contagious, since making contact with the diseased fabric of the city was revealed to be tantamount to exposing oneself to the risk of illness. Rome's old alter ego as the grave of civilisation (and hence site of Christian resurrection) had an all too real correlate in contemporary life. Yet it is remarkable how long the myth of Rome as a place of magical artistic transformation survived given the ubiquitous evidence of 'bad airs' damaging effects. Indeed, this carried through into the twentieth century after the nature of malarial fever had been discovered and a programme of education and eradication undertaken.

In a sense, art historians have contributed to this disavowal through accepting Romantic celebrations of Rome as the city of the melancholy soul as a form of lapidary witness, and insisting on the reinvention of Rome's topographical vocation as a site of untarnished ideal beauty in the form of the liberating nature of *plein air* painting, for which the *campagna* was deemed to be uniquely endowed with artistically propitious light and atmosphere. In so far as painting out of doors was equated with a new way to achieve visual truth, it was doubly endowed with art-historical prestige as a modernising mode of vision and technique which reinvented the innovative legacy of seventeenth-century antecedents. Because of its crucial transitional role between ideal landscape and modernity (destined to be heroically translated to Paris), this episode has obscured the degree to which it falls short of giving a more historically contextualised account of what it was to represent Rome and its landscape.

By emphasising the counter-image of Rome as filthy – an image that seeps through into and soils the more celebratory clichés recycled by tourists and artists alike – we are led to reconsider the relation between the senses in experiencing the city. Rome's reputation as a place of excitation where a benign ambience fostered exceptional imaginative activity was premised on a holistic conception of the dependence of bodies and therefore minds on climate and its components. However, once the legendary efficacy of the city as a privileged site of art-making and viewing was acknowledged not to render visitors immune to local 'intempéries', then the idea of influence took on a more complex role. More specifically, its medical function overlapped and indeed interfered with the more benign artistic version of influence which derived its mechanism from an originally Hippocratic model. The foul nature of Rome's streets could be allowed into view, but only so as to be sanitised by shifting focus onto the visual, as we saw in Henry James's yearning for 'colour' detached from the unpleasantness of stink. Equally, a parallel would be Ruskin's Roman trajectory: setting out with a desire to evade the clichés of tourism, a sense of mounting relish at the profusion of motifs he found down side streets, then recoil at the stench, shuddering at the touch of the city's 'pestilential' fabric, before retreating into the pre-existing conventions of the picturesque. In both cases, the initial willingness to embrace Rome as a gratifying sensory whole produced a self-protective reaction, consolidating a preference to remain on the level of visual experience so as to screen out distasteful intrusions. This could be seen as a reinvention of the notion of artistic influence as a mode of perception projected onto the fabric of the city in place of the earlier synoptic vision of a canonical set of prescribed great works.

A further dimension to this transformation of the notion of influence is the process of artworks' detachment from their surroundings so as to install them physically and conceptually within the academicised world of the museum. Of course, there is no little irony in this relocation: it was in Rome that the Museo Pio-Clementino offered a novel form of display for the papal collections, combining public access with an image of enlightened authority.[1] But it was also in Rome above all that the debate over the benefits of art's rootedness as opposed to its purported liberation from ideological servitude and physical neglect was played out (to this extent influence could be said to be an inherently political matter, in so far as it is constituted by a struggle over authority and dependence, a recognition Harold Bloom translated into an epic literary psycho-drama). Following the fall of Napoleon, Rome's treasures may have been restored to their home, but the rival model of curatorial and conservation expertise exemplified by the Louvre allied to the influential concept of the universal survey museum was to hold its place in the institutionalised cultural imagination. The evidence of nineteenth-century museum culture would seem to demonstrate how comprehensively claims that Rome possessed an artistically sustaining Gestalt seem to have lost their authority.

Yet one could argue that it was precisely the growing consensus that the museum was the proper home of art which sustained and gave a new impetus to Rome's reputation as an anomalous oasis of wholeness. On the one hand, this claim seemed to be borne out by the city's resolutely decrepid aspect, at least until such time as the new national capital was cleansed and refurbished. On the other hand, the very success of the museum provoked a fundamental critique of its rationale, to the effect that art risked being robbed of its life-giving qualities once consigned to institutional safekeeping. For Paul Valéry, the ordered displays of the Louvre caused a 'vertigo of the mixed-up' (vertige du mélange); such erudite categorisation was essentially unnatural, and he relished returning to the authenticity of 'la rue vivante'.[2] In affirming Valéry's judgement that museums killed art, Adorno extended the biological metaphor: once inside museums, artworks became 'objects to which the observer no longer has a vital relationship and which are in the process of dying'.[3] The idea that, in Rome, one could experience authentic and energising contact with art because it was embedded in its original envelope underpinned the city's talismanic status; and this was only intensified by the seeming normality of museums' homogenising spaces. Paradoxically, this reputation was further enhanced by the proliferation of foreign academies in the late nineteenth century; their official purpose was premised on a belief in the irreplaceable mystique of Rome as artistic source, an idea that spawned ever greater quantities of generic academic art.[4]

Belief in Rome's magical properties has been so strong that it has blinded historians of journeys to and sojourns in the city and their artistic consequences to the intrusion of debilitating and sometimes fatal aspects of the local environment. As Ménageot had been forced to reflect in 1788 when faced with a mounting list of casualties amongst his charges in the Académie de France, the 'cradle of art' might become the 'tomb of artists', so damaging was it proving to be to the sheer physical survival of France's élite young artists. Ménageot and his peers recognised that such realities were not merely external to the experience of art in Rome, but an integral aspect of how art was imagined as springing from some essential components of the local environment. We have seen how blurred were the distinctions between medical investigation of Rome's 'bad air' and the spectrum of cultural modes of perception and representation by means of which the phenomenon was acknowledged and neutralised.

Rome has always been treated as a particularly charismatic destination. But the preponderant literary and touristic discourses within which the city played so a potent role need situating within an historical perspective which connects such forms of representation to the complexities of local circumstances. Investigating ideas of influence within the particular context of Rome in the eighteenth and nineteenth centuries has shown that art-historical disinclination to engage with this term has been based on a short-sighted, not to say ahistorical, perspective. Above all, we have seen how insistently Rome's climate and environment impinged on the minds and bodies of all who spent time there, and the complex ways in which this compelled a response – whether evasion, confrontation, resignation, or disdain. Ultimately, Roman fever in all its forms seems to have become accepted as a risk worth taking in the pursuit of artistic revelation.

NOTES

ABBREVIATIONS

CDAFR   *Correspondance des directeurs de l'Académie de France à Rome, avec les Surintendants des Bàtiments (1666–1804)*, ed. Anatole de Montaiglon and Jules Guiffrey, 18 vols (Paris, 1887–1912). New Series: *Répertoires*, ed. Georges Brunel (Rome, 1979); *Suvée (1795–1807)*, ed. Georges Brunel et Isabelle Julia, 2 vols (Rome, 1984); *Guérin (1823–1828)*, ed. Antoinette Le Normand-Romain, François Fossier and Mehdi Korchane (Rome, 2005); *Vernet (1828–1834)*, ed. François Fossier, Isabelle Chave and Jacques Kuhnmunch (Rome, 2011).

Encyclopédie   *Encyclopédie, ou dictionnaire des sciences, des arts et des métiers*, ed. Denis Diderot and Jean Le Rond d'Alembert, 28 vols (Paris, 1751–72).

INTRODUCTION

1 A notable exception is Daniel Pick's study of Garibaldi, *Rome or Death: The Obsessions of General Garibaldi* (London, 2005).

I INFLUENCE

1 Inscriptions are unusual in Robert's Roman drawings. See *J. H. Fragonard e H. Robert a Roma* (Villa Medici, Rome, 1990), pp. 174–5, cat. no. 117. Robert spent 11 years in Rome from November 1754.

2 On Bellori, see Richard Spear, *Domenichino*, 2 vols (New Haven and London, 1982), vol. 1, pp. 155–7, cat. no. 33, plates 58, 59; Denis Mahon pointed out that the original source for the story is Mosini's preface to Giambattista Agucchi's *Trattato della pittura* (1610) (*Studies in Seicento Art and Theory* (London, 1947), p. 271 note 54).

3 Although there are no surviving drawings after these murals by Robert, J. P. Cuzin and Pierre Rosenberg note his use of figures from Domen-

ichino's *St Cecilia distributing Alms* (San Luigi dei Francesi, Rome) in a drawing, *Ruines antiques avec personnages* (sale Lille, 23 Nov. 1988, cat. no. 169, ill.), *Fragonard*, p. 174, cat. no. 117.

4 'l'une des belles choses qu'il y ait à Rome' (CDAFR, vol. 15, p. 278, 10 Sept. 1788). A previous director, Natoire, refers to 'plusieurs copies par nos élèves d'après les Raphael et Dominiquin' (CDAFR, vol. 11, p. 116, Feb. 1754).

5 'car cette belle fresque dépérit de jour en jour...une grande leçon de dessin, de pensée et d'expression' (ibid., pp. 360–1, where he estimates only eight to ten years before its disappearance). Spear, *Domenichino*, vol. 1, pp. 155–7, cat. no. 33, notes comments on its damaged state by Charles de Brosses from 1739–40 (*Lettres...*, 1798 edn, vol. 3, p. 118), and Charlotte Anne Eaton: 'the vestiges of the matchless frescoes of Domenichino and Guido – The spectres of painting, "the ghosts of what they were"' ([Charlotte Anne Eaton], *Rome in the Nineteenth Century...in a Series of Letters written...in the Years 1817 and 1818*, 3 vols (Edinburgh, 1820), vol. 2, pp.

321–5). Mariana Starke warned travellers who were concerned about their health to be wary of visiting this oratory: 'This Church and the Chapels are damp and cold' (Starke, *Letters from Italy between the Years 1792 and 1798*, 2 vols (London, 1800), vol. 2, pp. 361–2). Already in 1722, Jonathan Richardson (junior) described the oratory as 'Dirty, Injur'd, particularly by the Rain Water coming through the Ceiling, and running down' in *An Account of some of the Statues, Bas-reliefs, Drawings and Pictures in Italy, &c. with Remarks* (1722), p. 321, cit. Carol Gibson-Wood, *Jonathan Richardson: Art Theorist of the English Enlightenment* (New Haven and London, 2000), p. 220. In 1799, Henri Reboul mistakenly included San Gregorio Magno al Celio as one of the monuments belonging to the Académie de France, and which should therefore not be removed to France; he mentions Daniele da Volterra's *Deposition* fresco in Trinità dei Monti as being in the process of being removed (Henri Reboul to Minister of Interior, CDAFR, new series, ed. Georges Brunel and Isabelle Julia, vol. 2, Directorat de Suvée, 1795–1807 (Rome, 1984), pp. 172–3, 5 prairial an VII [24 May 1799]).

6 *Entretiens*, 2nd edn (1688), vol. 2, pp. 340ff., cit. Mahon, *Seicento*, p. 271 note 54. Elizabeth Cropper notes Delacroix's observation in his essay on Poussin, that his copying of the *Flagellation* led to friendship between the two artists. She illustrates another Granet drawing involving Poussin's copy of Domenichino's *Last Communion of St Jerome* in *The Domenichino Affair: Novelty, Imitation, and Theft in Seventeenth-Century Rome* (New Haven and London, 2005), pp. 16–17.

7 Deanna Petherbridge, *The Primacy of Drawing: Histories and Theories of Practices* (New Haven and London, 2010), fig. 201, pp. 292–3.

8 Victor Carlson quotes from the article on the French Academy in the 1777–9 edn of the *Encyclopédie* (no vol. given) (*Art in Rome in the Eighteenth Century*, ed. Edgar Peters Bowron and Joseph J. Rishel (London and Philadelphia, 2000), p. 550, cat. no. 397).

9 [Stephen Weston], *Viaggiana; or, Detached Remarks on the Buildings of Rome*, 3rd edn (London, 1797), p. 1.

10 For example, Guillaume Guillon Lethière was encouraged to copy Ribera's *Descent from the Cross*, in the Chartreux in Naples, because it was 'un des plus beaux tableaux d'Italie, pur et conservé', despite the fact the lighting was poor (CDAFR, vol. 15, p. 415, 21 April 1790, Ménageot to d'Angiviller; vol. 15, p. 462, 3 Nov. 1790); see also Ménageot to d'Angiviller, on Prince Giustiniani's refusal to let works be copied (vol. 15, p. 422, 2 June 1790).

11 *An Account of some of the Statues, Bas-reliefs, Drawings and Pictures in Italy, &c. with Remarks* (1722), p. 321, cit. Gibson-Wood, *Jonathan Richardson*, p. 220.

12 Francesco Algarotti, *Essai sur la peinture et sur l'Académie de France établie à Rome* (Paris, 1769), p. 268; first published as *Saggio sopra l'Accademia di Francia che è in Roma* (Livorno, 1763).

13 On Natoire and copying policy under his directorate of the Académie de France à Rome see Susanna Caviglia-Brunel, *Charles-Joseph Natoire (1700–1777)* (Paris, 2012), pp. 122–3 note 697. For a discussion of later ideas on this, see Paul Duro, 'The Lure of Rome: The Academic Copy and the Académie de France in the Nineteenth Century', in Rafael Cardoso Denis and Colin Trodd (eds), *Art and the Academy in the Nineteenth Century* (Manchester, 2000).

14 Sir Joshua Reynolds, *Discourses on Art*, ed. R. Wark (New Haven and London, 1997), pp. 135–42 (second discourse). On Reynolds's approach to copying, see Harry Mount, 'Reynolds, Chiaroscuro and Composition', in Paul Taylor and François Quiviger (eds), *Pictorial Composition from Medieval to Modern Art* (London and Turin, 2001), pp. 172–97. Hennequin reckoned that literal copies chilled the imagination (*Mémoires de Ph. A. Hennequin, écrits par lui-même* (Paris, 1933), p. 94). For a general account of drawings as copies, see Petherbridge, *Primacy of Drawing*, chapter 10, 'The complex contradictions of copying', pp. 260–85. For a magisterial survey of what it might mean to acquire, copy and reinvent the work of others, see Jeremy Wood, *Rubens. Copies and Adaptations from Renaissance and Later Artists*, Corpus Rubenianum Ludwig Burchardt, XXVI (2), 3 vols (London and Turnhout, 2010–11).

15 Ingres: 'Il y a sans doute beaucoup à profiter à Rome, mais je me suis fait une échelle de beauté qui me fait admettre ou regretter une chose belle ou moins, ce qui fait que les extraits que j'ai à faire ici seront moins nombreux et plus judicieusement

choisis. Mais j'espère toujours en retirer une belle moisson [emphasis in original]. Je n'ai, jusqu'ici, pas fait grand chose et il est impossible de faire autrement: on travaillerait sans cela sans discernement et tout à côté. Les beautés de tout genre sont ici les unes sur les autres et on est assommé de voir; ce n'est que peu à peu que l'on revient de son étonnement et que l'on voit bien' (H. Lapauze, *Le Roman d'amour de M. Ingres* (Paris, 1910), pp. 123–4, 21 Feb. 1807, to M. Forestier); Valenciennes warned artists contemplating a Roman sojourn that on their return 'il faut avoir bien employé son temps et fait une ample moisson' (*Elémens de perspective pratique à l'usage des artistes, suivis de réflexions et conseils à un élève sur la peinture et particulièrement sur le genre du paysage* (Paris, 1800), p. 606). On Turner's indefatigable activity and the drawings he produced in Rome, see Cecilia Powell, *Turner in the South: Rome, Naples, Florence* (New Haven and London, 1987), and John Gage, *J. M. W. Turner: 'A Wonderful Range of Mind'* (New Haven and London, 1987).

16 'je suis devenu subitement voyageur, et la fièvre de voir les Raphael m'a pris. Je suis donc en train d'avaler mon Italie' (letter to Mme Georges Charpentier, autumn 1881, cit. Barbara Ehrlich White, 'Renoir's Trip to Italy', *Art Bulletin*, vol. 60, December 1969, p. 346).

17 'Je veux voir les Raphael oui Monsieur, les Ra, les pha, les el. Après ça ceux qui ne seront pas contents....Je parie que l'on dira que j'ai été influencé!' (letter to Charles Dendon, autumn 1881, cit. White, 'Renoir's Trip', p. 347).

18 For example, Auguste Schoy, *Histoire de l'influence italienne sur l'architecture des Pays-bas* (Brussels, 1879).

19 Michael Baxandall, *Patterns of Intention* (New Haven and London, 1985), pp. 56–62.

20 Harold Bloom, *The Anxiety of Influence: A Theory of Poetry* (Oxford, 1973, 2nd edn 1997), and see now *The Anatomy of Influence: Literature as a Way of Life* (New Haven and London, 2011); Robert Douglas-Fairhurst, *Victorian Afterlives: The Shaping of Influence in Nineteenth-Century Literature* (Oxford, 2002).

21 Brian Grosskurth, review of Norman Bryson, *Tradition and Desire: From David to Delacroix* (Cambridge, 1984), in *Burlington Magazine*, vol. 127, no. 989, August 1985.

22 For an imperious put-down, see Rosalind Kraus, 'The Future of an Illusion', *AA Files*, no. 13, Autumn 1986.

23 Joseph Koerner, 'Albrecht Dürer: A Sixteenth-Century *Influenza*', in Giulia Bartrum et al., *Albrecht Dürer and his Legacy: The Graphic Works of a Renaisssance Artist* (Princeton, 2002). Jay Clarke kindly drew this to my attention. Modern contributions to thinking about how art depends on art choose different, more elaborate vocabularies, e.g. Michael Fried, *Manet's Modernism, or The Face of Painting in the 1860s* (Chicago, 1996), which includes the text of his earlier article with further reconsideration, 'Manet's Sources: Aspects of his Art 1859–1869', *Artforum*, vol. 7, no. 7, March 1969, pp. 28–82. While her account centres on the particular problem of plagiarism, there is much in Cropper's *Domenichino Affair*, which addresses aspects of influence as a historical phenomenon and how this relates to more general matters of art-historical method (see in particular her 'Coda: A Reflection on the History of Art').

24 Michel Foucault, *The Archaeology of Knowledge* (New York, 1972), p. 21.

25 A. P. Oppé (ed.), 'The Memoirs of Thomas Jones', *Walpole Society*, vol. 32, 1951, p. 55. In 1813, Franz Horny lauded the Olevano countryside as 'ein wahres Zauberland' (cit. Sarah Faunce, in Philip Conisbee et al., *In the Light of Italy: Corot and Early Open Air Painting* (Washington, D.C., 1996), p. 72).

26 [Weston], *Viaggiana*, p. 1.

27 Vivien Noakes, *Edward Lear: The Life of a Wanderer*, revised edn (Stroud, 2004), p. 48.

28 Allan Cunningham, *The Life of Sir David Wilkie*, 3 vols (London, 1843), vol. 2, p. 162.

29 Vivian Nutton, *Ancient Medicine* (London and New York, 2004).

30 Tony Halliday has discussed the late eighteenth-century updating of Galenic ideas on humoural theory in an important recent book, *The Temperamental Nude: Class, Medicine, and Representation in Eighteenth-Century France*, Studies on Voltaire and the Eighteenth Century (Oxford, 2010). See Richard Mead, *De imperio solis ac lunae in corpora humana et morbis inde oriundis* (London, 1704), *A Treatise concerning the Influence of the Sun and the Moon upon Human Bodies, and the Disease thereby Produced* (London, 1748).

31 Francis Balfour, *A Treatise on the Influence of the Moon in Fevers* (Calcutta, 1784; Edinburgh, 1785); William Falconer, *A Dissertation on the Influence of the Passions upon Disorders of the Body: Being the Essay to which the Fothergillian Medal Was Adjudged* (London, 1788); William Falconer, *Remarks on the Influence of Climate, Situation, Nature of Country, Population, Nature of Food, and Way of Life: On the Disposition and Temper, Manners and Behaviour, Intellect, Laws, Customs, Form of Government and Religion of Mankind* (London, 1781).

32 *Encyclopédie*, vol. 8, pp. 729–38.

33 'News from Rome of a contagious Distemper raging there, call'd the *Influenza*', *London Magazine*, vol. 12 1743, p. 145; these remarks equate influenza with a foreign form of political corruption. 'Everybody [in Rome] is ill of the *Influenza* and many die' (Mann, letter to Walpole, 12 Feb. 1743, in John Doran, *'Mann' and Manners at the Court of Florence, 1740–1786: Founded on the letters of Horace Mann to H[orace] Walpole*, 2 vols (1876), vol. I , p. 144). See [James Russel], *Letters from a Young Painter Abroad to his Friends in England*, 2 vols (1750), vol. 1, p. 232: 'Neither the apprehension of the *Influenza*, nor the terror of the pestilence…'. Other sources use the alternative French term 'la grippe' for the 1743 outbreak of illness (see *OED* 'influenza').

34 See also Jean-Pierre Peter, 'Malades et maladies à la fin du XVIIIe siècle', *Annales ESC*, vol. 22, no. 4, 1967, p. 732.

35 Bloom, *Anxiety of Influence* (1973), p. 95.

36 On the broader repercussions of contagion, see Andrew R. Aisenberg, *Contagion: Disease, Government, and the 'Social Question' in Nineteenth-Century France* (Stanford, 1999).

37 'myasmes ou sémences morbifiques…première origine ou la matrice des myasmes' (*Encyclopédie*, vol. 4, p. 110).

38 Dr Armstrong, 'Lectures on the Principles and Practice of Physic', *The Lancet*, vol. 7, no. 7, 21 May 1825, p. 194.

39 Saul Jarcho, *The Concept of Contagion in Medicine, Literature and Religion* (Malabar, Fl., 2000); Alison Bashford and Claire Hooker, *Contagion: Historical and Cultural Studies* (London, 2001); Allen Conrad Christensen, *Nineteenth-Century Narratives of Contagion: 'Our Feverish Contact'* (London, 2005); Claire L. Carlin (ed.), *Imagining Contagion in Early Modern Europe* (Basingstoke, 2005). 'The complexity and sense of compromise more characteristic of the whole period in question, were most obviously expressed in the widespread use of analogy' (Margaret Pelling, *Cholera, Fever, and English Medicine, 1825–1865* (Oxford, 1978), p. 303). Gérard Fabre has addressed contagion in terms of 'imaginaire social' in *Épidémies et contagions: L'Imaginaire du mal en Occident* (Paris, 1998).

40 David Hume, 'Of National Characters', in *Essays Moral, Political, and Literary*, ed. T. H. Green and T. H. Grose, 2 vols (London, 1898), vol. 1, p. 248, cit. Clarence J. Glacken, *Traces on the Rhodian Shore: Nature and Culture in Western Thought from Ancient Times to the End of the Eighteenth Century* (Berkeley, 1967), p. 586.

41 [James Elmes], *The Arts and Artists; or, Anecdotes and Relics of the Schools of Painting, Sculpture and Architecture*, 3 vols (London, 1825), vol. 2, pp. 44–5.

42 'Dans un tems où la contagion devenoit presque générale, quelles obligations n'avons-nous pas à quelques artistes d'un génie plus heureux et plus sage de nous avoir enfin rappellé au vrai goût, qui est celui de l'antique?' (*Observations sur les ouvrages de MM. de l'Académie de peinture et de sculpture exposés au Sallon du Louvre en l'année 1753* (Paris, 1753), cit. Wolfgang Herrmann, *Laugier and Eighteenth-Century French Theory* (London, 1962), p. 229).

43 Charles-Nicolas Cochin, *Lettre à un jeune artiste peintre, pensionnaire à l'Académie royale de France à Rome par M. C.* (Paris, 1773–4), pp. 43–4.

44 'tandis que leurs défauts sont très-contagieux' (Madame de Staël, *De la littérature considérée dans ses rapports avec les institutions sociales*, 2 vols (Paris, 1959), vol. 1, p. 170).

45 Quatremère de Quincy, 'Essai historique sur l'art du paysage à Rome', *Archives littéraires de l'Europe*, 1806, vol. 10, p. 207.

46 'Le préservatif ainsi que les modèles sont au-delà des Alpes' (report to Minister of Interior, 26 vendémiaire an IV, cit. H. Lapauze, *Histoire de l'Académie de France à Rome*, 2 vols (Paris, 1924), vol. 2, p. 2).

47 'l'influence stupéfiante de la villa Médicis' (*Le Vote universel*, 28 Jan. 1851, cit. Isabelle Julia, *La Campagne romaine à propos d'un tableau d'Hébert <u>La Mal'aria</u>*, Petit Journal des Grandes Expositions, new series, no. 93, 1980, Musée Hébert, Paris, p. 2).

48 William Bissell Pope (ed.), *The Diary of Benjamin Robert Haydon*, 5 vols (Cambridge, Mass, 1960–3), vol. 5, p. 27, cit. William Vaughan, '"David's Brickdust" and the Rise of the British School', in A. Yarrington and K. Everest (eds), *Reflections on Revolution: Images of Romanticism* (London, 1993), p. 135.

49 Hester Lynch Piozzi, *Observations and Reflections made in the Course of a Journey through France, Italy and Germany*, 2 vols (London, 1789), p. 148.

50 Thomas Moore, *The Life of Byron*, 2 vols (Philadelphia, 1851), vol. 1, p. 601, cit. James Buzard, *The Beaten Track: European Tourism, Literature, and the Ways to 'Culture', 1800–1918* (Oxford, 1993), p. 84.

51 Chloe Chard, *Pleasure and Guilt on the Grand Tour: Travel Writing and Imaginative Geography, 1600–1830* (Manchester, 1999), and 'Nakedness and Tourism: Classical Sculpture and the Imaginative Geography of the Grand Tour', *Oxford Art Journal*, vol. 18, no. 1, 1995.

52 Silvio Negro, *Seconda Roma 1850–1870* (Vicenza, 1966), pp. 13–36.

2 SUCCUMBING TO ROME

1 Jacques Thuillier, '"Il se rendit en Italie": notes sur le voyage à Rome des artistes français au XVIIe siècle', in *'Il se rendit en Italie': Études offertes à André Chastel* (Rome, 1987). See H. Lapauze, *Histoire de l'Académie de France à Rome*, 2 vols (Paris, 1924); *Maestà di Roma: Da Napoleone all'unità d'Italia; Da Ingres a Degas artisti francesi a Roma* (Rome, 2003).

2 CDAFR, vol. 3, p. 348, 20 Oct. 1708.

3 Ellis Waterhouse, *Three Decades of English Art 1740–1770* (Philadelphia, 1964), pp. 24–7, cit. David Solkin, *Richard Wilson: The Landscape of Reaction* (Tate Gallery, London, 1982), p. 38.

4 See Alison Yarrington, '"Made in Italy": Sculpture and the Staging of National Identities at the International Exhibition of 1862', in Manfred Pfister and Ralph Hertel (eds), *Performing National Identities: Anglo-Italian Cultural Transactions* (Amsterdam, 2008), p. 78.

5 Marquis d'Argens, *Réflexions critiques sur les différentes écoles de peinture* (Paris, 1752); see the riposte by Ridolfino Venuti, *Risposta alle reflessioni critiche sopra le differenti scuole di pittura del Sig. marchese d'Argens* (Lucca, 1755). Francesco Algarotti also replied in his *Saggio sopra l'Accademia di Francia che è in Roma* (Livorno, 1723; French trans. 1769). See Francis Haskell's introduction to the second edition of his *Patrons and Painters: Art and Society in Baroque Italy* (New Haven and London, 1980), where he rejects criticism that he had undervalued eighteenth-century Roman art (pp. xvi–xvii). Amongst the works which have guided subsequent re-evaluation and deeper understanding of Italian and specifically Roman art, see *Art in Rome in the Eighteenth Century*, ed. Edgar Peters Bowron and Joseph Rishel (Philadelphia, 2000) and the writings of the late Stefano Susinno, notably the compendious exhibition surveying art in nineteenth-century Rome which he conceived, *Maestà di Roma, da Napoleone all'unita d'Italia: Universale ed eternal; Capitale delle arti*, ed. Sandra Pinto, Liliana Barroero, Fernando Mazzocca, Giovanna Capitelli and Matteo Lafranconi (Milan, 2003).

6 Jeremy Black, *Italy and the Grand Tour* (New Haven and London, 2003), pp. 1–16, and Frank Felsenstein on 'The Splenetic Traveller and the Grand Tour', in his edition of Tobias Smollett, *Travels through France and Italy* ([1766] Oxford, 1979), pp. xv–xxv.

7 Christian Michel (ed.), *Le Voyage d'Italie de Charles-Nicolas Cochin (1758)* (Rome, 1991); Anne Bush, 'The Roman Guidebook as a Cartographic Space', in R. Wrigley (ed.), *Regarding Romantic Rome* (Oxford, 2007).

8 R. S. Pine-Coffin, *Bibliography of British and American Travel in Italy to 1860* (Florence, 1974); Gilles Bertrand, *Le Grand Tour revisité: Pour une archéologie du tourisme; Le voyage des Français en Italie (milieu XVIIIe siècle – début XIXe siècle)* (Rome, 2008); Jeremy Black, *The British Abroad: The Grand Tour in the Eighteenth Century* (Stroud, 1992, new edn 2003).

9 Stendhal, *Œuvres posthumes: Journal d'Italie*, ed. Paul Arbelet (Paris, 1911), p. 57; see also Stendhal, *Journal*, 4 vols (Paris, 1932), vol. 3, p. 208 (9 March 1811).

10 Pascal Griener, *La République de l'œil: L'Expérience de l'art au siècle des Lumières* (Paris, 2010), pp. 136–7.

11 Paul O'Keeffe, *A Genius for Failure: The Life of Benjamin Robert Haydon* (London, 2009), p. 189.

12 'un saisissement involontaire, une espèce de trouble inconnu....Il a fallu entrer dans Rome

pour nous guérir de Rome' (Auguste Creuzé de Lesser, *Voyage en Italie et en Sicile fait en 1801 et 1802* (Paris, 1806), preface, cit. Roland Mortier, *La Poétique des ruines en France: Ses Origines, ses variations de la Renaissance à Victor Hugo* (Geneva, 1974), p. 181 note 2).

13 Johann Wolfgang von Goethe, *Italian Journey* (14 March 1788), cit. W.D. Robson-Scott, *The Younger Goethe and the Visual Arts* (Cambridge, 1981), p. 119, where Goethe's tidying up of his reactions and aperçus is discussed.

14 Henk van Os, *Dreaming of Italy* (Mauritshuis, The Hague, 2006), p. 23, where the original German quotation is given without a source (p. 120 note 11).

15 On the modern attachment of the title to the drawing, see Gert Schiff, *Johann Heinrich Füssli, 1741–1825*, 2 vols (Zurich and Munich, 1973), cat. no. 666, pp. 478–9. See also John Knowles (ed.), *The Life and Writings of Henry Fuseli*, 3 vols (London, 1831), vol. 1, p. 147, where the artist's name change is attributed to Italianised pronunciation (having earlier in England adapted it to 'Fusseli' (ibid., p. 31); P. Tomory, *The Life and Art of Henry Fuseli* (London, 1972), p. 49. Jonah Siegel reads the title as if it was Fuseli's (*Desire and Excess: The Nineteenth-Century Culture of Art* (Princeton, 2000), p. 28). I am grateful to Asia Haut for discussing the significance of Fuseli's name.

16 Knowles, *Life and Writings of Henry Fuseli*, vol. 2, p. 181, cit. Elizabeth Cropper, *The Domenichino Affair: Novelty, Imitation, and Theft in Seventeenth-Century Rome* (New Haven and London, 2005), p. 186.

17 David Weinglass (ed.), *The Collected English Letters of Henry Fuseli* (New York and London, 1982), p. 17, 29 Sep. 1778. The drawing is catalogued in Schiff, *Johann Heinrich Füssli*, cat. no. 568. Rome could also be thought of as a place where a kind of making whole again could be symbolically effected; in 1815, J.L. David requested to be allowed to go into exile there (Richard Cantinelli, *Jacques-Louis David* (Paris, 1930), p. 11).

18 Siegel's proposed connection to the pose of a *Sleeping Faun* from Herculaneum may be relevant, but it does not in my view override the surely far more powerful link to the Laocoön (*Desire and Excess*, p. 49).

19 T. Matthews, *The Biography of John Gibson R.A., Sculptor* (London, 1911), pp. 28–9.

20 'Les siècles, les empereurs, les nations, tout ce que ce vaste mot de Rome contient de grand, d'imposant, d'intéressant, d'effrayant, sortoit successivement, ou à la fois, et environnoit mon âme' (Charles-Marguerite-Jean-Baptiste Mercier Dupaty, *Lettres sur l'Italie, en 1785*, 3rd edn (Paris, 1796), p. 150).

21 James Johnson, *Change of Air; or The Pursuit of Health; An Autumnal Excursion through France, Switzerland, and Italy, in the Year 1829, with Observations and Reflections on the Moral, Physical, and Medical Influence of Travelling-Exercise, Change of Scene, Foreign Skies, and Voluntary Expatriation* (London, 1831), p. 167.

22 J.J. Tobin (M.D.), *Journal of a Tour made in the Years 1828–1829, through Styria, Carniola, and Italy, whilst accompanying the late Sir Humphrey Davy* (London, 1832), p. 120.

23 Letter to his mother, cit. colnaghi.co.uk [Nov, 2010].

24 'Memoirs of the Painter Granet', trans. and annotated Joseph Focarino, in Edgar Munhall, *François-Marius Granet: Watercolors from the Musée Granet at Aix-en-Provence* (Frick Collection, New York, 1988).

25 'une fantôme effrayante…on aurait pu être quelqu'un de ces maîtres, chacun suivant son inclination' (Charles-Nicolas Cochin, *Lettre à un jeune artiste peintre, pensionnaire à l'Académie royale de France à Rome par M. C.* (Paris, 1773–4), p. 46).

26 [Charlotte Anne Eaton], *Rome in the Nineteenth Century containing a Complete Account of the Ruins of the Ancient City, the Remains of the Middle Ages, and the Monuments of Modern Times,…; in a Series of Letters Written during a Residence at Rome in the Years 1817 and 1818*, 3 vols (Edinburgh, 1820), vol. 2, pp. 321–5, cit. Richard E. Spear, *Domenichino*, 2 vols (New Haven and London, 1982), pp. 155–7, cat. on. 33, plates 58, 59.

27 John Izard Middleton, *Grecian Remains in Italy: A Description of Cyclopian Walls, and of Roman Antiquities; With Topographical and Picturesque Views of Ancient Latium* (London, 1812), p. 50.

28 J.E. Norton (ed.), *The Letters of Edward Gibbon to Edward Gibbon Sen.*, 3 vols (London, 1956), vol. 1, p. 184, 9 Oct. 1764; Georges A. Bonnard (ed.), *Gibbon's Journey from Geneva to Rome: His Journal from 20 April to 2 October 1764* (London, 1961).

29 24 July 1856, Richard Kendall, *Degas by Himself* (London, 1987), p. 14.

30 Johann Joachim Winckelmann, *History of the Art of Antiquity*, trans. Harry Francis Mallgrave (Los Angeles, 2006), p. 189.

31 Walter Benjamin, *The Arcades Project*, ed. Rolf Tiedemann, trans. Howard Eiland and Kevin McLaughlin (Cambridge, Mass., and London, 1999), p. 417. In German: 'Zieht nicht in Rom selbst das Träumen gebahnte Straßen?' (Walter Benjamin, *Das Passagen-Werk. Gesammelte Schriften*, vol. 5.1, ed. Rolf Tiedemann (Frankfurt / Main, 1991), p. 525). This is an adjustment of 'take the high road'; I am grateful to Dario Gamboni for helping me to revise this translation.

32 Munhall, *François-Marius Granet*, p. 20. On the convention of moonlit visits to the Colosseum, see Mortier, *La Poétique des ruines en France*, p. 196.

33 'tout ce qui séparent de l'Antique est assoupi et les ruines se relèvent' (letter of 7 February 1805, cit. Roland Mortier, *La Poétique des ruines en France*, p. 196. See more generally Robert Casillo, *The Empire of Stereotypes: Germaine de Staël and the Idea of Italy* (London, 2006).

34 A.P. Oppé (ed.), 'The Memoirs of Thomas Jones', *Walpole Society*, vol. 32, 1951, p. 55.

35 Marie Bonaparte, Anna Freud and Ernst Kris (eds), *The Origins of Psychoanalysis: Letters to Wilhelm Fliess, Drafts, Notes, 1887–1902 by Sigmund Freud* (London, 1954), p. 294, 27 Aug. 1899.

36 Ronald W. Clark, *Freud: The Man and the Cause* (London, 1980), p. 200.

37 Carl E. Schorske, *Fin-de-siècle Vienna: Politics and Culture* (London, 1980), p. 192. See also the account of Freud's travels by the psychiatrist Graziella Magherini, *Le Syndrome de Stendhal: Du Voyage dans les villes d'art* (Paris, 1990), pp. 123–52; Lawrence Simmons, *Freud's Italian Journey* (Amsterdam, 2006), pp. 119–43 (who notes that Jung too had a Roman phobia, p. 142 note. 11); Jonah Siegel, *Haunted Museum: Longing, Travel and the Art-Romance Tradition* (Princeton and Oxford, 2005), pp. 173–92; Jean Lombardi, *Le Compagnon des voyages de Freud* (Paris, 1988).

38 Noel Humphreys, *Rome and its Surrounding Scenery* (London, 1840), p. 1.

39 John Shearman, 'A Functional Interpretation of Villa Madama', *Römisches Jahrbuch für Kunstgeschichte*, vol. 20, 1983.

40 Mary Keele (ed.), *Florence Nightingale in Rome: Letters written by Florence Nightingale in Rome in the winter of 1847–1848* (Philadelphia, 1981), p. 27, 11 Nov. 1847. It was when passing the night in the posting inn at Storta in November 1537, the last stop before his momentous encounter with Rome, that Ignatius Loyola had had a vision; see Bruno Foucart (ed.), *Camille de Tournon: Le Préfet de la Rome napoléonienne 1809–1814* (Rome, 2001), p. 69.

41 Yves-Marie Bercé, 'Influence de la maladie sur l'histoire événementielle du Latium, XVI–XIXe siècles', in Neithard Bulst and Robert Delort (eds), *Maladies et société (XIIe–XVIIIe siècles): Actes du colloque di Bielefeld, Novembre 1986* (Paris, 1989), p. 235; Hanns Gross, 'L'Agro Romano', in *Rome in the Age of the Enlightenment: The Post-Tridentine Syndrome and the Ancien Régime* (Cambridge, 1990), p. 155. On travellers' traversal of the *campagna* see Attilio Brilli, *Il "Petit Tour": Itinerario minori del viaggio in Italia* (Milan, 1988), pp. 117–33.

42 'Savez-vous ce que c'est que cette campagne fameuse? C'est une quantité prodigieuse et continue de petites collines stériles, incultes, absolument désertes, tristes, et horribles au dernier point' (Abbé Charles de Brosses, *Lettres familières écrites d'Italie en 1739 et 1740*, 2 vols (Paris, n.d.), vol. 1, p. 308).

43 'Il m'est impossible...de vous dire ce qu'on éprouve, lorsque Rome vous apparaît tout-à-coup du milieu des ses royaumes vides....elle a l'air de se lever pour vous, de la tombe où elle était couchée' (letter to Fontanès, 10 Jan. 1804, cit. Yves Hersant (ed.), *Italies: Anthologie des voyageurs français aux XVIIIe et XIXe siècles* (Paris, 1988), p. 103.

44 'Le vetturino me dit tout-à-coup d'un air nonchalant, en se versant un verre de vin: "Ecco Roma signore!" Et, sans se retourner, il me montrait du doigt la croix de Saint-Pierre. Ce peu de mots opéra en moi une révolution complète; je ne saurais exprimer le trouble, le saisissement, que me causa l'aspect lointain de la ville éternelle, au milieu de cette immense plaine nue et désolée....Tout à mes yeux devint grand, poétique, sublime' (Hector Berlioz, *Mémoires*, 2 vols (Paris, 1966), vol. 1, p. 195). On Berlioz in Rome, see also David Cairns, *Berlioz: The Making of an Artist 1803–1832* (London, 1989), p. 464, and Brian Grosskurth,

'Solitude as Style', in Richard Wrigley (ed.), *Regarding Romantic Rome* (Basel and Oxford, 2007).

45 Augustus Hare, *Walks in Rome*, 15th edn, 2 vols (London and New York, 1902), vol. 1, pp. 5–6.

46 'commande l'enthousiasme…forcent à l'admiration…[l]es réalités qui lui manquent' (J.B. Michel, *Recherches médico-topographiques sur Rome et l'Agro romano* (Rome, 1813), p. 2).

47 'soupirait…depuis longtemps après l'Italie, cette terre promise de l'artiste…les mystères de l'art' (Paul Carpentier, 'Notice sur M. De Montabert, peintre et homme de lettres', in Paillot de Montabert, *L'Artistaire* (Paris, 1855), p. x).

48 'le plus grand nombre [of arrivals] n'aborde Rome qu'en frémissant, prévenus par je ne sais quelle voix ennemie qui leur a signalé la ville sainte comme un foyer perpétuel de fièvre et de mort!' (Dr Bérard, 'De l'hygiène de Rome, ou quelques avis utile à la santé des étrangers qui visitent cette ville', *Journal des connaissances médico-chirurgicales*, no. 5, Nov. 1847). On the way travellers flinched as they prepared for an 'assault' on their emotions, see Alfred J.B. Rivoire, *Essai sur la topographie et le climat de la ville de Rome et du bassin romain* (Montpellier, 1853), p. 22.

49 Attilio Brilli, *Il 'Petit Tour'* (Milan, 1988); Edward Chaney, *The Grand Tour and the Great Rebellion: Richard Lassels and 'The Voyage of Italy' in the Seventeenth Century* (Geneva, 1985).

50 'Mais rien ne me décourage; je sens que j'irois au bout du monde s'il le falloit' (Antoine Sérieys (ed.), (*Voyage en Italie de M. l'Abbé Barthélemy*, 2nd edn (Paris, 1802), p. 16).

51 Keele, *Florence Nightingale in Rome* p. 27, 11 Nov. 1847.

52 'Il faut que je commence par errer de [côté et d'autre, pour user cette première impatience de voir, qui m'empêcheroit toujours de regarder' (Charles-Marguerite-Jean-Baptiste Mercier Dupaty, *Lettres sur l'Italie en 1785* (Paris, 1788), p. 152).

53 'J'avais désiré trop vivement, le matin, d'arriver à Rome pour que mes impressions eussent conservé leur fraîcheur. J'entrai dans le faubourg de cette ville, comme j'aurais traversé Passy' (Etienne-Jean Delécluze, *Carnet de route d'Italie (1823–1824). Impressions romaines*, ed. Robert Baschet (Paris, 1942), p. 21).

54 'un chaos…de choses admirables et d'objets fort laids, de monuments de tous les siècles….couches de terres différentes que le temps et les révolutions naturelles ont accumulées à la surface du globe' (*Carnet de route*, p. 23).

55 Jean-Jacques Rousseau, *Confessions*, 2 vols (Paris, 1968), vol. 1, pp. 196–7. See J. Rustin and J.P. Schneider, 'Le Motif de l'arrivée à Paris dans les romans français du XVIIIe siècle', *Images de la ville au XVIIIe siècle* (Strasbourg, 1984).

56 Letter to Romain Colomb, 11 Nov. 1825, in Stendhal, *Correspondance de Stendhal, 1800–1842*, 3 vols (Paris, 1908), vol. 2, p. 397. See also Delécluze, *Carnet de route*, p. 22. On Montaigne's similar experience in 1580, see Eric Macphail, *The Voyage to Rome in French Renaissance Literature*, Stanford French and Italian Studies (Saratoga, Calif., 1990), p. 172.

57 'Non, cette ville, ce n'est pas Rome; c'est son cadavre; cette campagne, où elle gît, est son tombeau; et cette populace, qui fourmille au milieu d'elle, des vers qui la dévorent' (Dupaty, *Lettres*, p. 149). On Rome as a tomb see Margaret M. Macgowan, *The Vision of Rome in Late Renaissance France* (New Haven and London, 2000), pp. 188–90, 212–14, 228, 267–8, 281, 394 notes 33 and 35, 396 note 53.

58 'ossuaire des villes mortes' (Théophile Gautier, *Italia* (Paris, 1852), cit. Hersant, *Italies*, p. 415).

59 Umberto Apollonio, *Futurist Manifestoes* (London, 1973), p. 22.

60 Mrs Russell Barrington, *The Life and Letters of Frederic Baron Leighton of Stretton*, 2 vols (London, 1906), vol. 1, p. 191.

61 See Antoinette Le Normand, *La Tradition classique et l'esprit romantique: Les Sculpteurs de l'Académie de France à Rome de 1824 à 1840* (Rome, 1981), pp. 23–34.

62 Thomas W. Gaehtgens and Jacques Lugand, *Joseph-Marie Vien, peintre du Roi (1716–1809)* (Paris, 1988), pp. 294–6.

63 'qui nous fait trotter de plus belle tant que la journée dura, de sorte qu'en trois jours de temps nous avons parcouru tout Rome et une grande partie des églises' (Charles Clément, *Prud'hon: Sa Vie, ses œuvres et sa correspondance* (Paris, 1872), p. 102).

64 Charles Clément, *Léopold Robert d'après sa correspondance inédite* (Paris, 1875), p. 133.

65 'à courir comme des enfants à tout ce que [leur semble] curieux' (Stendhal, *Promenades dans Rome*, 3 vols (Paris, 1958), vol. 1, p. 11, cit. Le Normand, *La Tradition classique* p. 24). Elsewhere, Stendhal

explained that French visitors underwent a change of pace as the Roman climate had its effect on them: 'Il est de fait qu'un mois de séjour à Rome change l'allure du Français le plus semillant. Il ne marche plus avec la rapidité qu'il avait les premiers jours; il n'est plus précis pour rien. Dans les climats froids, le travail est nécessaire à la circulation; dans les pays chauds, le *divino far niente* est le premier bonheur' (Stendhal, *Vies de Haydn, Mozart, et Métastase* (Paris, 1928), pp. 401–2).

66 'J'ai couru tout ce jour' (F.R. Chateaubriand, *Œuvres romanesques et voyages*, ed. Maurice Regard, 2 vols (Paris, 1969), vol. 1, p. 1437).

67 H. James, *Letters*, vol. 1, 1843–1875, ed. Leon Edel, p. 160, Oct. 30, 1869 (London, 1974). Could this be an echo?

68 'l'ivresse des merveilles d'Italie' (C.L. de Saint-Yves, *Observations sur les arts* (Paris, 1748), cit. Jean Locquin, *La Peinture d'histoire en France de 1747 à 1785* (Paris, 1912, reprint 1976), p. 96).

69 'où trouver des mots pour peindre le bonheur parfaite goûté avec délices et sans satiété par un âme sensible jusqu'à l'anéantissement et à la folie?' (*Promenades dans Rome*, cit. Jytte Walker Ditlevsen, *Inspirations italiennes dans les œuvres de Chateaubriand, Stendhal, Barrès, Suarès* (Turin, 1962), p. 43). Elsewhere he wrote of 'ce divin mélange de volupté et d'ivresse morale' (*Promenades*, p. 49).

70 George Eliot, *Middlemarch* (Harmondsworth, 1965), p. 225. This passage is discussed in Q.D. Leavis, 'A Note on Literary Indebtedness: Dickens, George Eliot, Henry James', *The Hudson Review*, vol. 8, no. 3, Autumn 1955, and Patricia Meyer Spacks, '"Splendid falsehoods": English Accounts of Rome, 1760–1798', *Prose Studies*, vol. 3, no. 3, 1980, 3, p. 209.

71 'un terrible stimulant' (E. Viollet-le-Duc, *Lettres d'Italie 1836–1837, adressées à sa famille*, ed. Geneviève Viollet-le-Duc (Paris, 1971), p. 232 (13 Jan. 1837)).

72 'fièvre d'art', 'si féconde en progrès', 'une tempête intérieure, bien cruelle et bien violente' (ibid., p. 236 (17 Jan. 1837)).

73 'un terrible creuset d'où il faut qu'il sorte pur' (ibid., p. 246 (8 Feb. 1837)).

74 'une stupéfaction, un abalourdissement complet' (ibid., p. 187 (31 Oct. 1837)).

75 'Histoire de Julien de Parme racontée par lui-même' (1794), *L'Artiste*, 1862, new period, vol. 1, 15 Feb., 4th livraison, p. 85.

76 William Bemrose, *The Life and Works of Joseph Wright A.R.A., commonly called 'Wright of Derby'* (London and Derby, 1885), p. 32 (22 May 1774).

77 Ibid., p. 34 (4 May 1775).

78 William Hayley, *The Life of Romney* (London, 1809), p. 55; see also Bemrose, *Life and Works of Joseph Wright*, p. 28.

79 See Cecilia Powell, *Turner in the South: Rome, Naples, Florence* (New Haven and London, 1987), pp. 36–50, and James Hamilton, *Turner and Italy* (Edinurgh, 2009).

80 'Il y a sans doute beaucoup à profiter à Rome, mais je me suis fait une échelle de beauté qui me fait admettre ou regretter une chose belle ou moins, ce qui fait que les extraits que j'ai à faire ici seront moins nombreux et plus judicieusement choisis. Mais j'espère toujours en retirer une belle moisson. Je n'ai, jusqu'ici, pas fait grand chose et il est impossible de faire autrement: on travaillerait sans cela sans discernement et tout à coté. Les beautés de tout genre sont ici les unes sur les autres et on est assommé de voir; ce n'est que peu à peu que l'on revient de son étonnement et que l'on voit bien' (H. Lapauze, *Le Roman d'amour de M. Ingres* (Paris, 1910), pp. 123–4, 21 Feb. 1807, to M. Forestier).

81 C.N. Cochin, *Lettre à un jeune artiste peintre …* (Paris, 1773–4), p. 46.

82 'Sortis de France sans connaître ni les sites ni les productions de leurs pays, séduits en arrivant ici par le charlatanisme italien autant par la vue des monuments de l'antiquité, leurs yeux semblent pour la première fois s'ouvrir à la nature et aux arts' (André Thouin, *Voyage dans la Belgique, la Hollande et l'Italie* (Paris, 1841), p. 303 (the travels took place in 1796–8)).

83 'During the time he [Boucher] spent there [in Italy], the poor state of his health prevented him from pursuing all the studies he wished to do' ([Denis Pierre Papillon de la Ferté], *Extrait des différens ouvrages publiés sur les vies des peintres par M. P. D. L. F.*, 2 vols (Paris, 1776), vol. 2, pp. 657–62). The [Anon.], *Discours sur l'origine et l'état actuel de la peinture* (Paris, 1785) repeats this statement (p. 7), both trans. and cit. *François Boucher, 1703–1770* (Met-

ropolitan Museum of Art, New York, 1986), p. 46. Alaistair Laing puts it thus: '[Boucher] appears to have been unmoved by what he saw there, and also possibly prevented by illness from either succeeding in the Concorso Clementino or working on anything to be sent back to France' ('Boucher: The Search for an Idiom', ibid., p. 56. However, in the same volume, Pierre Rosenberg suggests that Boucher's selective approach may also be explained by his precocious artistic maturity ('The Mysterious Beginnings of the Young Boucher', ibid.).

84 'N'allez pas faire Rome, comme tant d'autres. Tachez de ne pas vous y couler, rappellez-vous sans cesse votre charmante composition de Senèque.…l'antique ne me séduira pas, il manque d'entrain, et ne remue pas!' (Louis Hautecoeur, *Louis David* (Paris, 1954), p. 31); the source is Jules David, who merely refers to 'un graveur'; Antoine Schnapper, *Jacques-Louis David, 1746–1824* (Réunion des Musées Nationaux, Paris, 1989), p. 41.

85 'étourdi de toutes les beautés' (autobiographical text, *c.*1800 (École des beaux-arts), cit. Daniel and Guy Wildenstein, *Louis David: Recueil de documents complémentaires au catalogue complet de l'œuvre de l'artiste* (Paris, 1973), p. 156).

86 'état d'anéantissement' (*David a Roma* (Académie de France à Rome, Rome, 1981), pp. 228–9). Jean-Baptiste Pierre ascribed David's harmful overwork to 'quelque passion violente', which he had resolved to sacrifice in order to come to Italy (ibid.). For a recent account of David in Rome which emphasises his connections to the local artistic context, see Christopher M.S. Johns, 'The Roman Experience of Jacques-Louis David, 1775–80', in Dorothy Johnson (ed.), *Jacques-Louis David: New Perspectives* (Newark, 2006), pp. 63–4. For evidence of David's improved perspective on Rome as viewed from Naples see David to Vien, 27 July 1778: 'Ce voyage m'étoit d'autant plus nécessaire qu'il m'a appris à apprécier Rome; il n'est point de choses ici que je n'y voye qui ne me fasse dire! Oh Rome, où es-tu? Je vois bien que tu es la seule dans le monde puisque Naples tant renommée n'est rien à côté de toye' (Gaehtgens and Lugand, *Joseph-Marie Vien*, p. 325). On Berlioz's flight from Rome in the interests of self-preservation, see David Cairns, *Berlioz*, vol. 1, *The Making of an Artist* (London, 1989), pp. 437–8.

87 Annie Becq, *Genèse de l'esthétique moderne: De la Raison classique à l'imagination créatrice, 1680–1814*, 2 vols (Pisa, 1984), vol. 2, pp. 695–740.

88 John Fleming, *Robert Adam and his Circle in Edinburgh and Rome* (London, 1962), p. 183.

89 Ibid., p. 191.

90 D. E. Williams, *Life and Correspondance of T. E. Lawrence*, 2 vols (London, 1831), cit. Kenneth Garlick, *Sir Thomas, Lawrence: A Complete Catalogue of the Oil Paintings* (London, 1989), p. 18, emphasis in original. Lawrence's comments are a positive version of satires on the spurious belief that those who succeeded in engaging in Italian travel would be transformed.

91 'que l'état inquiet de son esprit lui faisait éviter' (Jules David, *Le Peintre Louis David: Souvenirs et documents inédits*, 2 vols (Paris, 1880–2), vol. 1, p. 10).

92 Pierre Rosenberg and Udolpho van de Sandt, *Pierre Peyron, 1744–1814* (Paris, 1983), p. 15. On the question of David being in Naples with Quatremère see *David a Roma*, p. 238.

93 'Je suis pris trois ou quatre fois par mois d'une forte envie d'émigrer en Italie. J'ai renoncé à courir la chance du prix de l'Académie. Comme je ne désire pas aller à Rome pour y bien manger et y loger dans un palais, je saurais aussi m'y contenter de peu comme je le fais ici' (Raymond Escholier, *Delacroix, peintre, graveur, écrivain* (Paris, 1926), p. 58 (30 July 1821)).

94 'Cette idée me travaille continuellement…amitié, amitié et Rome!' (Eugène Delacroix, *Correspondance générale*, ed. André Jouin, 5 vols (Paris, 1935–8), vol. 1, p. 140, 15 April 1822).

95 'En Italie!…Je ne peux penser à y aller sans toi. C'est un des rêves que j'ai le plus caressé' (ibid., vol. 1, p. 175, 13 Feb. 1826). According to Anita Brookner, Stendhal invited Delacroix to accompany him to Italy in 1830 (*The Genius of the Future* (London, 1971), p. 54. Letter to Frederic Mercey, Trieste, 2 Nov. 1830: 'Comment passer les soirées? Voilà le grand probleme. Ce n'est pas l'Italie, ce n'est que l'antichambre. Je cherche à organiser un troupe pour l'hiver prochain si j'y suis. J'ai proposé l'engagement à MM. de Lacroix et de Sainte-Beuve' (Stendhal, *Correspondance de Stendhal* (Paris, 1967), p. 192). Delacroix's wanderlust took the form of a Roman painting (now Basel, Öffentliche Kunstsammlung, Kunstmuseum, Basel; *c.*1825, 32.5 ×

40 cm, painted for Alexandre Du Sommerard): 1827 Salon *livret*, 'Un pâtre de la campagne de Rome, blessé mortellement, se traîne au bord d'un marais pour se désaltérer'; entered in register of works submitted to Salon jury as 'Brigand se traînant près d'un ruisseau'; 'Brigand blessé' and 'La Mort du brigand' were used as titles on different states of the Mouilleron lithograph published during Delacroix's lifetime; see Lee Johnson, *The Paintings of Eugène Delacroix: A Critical Catalogue*, 6 vols (Oxford, 1981–9), vol. 1, pp. 171–2, cat. no. 162. Paul Joannides proposes the subject is 'clearly based on a passage from the second canto of [Byron's] *Lara*' ('Delacroix and Modern Literature', in Beth S. Wright (ed.), *The Cambridge Companion to Delacroix*, (Cambridge, 2001), p. 145).

96 'il ne me manque qu'un bon ami avec lequel je pourrais vivre et travailler' (Charles Clément, *Géricault: Étude biographique et critique* (Paris, 1868), p. 85).

97 'cuisine bourgeoise...qui engraisse leur corps et anéantit leur âme' (ibid., pp. 108–9 note).

98 Régis Michel, *Géricault*, 2 vols (Paris, 1996), vol. 1, p. 837.

99 Marc J. Gotlieb, *The Plight of Emulation: Ernest Meissonier and French Salon Painting* (Princeton, 1996), quoting Gustave Planche, 'Géricault,' *Revue des deux mondes*, vol. 2, 1851, pp. 518–21.

100 'Tout ici est néant pour moi....Adieu mon ami, une lettre de vous fera plus pour ma tranquillité que toutes ces beautés ruinés' (Clément, *Prud'hon*, p. 109).

101 See Helen Weston, 'Prud'hon in Rome: Pages from an Unpublished Sketchbook', *Burlington Magazine*, vol. 126, no. 970, Jan. 1984.

102 'Ah! Sans doute ces palais, ces monuments que l'orgueil des conquérants de l'univers a élevés pour dire à la postérité que leurs idées étaient aussi grandes que le monde....Mais ce que je ne retrouverai pas, ce sont mes amis' (Henri-Auguste Jouin, *David d'Angers, sa vie, son œuvre, ses écrits et ses contemporains*, 2 vols (Paris, 1878), vol. 2, p. 36 (6 June 1811)).

103 'Les jeunes artistes établis à Rome dans la Villa Médicis forment, dit-on, une oasis parfaitement isolée de la société italienne et où règnent despotiquement toutes les petites convenances qu'ont étiolés les arts à Paris' (Stendhal, *Promenades dans*

Rome, 2 vols (Paris, 1829), vol. 2, p. 282). See Kathy Mclauchlan, 'French Artists in Rome 1815–1863' (Courtauld Institute of Art, University of London, 2001).

104 'il n'existe parmi eux la même union que de ton tems; il y a des coteries; aussi sous ce rapport, le séjour de Rome a-t-il beaucoup perdu de ses agréments' (Schnetz in Rome to Navez in Paris, 30 July 1826, *Lettres inédites de Jean-Victor Schnetz à François-Joseph Navez: Une amitié italienne* (Flers, 2000), p. 80).

105 'Je crains votre Rome comme la peste' (Denis Coutagne, *François-Marius Granet 1775–1849: Une vie pour la peinture* (Paris, 2008), p. 114) originally published in 'Granet son entourage', *Archives de l'art Français*, new period, vol. 31, 1995, pp. 2–3 (Révoil to Granet, 25 May 1806).

106 'malheureuse manie de vivre comme un sauvage' (*Jean-Germain Drouais, 1763–1788* (Musée des Beaux-Arts, Rennes, 1985), p. 15). For a reading of David's relation to Drouais and Girodet in terms of oedipal claustrophobia, see Thomas Crow, *Emulation: Making Artists for Revolutionary France* (New Haven and London, 1995).

107 *Correspondance de François Gérard, peintre d'histoire*, ed. Henri Gérard, 2 vols (Paris, 1867), vol. 1, p. 59, 11 Aug. 1790.

108 Ménageot to d'Angiviller, 7 July 1790, CDAFR, vol. 15, p. 432.

109 'Si c'est un abrégé de l'école du monde, il me semble que les leçons sont ici fort rebutantes; elles ne changeront point mon être moral, elles n'influeront que sur l'habit ou l'enveloppe' (*Correspondance de François Gérard*, p. 63, 28 Sept. 1790).

110 Johann Wolfgang von Goethe, *Italian Journey, 1786–1788*, trans. W. H. Auden and Elizabeth Mayer (Harmondsworth, 1970), p. 345.

111 Roger de Piles, *Cours de peinture par principes* ([1708] Paris, 1989), p. 12. Jonathan Richardson (senior) never saw the Stanze, but still reckoned the Hampton Court tapestries were a better way to see them and that Raphael's cartoons were his best work; see Carol Gibson-Wood, *Jonathan Richardson: Art Theorist of the Enlightenment* (New Haven and London, 2000), pp. 223–4, where Vleughels's rebuttal of the French translation of *An Account of some of the Statues, Bas-reliefs, Drawings and Pictures in Italy, &c. with Remarks* (1722),

and the associated debate around freedom of judgement, is also discussed (p. 229). On Vleughels, see Bernard Hercenberg, *Nicolas Vleughels: Peintre et directeur de l'Académie de France à Rome, 1668–1737* (Paris, 1975).

112 Joseph Jérôme le Français de Lalande, *Voyage d'un français en Italie*, 10 vols (Paris, 1786), vol. 3, pp. 568–9. Murat, uninhibited by artistic niceties or apprehensions but nonetheless having made the Loggie his first visit in Rome, on seeing their poor condition had glazed windows installed within two weeks, according to Lady Morgan (*Italy*, 3 vols (London, 1821), vol. 2, p. 387).

113 Lapauze, *Histoire*, vol. 2, pp. 96–7, letter to chevalier Agricola [?], 28 Aug. 1812.

114 James Northcote, *The Life of Sir Joshua Reynolds*, 2 vols, (2nd edn (London, 1819), vol. 1, p. 33. William Hazlitt noted how he had seen 'all that is fine in the Vatican' first in the Louvre, apart from these immovable works ('The Vatican', in *Criticisms on Art* (London, 1844), p. 173).

115 'quoique tous ceux qui les voient s'écrient d'admiration, la plupart ne le font que parce qu'ils ont ouï dire que du consentement de tout le monde ce sont des choses admirables. Le plus grand nombre des ouvrages de ce grand maître ne cause pas ce subit étonnement' (C. N. Cochin, 'Sur l'utilité du voyage d'Italie', conférence 4 March 1752, Paris, ENSBA, MS no. 194), cit. Christian Michel, 'Les Relations artistiques entre l'Italie et la France (1680–1750): La contradiction des discours et de la pratique', *Studiolo*, no. 1, 2002, p. 13).

116 E. Malone, *The Works of Joshua Reynolds, Knt., Late President of the Royal Academy*, 5th edn, 2 vols (London, 1819), vol. 1, pp. x–xi. He adds that 'one of the first painters of France' had told him the same story.

117 Malone, *Works*, p. xxi. Reassuring James Barry (sometime before May 1769), Reynolds also reiterated the need for persistence in relation to the works of Michelangelo, those things which were the supreme justifications for being in Rome. 'If you should not relish them at first, which may probably be the case, never cease looking till you feel something like inspiration come at you, till you think every other painter insipid in comparison, and to be admired only for petty excellencies' (John Ingamells and John Edgecumbe (eds), *The Letters of Joshua Reynolds* (New Haven and London, 2000), p. 30).

118 'Ne vous affligez pas, si vous ne trouvez point encore Raphael tout ce qu'il est en effet. Comptez [?] que le soleil se lève pour vous, que vous entrez à votre réveil dans le plus bel endroit de la nature, que tout vous éblouit, et que les fleurs ou les objets les plus coloriés qui se trouvent plus près de vous sont les seuls objets dont vous soyez frappé, et que vous ne l'êtes point par les grands effets de l'air et du ciel, et qu'enfin, dans cet état d'éblouissement, les grands phénomènes de la nature doivent vous échapper. Je n'oserais avouer combien j'ai été de temps sans presque me douter des beautés et du sublime de ce même Raphael, et pendant quel espace de temps je ne l'ai vu que par ses défauts. Ne vous pressez point; il viendra quelque jour un coup de lumière dont vous serez éclairé; alors vous verrez et vous verrez bien' ('Lettre à [Louis] Lagrenée', 12 Jan. 1751, in André Fontaine (ed.), *Vie des artistes du XVIIIe siècle* (Paris, 1910), pp. 210–13).

119 Reported by Delafontaine, cit. Wildenstein, *Recueil*, p. 9 item 58, and Hautecoeur, *Louis David*, pp. 47–9. On cataract operations in the eighteenth century, see Arnold Sorsby, *A Short History of Opthalmology* (London, 1933), pp. 41–3. Jal wrote that David really only awoke to Rome after disappointment with Naples, where he went to recuperate after 'avoir été opéré de la cataracte' and to have understood that 'procéder comme les anciens et comme Raphael, c'est être vraiment artiste' (Auguste Jal, 'Notes sur Louis David, peintre d'histoire', *Revue étrangère*, vol. 55, Sept. 1845, p. 624, cit. Schnapper, *Jacques-Louis David*, p. 63).

120 Alexandre Lenoir, 'Fragonard', in *Biographie universelle et moderne* (Paris, 1816), cit. Jean-Pierre Cuzin, *Jean-Honoré Fragonard: Life and Work* (New York, 1988), p. 251 note 11. See also *J. H. Fragonard e H. Robert a Roma* (Académie de France à Rome, Rome, 1990).

121 Cuzin, *Fragonard*, p. 46. On Natoire's encouragement of copying (including another of the same painting by Bonvoison), see Susanna Caviglia-Brunel, *Charles-Joseph Natoire (1700–1777)* (Paris, 2012), pp. 122–3 note 697. Although Cortona was often singled out as having been responsible for the decline of seventeenth-century Italian art (e.g. 'le goût de ce même Cortone, tant vanté par les Ama-

teurs, a seul causé la décadence des Arts en Italie': *Journal de Paris*, 11 Sep. 1783, p. 1066), Fragonard's instructions relate to Cortona's classicising paintings, rather than the dramatic ceiling paintings such as that in the Palazzo Barberini. By the mid-eighteenth century such censure was selectively applied to his 'baroque' works. For example, David wrote of his artistic horizons on his arrival in Rome, 'Cortone, hélas, le dirai-je, avait encore des charme[s?] sur moi' (autobiographical text, c.1800, cit. Wildenstein, *Recueil*, p. 157). See Louis-Antoine Prat, '"Cortone, hélas…": Sur deux dessins de Jacques-Louis David', in Olivier Bonfait, Véronique Gerard Powell and Philippe Sénéchal (eds), *Curiosité: Études d'histoire de l'art en l'honneur d'Antoine Schnapper* (Paris, 1998). That this distinction within Cortona's work is the product of a relatively novel form of academic decorum is indicated by the fact that in the earlier part of the century Nicolas Vleughels, then director of the Académie, recommended both the St Paul and the Barberini ceiling to his students (Hercenberg, *Nicolas Vleughels*, p. 17). La Font de Saint-Yenne had included Cortona with Raphael and Domenichino as Italian artists who were desirable models for French artists in *Réflexions sur quelques causes de l'état présent de la peinture en France avec un examen des principaux ouvrages exposés au Louvre le mois d'Août 1746* (The Hague, 1747), pp. 10–11. Prud'hon made a copy of the Barberini ceiling; see Weston, 'Prud'hon in Rome' in Martin Myrone, *Bodybuilding: Reforming Masculinities in British Art 1750–1810* (New Haven and London, 2005), pp. 71–2, 81–2, on Nathaniel Dance's c.1766–7 copy and its contemporary critical context.

122 Johann Christian von Mannlich, *Histoire de ma vie*, ed. K.H. Bender and H. Kleber, 2 vols (Trier, 1989–93), vol. 1, p. 21, cit. Jo Hedley, *François Boucher: Seductive Visions* (London, 2004), p. 33.

123 Bergeret de Grancourt, *Voyage d'Italie, 1773–1774: Lettres écrites par M. Bergeret de Grancourt au cours de son voyage en compagnie de Fragonard*, ed. Jacques Wilhelm (Paris, 1948), pp. 94–5. See André Chastel, 'Michel-Ange en France', in *Fables, formes, figures*, 2 vols (Paris, 1978), vol. 1, pp. 189–207.

124 'il avait tremblé devant les maîtres d'Italie, qu'il avait alors douté de lui-même et avait été longtemps à se retrouver de son trouble' (Clément, *Géricault*, pp. 82–3).

125 'accès de nerfs' (letter to Louise Crozet, 20 Oct. 1816, cit. Brookner, *Genius of the Future*, p. 45).

126 Gustave Flaubert, *Correspondance*, 5 vols (Paris, 1973), vol. 1, p. 772.

127 Bemrose, *Life and Works of Joseph Wright*, p. 42. Cf. Julia Cartwright's encounter with Lord Leighton in the Sistine Chapel 'deep in study. He had been there since 9 o'clock and lay on his back and in all sorts of attitudes studying every part, true artist that he is!' (Angela Emanuel (ed.), *A Bright Remembrance: The Diaries of Julia Cartwright 1851–1924* (London, 1989), p. 118, 16 Oct. 1880).

128 Malone, *Works*, vol. 1, p. lxxxix.

129 Goethe, *Italian Journey*, p. 104.

130 Letter to the Herders, 2 Dec. 1786, cit. Robson-Scott, *The Younger Goethe*, p. 120. See Sophie Thomas on Goethe in *Romanticism and Visuality: Fragments, History, Spectacle* (London, 2007). Another example of Goethe's connection to artists' experience of Italy is found in Léopold Robert's report that he travelled south from the Alps singing 'Kennst du das Land?' (Félix-Sébastien Feuillet de Conches, *Léopold Robert, sa vie, ses œuvres et sa correspondance* (Paris, 1848), p. 36. This was likely to have been in the arrangement either by Johann Friedrich Reichardt or Carl Friedrich Zelter; see Steven Paul Scher, 'Mignon in Music', in Gerhart Hoffmeister (ed.), *Goethe in Italy, 1786–1986* (Amsterdam, 1988). Thanks to Donald Ellmann and Daria Santini for advice on lieder and Goethe respectively.

131 Goethe's text was not published until 1816; see further on this Robson-Scott, *The Younger Goethe*, pp. 110–49; see also Stefan Oswald, *Italienbilder: Beiträge zur Wandlung der deutschen Italienauffassung 1770–1840* (Heidelberg, 1985). I am grateful to Andreas Vejvar for fruitful discussion on German Romantic attitudes to Rome.

132 Leslie A. Marchand (ed.), *'So late into the night': Byron's Letters and Journals*, vol. 5, 1816–1817 (London, 1976), p. 221, Rome, 9 May 1817.

133 Carl Thompson, *The Suffering Traveller and the Romantic Imagination* (Oxford, 2007), notes Byron's awareness of guidebooks by Eustace and Forsyth etc.

134 'Le lieu est propre à la réflexion et à la rêverie: je remonte dans une vie passée; je sens le poids du présent, et je cherche à pénétrer mon avenir' (F.R.

Chateaubriand, *Œuvres complètes*, 26 vols (Paris, 1826–31), vol. 7, p. 169).

135 Alexander Dru (ed.), *The Letters of Jacob Burckhardt* (London, 1955), pp. 96–100.

136 'Tu ne peut t'imaginer comme l'Italie développe le goût que l'on peut avoir pour l'histoire. On vit ici triplement; on vit dans le présent, dans l'avenir (car l'imagination sans cesse en mouvement, crée et renchérit sur ce qu'elle voit), et surtout dans le passé; je me sens des journées entières en dehors du moment actuel; je *flâne* dans le passé, et ce sont là, je t'assure, de moments d'une douceur inexprimable; rien ne me distrait ici et tout, au contraire tend à me remettre sans cesse au milieu d'un passé poétique' (Viollet-le-Duc, *Lettres*, p. 159, 3 Oct. 1836).

137 *Promenades dans Rome*, cit. Ditlevsen, *Inspirations italiennes*, p. 43.

138 'Je me trouvai ce matin, 16 octobre 1832, à San Pietro in Montorio, sur le mont Janicule, à Rome, il faisait un soleil magnifique. Un léger vent de sirocco à peine sensible faisait flotter quelques petits nuages blancs au-dessus du mont Albane: une chaleur délicieuse régnait dans l'air, j'étais heureux de vivre' (Stendhal, *Vie de Henry Brulard*, ed. H. Martineau (Paris, 1927), p. 1).

139 '[t]oute Rome ancienne et moderne [qui] se déploie à la vue....une heure ou deux' (ibid., pp. 3–4). Hazlitt had used a reverse logic to satirise modern pretentiousness in Rome: 'We stand before a picture of some great master, and fancy there is nothing between him and us: we walk under the dome of St Peter's, and it seems to grow larger with a consciousness of our presence and with the amplitude of our conceptions' ('English students at Rome', p. 206).

140 'Il ne faut pas, cher père, prendre le découragement que j'ai éprouvé à Rome pour de la folie ou de la faiblesse. Il est impossible de se faire tout-à-coup à cette grande ville: avant qu'on ait pu prendre, au milieu de ce rendez-vous des arts de tous les âges, un parti, il peut se passer beaucoup de temps. Il faut, ici, se former le goût, reprendre, pour ainsi dire, ses études de leur base, et les recommencer avec la bonne foi et la soumission d'un écolier. Je regarderais comme incapable d'être artiste celui qui, à Rome, n'y éprouverait pas cette révolution' (Viollet-le-Duc, *Lettres*, p. 257).

141 'ce déchirement intérieure, cet abandon forcé de quelques systèmes que l'on pouvait prendre pour la vérité sous l'influence factice de Paris, ne peuvent pas se faire sans quelques découragements et sans quelques regrets en voyant qu'on a été si longtemps dans une *quasi-vérité*' (ibid. Emphasis in original).

142 'Rome a changé toutes mes idées; elle m'accable; je ne puis vous rien exprimer' (Sérieys, *Voyage en Italie de M. l'Abbé Barthélemy*, p. 29, 5 Nov. 1755).

143 'Vous ne scauriez croire combien mon voyage m'a humilié; j'ai vu tant de choses que j'ignorais, et que j'ignore encore, qu'il m'a paru fou de se savoir gré de quelques connoissances superficielles' (lettre XXI, cit. Jeremiah Donovan, *Rome, Ancient and Modern: And its Environs*, 4 vols (Rome, 1842–4), vol. 1, pp. xv–xvi).

144 'On s'y sent plus petit encore que dans le désert' (Flaubert, *Œuvres*, vol. 1, pp. 769–70, letter to mother, 8 April 1851). Byron also made the comparison to desert, a terrain both had encountered: 'Rome is as the desert, where we steer / Stumbling o'er recollections' (*Childe Harold*, IV, 726–7, cit. Timothy Webb, '"City of the Soul": English Romantic Travellers in Rome', in Michael Liversidge and Catharine Edwards (eds), *Imagining Rome: British Artists and Rome in the Nineteenth Century*, (London, 1996), p. 25.

145 Allan Cunningham, *The Life of Sir David Wilkie*, 3 vols (London, 1843), vol. 2, p. 213.

146 Amaury-Duval, *L'Atelier d'Ingres* (Paris, 1924), p. 115.

147 'je suis devenu subitement voyageur, et la fièvre de voir les Raphael m'a pris' (letter to Mme Georges Charpentier, autumn 1881, cit. Barbara Ehrlich White, 'Renoir's Trip to Italy', *Art Bulletin*, vol. 60, December 1969, p. 346).

148 '[à] mon arrivée dans la ville éternelle, je sens une certaine déplaisance et je crois un moment que tout est changé; peu à peu la fièvre des ruines me gagne, et je finis, comme mille autres voyageurs, par adorer ce qui m'avait laissé froid d'abord. La nostalgie est le regret du pay natal: aux rives du Tibre on a aussi le mal du pays, mais il produit un effet opposé à son effet accoutumé: on est saisi de l'amour des solitudes et du dégoût de la patrie' (F.R. Chateaubriand, *Memoires d'outre-tombe*, 3 vols (Paris, 1951), vol. 2, p. 612).

149 'C'est par l'amour pour les beaux-arts que l'on vient à Rome, et là...cet amour vous abandonne, et, comme à l'ordinaire, la haine est sur le point de le remplacer' (Stendhal, *Promenades dans Rome* (Paris, 1973), p. 134).

150 See the classic essay by Susan Sontag, *Illness as Metaphor* (New York, 1988), and Rudolph and Margot Wittkower, *Born Under Saturn: The Character and Conduct of Artists* (London, 1963, reissued New York, 2007). Girodet's poem *Le Peintre* emphasises the artist's close acquaintance with pathological states: 'Étude périlleux: une fièvre brulante / Verse tous ses poisons dans un sang qui fermente; / Mais, du peintre accablé le talent créateur / Avec lui veille encor [*sic*] sur son lit de douleur; / Souvent, même, il ne doit qu'aux tristes maladies / Ces pensers lumineux, ces images hardies, / Que son cerveau tranquille encor tenait cachés, / Qu'en un moment plus calme en vain il eût cherchés, / Et qui, brillans éclairs au sein des noirs orages, / Sont, comme eux, trop souvent suivis d'affreux ravages!', *Le Peintre*, 'chant second', pp. 106–7, cit. Neil Macgregor, 'Girodet's Poem *Le Peintre*,' *Oxford Art Journal*, vol. 4, no. 1, July 1981.

151 'Klassisch ist das Gesunde, romantisch das Kranke' (Johann Wolfgang von Goethe, *Maximen und Reflexionen*, no. 813, in *Goethes Werke: Hamburger Ausgabe*, ed. Erich Trunz, 14 vols (Munich, 1988), vol. 12, p. 487).

152 Hazlitt, 'English Students at Rome', p. 203.

153 Ibid.

154 Ibid.

155 Ibid., p. 216.

3   SOMETHING IN THE AIR

1 Clarence J. Glacken, *Traces on the Rhodian Shore: Nature and Culture in Western Thought from Ancient Times to the End of the Eighteenth Century* (Berkeley, 1967); Vivian Nutton, *Ancient Medicine* (London and New York, 2004).

2 Giorgio Vasari, 'Life of Perugino', *Lives of the Painters, Sculptors and Architects*, 4 vols (London, 1963), vol. 2, pp. 307–8.

3 Michelangelo reported the illness of his assistant, Giovansimone, with the comment: 'I don't think the air here agrees with him' (letter to Buonanoto di Ludovico Simoni in Florence, 2 July 1508); and later that Piero Basso, although ill, had left Rome 'so much fear of the air here was put into his head, that I could not have kept him' (29 July 1508), cit. E.H. Ramsden (trans. and ed.), *The Letters of Michelangelo*, 2 vols (London, 1963), vol. 1, pp. 45–6).

4 See André Chastel, 'L'Aria: Théorie du milieu à la Renaissance', in *Fables, formes, figures*, 2 vols (Paris, 1978).

5 Julia Cartwright [Mrs Ady], *The Painters of Florence: From the Thirteenth to the Sixteenth Century*, 2nd edn (London, 1910), p. vii. Isabelle Julia, in an excellent text on Hébert's *La Malaria*, observed that he had 'subi la poésie envoûtant de l'aria di Roma' (Isabelle Julia, *La Campagne romaine à propos d'un tableau d'Hébert 'La Mal'aria'*, Petit Journal des Grandes Expositions, new series, no. 93 (Musée Hébert, Paris, 1980), p. 2).

6 See Marquis d'Argens, *Réflexions critiques sur les différentes écoles de peinture* (Paris, 1752), and Ridolfino Venuti, *Risposta alle reflessioni critiche sopra le differenti scuole di pittura del sig. marchese d'Argens* (Lucca, 1755).

7 'Est-ce à [des] causes physiques ou causes morales, ou à la réunion des unes et des autres qu'on doit attribuer l'état de langueur où la Peinture et la sculpture sont actuellement en Italie?...Sont-ce les récompenses, les occasions, l'encouragement & et l'émulation, qui manquent aux Italiens? Car ce ne sont pas les grands modèles' ('École', in *Encyclopédie*, vol. 5, p. 334).

8 'Ne seroit-ce point plutôt un caprice de la nature, qui, en fait des talens & de génie, se plaît, pour ainsi dire, à ouvrir de tems en tems des mines, qu'elle renferme ensuite absolument pour plusieurs siècles? Plusieurs des grands Peintres de l'Italie & de Flandres ont vécu & sont morts dans la misère: quelques-uns ont été persécutés, bien loin d'être encouragés. Mais la nature se joue de l'injustice de la fortune, et de celle des hommes; elle produit des génies rares au milieu d'un peuple de barbares, comme elle fait naître les plantes précieuses parmi des sauvages qui en ignorent la vertu' (ibid.).

9 'le génie de arts est un espèce d'épidémie morale?' (J.B.A. Suard, *Correspondance littéraire de Suard avec la margrave de Bayreuth, fragments inédits* [1773], ed. G. Bonno, University of California Publications

in Modern Philology, vol. 18, no. 2 (Berkeley, 1934), pp. 145–6, 166–7).

10 'Vous me demandez sans doute quelle est la raison de ces changements, et comment ces fameux écoles de Rome, de Boulogne, de Venise, ont pu cesser tout-à-coup. Je vous répondrai qu'il en est des grands hommes qui excellent dans les arts comme de ces feux aëriens qui ne paraissent que dans certaines saisons, ou comme des prodiges qui ne sont produit que dans une longue suite de siècles....génie supérieur...'[le] Ciel'...comme une fleur brillante qu'un même jour voit éclore et flétrit' (Marquis d'Argens, *Mémoires du marquis d'Argens* (Paris, 1807), p. 344).

11 'Redoublez tous vos soins pour la culture d'une si belle plante qui fera honneur à votre direction et aux arts en France', CDAFR, vol. 11, p. 365, 20 Nov. 1760; Jean-Pierre Cuzin, *Jean-Honoré Fragonard: Life and Work; Complete Catalogue of the Paintings* (New York, 1988), p. 57.

12 P.J.G. Cabanis, *Rapports du physique et du moral de l'homme* (Paris, 1802), pp. 411–12.

13 'plante qui végète comme les ronces du Colisée, plus vivace dans les ruines que dans les sillons....La plante homme naît plus forte et plus robuste en Italie qu'ailleurs....La cendre des siècles est féconde comme celle des incendies....Je sentis que l'air même de cette contrée était littéraire, et qu'on pouvait lui enlever la liberté, mais jamais le génie' (Alphonse de Lamartine, *Cours familier de littérature* (Paris, 1856–69), cit. Yves Hersant (ed.) *Italies: Anthologie des voyageurs français aux XVIIIe et XIXe siècles* (Paris, 1988), pp. 430–1). La Mettrie coined the term, *L'Homme-plante* (Potsdam, n.d.). Alfieri's formulation occurs in the context of a discussion of the possible reappearance of a republic in Italy, and the way that virtue and liberty would stimulate Italians: 'perche la pianta uomo in Italia essendovi assai piu robusta che altrove' (*Tragedie di Vittorio Alfieri*, 6 vols (Pisa, 1819), vol. 6, p. LIV). Byron quoted this in the preface to Canto XXX of *Childe Harold's Pilgrimage*: 'It has been somewhere said by Alfieri, that "La pianta uomo nasce piu robusta in Italia che qualunque terra – e que gli stessi atroci delitti che vi si commettono ne sono una prova" (*Childe Harold's Pilgrimage*, 2 vols (Brussels, 1829), vol. 1, p. 129). See Jacques Misan, *L'Italie des doctrinaires, 1817–1830: Une Image en élaboration* (Florence, 1978).

14 'Les différentes idées sont comme des plantes et des fleurs qui ne viennent pas également bien en toutes sortes de climats. Peut-être notre terroir de France n'est-il pas propre pour les raisonnements que font les Egyptiens, non plus que pour leurs Palmiers; et sans aller si loin, peut-être que les orangers qui ne viennent pas ici aussi facilement qu'en Italie, marquent-ils qu'on a en Italie un certain tour d'esprit que l'on n'a pas tout-à-fait semblable en France. Il est toujours sûr que par l'enchaînement et la dépendance réciproque qui est entre toutes les parties du monde matériel, les différences des climats qui se font sentit dans les plantes, doivent s'étendre jusques aux cerveaux, et y faire quelque effet' ([J.B.] Dubos, *Réflexions critiques sur la poésie et sur la peinture*, 7th edn, 3 vols (Paris, 1770), vol. 2, pp. 156–7; Glacken, *Traces on the Rhodian Shore*, p. 555; Fontenelle's remarks come from 'Digression sur les Anciens et les Modernes' (1687), in *Œuvres*, 3 vols (The Hague, 1728–1729), vol. 2, p. 127.

15 'sont poètes et musiciens, parce que l'air vif et serein de ces régions subtilise leur sang' (Dubos, *Réflexions critiques*, vol. 1, pp. 22, 183, vol. 3, pp. 3, 56, cit. Alfred Lombard, *L'Abbé Dubos, un initiateur de la pensée moderne, 1670–1742* (Paris, 1913), p. 250).

16 [Anon.], *A Comparative Sketch of England and Italy, with Disquisitions on National Advantages*, 2 vols (London, 1793), vol. 1, p. 103. This idea sustained the formula later recycled by the Goncourts as regards the 'soleil purement artiste de Rome, qui ne fait que des fleurs et pas de légumes' (Edmond de Goncourt, *Journal: Mémoires de la vie littéraire*, 9 vols (Paris), vol. 3, 1887–1896, p. 93, 1 May 1867.

17 'la puanteur et l'infection qui s'en exhalent, leur donnent souvent des maladies mortelles' (Dubos, *Réflexions critiques*, vol. 2, pp. 292–4). Abbé Espiard followed Dubos in believing that the climate since antiquity was milder but more unhealthy because of natural causes and 'l'industrie des hommes' (*Essais sur le génie et le caractère des nations*, 3 vols (Brussels, 1743), vol. 3, pp. 57–61, 154–6, cit. Jean Ehrard, *L'Idée de nature en France dans la première moitié du XVIIIe siècle*, 2 vols (Paris, 1963), vol. 2, pp. 715–17).

18 The pernicious effects of sulphur and alum in the Roman hinterland were also cited by Baron Alexis von Krüdener, *Voyage en Italie en 1786: Note sur l'Italie, la Savoie, Lyon et la Suisse*, trans. and ed. Francis Ley (Paris, 1983), p. 200.

19 Cit. Glacken, *Traces on the Rhodian Shore*, p. 560. Alfred Lombard perhaps exaggerates Dubos's claims to innovation with regard to analysis of climate; see his *L'Abbé Dubos* and Armin Hajman Koller, *The Abbé Dubos: His Advocacy of the Theory of Climate; A Precursor to Johann Gottfried Herder* (Champaign, Ill., 1937). David Hume agreed that the Italian climate had grown warmer, but attributed this to the 'better cultivation of the land, and that woods are cleared, which formerly threw shade upon the earth, and kept the rays of the sun from penetrating to it' ('On the Populousness of Ancient Nations', in *Essays Moral, Political, and Literary*, ed. Eugene F. Miller (Indianapolis, 1985), pp. 448–51).

20 Etienne Fournel, *Bodin, prédécesseur de Montesquieu* (Paris, 1896), and Marian J. Tooley, 'Bodin and the Medieval Theory of Climate', *Speculum*, vol. 28, no. 1, 1953.

21 Robert Shackleton, *Montesquieu: A Critical Biography* (Oxford, 1961), p. 303. For fuller discussion, see Robert Shackleton, 'The Evolution of Montesquieu's Theory of Climate', *Revue internationale de philosophie*, 1955, vol. 9, nos 33–4, and R. Mercier, 'La Théorie des climats des *Réflexions critiques à L'Esprit des lois*', *Revue d'histoire littéraire de la France*, vol. 53, Jan.–March, April–June 1953; and for a larger context, Ehrard, *L'Idée de nature*, vol. 2, pp. 692–717.

22 Shackleton, *Montesquieu*, pp. 309–10.

23 Ibid., p. 313.

24 See Margot and Rudolph Wittkower, *Born under Saturn: The Character and Conduct of Artists; A Documented History from Antiquity to the French Revolution* (London, 1963, reissued New York, 2007).

25 Montesquieu, *Œuvres complètes*, 2 vols (Paris, 1949–51), vol. 1, p. 663.

26 'parties malignes' (ibid., 19 Jan. 1729). His employment of the theory of fibres probably came via Arbuthnot, who believed that it was through this means that the body was influenced by the specific qualities of a location's air; see Shackleton, 'Evolu-

tion, p. 323. Shackleton identifies the importance of Espiard de La Borde's *Essais sur le génie et le caractère des nations* (p. 325).

27 Montesquieu, 'Voyage de Gratz à La Haye', *Œuvres complètes*, vol. 1, p. 663, 19 Jan. 1729.

28 In Giovanni Maria Lancisi, *De noxiis paludum effluviis, eorumque remediis*, in *Opera*, 3 vols (Geneva, 1718). It is somewhat piquant to note that Jean-André Venel, in his *Encyclopédie* article on climate, observed wearily that Montesquieu's acknowledgement of the role played by climate in shaping the 'physique des passions, des goûts, des moeurs' was well known to all doctors (vol. 3, p. 534).

29 'chacun défend ses espérances en prenant un soin continuel de sa santé, et Rome est un peuple de convalescans' (Montesquieu, 'Réflexions sur la sobriété des habitants de Rome comparée à l'intempérance des anciens Romains, mémoire académique', *Œuvres complètes*, 3 vols (Paris, 1950–5), vol. 3, p. 360). This was read in December 1732 at the Académie in Bordeaux after his Italian trip. On a sheet attached to the manuscript, Montesquieu had noted: 'Pour mon ouvrage sur l'air de la Campagne de Rome'.

30 'font que tous le monde est à son aise, excepté ceux qui travaillent, excepté ceux qui font de l'industrie, excepté ceux qui cultivent les arts, excepté ceux qui ont des terres, excepté ceux qui font le commerce' (Montesquieu, *Œuvres*, 3 vols (Amsterdam and London, 1758), vol. 2, p. 79).

31 Johann Joachim Winckelmann, *History of the Art of Antiquity* (Los Angeles, 2006), p. 186. Mme Dacier had pointed to situation and climate when championing Homer: 'il est des nations si heureusement situées, que le soleil regarde si favorablement, qu'elles ont été capables d'imaginer et d'inventer d'elles-mêmes, et d'arriver à la perfection. D'autres, par contre, ensevelies dans un air plus épais, ont dû imiter' (*Des causes de la corruption du goût* (1715), p. 12, cit. Lombard, *L'Abbé Dubos*, p. 245).

32 'Il semble que la nature ait une force dans la Grèce qu'elle n'a pas dans les autres contrées' (Dubos, *Réflexions critiques*, Deuxième réflexion, p. 220, cit. Ehrard, *L'Idée de nature*, vol. 1, p. 708). That Athens's air generated genius was, for example, reiterated by Tommaso Maria Celoni, *Ragionamento sull'aria del Vaticano di Arenio Triense P.A., recitato in*

una general Adunanza tenuta degli Arcadi nella sala del Serbatojo (Rome, 1780) p. 5.

33 David Bindman, *Ape to Apollo: Aesthetics and the Idea of Race in the Eighteenth Century* (Ithaca, N.Y., 2002), p. 83.

34 Carlo Fea, *Discorso intorno alle belli arte in Roma* (Rome, 1797), p. VI.

35 Ibid., pp. 21–2, 27–8. Catherine Guégan kindly drew this reference to my attention. The argument was to be deployed after Rome became the new nation's capital; see also G. Taussig, *The Roman Climate, its Influence on Health and Disease, Serving as an Hygienical Guide* (Rome, 1870): 'Thus the culture of the fine arts is carried on in every part of Rome and elevates and enobles the feelings of even the lower classes' (p. 42).

36 Dr Johnson had anticipated this proud assertion of independence from climate: 'surely nothing is more reproachful to a being endowed with reason, than to resign its power to the influence of the air' (*The Idler*, 14 June 1758, cit. Jan Golinski, *British Weather and the Climate of Enlightenment* (Chicago and London, 2007), p. 156).

37 'En Grèce…tout est adouci, tout est plein de calme dans la nature, comme dans les écrits des anciens.…Dans cette patrie des Muses, la nature ne conseille point les écarts; elle tend au contraire à ramener l'esprit à l'amour des choses uniformes et harmonieuses' ([J. N.] Paillot de Montabert, *Traité complet de la peinture*, 9 vols (Paris, 1829–51), vol. 3, p. 363).

38 'délicieux' (ibid., vol. 2, p. 208).

39 'David a changé l'art, parce qu'à trente ans il changea de doctrine: ce n'est point parce qu'il a été influencé par les moeurs de son pays, car ce fût en Italie et à Rome qu'il se perfectionna, mais c'est parce qu'il eût recours à d'autres d'idées et à une autre théorie.…Tout ce qu'on pourrait dire sur l'influence du climat, semble devoir être réduit à deux ou trois idées fort simples et que suggère naturellement le bon sens, savoir que dans les pays où le climat est extrême, il doit être un obstacle au perfectionnement des ouvrages d'imagination; que dans les pays réellement tempérés, cet obstacle est nul; et que dans les pays favorisés par un climat pur, par un ciel bienfaisant, non-seulement l'esprit des hommes n'a point de pareils obstacles à

vaincre, mais leur imagination est excitée même par cette beauté du ciel, beauté qui s'étend sur toute la nature' (ibid., vol. 3, p. 360).

40 'Il faut donc reconnaître seulement que la beauté du climat favorise toutes les dispositions pour les arts, et c'est ce qu'on ne saurait nier. En effet, la douceur du ciel et le bel aspect de la nature non-seulement soutiennent les idées, mais elles les vivifient, les renouvellent. Un ciel pur semble nous purifier nous-mêmes.…[L]es douceurs dans les beaux climats sont pour tous, et c'est là seulement qu'on devrait dire que le soleil luit pour tout le monde' (ibid., vol. 3, p. 362).

41 Ibid., vol. 3, p. 365.

42 Ibid., vol. 3, p. 363. This emphasis on human independence in the face of a challenging environment, based on reason, conscience and will, is a keynote of P. Foissac, *De la Météorologie dans ses rapports avec la science de l'homme et principalement avec la médecine et l'hygiène publique*, 2 vols (Paris, 1854), vol. 2, p. 509.

43 'sous le plus beau ciel de la terre' (Paillot de Montabert, *Traité*, vol. 3, p. 366).

44 'Alors, à Rome, il ne voit que Paris' (ibid., vol. 3, p. 432). The young Ingres exemplifies this Parisian arrogance: 'Je déteste bien cordialement la ville de Rome, telle belle qu'elle est d'ailleurs, car elle est bien belle, mais pour dire en peu de mots, tout est la province a cote de Paris la grand-ville et cela en toutes choses' (letter to Julie Forestier, Rome, 23 Nov. 1806, cit. H. Lapauze, *Le Roman d'amour de M. Ingres* (Paris, 1910), p. 58). See also Valérie Bajou, *Monsieur Ingres* (Paris, 1999), p. 87.

45 Ehrard, *L'Idée de nature*, vol. 1, p. 706.

46 See R. Naves, 'Un adversaire de la théorie des climats au XVIIe siècle, Adrien Baillet', *Revue d'histoire littéraire de la France*, vol. 43, no. 3, 1936.

47 'encore un objet de litige entre des hommes d'ailleurs très-éclairés' (Cabanis, *Rapports*, p. 413).

48 Stendhal, *Promenades dans Rome* (Paris, 1996), chapters 92–100, pp. 264–98.

49 Michel Crouzet, *Stendhal et l'italianité: Essai de mythologie romantique* (Paris, 1982), p. 39.

50 Paul Arbelet, *L'Histoire de la peinture en Italie et les plagiats de Stendhal* (Paris, 1914). James G. Shields, 'Stendhal et Cabanis: Le Mythe italien à travers le prisme de physiologie', in V. Del Litto and J. Dérens

(eds), *Stendhal, Paris et le mirage italien: Colloque pour le cent-cinquantième anniversaire de la mort de Stendhal* (Paris, 1992).

51 'le soleil…réclame si hautement tout ce qui tient à la beauté, que les artistes du Nord ont, dans tous les temps, senti le besoin d'un autre climat; tous ceux qui se sont distingués dans la carrière des beaux-arts, se sont formés en Italie; ou du moins, ont senti comme par instinct le besoin d'y vivre' (Charles Victor Bonstetten, *L'homme du midi et l'homme du nord, ou L'influence du climat* (Geneva and Paris, 1824), p. 76).

52 Quatremère de Quincy, *Lettres à Miranda sur le déplacement des monuments de l'art de l'Italie* [1796], ed. Édouard Pommier (Paris, 1989). For a fuller account of the arguments around this episode, see also Pommier's *L'Art de liberté: Doctrines et débats de la Révolution française* (Paris, 1991), pp. 397–466.

53 'ce concert de choses et d'idées, de formes et de sentiments, d'admiration publique, d'affections, de sympathie, qui forment comme l'atmosphère des modèles de beau….Excepté Rome, il n'est pas de ville dans l'Europe qui puisse présenter à ces chefs-d'œuvre un hospice digne d'eux, ni un temple propre au recueillement qu'exige leur étude. Ce n'est ni au milieu des brouillards et des fumées de Londres, des pluies et de boues de Paris, des glaces et des neiges de Pétersbourg; ce n'est ni au milieu du tumulte des grandes villes de l'Europe, ni au milieu de ces chaos de distractions d'un peuple nécessiteusement occupé de soins mercantiles, que peut se développer cette profonde sensibilité pour les belles choses, ce sixiéme sens que la contemplation et l'étude du beau donnent aux élèves des arts. Quelque-chose qu'on fasse, il faudra toujours que ceux qui s'y livrent aillent respirer un air dégagé de toutes ces vapeurs qui obscurcissent à nos yeux les images du beau et du vrai' (Quatremère de Quincy, *Lettres à Miranda*, p. 116). The idea that aesthetic judgement is equivalent to a sixth sense is anticipated by, if not derived from, Dubos; see Lombard, *L'Abbé Dubos*, p. 249. On the philosophical and medical tradition which refers to a sixth sense, see Brian Dillon, *Tormented Hope: Nine Hypochondriac Lives* (London, 2009), pp. 201–3. Paillot de Montabert suggested that the Greeks had possessed a 'sentiment' for art which

had developed because of their successful fostering of art as a general phenomenon; he argued it was this, not climate, which lay behind Greek aesthetic superiority (*Traité*, vol. 1, p. 107).

54 'éclat…charme…tout ce qui tient à l'histoire, au monde, à la politique.…Monuments inséparables de l'histoire, que deviendrez-vous, si l'on vous arrachait du lieu témoin de votre antique splendeur?' (Louis-Pierre Deseine, *Opinion sur les musées où se trouvent retenus tous les objets d'arts, qui sont la propriété du temples consacrés à la religion catholique* (Paris, Floréal an XI [April 1801]), in *Notices historiques sur les anciens académies royales de peinture, sculpture, et celle d'architecture: Suivies de deux écrits qui ont déjà été publiés, et qui ont pour l'objet la restitution des monumens consacrés à la religion catholique* (Paris, 1814), pp. 241–4. See Werner Szambien, 'Le Musées tueront-ils l'art? A propos de quelques animadversions de Deseine', in Jacques Guillerme (ed.), *Les Collections: Fables et programmes* (Paris, 1993), p. 338; Andrew McClellan, *Inventing the Louvre: Art, Politics, and the Origins of Modern Museum Culture in Eighteenth-Century Paris* (Cambridge, 1994), p. 195; and Dominique Poulot, '*Surveillir et s'instruire*': La Révolution française et l'intelligence de l'héritage historique (Oxford, 1996), pp. 489–91, 494–5.

55 Carol Gibson-Wood, *Jonathan Richardson: Art Theorist of the English Enlightenment* (New Haven and London, 2000), pp. 223–4.

56 'les chefs d'œuvres des grands maîtres ainsi semées dans le désert.…Je me désole qu'on ait réunit les tableaux de Rome dans un musée' (Chateaubriand, *Mémoires d'outre-tombe*, cit. Hersant, *Italies*, p. 507).

57 Cecil Gould, *Trophy of Conquest: The Musée Napoleon and the Creation of the Louvre* (London, 1965), pp. 123–4. See also Élizabeth Décultot, 'Le Cosmopolitisme en question: Goethe face aux saisies françaises d'œuvres d'art sous la Révolution et sous l'Empire', *Revue germanique internationale*, no. 12, 1999.

58 'ces restes de monuments qui tiennent au sol de l'ancienne Rome' (CDAFR, vol. 17, p. 200, Fructidor an VI / August–September 1798, *Rapport présenté au ministre de l'Intérieur*).

59 A.V. Arnault, *Souvenirs d'un sexagénaire*, 4 vols (Paris, 1833), vol. 4, pp. 288–9. Farington notes two

letters by Flaxman against French art plunder, published in the *Morning Chronicle* (Kenneth Garlick and Angus Macintyre (eds), *The Diary of Joseph Farington*, vol. 3 (New Haven and London, 1979), p. 747, 14 Jan. 1797).

60 Pommier, *L'Art de liberté*, p. 413.

61 Anne-Louis Girodet, *Œuvres posthumes de Girodet-Trioson, suivies de sa correspondance*, ed. Pierre A. Coupin, 2 vols (Paris, 1829), vol. 1, p. 266; for example, William Hazlitt compared Rome's galleries unfavourably to the Louvre, where he had first seen Italian art en masse (*Notes of a Journey through France and Italy* ([1826] New York, 1983), p. 232).

62 'feu du génie' (E.J. Delécluze, 'Sur l'exposition des ouvrages de peinture, sculpture, architecture et gravure des artistes vivans', *Le Lycée français* (Paris, 1819), vol. 1, p. 273); Robert Baschet (ed.), *Journal de Delécluze 1814–1828* (Paris, 1948), p. 295, 4 Jan. 1826. On debates around repatriation and legitimacy, see Christopher M.S. Johns, *Antonio Canova and the Politics of Patronage in Revolutionary and Napoleonic Europe* (Berkeley, Los Angeles, London, 1998), pp. 171–94.

63 *Age of Neoclassicism* (London, 1972), p. lxxxiii.

64 'Il n'y a pas de prose dans cet air, tout y est musique, mélodie, extase ou poème!' (Lamartine, *Cours familier de littérature*, vol. 2, 1856, p. 49).

65 'ce qu'il y a de singulier, c'est qu'on respire dans cette ville le goût des arts, et que l'homme qui y est arrivé avec le plus grand éloignement pour eux finit assez promptement par en devenir très amateur' (Auguste Creuzé de Lesser, *Voyage en Italie et en Sicile fait en 1801 et 1802* (Paris, 1806), p. 325).

66 Joseph Forsyth, *Remarks on Antiquities, Arts, and Letters, during an Excursion in Italy in the Years 1802 and 1803*, 4th edn (London, 1835), p. 245.

67 'On venait y respirer ce même air qui avait su puissamment inspiré les grands peintres italiens' (Théodore Gudin, *Souvenirs du Baron Gudin, peintre de la marine (1820–1870)* (Paris, n.d.), p. 102). In 1846, the composer Charles Gounod urged the painter Jules Richomme to enjoy Rome 'par tous les pores' (André Beaunier, 'Quelques lettres de Charles Gounod', *La Revue hebdomadaire*, vol. 12, Dec. 1908, p. 469, cit. Anne Christine Faitrop-Porta, *Rome au XIXe siècle, vu par les grands compositeurs pensionnaires à la Villa Médicis et par leurs contemporains* (Paris, 1996), n.p.

68 'Je sens par tous les pores que ce pays est la patrie des arts' (Stendhal, *Œuvres intimes* (Paris, 1955), p. 1122). More scientific statements of the priority given to the skin's pores as a means of access to air and its constituent elements are: 'Cet Air s'insinue dans nos corps par toutes les ouvertures qui lui sont présentés' (Boissier de Sauvage, *Dissertation où l'on recherche comment l'air suivant ses différent qualités agit sur le corps humain* (Bordeaux, 1753), p. 2); 'It appears that the skin imbibes and exhales air' (Thomas Beddoes, *Considerations on the Medicinal Uses and on the Production of Factitious Airs* (Bristol, 1795), part I, p. 12).

69 'Le climat est ici le plus grand des artistes' (Stendhal, *Promenades dans Rome* (Paris 1996, 30 August 1827, p. 49).

70 'je me demande, je cherche quel est le génie qui a pu inspirer aux artistes anciens cette beauté de proportion, cette pureté de forme, cette vigueur d'exécution qui a présidé à leurs monuments, et je ne sais où en trouver la source. L'air (si je puis parler ainsi) a encore à Rome, conservé quelque chose de son parfum d'art des temps heureux de sa prospérité' (Eugène Viollet-le-Duc, *Lettres d'Italie 1836–1837, adressées à sa famille*, ed. Geneviève Viollet-le-Duc (Paris, 1971), p. 187, 31 Oct. 1836).

71 Hazlitt, *Notes*, p. 233.

72 Henry Matthews, *The Diary of an Invalid, being the Journal of a Tour in Pursuit of Health, in Portugal, Italy, Switzerland, and France in the Years 1817, 1818, and 1819* (London, 1820), p. 389.

73 William Wetmore Story, *Roba di Roma*, 2 vols (London, 1863), vol. 1, p. 351.

74 Henry James, *Italian Hours* (New York, 1979), p. 205.

75 My thanks to Agnès Bouvier for guiding me towards Flaubert's Roman letters. Frederic Leighton's disappointment in Rome was all the more galling as he had expected to find 'an atmosphere of high art' (Mrs Russell Barrington, *The Life and Letters of Frederic Baron Leighton of Stretton*, 2 vols (London, 1906), vol. 1, p. 96, letter to his mother, 25 Nov. 1852).

76 'J'ai vécu à Rome, c'est sûr, du temps de César ou de Néron....C'est là qu'il faut vivre, vois-tu? On n'a d'air que [de?] là et on en a, de l'air poétique, à pleine poitrine comme sur une haute montagne, si bien que le coeur vous en bat' (Gustave Flaubert, *Correspondance*, 5 vols, ed. Jean Bruneau (Paris,

1973–2007), vol. 1, p. 266, May 1846). Michelet himself found something disturbing in Rome's air: 'Et il faut dire aussi qu'il y a dans l'air de cette ville quelque chose d'orageux, d'immoral et frénétique'; 'Je ne m'étonne pas que tant d'Empereurs y soient devenus fous et qu'Hoffmann y ait mis les scènes de ses contes fantasques' (journal, 14 April 1830, cit. Theodora Scharten, *Les Voyages et séjours de Michelet en Italie: Amitiés italiennes* (Paris, 1934), pp. 31, 215).

77 'La patrie c'est la terre, c'est l'univers, ce sont les étoiles, c'est l'air. C'est la pensée elle-même, c'est-à-dire l'infini dans notre poitrine' (Flaubert, *Correspondance*, vol. 1, p. 418). Lamartine used a similar atmospheric vocabulary: 'L'Italie pour moi n'est pas un pays, c'est un mirage! Ce n'est pas de l'air qu'on y respire, c'est de l'âme!' (*Cours familier de littérature*, 1856, vol. 2, p. 48).

78 'C'est bien la ville de artistes. On peut y passer l'existence dans une atmosphère complètement idéale, en dehors du monde, au dessus' (Flaubert, *Correspondance*, vol. 1, p. 772, 9 April 1851 to Louis Bouilhot).

79 'Eh bien, vieux, je suis fâché de l'avouer: ma première impression a été défavorable. J'ai eu, comme un bourgeois, une désillusion. Je cherchai la Rome de Néron et je n'ai trouvé que celle de Sixte-Quint. L'air prêtre emmiasme d'ennui la ville des Césars' (ibid.).

80 'il faudrait être aveugle ou de mauvaise foi pour ne pas avouer que c'est un climat et une ville intarissables en beautés de tout genre, en architecture pittoresque et surtout en beaux effets. C'est un Babylone' (letter to Julie Forestier, Rome, 25 Dec. 1806, cit. Lapauze, *Le Roman d'amour de M. Ingres*, pp. 69–70); see also Bajou, *Monsieur Ingres*, p. 87.

81 'Je suis las de mon séjour en Italie; il me semble que le climat me tue; et cependant il est si beau!' (cit. L. Becq de Fouquères, *Isidore-Alexandre Auguste Pils: Sa Vie et ses œuvres* (Paris, 1876), p. 20). I am extremely grateful to Kathy Mclauchlan for drawing this reference to my attention.

4 CONFRONTING *MAL'ARIA*

1 'L'air est l'agent le plus universel et le plus fort qu'il y ait dans la Nature, c'est son instrument principal dans toutes ses opérations sur le surface de la terre et dans son intérieur, rien ne peut être produit, vivre ou croître sans air' (Abbé Jérôme Richard, *Histoire naturelle de l'air et de ses météores*, 10 vols (Paris, 1770–1), vol. 2, p. 67).

2 Barbara Maria Stafford, *Voyage into Substance: Art, Science, Nature, and the Illustrated Travel Account, 1760–1840* (Cambridge, Mass., 1984), pp. 191–4.

3 'il ne faut pas croire que l'action des climats, sur ceux qui les habitent, ne tienne qu'aux qualités sensibles de l'atmosphère, à sa température, à son aquosité, à ses météores etc.; elle tient aussi aux qualités occultes, ou indiscernables, à des mélanges d'autres éléments invisibles, insaisissables par tous les instruments' (Pierre Thouvenel, *Traité sur le climat de l'Italie considérée sous ses rapports phisiques, météorologiques et médicinaux*, 4 vols (Verona, 1797–8), vol. 2, p. 203).

4 See James C. Riley, *The Eighteenth-Century Campaign to Avoid Disease* (Basingstoke and London, 1987), pp. 50–5, Alain Corbin, *Le Miasme et la jonquille: L'Odorat et l'imaginaire social XVIIIe–XIXe siècles* (Paris, 1982), pp. 15–16, and S. Schaffer, 'Measuring Virtue: Eudiometry, Enlightenment and Pneumatic Medicine', in A. Cunningham and R. French (eds), *The Medical Enlightenment in the Eighteenth Century* (Cambridge, 1990).

5 'n'ont envisagé ces effets [of air on a human body] que sous le rapport physique, ou d'après les principes de la physiologie admise par les humoristes.... Quand on a voulu porter ses regards sur les qualités que lui communiquent les corps hétérogènes répandus dans cette vaste mer de fluides électriques, des hypothèses, des idées abstraites, des expressions vagues ont tenu lieu pendant longtemps de connoissances exactes et d'un langage plus précis. On a attribué à des molécules salines, nitreuses, sulfureuses, à des miasmes délétères, etc., etc., etc., le plus grand nombre des phénomènes dont on ne pouvait se rendre raison que par l'analogie de quelques expériences inexactes ou d'après l'idée qu'on se formait de l'action des substances dont l'existence n'était souvent que supposé' (Louis Dominique Amable Bouffey, *Recherches sur l'influence de l'air dans le développement, le caractère et le traitement des maladies* (Paris, 1813), part 1, pp. 118–19).

6 'La sapienza proviene al cervello dall'aria' (Giovanni Maria Lancisi, *De noxiis paludum effluviis*

eorumque remediis, trans. Elvira Valentini (Milan and Rome, 1942), p. 94.

7   Owsei Temkin, *Galenis:. Rise and Decline of a Medical Philosophy* (Ithaca and London, 1973), p. 26.

8   F. Dagognet, 'La Cure d'air: Essai sur l'histoire d'une idée en thérapeutique', *Thalès*, vol. 10, 1959, p. 75.

9   'Depuis les murs Saturniens, citadelle du temps, qui couronnent le mont Circe, jusqu'aux jardins et au palais Poniatowski et au village de San Felice, l'air pur, léger, vital, embaumé, exhalent l'éther des tropiques; en le respirant après celui des Maremmes, on sent qu'il a sa source dans la haute région du ciel, à laquelle ne peuvent atteindre les pesantes et méphitiques vapeurs de la terre' (Baron Jacques Marquet de Montbreton Norvins et al., *L'Italie pittoresque* (Paris, 1834), p. 21).

10 William Falconer, *Remarks on the Influence of Climate...* (London, 1781), p. 161.

11 See chapter 6 on the characterisation of Rome's air in terms of pleasing smells, and the problem of perfume.

12 'Respirer un air doux et pur' (Stendhal, *Correspondance,* 10 vols, ed. H. Martineau (Paris, 1933–4), vol. 6, p. 180, 10 Oct. 1824, to sister Pauline and cousin).

13 Alphonse de Lamartine, *Cours familier de littérature. Revue mensuelle*, vol. 7, 1859, p. 28.

14 'Je suis dans un calme de passion qui me charme; je philosophe tout seul bien doucement, en contemplant notre belle plaine de Rome, l'horizon et le ciel, et je respire avec un véritable ravissement, l'excellent air que nous avons ici' (L. Robert, letter to Schnetz, Frascati, 15 Sept. 1830, cit. E. Carrière, *Le Climat de l'Italie sous le rapport hygiénique et médical* (Paris, 1849), p. 384; no source is given but this is from Felix-Sébastien Feuillet de Conches, *Léopold Robert, sa vie, ses œuvres et sa correspondance* (Paris, 1848), p. 143).

15 James Clark, *Medical Notes on Climate, Diseases, Hospitals, and Medical Schools, in France, Italy, Switzerland, comprising an Inquiry into the Effects of a Residence in the South of Europe in Cases of Pulmonary Consumption...* (London, 1820), p. 71.

16 William Bemrose, *The Life and Works of Joseph Wright A.R.A., commonly called 'Wright of Derby'* (London and Derby, 1885), p. 30, 12 Feb. 1774,

17 'Je n'ai jamais entendu dire que l'air de Rome fût bon à rien' (Chateaubriand, *Correspondance*, ed. P. de Raynal (Paris, 1862), p. 104, cit. Chateaubriand, *Lettre à M. Fontanes sur la campagne romaine*, ed. J.M. Gatier (Geneva, 1951), p. xxvi note. 4).

18 Clark, *Medical Notes on Climate*.

19 T. H. Burgess, *Climate of Italy in relation to Pulmonary Consumption: With Remarks on the Influence of Foreign Climates upon Individuals* (London, 1852), pp. 165–6; Dr Armstrong, 'Lectures on the Principle and Practice of Physic', Lecture 26, 'On the Origins of Typhus Fever, in which its Contagious or Non-contagious Nature is Considered', *The Lancet*, vol. 7, no. 7, 21 May 1825, p. 194.

20 'Par miasme on entend des corps extrèment subtils, qu'on croit être les propagateurs des maladies contagieuses....la nature, les propriétés, et la façon d'agir de ces particules contagieuses ou miasmes sont entièrement inconnues...comme placés sur les confins qui séparent la matière des êtres abstraits' ('Miasme', *Encyclopédie*, vol. 10, pp. 484–5).

21 See James Johnson, *Change of Air, or The Pursuit of Health; An Autumnal Excursion through France, Switzerland, and Italy; in the Year 1829 with Observations and Reflections on the Moral, Physical, and Medicinal Influence of Travelling-Exercise, Change of Scene, Foreign Skies, and Voluntary Expatriation* (London, 1831), pp. 29–30; P. Foissac, 'Le Miasme paludéen...échappent à tous les instruments' (*De la Météorologie dans ses rapports avec la science de l'homme et principalement avec la médecine et l'hygiène publique*, 2 vols (Paris, 1854), vol. 2, p. 509.

22 John Macculloch, *On Malaria: An Essay on the Production and Localities of the Places by which it is produced; With an Enunciation of the Diseases caused by it, and the Means of Preventing or Diminishing Them, both at Home, and in the Naval and Military Service* (London, 1827), pp. 6, 381. John Henner strikes a similar note in characterising the conflict between cultural historical reputation and medical reality of the Mediterranean: 'To the Medical Topographer, belongs the less pleasing task of describing these far-famed scenes as they at present exist: – no longer the seat of science, the chosen residence of demi-gods, and the fruitful nursery of sages and heroes; but now, alas! too often the residence of squalid misery and sordid ignorance; immersed in the noisome vapour of untrodden marshes, and fanned by no zephyrs but those which scatter disease and health from their wings' (*Sketches of*

Medical Topography of the Mediterranean: Comprising an Account of Gibraltar, the Ionian Islands, and Malta; To which is prefaced a Sketch of a Plan for Memoirs on Medical Topography (London, 1830), p. 1).

23 Cit. in review of Jacob Frédéric Sullin de Châteauvieux, *Lettres écrites d'Italie en 1812 et 13 à C. Pictet*, 2 vols (Paris, 1816), *Edinburgh Review*, vol. 28, no. 55, March 1817, p. 43.

24 Macculloch, *On Malaria*, p. 423.

25 William Falconer, *Remarks on the Influence of Climate, Situation, Nature of Country, Population, Nature of Food, and Way of Life on the Disposition and Temper, Manners and Behaviour, Intellect, Laws, Customs, Form of Government and Religion of Mankind* (London, 1781), pp. 160–1.

26 'L'influence maligne ne se fait sentir par aucun signe extérieur: vous respirez un air qui semble pur et qui est très-agréable; la terre est riante et fertile; une fraîcheur délicieuse vous repose le soir des chaleurs brûlantes du jour!: et tout cela, c'est la mort!' (Germaine de Staël, *Corinne ou l'Italie* (Paris 1872), p. 110). James Fenimore Cooper was 'singularly struck by the existence of this subtle and secret danger in the midst of a scene otherwise so lovely' [i.e. the view of Ostia from his vessel] (*Excursions in Italy*, 2 vols (Paris, 1838), vol. 1, p. 197).

27 'tout ce qui tient trop à l'enthousiasme ou au merveilleux, et surtout au prestige reproché aux voyageurs: *multum mentitue qui multum vidit*' (Louis Valentin, *Voyage en Italie fait en l'année 1820: Deuxième édition, corrigée et augmentée de nouvelles observations faits dans un second voyage en 1824* (Paris, 1826), p. 8).

28 'Il y a dans l'air de la campagne de Rome, une cause de maladie dont personne n'a calculée encore la force réelle' (C.V. Bonstetten, *Voyage sur la scène…Énéide* (Geneva, an XIII (1805)), p. 234). He was of the view that though there may well be in the area's air 'une disposition à la fièvre', it only become dangerous when exacerbated by other circumstances (p. 268). Rather 'la grande cause de la morbidité croissante de Rome moderne, il faut la chercher dans la pauvreté de ses habitans' (p. 235).

29 'La malaria e una potenza nociva piu sentita che intesa' (G. Baccelli, 'La Malaria di Roma', *Monografia della città di Roma e della campagna romana presentata all'Esposizione universale di Parigi del 1878*, 4 vols (Rome, 1879), vol. 1, p. 170.

30 [Anon.], *A Comparative Sketch of England and Italy, with Disquisitions on National Advantages*, 2 vols (London, 1793), vol. 1, p. 100.

31 'Ils sont tous pâles, et même plus que pâles, car ils ont l'air des habitants de quelque infermerie' ([Dr Maihows], *Voyage en France, en Italie…trad. de l'anglais de M. de Puisieux*, 4 vols (Paris, 1763), vol. 1, pp. 42–3). [Chateaubriand, *Lettre à M. Fontanes sur la campagne romaine*, ed. J.M. Gautier (Geneva and Paris, 1961), p. xlvii].

32 'une partie des habitans du centre des marais avoit, avant 1777, les chairs, sur la surface entière du corps, tellement oedémateuses, et le systeme musculaire tellement dépourvu d'élasticité, que l'impression du doigt appuyé sur la peau y laissoit un enfoncement qui ne s'effaçoit qu'après un espace de temps sensible; un pareil effet suppose une atonie générale, une foiblesse d'organisation, que rend l'état de vie très-voisin de l'état de mort' (Gaspard de Prony, *Description hydrographique et historique des marais Pontins*, 2 vols (Paris, 1822–3), p. xxviii note). On Prony see Margaret Bradley, 'Prony the Bridge Builder: The Life and Times of Gaspard de Prony, Educator and Scientist', *Centaurus*, vol. 37, no. 3, July 1994.

33 'Quella stizza e quel mal talento da cui sono dominanti coloro che covano delle vene il germe della febbre maremmana, quella proclività a concentrarsi ne' loro cupi pensieri, quelle fisionomie torbide e sinistre ci rendano abbastanza convinti de questa verita' (Giovanni Battista Brocchi, *Dello stato fisico del Suolo di Roma* (Rome, 1820), p. 250).

34 Crauford Tait Ramage, *The Nooks and By-Ways of Italy: Wanderings in Search of its Ancient Remains and Modern Superstitions*, in *Ramage in South Italy*, ed. Edith Clay (London, 1965), p. 218, Rome, 2 Aug. 1828.

35 'la condizione igienica vera della romanità ….Del resto, basterebbe uno sguardo solo alla *nostra* città per far giustizia sommaria di tutte le accuse che le furono mosse' (Baccelli, *Monografia*, pp. 150–1).

36 'Il soggiorno di Roma, per la sanità del suo clima, e ora, decantato da tutti. E la gente di Roma rispecchia questa sanità con la robustezza, il colorito, il vigore dei giovani, la fierezza del suo popolo' (Dr G. Pecori, 'La malaria dell'Urbe nei tempi passsati e la sua salubrita attuale', *Capitolium*, vol. 2, 1925–6, p. 509).

37 'bastava lo sguardo a misurare la limpidezza…senza passare alle chimiche osservazioni ed esperimenti' (cit. Andreina de Clementi, *Vivere nel Latifondo: Le comunità della campagna laziale fra 1700 e 1800* (Milan, 1989), p. 51).

38 'Comment pourrait-il saisir le vrai caractère de ces maladies qui se cachent sous les apparences d'affections morales, de ces altérations morales qui se présentent sous l'aspect de certaines maladies?' (P.J.G. Cabanis, *Coup d'œil sur les révolutions et sur la réforme de la médecine* (Paris, 1804), cit. Jean-François Dancel, *De l'Influence de voyages sur l'homme et sur les maladies* (Paris, 1846), p. 105). In a sense the resort to aestheticised descriptions was a way to offset the uncertainties which followed from a commitment to close visual scrutiny, which yet frequently failed to provide diagnostic answers.

39 For example, Francis Boott, *Memoir of the life and medical opinions of John Armstrong; to which is added an enquiry into the facts connected with those forms of fever attributed to malaria or marsh effluvium* (London, 1833–4). Andrew Ure, *The General Malaria of London and the Peculiar Malaria of Pimlico: Investigated, and the Means of their Economical Removal Ascertained* (London, 1850); Thomas Herbert Baker, *On Malaria and Miasmata and their Influence in the Production of Typhus and Typhoid Fevers, Cholera, and the Exanthemata* (London, 1868). L.J. Bruce-Chwatt, 'Ague as Malaria', *Journal of Tropical Medicine and Hygiene*, vol. 79, 1976.

40 'il est d'une complexxion [*sic*] assés délicate et je ne croy pas que cet air luy soit favorable; comme il est assés grossier et fort inconstant il n'accomode pas tout le monde. Les gens du pays disent assés plaisamment qu'il luy faut porter respect: si deve portare rispetto a l'arria, voulant dire sans doute, qu'il faut s'y mesnager pour n'en estre pas maltraitté' (CDAFR, vol. 2, p. 424, La Teulière to Villecerf, 14 Oct. 1698).

41 'que le vulgaire a imaginées pour distinguer l'air de la plaine, des lieux bas et voisins des marais et du littoral d'avec [*sic*] celui des pays situés sur le sommet de la montagne' (J.B. Michel, *Recherches médico-topographiques sur Rome et l'Agro romano* (Rome, 1813), p. 56).

42 C. de Tournon, *Études statistiques sur Rome et la partie occidentale des états romains*, 2 vols ([1831] Paris, 1855), vol. 1, pp. 238–9; cf. William Gell, *The Topography of Rome and its Vicinity*, revised and enlarged by Edward Herbert Bunbury (London, 1846), p. 128: 'The air of Bracciano, without being pronounced absolutely dangerous, is, in the summer, what the natives call "suspected".'

43 James Clark, *The Sanative Influence of Climate*, 3rd edn (London, 1841), p. 225. See Mary J. Dobson, *Contours of Death and Disease in Early Modern England* (Cambridge, 1997), and Mary Dobson, "Marsh Fever" - The Geography of Malaria in England', *Journal of Historical Geography*, vol. 6, 1980.

44 Jean-Jacques Ampère, *Histoire romaine à Rome*, 4 vols (Paris, 1862–4), vol. 2, pp. 60–1; 'one of the chief predisposing causes of the Roman fever is the inconceivable filthiness of the people and their dwellings' (George Augustus Sala, *Rome and Venice with other Wanderings in Italy, in 1866–67* (London, 1869), p. 448).

45 W. North, *Roman Fever: The Results of an Inquiry during Three Years' Residence on the Spot into the Origin, History, Distribution and Nature of the Malarial Fevers of the Roman Campagna, with Especial Reference to their Supposed Connection with Pathogenic Organisms* (London, 1896), p. 381.

46 Christopher Hoolihan uses the term without discussing its terminological context ('Health and Travel in Nineteenth-Century Rome', *Journal of the History of Medicine and Allied Sciences*, vol. 44, no. 4, 1989). Wharton's story was originally published in the magazine *Liberty* in 1934. Wharton's story is discussed in Annamaria Formichella Elsden, *Roman Fever: Domesticity and Nationalism in Nineteenth-Century American Women's Writing* (Columbus, 2004). Nathaniel Hawthorne had played on the blurring of emotional and atmospheric dimension in *The Marble Faun*; see Willian Vance's discussion in *America's Rome*, 2 vols (New Haven and London, 1989) vol. 1, p. 120.

47 'Malaria is indeed an Italian word; but I know not that Miasma would have served the purpose better' (Macculloch, *On Malaria*, pp. 278–9).

48 On the currency of a miasmatic orthodoxy until mid-1880s, see Frank Snowden, *The Conquest of Malaria: Italy, 1900–1962* (New Haven and London, 2006), pp. 27–35; Michael Worboys, 'From Miasma to Germs: Malaria 1850–1879', *Parassitologia*, vol. 36, nos 1–2 August 1994, p. 61, and *Spreading Germs:*

Disease Theories and Medical Practice 1865–1900 (Cambridge, 2000); Pierre Darmon cites the *Dictionnaire encyclopédique des sciences médicales*, 2nd series, vol. 7, p. 511, in his *L'homme et les microbes XII–XXe siècle* (Paris, 1999), p. 80.

49 John Charles Atkinson, *Change of Air: The Fallacies Regarding It* (London, 1848), p. 18.

50 Saul Jarcho, 'A Cartographic and Literary Study of the Word *Malaria*', *Journal for the History of Medicine*, vol. 25, no. 1, 1970. Italian etymological dictionaries state that the term 'mal'aria' was used by Francesco Sansovino, *Della agricoltura di M. Giovanni Tatti* (Venice, 1560), fol. 11, but to mean 'bad air', not a disease. The claim that Francesco Torti (associated with the use of quinine) was the first to use it is wrong; Jarcho p. 34 note 17. J.A.H. Murray (ed.), *New English Dictionary on Historical Principles* [1888–1933], records 'mal'aria' as late as 1813; beginning in 1818 all uses recorded omit apostrophe, thus malaria.

51 Pietro Balestra, *L'Igiena nella campagna e città di Roma* (Rome, 1875), pp. 4–5.

52 Colin proposed 'intoxication tellurique', and notes that this was invented by Lucien-Prosper Lacroix, *Une Idée nouvelle sur la manière d'envisager les fièvres intermittentes, ou Considérations générales sur le rôle que joue l'élimination séreuse dans les diverses manifestations de l'intoxication tellurique, par le Dr Lacroix (des Rousses)* (Paris, 1854) (Lèon Colin, *Traité des fièvres intermittentes* (Paris, 1870), p. IX note 1).

53 Giovanni Berlinguer, (brother of Enrico, leader of the PCI, 1972–84), *Malaria romana: Patologia delle metropoli* (Milan, 1976), p. 11.

54 W.H.S. Jones and R. Ross, *Malaria: A Neglected Factor in the History of Greece and Rome* (London, 1907), p. 62.

55 Angelo Celli, *The History of Malaria in the Roman Campagna from Ancient Times*, ed. Anna Celli-Fraentzel (London, 1933).

56 Arcangelo Ilvento, *Storia delle grandi malattie epidemie con speciale riguoardo alla malaria* (Rome, 1936; anno XVI).

57 Robert Sallares, *Malaria and Rome: A History of Malaria in Ancient Italy* (Oxford and New York, 2002). However, if his review of ancient sources for clues to the presence of malaria in Rome is carried through scrupulously, the extension of this procedure to include comments from early modern and nineteenth-century sources risks losing historical purchase on the material.

58 'Il disoit "qu'on ne voïoit rien de Rome que le ciel sous lequel elle avoit esté assise et le plan de son gîte;…que ceux qui disoint qu'on n'y voyoit au moins les ruines de Rome en disoint trop; car les ruines d'une si espouvantable machine rapporteroint plus d'honneur et de reverence à sa mémoire; ce n'estoit rien que son sepulcre"' (Montaigne, *Journal de voyage en Italie par la Suisse et l'Allemagne en 1580 et 1581*, ed. Maurice Rat (Paris, 1955), p. 103; see Margaret M. McGowan, *The Vision of Rome in Late Renaissance France* (New Haven and London, 2000), p. 229. A comparison here is Du Bellay's celebration of the Tiber as a constant presence despite a condition of general ruination: 'Le Tybre seul, qui vers la mer s'enfuit, / Reste de Rome. / O mondaine inconstance! / Ce qui est ferme, est par le temps destruit, / et ce qui fuit, au temps fait resistance' (poem no. 3, from *Les Antiquitez de Rome*, in *Œuvres poétiques*, 2 vols (Paris, 1934), vol. 2, p. 6). As expressed by Luigi Biondi, an indigenous perspective could celebrate such physical continuity: not only were foreigners right to be jealous of Rome's past glories, but also the fact that modern Romans were 'coperti da questo cielo, respiriamo quest'aria, calchiamo questa terra immortale, beviamo le acque che bevevano que'buoni antichi' (*Osservazioni del Conte Luigi Biondi Marchese di Badino sull'opera di S.E.R. Niccolo Maria Nicolai uditore generale della C.R. intorno alla Presidenza della strade ed acque* (Rome, 1829), p. 14).

59 'Je ne sçai comme les autres se trouvent de l'air de Rome: moi je le trouvois très plesant et sein.' The French here is translated from Montaigne's original Italian (Montaigne, *Journal de voyage en Italie*, p. 127).

60 'Ce ciel sous lequel on vient respirer un air doux et salutaire aux poitrines affaiblies était un ciel inclément; ces hivers tièdes aujourd'hui étaient des hivers rigoureux' (Ampère, *Histoire romaine*, vol. 2, pp. 60–1.)

61 'le sol même qu'ils labouraient, l'air que respirer leur poitrine. Ils en triomphèrent comme ils devaient triompher de tout; le ciel leur avait fait une rude destinée: c'est pour cela qu'elle fût grande' (ibid., vol. 2, p. 72). Cabanis noted that those who sought refuge from Attila amongst the

'marais infects...devroient absolument changer la face de ces marais infects, ou périr moissonnés par les maladies pestilentielles et par la misère' (*Rapports du physique et du moral de l'homme* (Paris, 1844, 8th edn, pp. 260–1).

62 'Un trait du climat romain, que le temps n'a malheureusement effacé, c'est la malaria; c'est cette influence funeste qui, pendant quelques mois de l'année, plâne sur la ville et principalement sur la campagne romaine; c'est cette fièvre de Rome, que l'on peut éviter avec des précautions, mais à laquelle la moindre imprudence vous expose à succomber; qui frappe les habitants, chasse les étrangers, fait de la plaine qui entoure Rome un désert et répand sur elle comme une poésie formidable' (Ampère, *Histoire romaine*, vol. 2, pp. 60–1).

63 'l'exhalation de la peau' (A.J.C.A. Dureau de la Malle, *Économie politique des romains*, 2 vols (Paris, 1840), vol. 2, pp. 30–1). In 1854, Frederic Leighton reassured his mother that he would revert to wearing flannel in Rome 'as I see reason to believe that it is a great preservative against fever' (Mrs Russell Barrington, *The Life and Letters of Frederic Baron Leighton of Stretton*, 2 vols (London, 1906), vol. 1, p. 146, 29 April 1854).

64 Francesco Cancellieri, *Lettera di Francesco Cancellieri al Ch. Sig. Dottore Koreff, Professore di Medicina nell'Universitá di Berline sopra il tarantismo, l'aria di Roma, e della sua campagna ed. i Palazzi Pontificij entro e fuori di Roma, con le Notizie di Castel Gandolfo, di Paesi circonvicini* (Rome, 1817). Cancellieri also gathers texts on air in other places, making this the single most inclusive historical bibliography on the subject of its time. I am very grateful to Olivier Michel for drawing this text to my attention.

65 Ibid., p. 38, citing Paolo Sanquirico, *Parere dell'aere di Borgo* (Rome, 1670), and Tommaso Maria Celoni, *Ragionamento sull'aria del Vaticano...*(Rome, 1780).

66 Alessandro Petronio, *Del vivere delli Romani et di conservare la sanità* (book 5), (Rome, 1592): Marsilio Cagnati, 'De Romani aeris salubritate' (1599), in *Opuscula varia* (Rome, 1603); Domenico Panarolo, *Aërologia o discorso dell'aria* (Rome, 1642); Jo. Bapt. Doni, *De restituenda salubritate Agri Romani* (Florence, 1664).

67 *Rapports*, p. 447. Jean-Baptiste Michel also uses this as the motto for his book *Recherches médico-*

topographiques sur Rome et l'Agro romano (Rome, 1813).

68 Frank A. Barrett, 'Finke's 1792 Map of Human Diseases: The First World Disease Map?', *Social Science and Medicine*, vol. 50, nos 7–8, April 2000; Nicholaas A. Rupke (ed.), *Medical Geography in Historical Perspective*, *Medical History* supplement no. 20 (London, 2000); Gilles Palsky, *Des chiffres et des cartes. Naissance de la cartographie quantitative Français au XIXe siècle* (Paris, 1996); for a larger context see Laurence Brockliss and Colin Jones, *The Medical World of Early Modern France* (Oxford, 1997), pp. 463–5, 751–4.

69 See C.F. de Volney, 'Questions de statistique à l'usage des voyageurs' (1795) in *Œuvres complètes* (Paris, 1846), pp. 748–52, and Riley, *Eighteenth-Century Campaign*, chapter 2, 'Medical Geography and Medical Climatology', pp. 31–52.

70 'mon attention constante a été de ne poser le pied que là où je n'apercevais aucun empreinte' (Camille de Tournon, *Études statistiques sur Rome et la partie occidentale des états romains*, 2 vols (Paris, 1855), vol. 1, pp. viii, xi); cf. James Buzard's discussion of anti-tourism, in *The Beaten Track: European Tourism, Literature, and the Ways to 'Culture', 1800–1918* (Oxford, 1993).

71 Marsilio Cagnati, 'De Romani aeris salubritate' (1599), in *Opuscula varia* (Rome, 1603), unpaginated [p. 55].

72 Joseph Guislain, *Lettres médicales sur l'Italie, avec quelques renseignements sur la Suisse: Résumé d'un voyage fait en 1838* (Ghent, 1840), p. 102.

73 See Giorgio Cosmacini, *Soigner et réformer: Médecine et santé en Italie de la grande peste à la première guerre mondiale*, trans. Françoise Felce (Paris, 1992), pp. 221–5, originally published as *Storia della medicina e della sanità in Italia: Dalla peste europea alla guerra mondiale, 1348–1918* (Rome and Bari, 1978).

74 G. M. Lancisi, *De noxiis paludum effluviis, eorumque remediis*, in *Opera*, 3 vols (Geneva, 1718), vol. 1, pp. 124–5.

75 *Journal des scavans*, vol. 32, 1719, p. 506, review of *Jo. Maria Lancisii intimi cubicularii & archiatri Pontificii dissertatio de nativis, deque adventtitiis Romani coeli qualitatibus, cui accedit Historia Epidemiae Rheumaticae, quae per hiemem anni 1709 vagata est* (Geneva).

76 G. M. Lancisi, *Dissertatio de nativis atque adventitiis coeli qualitatibus: Cui accidit historia epidemiae rheu-*

maticae que per hyemem anni 1709 vagata est (Rome, 1711).

77 I refer to Lancisi, *De noxiis paludum effluviis* 1942). I am most indebted to Marco Fiorillo for providing me with a copy.

78 Ibid., Ch. XV, p. 69.

79 Ibid., Ch. XIII, p. 66.

80 Ibid., p. 115.

81 See 'La campagna romana con indicazione delle paludi e delle selve' (1802), Archivio di Stato di Roma, Stampe incornicate, n. 105, 65 × 81 cm, and 'Le selve di Cisterna e Sermoneta' (1714), Bibl. Naz. Rome, Miscellanea Valenti, 920, 23 × 38.5 cm, illustrated in Marina Petrucci, 'Alberi e venti: La vertenza di Cisterna e Sermoneta nel secolo XVIII', in Fondazione Lelio e Lisli Basso-Issoco, *L'Ambiente nella storia d'Italia: Studi e immagini* (Venice, 1989).

82 This episode has been treated in detail by Petrucci, 'Alberi e venti', and Elio Lodolino, 'Le "selve" nello Stato pontificio (secc. XV–XVIII): Legislazione e fonti archivistiche', in Simonetta Cavaciocchi (ed.), *L'uomo e la foresta: Secc. XIII–XVIII* (Florence, 1996). See more generally Renato Sansa, *L'Oro verde: I boschi nello stato pontificio tra XVIII e XIX secolo* (Bologna, 2003).

83 Elio Lodolino, 'Il brigantaggio nel Lazio medidionale (1814–1825)', *Archivio della società romana di storia patria*, vol. 83, 1960. This context may have contributed to modern Romans' 'horreur des arbres' (Ampère, *Histoire romaine*, vol. 2, p. 61).

84 See *Les Bois sacrés: Actes du colloque international organisé par le centre Jean Bérard, Naples, 1989* (Naples, 1993). Keith Thomas, 'The Worship of Trees', in *Man and the Natural World: Changing Attitudes in England 1500–1800* (London, 1983), pp. 212–23. See Enrico Coleman's *campagna* watercolours, *Bosco sacro* (1906); *Bosco sacro d'Egeria* (1910), ill. Renato Mammucari and Rigel Langella, *I Pittori della malaria dalla Campagna romana alle Palude Pontine* (Rome, 1999), p. 32.

85 On this occasion, another medical authority was consulted, Domenico Morichini; see his 'Rapporti alla congregazione di Sanita: Selva di Cisterna', in *Raccolti di scritti editti ed inediti del Cavaliere D. Morichini*, 2 vols. (Rome, 1857), vol. 2, pp. 180–96, cit. Petrucci, 'Alberi e venti', pp. 257–9, and Lodolino, 'Le "selve"', p. 532. In 1780, Sermoneta was noted as particularly unhealthy ('si dangereux par le

mauvais air') by Joseph François; see R. Vander Burght, *Joseph François, peintre belge: Émule de David 1759–1851: Les Manuscrits de ses deux voyages en Italie: Les Lettres du Prince Louis et de la princesse Pauline d'Arneberg* (Brussels, 1948), p. 35. Gell noted that at Cisterna, although near the Pontine marshes, it 'does not appear that the air is by any means of the most dangerous quality' (p. 165); he also referred to the 'Bosco di Cisterna' as an example of 'lavish destruction' (Gell, *Topography*, p. 146).

86 'des chaleurs accablantes qu'on éprouve dans certains jours, où il semble qu'on ait les bras et les jambes rompus, avec des tiraillemens dans le nerfs, une lassitude et un abattement universel' (Joseph Jérôme le Français de Lalande., *Voyage d'un français en Italie*, 10 vols (Paris, 1786), vol. 6, pp. 255–6).

87 Arthur Young, *Voyage en Italie pendant l'année 1789*, trans. François Soules (Paris, 1796), p. 344; Michel also cited corrosion (*Recherches*, p. 61).

88 William Parsons, 'Ode on the Siroc', in [Anon.], *The Florence Miscellany* (Florence, 1785), pp. 126–8: 'The siroc is a south east wind, the same as the latin Syrus, which is much dreaded by the Italians, on account of its oppressive heat, and the extraordinary melancholy it occasions' (p. 126): 'Die Fevers rage – the parched throat / And alt'red pulse their sway denote; / The Soul's oppress'd with gloom; / And mid such woes, with tempting mien, / Pale Suicide, by Fancy seen, / Points to a friendly tomb!' (p. 128).

89 'chiroco continuel qui absorbe tous les facultés et qui cause les nombreuses maladies qu'il y a dans Rome' (CDAFR, vol. 15, p. 432, 7 July 1790).

90 On the debate on this, see Stafford, *Voyage into Substance*, p. 191, and Gaetano Moroni, *Dizionario di Erudizione storico-ecclesiastica*, 103 vols (Venice, 1840–61), vol. 50, pp. 203–31; [Ferber], *Lettres sur la minéralogie et sur les divers objets de l'histoire naturelle de l'Italie, écrites par Mr. Ferber à Mr. le Chev. De Born*, trans. B. De Dietrich (Strasbourg, 1776): 'L'air d'un pays inculte n'est pas purifié par les émanations des végétaux (voyez dans le LXII vol. des Transactions philosophiques les observations de Mr. Priestley)' (pp. 2–3).

91 N.M. Nicolai, *Memorie, leggi, ed osservazioni sulle campagne e sull'annona di Roma*, 3 vols (Rome, 1803), vol. 3, p. 252. Nicolai recorded that 70,000 trees were planted on the road from Torre Tre Ponti as

part of Pius VI's campaign to cleanse the Pontine marshes (*Sulle presidenze delle strade ed acque e su giurisdizione economica*, 2 vols (Rome 1829), p. 134). See also Jean Senebier, *Recherches sur l'influence de la lumière solaire pour métamorphoser l'air fixe en air pur par la végétation* (Geneva, 1783).

92 Joseph Forsyth, *Remarks on Antiquities, Arts, and Letters, during an Excursion in Italy in the Years 1802 and 1803*, 4th edn (London, 1835), p. 274.

93 On the claims made for the benefits of planting eucalyptus see Dr Gimbert (de Cannes), *L'Eucalyptus globulus, son importance en agriculture, en hygiène et en médecine* (Paris, 1870), and *Étude sur l'influence des plantations d' "Eucalyptus globulus" dans les pays fiévreux et sur le traitement des accidents intermittents par ce végétal, par le Dr Gimbert,... Mémoire présenté à la Société de médecine de Paris* (Paris, 1875); Luigi Torelli, *L'Eucalyptus e l'agro romano* (Rome, 1878). Lucien Chancerel, *Influence hygiénique des végétaux sur le climat et leur action spéciale sur la malaria et le tuberculose* (1896). Dr L. Aitken, in *British Medical Journal* (27 Sept. 1884) denied repeated claims that planting eucalyptus had been beneficial. Aitken is cited in an anonymous article 'Blue Gum' in Royal Botanic Gardens Kew, *Bulletin of Miscellaneous Information*, 1903, no.1, pp. 1–10, in which further evidence challenging the tree's reputation as a preventative of 'malaria' was gathered for Rome and elsewhere. Tommasi-Crudeli cites an article by Gimbert on 'Sanitary Improvements of Marshy Districts by Means of Eucalyptus globulus' (*Comptes rendus hebdomadaires des sciences de l'Académie des Sciences*, 29 Sept. 1873), which he disputes. Corrado Tommasi-Crudeli, *The Climate of Rome and Roman Malaria* (London, 1892), pp. 98–9.

94 Lady Morgan, *Italy*, 2 vols (New York, 1821), vol. 2, p. 321.

95 William Wetmore Story, *Roba di Roma*, 2 vols (London, 1863), vol. 1, p. 351.

96 Atkinson, *Change of Air*, pp. 9–10.

97 Giacomo Barzellotti, 'connaisseur des mauvais airs de la Maremme toscane', cit. Yves-Marie Bercé, *Le Chaudron et la lancette: Croyances populaires et médecine préventive 1798–1830* (Paris, 1984), p. 233; 'The pestilential *Miasmata* may be broke and destroyed by the Occursion of others' (John Quincy, trans. Nathaniel Hodges, *Loimologia: or, An Historical Account of the Plague in London in 1665; To Which Is Added, An Essay on the Different Causes of Pestilential Diseases, by J. Quincy* (London, 1720), p. 54).

98 See the review in *Journal des savants*, 1719, vol. 32, pp. 505–10, vol. 35, pp. 553–5, vol. 36, pp. 567–70. Lalande, *Voyage*, vol. 6, p. 255.

99 'l'absence de l'hygiène publique et privée, dans l'incurie de government pour ce qui concerne la police médicale, dans l'éducation physique et morale de ses habitants' (Valentin, *Voyage en Italie*, p. 97). He added that Rome's hot, humid atmosphere, combined with the persistent flooding, 'la malpropreté que j'ai vue dans des cours et des allées de plusieurs maisons des quartiers populeux', impermeable 'tuf', blocked canals and aqueducts, all caused unhealthiness and deadly annual fevers.

100 See G. De Matthaeis, *Sul culto reso degli antichi romani alla dea Febbre* (Rome, 1814), and his *Sulle infermerie degli antichi e loro differenza dai moderni ospedali. Dissertazione letta il Dì 24 Luglio 1828 nell'Accademia di archaeologia* (Rome, 1829). De Matthaeis is noted by Stendhal (*Promenades* (1996), p. 34), Louis Valentin (*Voyage en Italie*, p. 100), J.B. Michel, (*Recherches*, p. 18), and Maria Graham (*Three Months passed in the Mountains East of Rome, during the Year 1819* (London, 1921), p. 26), where she compliments him on his 'elegant paper on The Goddess Fever'.

101 Michel, *Recherches médico-topographiques*, pp. 111–55.

102 Mary Dobson pointed out to me that this kind of unpredictable distribution conforms to the habits of mosquitoes. Her comments on early modern England bear quoting here as a curious echo of her predecessors' uncertainties: 'This book sets out to produce the type of regional and medical topography and chronology envisaged, but never produced on a large scale in England during the seventeenth and eighteenth centuries. Its findings ironically serve to reinforce the convictions, the certainties, and the confusions of the early modern medical environmentalists' (*Contours of Death*, pp. 41–2).

103 Montaigne, *Journal de voyage en Italie parle Suisse et l'Allemagne en 1581*, ed. Maurice Rat (Paris, 1955), p. 133.

104 Joseph Forsyth, *Remarks on Antiquities, Arts, and Letters, during an Excursion in Italy in the years 1802 and 1803* (London, 1813), p. 248.

105 'Ce que je trouve d'étonnant, c'est que l'air mauvais soit si près du bon. Vous voyez une maison dans un bon air. A 20 ou 30 pas de là, il y en a une autre en mauvais air. C'est que l'une est plus haut; l'autre, plus bas' ('Voyage de Gratz à La Haye', in Montesquieu, *Œuvres complètes*, 2 vols (Paris, 1949–51), vol. 2, p. 753). The baffling inconsistency of cholera's localised impact in 1837 was noted by Edward Lear: 'Sometimes it carried off whole houses – at others only one or two inmates; the unhealthy often survived; and the stout were victims. Of the surrounding villages, most shut their gates and kept a cordon – but to no purpose; Velletri, alone, opened its gates all the time, and scarcely had any case of the cholera! – so unaccountable on human principles was the process of the disease!' (Vivien Noakes (ed), *Edward Lear: Selected Letters*, (Oxford, 1990), p. 25).

106 Michel, *Recherches médico-topographiques*, pp. 16, 30.

107 According to Decaisne, few places were as prone to 'perturbation' (rivals being Genoa, Milan and Florence) and extreme climatic contrast though year (A.E.L. Decaisne, *Guide médical et hygiénique du voyageur* (Paris, 1864), p. 196).

108 'fièvres endémiques intermittentes…les fièvres simples et pernicieuses pouvant se développer par tout où il n'y a pas de marais pourvu que le système nerveux acquiert cette diathèse prédisposante qui leur convient et qui leur est propre.…diverses contractilités…son influence relâchante et débilitante sur nos organes dont il sembler paralyser l'action. Il engourdit tout le système vivante, et cause une très-grande prostration, de force, une tendance au sommeil, et devient ainsi une puissante cause prédisposante à toutes les maladies nerveuses' (Michel, *Recherches médico-topographiques*, p. 56; where he cites the authority of Giuseppe Giannini, *Della natura delle febbri, e dei metodi di curarle*, 2 vols (Naples, 1817)).

109 'M. Metaxa, je crois, médecin célèbre et homme d'esprit…rien n'est baroque comme les contours de la contagion sur cette carte. Beau sujet à approfondir, mais raisonnablement, et non pas avec de jolies phrases vagues et élégantes' (*Promenades* (1973), p. 400). Stendhal's reference is cited in Ferdinand Braudel, *The Mediterranean and the Mediterranean World in the Age of Phillip II*, 2 vols (French edn 1949; Princeton, 1995), vol. 1, p. 66 note 218.

Luigi Metaxa's map is also noted by Guislain, *Lettres médicales sur l'Italie*, p. 56. For later post-unification maps of malaria see: Eugenia Tognotti, 'La carta della malaria d'Italia (1880–82)', *Quaderni internazionali di storia della medicina e della sanità*, vol. 1, no. 2, 1992, pp. 23–34.

110 François Balley, *Endémo-epidémie et météorologie de Rome: Étude sur les maladies dans leurs rapports avec les divers agents météorologiques* (Paris, 1863). Balley notes that much of his work was based on information from Th. Mayer, 'médecin en chef de l'armée de l'occupation', who had practised in Africa, Rome and Greece over 11 years. See Philip D. Curtin, *Disease and Empire: The Health of European Troops in the Conquest of Africa* (Cambridge, 1998).

111 As its title makes clear, Macculloch's innovative text on 'malaria' was also informed by British military experience abroad: *On Malaria: An Essay on the Production and Localities of the Places by which it is produced: With an Enunciation of the Diseases caused by it, and the Means of Preventing or Diminishing Them, Both at Home, and in the Naval and Military Service* (London, 1827). See William B. Cohen, 'Malaria and French Imperialism', *Journal of African History*, vol. 24, 1983.

112 'un vent inférieur, léchant le sol' (Léon Colin, *Traité des fièvres intermittentes* (Paris, 1870), p. 72 note 3).

113 François Balley, *Météorologie et météographie, pathogénie et nosographie, ou, Eléments de recherches sur la connexion entre les divers agents météorologiques et la pathogénie civile et militaire à Rome, de 1850 à 1861: atlas* (Paris, 1863); *Annexé aux nos 41 et 42 du Recueil de mémoires de médecine, de chirurgie et de pharmacie militaires*. Colin's map of malaria distribution and barracks, based on casualty figures from the latter, printed in *Traité des fièvres intermittentes*, is based on one 'gravé au dépôt de la guerre in Rome', and another done by the Austrian military (preface, p. ix).

114 Colin, *Traité*, p. 71.

115 Forsyth, *Remarks* (1813), p. 266), cit. *Oxford English Dictionary* 'Malaria'.

116 Forsyth, *Remarks* (1813), p. 247.

117 'la carte de l'aria cattiva étoit tout à fait changé. En 1775, les hauteurs de Trinità del Monti étoient réputées à l'abri du mauvais air, et en 1802 elle ne l'étoient plus' (C.V. Bonstetten, *Voyage sur la scène … Énéide* (Geneva, an XIII (1805)), p. 231).

118 Michel, *Recherches médico-topographiques,* pp. 113–14. Doni, *De restituenda salubritate Agri romani,* published posthumously in 1664.

119 Frédéric Lullin de Châteauvieux, *Lettres écrites d'Italie en 1812 et 1813 à Mr Charles Pictet, l'un des rédacteurs de la Bibliothèque britannique* (Geneva and Paris, 1820), quoted in *Edinburgh Review,* vol. 28, March 1817, pp. 56–8. André Vieusseux, *Italy and the Italians in the Nineteenth Century,* 2 vols (London, 1824), vol. 2, p. 165. This source clearly had a certain authority, being noted by Clark, *Medical Notes,* p. 79; Johnson, *Change of Air,* pp. 122–4; and Macculloch, *On Malaria,* pp. 253–5. However, writing in 1859 Denis O'Donovan noted that the Villa Pamfili-Doria was known popularly as Bel Respiro (Denis O'Donovan, *Memories of Rome* (London, 1859), p. 225).

120 Gell, *Topography,* p. 260.

121 'Ce mauvais air fait, pour ainsi dire, le siège de Rome; il avance chaque année quelques pas de plus, et l'on est forcé d'abandonner les plus charmantes habitations à son empire' (de Staël, *Corinne,* p. 110).

122 Clark, *Medical Notes,* p. 79.

123 Morgan, *Italy,* vol. 1, p. 439.

124 A.V. Arnault, *Souvenirs d'un sexagénaire,* 4 vols (Paris, 1833), vol. 3, pp. 269–70.

125 James Johnson, *Change of Air,* 3rd edn (London, 1835), p. 162.

126 He notes as previously good but now bad ('inhabitables'): Monti, Del Borgo, Trastevere, Mont Coelius, Aventin, Gianicolo; the upper part of Strada Pia and Piazza del Popolo and the ends of the streets leading off it were risky: 'Ainsi c'est par une transition presque insensible qu'on passe dans les villes des points malsains à ceux où la santé n'a pas d'atteinte à redouter, et le danger va toujours en diminuant à mesure qu'on se rapproche de la masse des habitations' (Tournon, *Études statistiques,* p. 202).

127 E. Carrière reviews the literature: *Fondements et organisation de la climatologie médicale* (Paris, 1869). See also Foissac, *De la Météorologie,* and his *De l'Influence des climats sur l'homme et des agents physiques sur le moral* (Paris, 1867). See also John Pemble, *The Mediterranean Passion: Victorians and Edwardians in the South* (Oxford, 1987) and especially Vladimir Janković, *Confronting the Climate: British Airs and the making of Environmental Medicine* (New York and Basingstoke, 2010).

128 See David Young, *Rome in Winter, the Tuscan Hills in Summer* (London, 1880).

129 Burgess, *Climate of Italy,* p. 1.

130 Decaisne, *Guide médicale,* p. 195.

131 [Anon.], *A Comparative Sketch of England and Italy,* vol. 1, pp. 105–6.

132 'L'usage à Rome, dans la saison des chaleurs, est de coucher nu. Le Poussin est censé préoccupé de la composition de son beau tableau du *Testament d'Eudamidas.* Une idée heureuse lui est survenue pendant la nuit: il s'est levé précipitamment pour la fixer, et s'est contenter de se couvrir de son manteau' (1804 Salon *livret,* no. 642); the lost plaster had been shown at the 1789 Salon, no. 228. See Michael Preston Worley, *Pierre Julien: Sculptor to Queen Marie-Antoinette* (New York, 2003), pp. 102–11, and *Pierre Julien 1731–1804* (Musée Crozatier, Le Puy-en-Velay, 2004), pp. 62–5.

133 Bemrose, *Life and Works of Joseph Wright,* p. 31.

134 Allan Cunningham, *The Life of Sir David Wilkie,* 3 vols (London, 1843), vol. 2, pp. 141–4, 151–2, 30 Aug. 1825.

135 Ibid., vol. 2, p. 149.

136 Ibid., vol. 2, p. 204, 8 Dec. 1825. See below (note 187) on Charles Eastlake's affinity for heat.

137 'Je ne peux imaginer l'origine de tout cela, sinon dans une réaction qui ne lui est propre, mais qui s'est vue aussi chez d'autres. La voici: cela paraît une chose étonnante et mystérieuse [cosa mirabile e occulta di natura], mais le fait est que changer de pays ou de séjour, c'est comme changer de nature, de capacité de moeurs et d'usages personnels, de sorte que parfois on n'est plus soi-même; on devient un autre et on est tout ahuri et abasourdi. C'est ce qui a du arriver à Rosso dans le milieu de Rome [nell'aria di Roma], en raison des ouvrages étonnants d'architecture et de sculpture qu'il y put voir et des œuvres peintes et sculptés de Michel-Ange qui l'ont peut-être faire sortir de lui-même. Les mêmes troubles amenèrent à quitter Rome, sans leur permettre de réaliser quoi que ce soit, Fra Bartolommeo di S. Marco et Andrea del Sarto' (André Chastel, 'L'aria: Théorie du milieu à la Renaissance', in *Fables, formes, figures,* 2 vols (Paris,

1978), vol. 1, p. 395 (originally in *L'uomo e suo ambiente* (Quaderni di S. Giorgio, no. 34) (Florence, 1973), pp. 161–79), translated from Giorgio Vasari, *Le vite de' piú eccellenti pittori, scultori e architettori*, Club del Libro, 9 vols (Milan, 1962–6), vol. 4, p. 439).

138 'S'il est resté longtemps loin de Florence, c'était uniquement en raison de la qualité de l'air [per la qualità dell'aria], car l'expérience lui avait appris que celui de Florence, tout vif et subtil qu'il est [per essere acuta e sottile] était très nocif à son tempérament, et celui de Rome plus doux et tempéré l'avait gardé en parfaite santé jusqu'à quatre-vingt-dix-ans avec une entière activité de ses sens et avec de forces qui, malgré l'âge, lui ont permis de travailler jusqu'à son dernier jour' (Vasari, *Le vite*, vol. 7, p. 250, cit. Chastel, 'L'aria', p. 393).

139 G. Baglivi, *The Practice of Physick* (London, 1723), p. 178.

140 'On est si peu surpris de voir mourir celui qui, en arrivant de la campagne, loge dans les endroits où l'air est corrompu, et même ceux qui dans ce tems-là y viendront habiter des endroits de la ville où l'air demeure sain, que de voir mourir l'homme qu'un boulet de canon a touché' ([J.B.] Dubos, *Rèflexions critiques sur la poésie et sus la peinture*, 7th edn, 3 vols (Paris, 1770), vol. 2, pp. 292–4).

141 'L'air natal est un remède pour nous' (ibid., vol. 2, p. 242).

142 *Journal des scavans*, vol. 32, 1719, p. 508. Baglivi, *Practice of Physick*, p. 174.

143 Johnson, *Change of Air* (1831), and his *The Recess, or Autumnal Relaxation in the Highlands and Lowlands; Being the Home Circuit versus Foreign Travel; A Tour... to the Highlands and Hebrides* (London, 1834).

144 His source was Giuseppe Mosca, *Dell'aria e de' morbi dall'aria dipendenti*, 2 vols (Naples, 1746–9), cit. Cancellieri, *Lettera*, p. 82.

145 'La liberté même a paru insupportable à des peuples qui n'étaient pas accoutumés à en jouir. C'est ainsi qu'un air pur est quelquefois nuisible à ceux qui ont vécu dans les pays marécageux' (Montesquieu, *L'Esprit des lois*, XIX, 2, cit. Tzvetan Todorov, *Nous et les autres: La Réflexion française sur la diversité humaine* (Paris, 1989), p. 420).

146 Dureau de la Malle, *Économie politique de Rome*, vol. 2, p. 38.

147 'maladies nerveuses...se plaignent d'affections hystériques' (Michel, *Recherches médico-topographigques*, p. 30).

148 'C'est ainsi que le climat inconstant et l'atmosphère toujours humide de Rome développent des tempéraments nerveux, et qu'ils diminuent en même temps la tonicité des organes et l'énergie des forces musculaires' (Michel, *Recherches médico-topographiques*, p. 17; he cites Giuseppe Calanchelli and Andrea Conti, *Opuscoli Astronomici* (Rome, 1813) on climate (p. 18)).

149 Michel, *Recherches médico-topographiques*, p. 15; Léon Colin held the same view, based on experience in Rome and North Africa (*Traité*).

150 *Dictionnaire encyclopédique des sciences médicales*, vol. 5, p. 330, 'Climat'.

151 Edward Trelawny, *Records of Shelley, Byron and the Author* (Harmondsworth, 1973), p. 99.

152 'L'habitude des déplacements et l'activité du travail intellectuel impriment aux organismes une sorte de tempérament nouveau...loin d'échapper aux agents météorologiques, ils en deviennent les jouets en attendant d'en être les victimes' (Carrière, *Fondements*, pp. 24–5).

153 C.M. de La Condamine, *An Extract from the Observations made in a Tour to Italy, by the Chevalier La Condamine, translated by a Fellow of the Royal Society* (London, 1767), pp. 79, 81. J.G. Keysler noted tenants and lodgers 'cannot be compelled to leave a house between St Peter's and Saints day' (*Travels through Germany, Bohemia, Hungary, Switzerland, Italy and Lorrain,* trans. from 2nd edn of German original, 4 vols (London, 1756–7), vol. 2 p. 128).

154 La Condamine, *An Extract*, pp. 1, 131.

155 H.L. Piozzi, *Observations and Reflections made in The Course of a Journey through France, Italy and Germany* (Dublin, 1789), p. 416.

156 Hoolihan, 'Health and Travel', p. 483.

157 Giacomo Barzellotti, *Avvisi agli stranieri che amano di viaggiare in Italia o dimorarvi per conservare o recuperare la salute* (Florence, 1838).

158 Karl Baedeker, *Italy: Handbook for Travellers, First Part, Northern Italy* (Leipzig and London, 1877), p. xxii.

159 Ibid., p. xxiii. 'None but dogs, idiots and Frenchmen walk the streets in the day time' (Keysler, *Travels*, vol. 2, p. 128).

160 *A Handbook of Rome and its Environs; Forming Part II of the Handbook for Travellers in Central Italy*, 5th edn (London, 1858), p. 283.

161 Henry James, *Daisy Miller* ([1878] Harmondsworth, 1986), p. 84.

162 F. L. Jones (ed.), *The Letters of Percy Bysshe Shelley*, 2 vols (Oxford, 1964), vol. 2, p. 34; Armstrong, 'Lectures, p. 194. See also Worboys, 'From Miasmas to Germs', pp. 61–8. Bynum notes that miasmata and contagion are complementary not alternative explanatory entities (W. F. Bynum, 'Cullen and the Study of Fevers in Britain, 1760–1820', in W. F. Bynum and V. Nutton (eds), *Theories of Fevers from Antiquity to The Enlightenment, Medical History* supplement no. 1 (London, 1981), p. 142). And we should note that in 1851 the subtitle given in the Salon *livret* to Ernest Hébert's painting *Malaria* was 'une famille fuyant la contagion'. See also Bercé, 'Les mythes de la contagion', in *Le Chaudron et la lancette*, pp. 204–9.

163 'on fuit avec une terreur superstitieuse le contact avec des mourants' (Prosper Mérimée, *Portraits historiques et littéraires* (Paris, 1874), p. 289). See De Matthaeis's case notes in *Sulle infermerie*.

164 Clark, *Medical Notes*, p. 94.

165 Christine Stevenson, *Medicine and Magnificence: British Hospital and Asylum Architecture, 1660–1815* (New Haven and London, 2000), p. 217. Santo Spirito only accepted male patients; women were treated by San Salvatore. See Edward Chaney's chapter, '"Philanthropy in Italy": English Observations on Italian Hospitals' in *The Evolution of the Grand Tour* (London, Portland OR, 1998), pp. 239–77; and Anna Lia Bonella, 'Gli Ospedali romani nell'età della Restaurazione', in *Archivi e archivista a Roma dopo l'Unita. Genesi storica, ordinamenti, interrelazioni* (Rome, 1994), pp. 485–503.

166 Baedeker, *Italy*, p. xxiii. See also Hoolihan, 'Travel and Health', p. 484.

167 *A Handbook of Rome and its Environs*, p. 283.

168 See also Dr Mendini, *Doctor Mendini's Hygienic Guide to Rome*, translated from the Italian and edited with an additional chapter on 'Rome as a Health Resort' by John J. Eyre (London, 1897), translator's preface.

169 For example, Florentines who resented Rome's new status played up its malarial reputation; see Laura Rossi, 'Appunti per una storia della malaria nell'Agro Romano nella seconda metà dell'Ottocento', in Maria Luisa Betri and Ada Gigli Marchetti (eds), *Salute e classi lavoratrici in Italia dell'Unità al fascismo* (Milan, 1982), p. 247.

170 Laura D. Lane, 'Malaria: Medicine and Magic in the Roman World', in David and Noelle Soren (eds), *A Roman Villa and a Late Roman Infant Cemetery: Excavation at Poggio Gramignano Lugnano in Teverna* (Rome, 1999). See also Frederick S. Paxton, 'Liturgy and Healing in an Early Medieval Saint's Cult: The Mass *in honore sancti Sigismundi* for the Cure of Fevers', *Traditio*, vol. 49, 1994; Mary Dobson, 'Bittersweet Solutions for Malaria: Exploring Natural Remedies from the Past', *Parassitologia*, vol. 40, nos 1–2, 1998.

171 Lancisi, *De noxiis paludum effluviis* (1942), pp. 149–61. See Keysler, *Travels*, vol. 2, pp. 130–1.

172 Brocchi, *Suolo di Roma*, p. 280.

173 Valentin, *Voyage en Italie*, p. 105.

174 'Je m'inondai du vinaigre des quatre voleurs en traversant les marais Pontins' (Stendhal, *Journal*, 4 vols ([1811] Paris, 1932), vol. 4, p. 127).

175 Mariana Starke, *Letters from Italy, between the Years 1792 and 1798, containing a View of the Revolutions in that Country; from the Capture of Nice by the French Republic to the Expulsion of Pius VI from the Ecclesiastical State*, 2 vols (London, 1800), vol. 1, pp. 332–3. Pietro Balestra lists further 'préjugés et superstitions du peuple en fait de preservatifs' (*L'Hygiène dans la ville de Rome et dans la campagne romaine* (Paris, 1876), p. 167).

176 A suitably revolting recipe for Helmont's anti-plague amulets is given in Francis Barrett, *The Magus or Celestial Intelligencer* (London, 1801), pp. 26–7.

177 'Poi di ogni altra cosa bisogna implorare il divino aiuto…l'anima forte e costante, e la speranza del bene nelle cose averse, fa in maniera che i villi del cervello e del cuore siano eccitati ad un vivace contrarsi, amico della natura; per cui il succo dei nervi suol essere dolcemente mosso, e piu felicemente e velocemente la sua materia scorre nei precordi. Il sangue con la sua forza e vitalita afferra gran parte dei nocivi effluvi, che si sforzano di aggirarsi nei visceri. E non lodiamo l'ilarita quale antidoto dei morbi pestilanzi per ragionamenti, ma perche ne siamo mossi da esperienze….l'anima forte e costante, e la speranza del

bene nelle cose averse, fa in maniera che i villi del cervello e del cuore siano eccitati ad un vivace contrarsi, amico della natura; per cui il succo dei nervi suol essere dolcemente mosso, e piu felicemente e velocemente la sua materia scorre nei precordi. Il sangue con la sua forza e vitalita afferra gran parte dei nocivi effluvi, che si sforzano di aggirarsi nei visceri. E non lodiamo l'ilarita quale antidoto dei morbi pestilanzi per ragionamenti, ma perche ne siamo mossi da esperienze….di non aver visto nessun malato de peste…che non l'avesse contratta per il timore di essa' (Lancisi, *De noxiis paludum effluviis* (1942), pp. 159–60).Catherine J. Kudlick notes a similar alignment of mental state and susceptibility in ideas about cholera in Paris in 1832: 'Officials warned that cholera and panic fed one another as they spread from person to person, reducing a person's ability to resist whatever organism caused the disease' (*Cholera in Post-Revolution Paris. A Cultural History* (Berkeley, Los Angeles, London, 1996), p. 14.)

178 Johnson, *Change of Air* (1835), pp. 119–20. He made the modern comparison with the British army at Flushing, which remained healthy until inactive. Similarly, Montesquieu remarked that northerners were less effective in the south during the War of the Spanish Succession because they were in an alien climate (*L'Esprit des lois*, in *Œuvres complètes*, 3 vols (Paris, 1870), vol. 1, pp. 314–15).

179 Peter Quennell, *Byron, the Years of Fame: Byron and Italy* (London, 1974), p. 299.

180 W.S. Rose, *Letters from the North of Italy, addressed to Henry Hallam* (London, 1819), p. 101.

181 Trelawny, *Records*, p. 66.

182 Equally, there were recommended techniques for avoiding malaria in these circumstances; hunters in Terracina believed they could escape infection by changing their clothes after the sweaty exertions of the hunt (Giuseppe Minzi, *Sopra la genesi della febbri intermittenti* (Rome, 1844), pp. 67–8). It is interesting that one of the first accounts of the campagna was written by Leo X's chief huntsman, Domenico Boccamazza, *Della caccia* (Rome, 1548), as noted by Thomas Ashby, *The Roman Campagna in Classical Times* (London, 1927), p. 5. See also Cesare De Cupis, *La Caccia nella Campagna Romana secondo la storia e i documenti* (Rome, 1922).

183 'Il me fallut passer toute la nuit à la fenêtre et dans l'agitation: sans doute ces mouvemens convulsifs m'auront garanti de l'influence maligne de l'air' (Etienne de Jouy, *L'Hermite en Italie*, 4 vols (Paris, 1824), vol. 3, pp. 262–3). An example of the belief in the danger of windows is the Belgian artist Joseph François. In 1781, he described how, having removed his hat while standing at a Roman window, 'Je sentis un coup sourd sur la tête et je me retira précipitemment en arrière tout étourdi', which resulted in a fortnight's fever (Vander Burght, *Joseph François*, pp. 44–5). In 1773 Lord Winchelsea attributed a bout of 'Ague' to going out into the sun (Brinsley Ford Papers, 'Illness').

184 'L'année dernière, mon frère et moi avons déjà fait une reconnaissance dans ces endroits peu connus par les étrangers, mais comme nous n'étions que les deux, nous étions trop peu pour l'être tout fait à l'abri du danger ou, pour mieux dire, de la crainte du danger'.

185 'J'aime, disait Oswald à Corinne, ce danger mystérieux, invisible, ce danger sous la forme des impressions les plus douces. Si la mort n'est, comme je le crois, qu'un appel à une existence plus heureuse, pourquoi le parfum des fleurs, l'ombrage des beaux arbres, le souffle rafraichissant du soir, ne seraient-ils pas chargés de nous en apporter la nouvelle?…Je conçois facilement que les habitants et les étrangers ne se degoûtent point de Rome par le genre de péril que l'on y court pendant les plus belles saisons de l'année' (de Staël, *Corinne* (Paris, 1872), p. 110).(Robert to Marcotte, 10 Aug. 1829, p. 67).

186 Leigh Hunt, *Lord Byron and some of his Contemporaries; With Recollections of the Author's Life*, 2 vols (London, 1828), vol. 1, p. 102., cit. Carl Thompson, *The Suffering Traveller and the Romantic Imagination* (Oxford, 2007), p. 1.

187 C.L. Eastlake, *Contributions to the Literature of the Fine Arts*, 2nd edn (London, 1870), p. 70, cit. John Gage, '"More French than the French": British Romantics and the Roman Landscape', in *Corot, un artiste et son temps* (Paris, 1998), p. 531.

188 'L'aria cattiva des marais Pontins n'est qu'un mauvais quart d'heure à passer; elle ferme ses glaces, ne s'endort point sur la route, et, insouciante du fléau, elle va sans cesse de Rome à Naples et de Naples à Rome….Rome gagne donc à ce

grand malaise de l'Europe impatiente de venir respirer le parfums de ses autels, de sa gloire, et de son climat'. He also described it as: 'le Lazareth nécessaire de la maladie qui tourmente en sens différens les esprits et les âmes' (Baron Jacques Marquet de Montbreton Norvins et al., *L'Italie pittoresque*, 4th edn (Paris, 1850), p. 1).

189 Johnson, *Change of Air* (1831), pp. 141–2.

190 Agucchi to Canon Dulcini in Bologna, from Rome, 15 July 1609, M. and R. Wittkower, *Born under Saturn: The Character and Conduct of Artists; A Documented History from Antiquity to the French Revolution* ([1963] New York, 2007), p. 113.

191 Mary Shelley, letter from Pisa to Medwin in Geneva, in Trelawny, *Records*, p. 199.

192 J.-F. Dancel, *De l'Influence des voyages sur l'homme et sur les maladies* (Paris, 1846), p. 63; Decaisne, *Guide médical*, p. 198.

193 James Whiteside, *Italy in the Nineteenth Century*, 3 vols (London, 1848), vol. 2, p. 52.

194 Clark, *Medical Notes*, p. 106.

195 Burgess, *Climate of Italy*, p. 106; he noted that St Peter's was an exception to these problems with cold, damp churches; its huge volume of air seemed to remain mild in winter, and cool in summer (p. 172). In the Vatican interior, 'perpetual spring reigns' (Celoni, *Ragionamento*, p. 28).

196 Louis Simond, *Voyage en Italie et en Sicile*, 2 vols (Paris, 1828), vol. 1, p. 274.

197 Pucinotti, *Storia*, who pointed out that the vicinity of the Piazza del Popolo was in general bad because exposed to wind, cit. Colin, *Traité*, p. 68.

198 Starke, *Letters*, vol. 2, pp. 43–4.

199 See Robert Casillo, *The Empire of Stereotypes: Germaine de Staël and the Idea of Italy* (London, 2006).

200 *Encyclopédie*, 'Influence', vol. 8, p. 735.

201 Anna Jameson, *Diary of an Ennuyée* (London, 1826; Boston, 1846), p. 175. Chloe Chard kindly gave me this reference.

202 Burgess, *Climate of Italy*, pp. 175–6.

203 James, *Daisy Miller*, p. 81.

204 Johnson, *Change of Air*, p. 127.

205 Burgess, *Climate of Italy*, p. 106. The most notorious cognate modern form of this recognition has been dubbed the 'Stendhal syndrome'; see G. Magherini, *Le Syndrome de Stendhal: Du Voyage dans les villes d'art* (Paris, 1990).

206 'The air of Bracciano, without being pronounced absolutely dangerous, is, in the summer, what the natives call "suspected"' (Gell, *Topography*, p. 128); at Isola Farnese the 'air is reputed unwholesome', and the population was half that at the last census (p. 278). See A. Wallace-Hadrill, L. Haselberger and J. Humphrey, 'Roman Topography and the Prism of Sir William Gell', in L. Haselberger and J. Humphrey (eds), *Imaging Ancient Rome: Documentation, Visualization, Imagination* (Portsmouth, R.I., 2006).

207 See Celli, *History of Malaria*, p. 121 (on the illness of workers at the archaeological excavations at Ostia in 1857), and p. 136, citing Keysler, *Travels through Germany*, vol. 2, pp. 25–7, 30, 337). Corbin, *Le Miasme et la jonquille*, p. 13, on fear of fissures' release of noxious emanations.

208 See Johnson, *Change of Air* (1831), p. 119. Edward Diccy extended this idea to reclaiming the *campagna*, suggesting that one solution would be to pave it over, so as to seal off the rising miasmas (*Rome in 1860* (Cambridge and London, 1861), pp. 46–7.) This reference was kindly pointed out by Kathy Maclauchlan. On the role of paving as a barrier to the exhalation of 'mal'aria', see Pietro Balestra, *L'Hygiène dans la ville de Rome et dans la campagne romaine* (Paris, 1876), pp. 205–7.

209 'un centre d'émanation d'air délétère….J'ai été moi-même attaqué deux fois de la fièvre, l'année dernière, pour avoir séjourné deux ou trois fois dans les fouilles….les exhalaisons de la tourbe qui y étoit mise en contact avec l'air, exhalaisons dont l'abondance est indiquée par la diminution de volume qu'éprouve la tourbe déssechée' (Prony, *Marais Pontins*, p. xxxiv note). Celli had written of similar archaeological problems at Ostia in 1857 (Celli, *History of Malaria*, p. 121).

210 Keysler, *Travels*, vol. 2, p. 26; he notes Seneca, 'Natural Questions', Book iii, chapter 19: 'The eating of fish which have lived in subterraneous, stagnated and foul waters, is very pernicious, and has often proved fatal.' Mariana Starke echoes Keysler closely: 'The stupendous common-sewers, through which the offal of Rome was conveyed into the Cloaca-maxima, are many of them choaked up, even the Cloaca-maxima itself is in bad order; this causes pestilential air; and workmen who, by digging deep, have opened apertures to the above-

mentioned common-sewers, not unfrequently have lost their lives from the putrid effluvia' (*Letters*, vol. 1, pp. 330–1). On Starke, see Jeanne Moskal, 'Politics and the Occupation of a Nurse in Mariana Starke's *Letters from Italy*', in Amanda Gilroy (ed.), *Romantic Geographies: Discourse of Travel, 1775–1844* (Manchester, 2000), p. 159. See also Anne Janowitz, *England's Ruins: Poetic Purpose and the National Landscape* (Oxford, 1990), chapter 2, 'Ruinists in Rome', pp. 38–9.

211 Charles-François Poerson 1704–25, Nicolas Vleughels, 1725–37, François De Troy, 1738–51.

212 'Rome est un pays d'étude et notre maison, par tout ce qui s'y trouve de beau et de bon y convie' (Olivier Michel and Pierre Rosenberg (eds), *Subleyras 1699–1749* (Paris, 1987), p. 66).

213 'l'oisiveté que les jeunes gens contractent aisément dans ce païs' (Bernard Hercenberg, *Nicolas Vleughels: Peintre et directeur de l'Académie de France à Rome 1668–1737* (Paris, 1975), p. 17).

214 'Il n'est point étonnant que vos jeunes gens soient malades; il semble que tout le monde l'est, surtout dans les premiers tems que l'on y habite' (CDAFR, vol. 3, p. 403, d'Antin to Poerson, 3 July 1710).

215 CDAFR, vol. 7, p. 88, Poerson to d'Antin, 14 Nov. 1724.

216 'la chaleur et le froid s'y font sentir tour à tour d'une manière incommode' (Lalande, *Voyage*, vol. 3, pp. 591–5); cit. R. Michea, 'Quelques détails inédits sur le voyage en Italie de Greuze et de Gougenot', *Études italiennes*, vol. 4, 1934, p. 140.

217 CDAFR vol. 15, p. 369.

218 CDAFR, new series, vol. 2, p. 555, 4 vend. An XIII / 26 Sept. 1804.

219 'l'air de Rome est contraire au Sr Gauffier' (CDAFR, vol. 15, p. 239, Ménageot to d'Angiviller, 19 March 1788).

220 'l'intempérie de Rome' (CDAFR, vol. 15, p. 417, 5 May 1790).

221 'Le berceau des arts finiroit par devenir le tombeau des artistes' (CDAFR, vol. 15, pp. 246–7, 9 April 1788). Van de Sandt and Rosenberg note some examples (Pierre Rosenberg and Udolpho van de Sandt, *Pierre Peyron, 1744–1814* (Paris, 1983), pp. 29–32). For Guillaume Lethière's comments on this, CDAFR, new series, vol. 2, p. 181, 23 July 1810. For a later case study see the sculptor James

Pradier: Douglas Siler (ed.), *James Pradier, Correspondance*, 2 vols (Geneva, 1984), vol. 1, pp. 13–14.

222 'est à considerer à Rome' (CDAFR, vol. 17, pp. 155–6).

223 'un local commode, sain et tranquille' (CDAFR, new series, vol. 2, p. 165); on the Villa Medici sickbay, see also Beatrice Bouvier and François Fossier (eds) *Procès-Verbaux de l'Académie des Beaux-Arts, Volume 3: 1821–25* (Paris, 2003), p. 388.

224 Celli, *History of Malaria*, p. 113.

225 Clark, *Medical Notes*, p. 76.

226 Hazlitt, *Notes of a Journey through France and Italy* ([1826] New York, 1983), p. 231; *A Handbook of Rome and its Environs*, p. 285. See also Macculloch, *On Malaria*, pp. 253–7.

227 William H. Pease and Jane H. Pease (eds), *The Roman Years of a South Carolina Artist: Caroline Carson's Letters Home, 1872–1892* (Columbia, S.C., 2003), p. 99, 26 Jan. 1876.

228 Hector Berlioz, *The Memoirs of Hector Berlioz, Member of the French Institute, including his Travels in Italy, Germany, Russia and England 1803–1865*, trans. and ed. David Cairns (London, 1970), p. 176.

229 C.J. Glacken, *Traces on the Rhodian Shore: Nature and Culture in Western Thought from Ancient Times to the End of the Eighteenth Century* (Berkeley, 1967), p. 560.

230 Augustus von Kotzebue, *Travels through Italy, in the Years 1804 and 1805*, 4 vols (London, 1806), vol. 3, pp. 248–9.

231 Bonstetten, *Voyage*, p. 231.

232 Augustus Hare, *Walks in Rome*, 2 vols (London, 1893), vol. 2, p. 431, quoting de Staël; also Valentin, *Voyage en Italie*, p. 108.

233 Michel, *Recherches médico-topographiques*, vol. 1, p. 125.

234 'fièvres annuelles': 'L'année dernière, sur vingt-deux élèves, il y en a dix-sept malades; l'air de cette villa Medici était sain avant que la villa Borghese, qui en est assez près, eût des eaux, et le deviendrait encore probablement, si ces eaux n'y étaient amenées' (Simond, *Voyage*, vol. 1, pp. 359–60).

235 'l'influence des causes morbifiques…tiennent au sol de Rome' (Etienne-Martin Bailly (1796–1837), *Traité anatomico-pathologique des fièvres intermittentes simples et pernicieuses, fondé sur des observations cliniques, sur des faits de physiologie et de pathologie*

comparées, sur des autopsies cadavériques, et sur des recherches statistiques, recueillies en Italie; et principalement à l'Hopital du Saint-Esprit de Rome, pendant les années 1820, 1821, et 1822 (Paris, 1825), p. 138).

236 Guislain, *Lettres médicales sur l'Italie*, p. 57.

5 FATAL PROSPECTS

1 'étonné prodigieusment…la mère-ville du monde…désert…les grands Romains' (Charles Clément, *Léopold Robert d'après sa correspondance inédite* (Paris, 1875), p. 125).

2 Thomas Ashby, *The Roman Campagna in Classical Times* (London, 1927), p. 18.

3 Mirka Beneš uses photographs of livestock and landscape to illustrate her study of pastoralism in the baroque villa and its relation to Claude's landscape art; Robert Sallares includes contemporary views of the *campagna* in his study of malaria and ancient Rome: Mirka Beneš, 'Pastoralism in the Roman Baroque Villa and in Claude Lorrain: Myths and Realities of the Roman *Campagna*', in Mirka Beneš and Dianne Harris (eds), *Villas and Gardens in Early Modern Italy and France* (Cambridge, 2001); Robert Sallares, *Malaria and Rome: A History of Malaria in Ancient Italy* (Oxford and New York, 2002).

4 'quoique défigurée, existe encore dans le paysage' (Charles Bonstetten, *Voyage sur le scène des six derniers livres de l'Enéide* (Geneva, 1971), pp. 7–8). Breislak made the same point as regards an exclusive focus on antiquity causing the neglect of proper observation of natural historical phenomena (Scipion Breislak, *Voyages physiques et lythologiques dans la Campanie: Suivi d'une mémoire sur la constitution physique de Rome*, 2 vols (Paris, an IX [1801]), vol. 1, p. 232).

5 Alfred von Reumont gives a list of landowners (*Della Campagna romana* (Florence, 1842), pp. 35–6 note 9), as does Ashby, *Roman Campagna*, p. 17.

6 Gross treats the Campagna Romana and Agro Romano as equivalent (Hanns Gross, *Rome in the Age of Enlightenment: The Post-Tridentine Syndrome and the Ancien Règime* (Cambridge, 1990)). A useful if provisional distinction is between the classical sites to the south-east and north of Rome, which

attracted landscape artists, the Pontine marshes to the south, and the northern *campagna*. See maps showing favoured itineraries in Peter Galassi, *Corot in Italy: Open Air Painting and the Classical Landscape Tradition* (New Haven and London, 1996), p. 132, plate 158, and Philip Conisbee et al., *In the Light of Italy: Corot and Early Open Air Painting* (Washinton, D.C., 1996), p. 70.

7 Silvio Negro, *Seconda Roma, 1850–1870* (Vicenza, 1966).

8 Letter from Humboldt to Goethe (24 Aug. 1804), in Goethe, 'Winckelmann' (1805), in H.B. Nisbet (ed.), *German Aesthetic and Literary Criticism: Winckelmann, Lessing, Hamann, Herder, Schiller, Goethe* (Cambridge, 1985), p. 244.

9 Jacques Moulard (ed.), *Lettres inédites du comte Camille de Tournon, préfet de Rome, 1809–1814, 1ere partie: La Politique et l'esprit publique* (Paris, 1914), Tournon to his mother, 9 March 1810, cit. Michael Broers, *The Napoleonic Empire in Italy, 1796–1814: Cultural Imperialism in a European Context?* (Basingstoke, 2005), p. 218.

10 Jerome McGann, 'Rome and its Romantic Significance', in Annabel Patterson (ed.), *Roman Images: Selected Papers of the English Institute, 1982*, (Baltimore, 1984).

11 On Hackert, see *Art in Rome in the Eighteenth Century*, ed. Edgar Peters Bowron and Joseph J. Rishel (Philadelphia and London, 2000), p. 517, cat. no. 362. Lusieri is discussed in *Paysages d'Italie: Les Peintres du plein air* (Paris, 2001), p. 73, cat. no. 46, in the company of his similarly constructed *Rome vue depuis les jardins de la Villa Mellini sur le Monte Mario* (1793), p. 72, cat. no. 45.

12 John Izard Middleton, *Grecian Remains in Italy: A Description of Cyclopian Walls, and of Roman Antiquities: With Topographical and Picturesque Views of Ancient Latium* (London, 1812), in chapter V, 'Road from Rome to Albano', pp. 17–19, plate no. 2 (dated 1811). This georgic imagery, combining ruin, agriculture and a sense of easy, intimate cohabitation, arrayed as a pleasing spectacle, was common in the later eighteenth century, for example in Houël's depictions of southern Italian remains: 'Bain antique', 'Reste d'un Bain antique ville de Caucana, à Ste Croix' (Jean-Pierre-Laurent Houël, *Voyage pittoresque des isles de Sicile, de Malte et de Lipari; où*

l'on traicte des antiquités qui s'y trouvent encore, des principaux phénomènes que la nature y offre, du costume des habitans, et de quelques usages, 4 vols (Paris, 1782–7), vol. 4, pp. 12/13, plate 212). His text, however, sets up a conflict between survival and contemporary activity: 'La terre est labourée autour de cet edifice et n'offre aucun reste des bâtimens qui ont dû l'accompagner' (p. 13).

13 Yet so strong was the area's negative image that *L'Artiste* in 1844 ignored the evidence of agriculture and claimed it 'respire toute la mélancholie de la campagne romaine': cit. Marie-Madeleine Aubrun, *Théodore Caruelle d'Aligny 1798–1871: Catalogue raisonné de l'œuvre peint, dessiné, gravé* ([Paris] 1988), p. 446. The print was probably exhibited in the 1846 Salon no. 2288, and previously in 1839 (no. 17), where the title included 'entre Rome et Albano'. Bartolomeo Pinelli constructed a similar visual overcompensation, by filling his image of *Harvesters stacking a Roman Hay Cart* (1820) with brawny labourers struggling with an abundance of hay (Victoria and Albert Museum, London, 13935, 0.6.3 (1) Pageants etc.).

14 For example, Anon., *Tempio di Minerva Medica and Gardens*, c.1865, albumen print, ill Negro, *Seconda Roma*, p. 80–1.

15 James Northcote, *The Life of Sir Joshua Reynolds*, 2nd edn, 2 vols (London, 1819), vol. 1, p. 23.

16 Noel Humphreys, *Rome and its Surrounding Scenery* (London, 1840), pp. 4, 7.

17 'Peu à peu tous les arbres disparaissent et, dans l'immense plaine que nous avions devant nous, on ne voyait ni bâtiments, ni habitants, ni voyageurs, ni eau, ni aucune trace de vie. Dans ce silence universel, on remarque le bruit de ses pas, et mes yeux se fixaient involontairement sur quelques nuées poussées par le vent, comme sur le seul objet qui représentât encore le mouvement et la vie' (Charles Bonstetten, *Voyage dans le Latium* (Geneva, an III [1795]) pp. 215–16).

18 'Si vous voyez cette grande solitude des campagnes romaines, le Tibre qui coule presque inconnu dans ses rives abandonnées, vous seriez frappé comme moi de cette unique idée qui me suit partout, le néant des choses humaines' (Chateaubriand, *Œuvres romanesques et voyages*, ed. M. Regard, 2 vols (Paris, 1969) vol. 1, p. 1420, letter to Mole, 16 July 1803, before death of Pauline de Beaumont Montmorin, whose monument in San Luigi dei Francesi records her as having been 'consumée d'une maladie de langueur').

19 'éminemment la cité de l'âme…banlieu en repos, qui a la majesté du désert sans en avoir l'âpreté mélancholique et nu…interceptant les bruits du monde autour de la ville sainte…grand cloître de Chrétienté' (Philippe Olympe Gerbet, *Esquisse de Rome chrétienne*, 3 vols (Paris, 1844–50), cit. W. Wetmore Story, *Roba di Roma*, 2 vols (London, 1863), vol. 1, pp. 353–4).

20 'inculte, vide, maudit, comme le désert, avec ses grands morceaux d'aqueduc et ses troupeaux de boeufs à large envergure.…L'antique subsiste dans la campagne.…Ça c'est vraiment beau et du beau antique rêvé' (*Correspondance*, vol. 5, p. 772).

21 Lady Morgan, *Italy*, 2 vols (New York, 1821), vol. 2, p. 320.

22 Ibid, vol. 2, p. 326. Eugène Sue describes Gudin's view of the Pontine marshes (which he notes no longer belonged to France) as including a shepherd and a gibbet ('Peintres contemporains – Louis et Théodore Gudin', *Revue de Paris*, vol. 1, 1833 [pub. 1835], p. 226). Géricault's *Italian Landscape* (Petit Palais, Paris), contains the same motif of severed limbs hanging from a gibet.

23 'quadro incantevole…squallido contadino' (A. Nibby, *Analisi topografico-antiquaria della carta de dintorni di Roma*, 3 vols (Rome, 1837), vol. 1, p. 464).

24 'où des animaux immondes habitent avec les cendres des maîtres de la terre' (Bonstetten, *Voyage sur le scène*, p. 45).

25 H.W. Carter, *A Short Account of some of the Principal Hospitals of France, Italy, Switzerland and the Netherlands, with Remarks upon the Climate and Diseases of these Countries* (London, 1819), p. 111. See Stephen Bann, 'Envisioning Rome: Granet and Gibbon in Dialogue', in Catharine Edwards (ed.), *Roman Presences: Receptions of Rome in European Culture, 1789–1945* (Cambridge, 1999), for an alternative form of painterly recuperation. André Vieusseux observed that the arrival of the French in 1809 has caused an exodus, at a stroke turning Rome into a sparsely populated provincial town (*Italy and the Italians in the Nineteenth Century*, 2 vols (London, 1824), vol. 2, p. 165).

26 See [Léon Cogniet], *Léon Cogniet 1794–1880* (Musée des beaux-arts, Orléans, 1990), p. 159.

27 'Carte topografiche della campagna romana', Giuseppe Tomassetti, *La Campagna romana antica, medioevale e moderna*, ed. Luisa Chiumenta and Fernando Bilancia, 4 vols ([1910] Rome, 1975–6), vol. 1, pp. 209–21. Nibby, *Analisi storico-topographico-antiquria*, vol. 1, p. 1, regarding Gell's map as paid for by Count Blessington, 1827.

28 Filippo Luigi Gilii, *Agri Romani historia naturalis tres in partes divisa, sive methodica synopsis naturalium rerum in agro Romano existentium Pars I. Regnum animale*, vol. 1, *Ornithologia, in qua de priori avium classe* (Rome, 1781). Luigi Metaxa, *Monografia de' serpenti di Roma e suoi contorni* (Rome, 1823).

29 Ashby, *Roman Campagna*, pp. 17–18.

30 Corrado Tommasi-Crudeli, *The Climate of Rome and the Roman Malaria*, trans. C. Cramond Dick (London, 1892), p. 54. Founder of the Istituto di Igiene Sperimentale in Rome, 1885, and parliamentarian.

31 Allan Cunningham, *The Life of Sir David Wilkie*, 3 vols (London, 1843), vol. 2, p. 189.

32 Cunningham, *Wilkie*, vol. 2, p. 255, 25 Feb. 1826.

33 Cecilia Powell, *Turner in the South: Rome, Naples, Florence* (New Haven and London, 1987), pp. 29–31.

34 John Gage, *J.M.W. Turner: A Wonderful Range of Mind* (New Haven and London, 1987), p. 49.

35 See *La Campagna Romana da Hackert a Balla* (Museo del Corso, Rome, 2001), cat. nos 58, 100. Caffi ascended at 6.00 p.m. and stayed aloft for one and a half hours.

36 'La campagne de Rome que par politesse sans doute on a appelée campagna, car ce n'est de toutes côtés qu'une lande infecte et souvent stérile' (Bonstetten, *Voyage dans le Latium*, p. 2).

37 William Hazlitt, 'English Students at Rome', in *Criticisms on Art* (London, 1844), p. 222.

38 Morgan, *Italy*, vol. 2, p. 374.

39 'la surface de cette campagne est presque entièrement dénuée d'habitations et de haute végétation; à peine aperçoit-on ça et là quelque oasis, et quelques misérables maisons; la solitude commence aux portes même de la ville, et, comme l'a dit justement un écrivain moderne, Rome est peut-être la seule grande ville qui n'ait pas de banlieue. Cette nudité complète du sol, cette absence de barrières naturelles ou artificielles semblent favorables à la pénétration dans l'atmosphère de Rome d'exhalaisons palustres dont les foyers sont situés à une certaine distance de la ville, soit en dehors des limites de cette campagne, soit dans l'Agro romano lui-même' (Léon Colin, *Traité des fièvres intermittentes* (Paris, 1870), p. 28). For a similar description of the *campagna* see F. Balley, *Endémo-épidémie et météorologie de Rome: Étude sur les maladies dans leurs rapports avec les divers agents météorologiques* (Paris, 1863), p. 10.

40 Jean-Jacques Ampère, *Histoire romaine à Rome*, 4 vols (Paris, 1862–4), vol. 2, p. 72. See now the authoritative account by Sallares, *Malaria and Rome*, and also the classic texts by W.H.S. Jones and Ronald Ross, *Malaria: A Neglected Factor in the History of Greece and Rome* (London, 1907), and Angelo Celli, *The History of Malaria in the Roman Campagna from Ancient Times*, ed. Anna Celli-Fraentzel (London, 1933).

41 'l'homme paisible s'est retiré du tumulte des villes et des foyers de l'intrigue, pour s'adonner à la culture des terres' (Arthur Young, *Voyage en Italie pendant l'année 1789*, trans. François Soules (Paris, 1796), p. vii).

42 Paula Rea Radisich, 'Eighteenth-Century Plein-Air Painting and the Sketches of Pierre-Henri de Valenciennes', *Art Bulletin*, March 1982.

43 Cacherano also wrote on growing grain and building storehouses for it. See Silvia Bordini, 'Un'ipotesi di razionalizzazione tardo-illuminista: I "villaggi agrari" della *campagna* romana', *Quaderni sul Neoclassico*, vol. 3, 1975 (Miscellanea), and for a larger context, E. Piscitelli, *La riforma di Pio VI e gli scrittori economici romani* (Milan, 1958); Fiorella Bartoccini, *Roma nell'Ottocento*, Storia di Roma, vol. xvi (Bologna, 1985), p. 235.

44 Pierre Thouvenel, *Traité sur le climat de l'Italie considerée sous ses rapports phisiques météorologiques et médicinaux*, 4 vols (Verona, 1797–8), vol. 2, p. 225, and vol. 4, p. 3, article supplémentaire no. V. For Italian political emigration at this period, see Anna Maria Rao, *Esule: L'emigrazione politica in Francia 1792–1802* (Naples, 1992).

45 Tommasi-Crudeli, *Climate of Rome*, p. 125; he cites the example of Eleanor Frances Poynter, *Madame de Presnel*, 2 vols (London, 1885).

46 Chateaubriand's 'Lettre à M. Fontanes' was originally published in the *Mercure*, 3 March 1804, not

1803 as he claims. See *Lettre à M. de Fontanes sur la campagne romaine*, ed. J.M. Gautier (Geneva, 1951). He mentions the rejection of an English company's proposed 'défrichement' of the *campagna* in the winter of 1829 as not economical, citing N.M. Nicolai, *Memorie, leggi ed osservazioni campagna annona*, 3 vols (Rome, 1803). The fourth unpublished volume of Nicolai's *Memorie* was published by A. Canaletti Gaudenti, *La politica agraria e annonaria dello Stato Pontificio da Benedetto XIV a Pio VII* (Rome, 1947).

47 A French finance company represented by Augusto Guichard, a Paris banker, and Pietro Tullien, consular agent of the French king in Rome, presented a plan for a perpetual concession to a 'Società di Colonizzazione dell'Agro Romano' to Leo XII, then Pius VII (Carlo M. Travaglini, *Il dibattito sull'agricultura romana nel secolo XIX (1815): Le Accademie e le società agrarie* (Rome, 1981), p. 18.

48 For example, G. de Giovanni, *Difesa del Popolo romano sull'abandono della campagna del. Can. Gioacchino de Giovanni parroco di S. Marco* (Rome, 1848).

49 'cadre magnifique que cette splendide nature, ces marais Pontins, cet infini solennel de la campagne romaine pour ces grands ossemens du passé!' (F.S. Feuillet de Conches, *Léopold Robert, sa vie, ses œuvres et sa correspondance* (Paris, 1848), pp. 68–9).

50 'On se promène en ce pays comme en un vaste Salon d'exposition publique où sont rassemblés les chefs-d'œuvre des grands maîtres du temps de Léon X, et les monuments de l'antiquité: pour le peuple, on n'y songe seulement pas. Sous l'épée française, ou sous le baton autrichien, qu'importe cet esclave malheureux et pourtant si plein de génie? Qu'est-ce que cela fait à l'artiste, au poète, au rêveur?' (*Le Globe*, 2 Nov. 1824, p. 97, cit. Jacques Misan, *L'Italie des doctrinaires, 1817–1830: Une Image en élaboration* (Florence, 1978), p. 29).

51 Beneš, 'Pastoralism in the Roman Baroque Villa'.

52 Helen Langdon, 'The Imaginative Geographies of Claude Lorrain', in Chloe Chard and Helen Langdon (eds), *Transports: Travel, Pleasure, and Imaginative Geography* (New Haven and London, 1996), p. 161. A recent illustration of the resilience of the association of Roman landscape and the ideal was the exhibition and catalogue *Nature et idéal. Le Paysage à Rome* (Paris, 2011).

53 Sabrina Norlander Eliasson, *Portraiture and Social Identity in Eighteenth-Century Rome* (Manchester, 2009).

54 Lisa Beaven, 'Landscapes of Death: Claude Lorrain and the Roman Campagna', unpublished paper, delivered British School at Rome, 2003; see also her 'Cardinal Camillo Massimo and Claude Lorrain: Landscape and the Construction of Identity in Seicento Rome', *Storia dell'Arte*, no. 112, April 2006.

55 'Nicola Poussin e Claudio Lorena non oseron spingersi troppo oltre fuori Porta del Popolo, over abitavano et dipingevano' (Pierre de Nolhac, *Souvenirs d'un vieux romain* (Paris, 1921), pp. 67–8, quoting Ugo Fleres; the unstated source is *La Campagna romana* (Bergamo, 1904), p. 18. Angelo Celli notes that in 1609 Domenichino refused to paint the interior of the convent at Grottaferrata as long as the air remained bad (*History of Malaria*, p. 123).

56 *Liber Veritatis* (1777), introduction, cit. David Solkin, *Richard Wilson: The Landscape of Reaction* (Tate Gallery, London, 1982), p. 41.

57 An essentially unpicturesque and agriculturally literal exception to this is *A Flock of Sheep in the Campagna*, 1656, oil on canvas, 35 × 44.5 cm, Gemäldegalerie der Akademie der bildenden Künste, Vienna, ill. Richard Rand, *Claude Lorrain: The painter as Draftsman: Drawings from the British Museum* (New Haven and London, 2006), fig. 10, p. 37. There is a curious echo of this in a painting formerly attributed to Léon Cogniet (*Vue de la campagne de Rome, avec un berger gardant des moutons près de grottes aménagées en étable*, c.1820, oil on papier marouflé, 24.8 × 38.3 cm; see *Le Temps des passions: Collections romantiques des musées d'Orléans* (Orléans, 1997), p. 327, cat. no. 33).

58 'aux genres d'antiquités, de ruines et de paysages, [qui] marchent sur les traces de leurs dévanciers, et ne s'attachent qu'aux vues et aux sites qui ont été peints' (P.H. Valenciennes, *Éléments de perspective pratique à l'usage des artistes...*(Paris, 1799), p. 606).

59 In addition to his painting of this motif, we might also note the Julliens' observation that the roads Corot followed on his way to and amongst the Castelli romani were for the most part antique in origin; see André and Renée Jullien, 'Corot dans les Castelli romani', *Gazette des beaux-arts*, vol. 110, 1987.

60 See Richard Verdi, 'Poussin's Critical Fortunes: The Study of the Artist and the Criticism of his Works from c.1690 to c.1830 with Particular Reference to France and England', Ph. D. thesis, University of London, 1976, p. 175, for a thorough account of this topic; and Galassi, *Corot in Italy*, pp. 162–5. For Poussin's walks around Rome see André Félibien, *Entretiens sur les vies et sur les ouvrages des plus excellens peintres anciens et modernes*, 2 vols (Paris, 1685–8), vol. 2, pp. 318ff.; for an anecdote about Poussin's promenades around Rome, see Jean-Baptiste Deperthes, *Histoire de l'art du paysage*…(Paris, 1822), p. 100.

61 The site's representations include: Guillaume Bodinier, *Vue de la fabrique du Poussin*, drawing, dated 3 August 1823 ([Bodinier], *Guillaume Bodinier: Paysages d'Italie, dessins de 1823 a 1826* (Musée des beaux-arts, Angers, 2004), p. 18, cat. no. 3, and an interior view, dated 19 January 1824, p. 20, cat. no. 5. Constant Bourgeois: *Villa Crescenza*, engr. *Vues et fabriques d'Italie* (Paris, 1803), no. 5: the Villa Crescenza, from the end of the fifteenth century, was built between via Flaminia and via Cassia 'dans la vallée autrefois connus sous le nom de "Val de Poussin", où coule une petite rivière, le Fosco della Crescenza'. Giacomo Caneva: *Campagna romana: La Crescenza, detta Valle del Poussin*, 1850–2, salt print, 20 × 27.6 cm. Fotomuseo Giuseppe Panini, Modena, inv. 60, ill. *Roma 1840–1870: La fotografia, il collezionista e lo storico; Fotografie della collezione Orsola e Filippo Maggia* (Modena, 2008), pp. 117, 148, cat. no. 31. J.B.C. Corot: drawing RF 9009; Alfred Robaut *L'Œuvre de Corot*, 4 vols (Paris, 1905), cat. 2481; painting RF 1941–6, Robaut, cat. no. 53. Ernest Hébert: see *Promenades italiennes: Études d'Ernest Hébert* (La Tronche, Grenoble, 2006), cat. no. 18. Edward Lear made at least two views of La Crescenza: a vignette, 'Crescenza', to which is attached 'note a': 'A tenimento four miles from Rome, to the left of the Flaminian Way, belongs to the family of the Raggi-Crescenzi, perhaps descended from the Crescenzi, Prefects of Rome in the tenth century (Nibby, *Analisi topografico-antiquaria della carta de dintorni di Roma*, vol. 1, p. 528); Crescenza is more usually known by the name of Poussin's Castle', in Lear's *Illustrated Excursions in Italy*, 2 vols (London, 1846), vol. 2, p. 38; and a watercolour, 29.2 × 49.9 cm, dated 17

March 1867, British Museum, London, 1929.0611.69). Claude Lorrain: *View of la Crescenza*, 1677, pen and brown ink; 19.6 × 25.7 cm, British Museum, London, 1957, 1214.124; record of a painting formerly in Downton Castle (Shropshire), Kincaid-Lennox Collection, from the *Liber Veritatis*. A.E. Michallon drawing: annotated 'Fabrique dite du Poussin Rome 1820' (Louvre, Paris, RF 13968).

62 'à la tête de tous les paysagistes.…Les qualités dont la réunion feroit la perfection peut-être chimérique du paysage, sont très nombreuses, et peut-être y en a-t-il dans le nombre d'incompatibles entre elles.…Lui seul, dans cet art, a su dérober à la nature le secret de ce mouvement calme, de ces magiques effets de l'air et la lumière, qui sont la vie du paysage.…On ne voit pas ses tableaux; on y est, on en respire l'air, on est enveloppé de leur atmosphère' (Quatremère de Quincy, 'Essai historique sur l'art du paysage à Rome', based on his review of Goethe's *Winckelmann und sein jahrhundert* and Johann Heinrich Meyer's *Essai sur l'histoire de l'art au dix-huitième siècle* in *Archives littéraires de l'Europe*, vol. 10 (Paris, 1806), pp. 203–4).

63 'prétention mesquine et rétrécie…représenter fidelement des sites donnés, et de faire ce qu'on appelle un portrait de la nature…il faut dire que rien n'a plus contribué à éteindre le génie et l'invention poétique dans le paysage.…véritables ouvrages…imitation servile d'aucun point de vue' (ibid, pp. 207–8).

64 'momens de calme' (Deperthes, *Histoire de l'art du paysage*, p. 160). These remarks resemble those of Louis-Sébastien Mercier on the physiognomic truth revealed when human features relaxed during sleep (*Le Nouveau Tableau de Paris*, 6 vols (Paris, 1797), vol. 6, chapter 228, cit. Richard Wrigley, 'The Afterlife of an Academician', in Nicola Kalinsky (ed.), *Courage and Cruelty: Le Brun's Horatius Cocles and the Massacre of the Innocents* (Dulwich Picture Gallery, London, 1990), p. 39.

65 'Une vapeur particulière, répandue dans les lointains, [qui] arrondit les objets et dissimule ce qu'ils pourraient avoir de dur ou de heurté dans leurs formes' (letter to Fontanés, 10 Jan. 1804, cf. Hersant, *Italies*, pp. 103–4); Alfred J.B. Rivoire singled out the 'doux éclat qui n'offense par la vue et se caractérise par sa moittur' (*Essai sur la topog-*

NOTES TO PP. 115–123

raphie et le climat de la ville de Rome et du bassin romain (Montpellier, 1853), p. 35.

66 'Vous avez sans doute admiré dans les paysages de Claude Lorrain, cette lumière qui semble idéale et plus belle que la nature? Eh bien, c'est la lumière de Rome!' (ibid.).

67 Claude's reputation as habitué of the *campagna* was the subject of Bergeret's 'Claude Lorrain et Innocent X: Ce Pape professait le plus haute estime pour le Lorrain; il aimait à le rencontrer dans ses promenades aux environs de Rome, et le regardait souvent étudier en s'entretenant avec lui' (1831 Salon, no. 123), a fantasy of aesthetic communion in the *campagna*.

68 'l'air toujours chargé de vapeurs produit pour la perspective aérienne des effets sûrs et décidés' ('Observations sur l'Ecole française des arts à Rome' to Minister of the Interior from 'Directeur par interim', 8 Oct. 1807, cit. H. Lapauze, *Histoire de l'Académie de France à Rome*, 2 vols (Paris, 1924), vol. 2, p. 76). He also hoped the example of landscape painters inspired by environs would encourage history painters to treat landscape in their works not just 'en accessoire'. Yet Ménageot had noted that too many landscape painters had come to Rome, where there was insufficient work to sustain them (CDAFR, vol. 15, p. 290).

69 D.E. Williams, *The Life and Correspondence of Sir Thomas Lawrence*, 2 vols (London, 1831), vol. 2, pp. 160–1.

70 Ibid., vol. 2, p. 190; he goes on to make a comparison with Claude. Wilson admired Claude for 'air' (and Dughet for 'composition'), according to Sir W. Beechey, cit. W. Whitley, *Artists and their Friends in England 1700–1799*, 2 vols (London, 1928), vol. 1, p. 380, cit. Solkin, *Wilson*, p. 15.

71 W. Gell, *The Topography of Rome and its Vicinity*, revised and enlarged by E.H. Bunbury (London, 1846), p. 36.

72 Morgan, *Italy*, vol. 2, pp. 224–5.

73 William Hazlitt, 'On Gusto', *The Complete Works of William Hazlitt*, ed. P.P. Howe, 21 vols (London, 1930–4), vol. 4, p. 79, cit. Claire Pace, 'Claude the Enchanted: Interpretations of Claude in England in the earlier Nineteenth Century', *Burlington Magazine*, vol. III, no. 801, Dec. 1969. Further on Hazlitt and Claude, see Kathleen Nicholson, 'Turner, Claude, and the Essence of Landscape',

in David Solkin (ed.), *Turner and the Masters* (London, 2009).

74 'Les Ateliers des peintres sont disposés à manière à pouvoir jouir successivement de la ville de Rome et de la campagne la plus étendue, aussi variée dans ses formes que dans ses effets' (CDAFR, new series, ed. Georges Brunel and Isabelle Julia, vol. 2, Directorat de Suvée, 1795–1807 (Rome, 1984), Suvée to Institut, Classe des beaux-arts, 4 vend. An XIII / 26 Sept. 1804, p. 555).

75 'Voyez à Rome la vie solitaire de l'artiste; il y vit tellement enfermé dans son étude [studio] qu'on le prendrait pour un saint ermite. Ses fenêtres, fermées du coté de la terre, ne lui laissent voir qu'un ciel presque toujours serein, ou variée par des nuages tantôt brillants et tantôt orageux' (C.V. Bonstetten, *L'Homme du midi et l'homme du nord, ou l'influence du climat* (Geneva and Paris, 1824), p. 79).

76 Galassi, *Corot in Italy*, p. 95. See Kim Sloan below, note 108.

77 Pace, 'Claude the Enchanted'.

78 Henry Matthews, *The Diary of an Invalid…* (London, 1820), p. 239.

79 See Humphrey Wine, *The Seventeenth-century French Paintings*, National Gallery catalogues (London, 2001), pp. 64–81.

80 *Modern Painters*, 2nd edn, preface, in John Ruskin, *The Works of John Ruskin*, ed. E.T. Cook and Alexander Wedderburn, 39 vols (London, 1903–12), vol. 3, pp. 42–3. For a discussion of this passage in terms of changing attitudes to landscape painting and its conventions which nevertheless ignores the problems posed by the prospect of a poisoned landscape, see Malcolm Andrews, *Landscape and Western Art* (Oxford, 1999), pp. 182–3. Robert Browning was also struck by the terrain's covering of grass: 'The Champaign, with its endless fleece / of feathery grasses everywhere', cit. Mrs Russell Barrington, *The Life and Letters of Frederic Baron Leighton of Stretton*, 2 vols (London, 1906), vol. 1, p. 146, 29 April 1854.

81 *Modern Painters*, in Ruskin, *Works*, vol. 3, p. 189.

82 Steven Adams, *The Barbizon School: The Origins of Impressionism* (London, 1994), p. 35.

83 'Revenant d'Italie, où ils [paysagistes] avaient mené, loin de la fièvre combative des ateliers parisiens, loin de toute préoccupation provocatrice, des journées paisibles et réfléchies, ils en rappor-

taient une gravité et une sérénité d'art dont on ne soupçonnait pas le rôle prochain' (Prosper Dorbec, 'La Tradition classique dans le paysage au milieu du XIXe siècle', *Revue de l'art ancien et moderne*, vol. 24, no. 139, Oct. 1908, cit. *Paysages d'Italie*, p. xxxvii).

84 'il esperienza catartica del plein air, con il suo lascito vitale per l'ottocento' (Anna Ottani Cavina and Emilia Calbi (eds), *La pittura di paesaggio in Italia: Il settecento* (Milan, 2005), p. 13).

85 Conisbee et al., *In the Light of Italy*, pp. 76, 151.

86 *De Corot à l'art moderne. Souvenirs et variations* (Musée des Beaux-Arts, Rheims, 2009), p. 53.

87 'chargées d'irréalité, qui ne jaillissaient plus des lieux géographiques' (*Paysages d'Italie*, p. xxxv).

88 On Rome as originary site for painting out of doors from nature, see, for example, Luciana Martins, 'The Art of Tropical Travel 1768–1830', in Miles Ogborn and Charles W.J. Withers (eds), *Georgian Geographies: Essays on Space, Place and Landscape in the Eighteenth Century* (Manchester, 2004).

89 Galassi, *Corot in Italy*, p. 141.

90 'Tu ne peux te faire une idée du temps que nous avons à Rome. Voilà un mois que je suis chaque matin réveillé par l'éclat du soleil qui frappe sur le mur de ma chambre. Enfin, il est toujours beau. Mais aussi, en revanche, ce soleil répand une lumière désespérante pour moi. Je sens toute l'impuissance de ma palette. Apporte des consolations à ton pauvre ami, qui est tant tourmenté de voir sa peinture si misérable, si triste auprès de cette éclatante nature qu'il a sous les yeux. Il y a des jours, véritablement, où on jetterait tout au diable' (*Corot par lui-même*, 2 vols (Paris, 1924), vol. 1, pp. 16–17). See also Michael Clarke, *Corot and the Art of Landscape* (London, 1991), p. 28.

91 'partir pour faire une campagne' (letter to Abel Osmond, May 1826, *Corot par lui-même*, vol.1, p. 17). Corot considered his studies as just that, 'instruments de travail', only later thinking to leave them to a museum (André and Renée Jullien, 'Les Campagnes de Corot au nord de Rome (1826–1827)', *Gazette des beaux-arts*, vol. 99, May–June 1982, p. 194). See Linda Freeman Bauer, 'Oil Sketches, Unfinished Paintings, and the Inventories of Artists' Estates', in Hellmut Hager and Susan Scott Munshower (eds), *Light on the Eternal City: Observations and Discoveries in the Art and Architecture of Rome* (Philadelphia, 1987).

92 'Mais avant d'avoir à lutter contre ces redoutables voisins, ils eurent à combattre d'autres ennemis, le sol même qu'ils labouraient, l'air que respirait leur poitrine. Ils en triomphèrent comme ils devaient triompher de tout; le ciel leur avait fait une rude destinée: c'est pour cela qu'elle fût grande' (Ampère, *Histoire romaine à Rome*, vol. 2, p. 72).

93 'L'Italie le frappa beaucoup par son climat éclatant, par ses vigoureux contrastes de lumière et d'ombre, par la manière grandiose dont les masses se dessinent sous son beau ciel....les contrées d'un aspect voilé....violence du climat italien...soleil implacable...justesse' (T. Silvestre, *Histoire des artistes vivants français et étrangers: Études d'après nature* (Paris, 1855–6), pp. 90–1). Peter Galassi also uses this metaphor; see *Corot en Italie* (Paris, 1999), p. 74. This is curiously similar to the way Planche censured Léopold Robert's technique in the *Arrival of the Harvesters*. Robert copied everything which seduced him in the *campagna*: 'la passion du naturel, exploitée trop en détail, séduit l'imagination de l'artiste à n'être plus qu'une mosaïque plus ou moins ingénieuse' (Gustave Planche, *Salon de 1831* (Paris, 1831), p. 95). There are still traces of this attempt to confront the conditions of overexposed light in work from his third Italian trip in 1843. *Genzano* (oil on canvas, 35.8 × 57.1 cm, Philips Collection, Washington, D.C.), for all its framing bushes and scrub, and the stripy veiled sky above, has a central core of hot, sandy rock which bulges out from the painting's centre.

94 'Ce mélange d'antique et de moderne, cet assemblage d'irrégularité et de symétrie, d'incohérence et d'harmonie, de folie et de raison, forme un tout original que l'on ne trouve qu'à l'Italie et sur-tout à Rome' (Valenciennes, *Éléments*, pp. 595–6).

95 [Schirmer], *Johan Wilhelm Schirmer und seine Zeit: Landschaft im 19. Jh. zwischen Wirklichkeit und Ideal* (Kunsthalle Karlsruhe/Suermont-Ludwig-Museum Aachen, Heidelberg, 2002). [Schirmer], *Johan Wilhelm Schirmer: Von Rheinland in die Welt*, ed. Marcell Perse et al. (Petersberg, 2010). See also *Sehnsucht Italien: Corot und die frühe Freilicht 1750–1850* (Baden, 2004).

96 'beaucoup plus salutaire qu'autrefois...la grande sympathie de la nature solitaire nourrit et en même temps satisfait un désir qui...très facilement peut

devenir lourd' (Christoph Heilmann in *Paysages d'Italie*, p. 241).

97 'une nature forte, puissante, où la vie, la lumière et la chaleur débordent de toutes parts' ([Anon.], 'Beaux-arts: Salon de 1831; Réouverture. Léopold Robert', *L'Artiste*, vol. 1, 1831, p. 233).

98 'cette teinte savante qui plaît tant aux peintres, tous en les désespérant. Ce ciel est constamment beau' (J.B. Guinan Laoureins, *Tableau de Rome vers la fin de 1814* (Brussels, 1816), p. 219).

99 *Isidore-Alexandre Auguste Pils: sa vie et ses œuvres* (Paris, 1876), p. 20). I am extremely grateful to Kathy Mclauchlan for drawing this reference to my attention.

100 Richard W. Thomas, 'Photography in Rome', *The Art-Journal*, May 1852, p. 159.

101 [Anon.] 'Photographs of Rome', *The Art Journal*, new series, vol. 1, 1862, p. 227.

102 Colin, *Traité des fièvres intermittentes*, preface, pp. vii–ix, 59.

103 Enrico Prampolini, 'Incontro con Picasso', in *Cinquanta Disegni di Pablo Picasso (1905–1938)* (Novara, 1943), cit. Marilyn McCully (ed.), *A Picasso Anthology: Documents, Criticism, Reminiscences*, (London, 1981), p. 123.

104 'Enfin je [ne] suis descendu du Janicule que lorsque la légère brume du soir est venue m'avertir que bientot je serais saisi par le froid du soir subit et fort désagréable et malsain qui en ce pays suit immédiatement le coucher du soleil' (Stendhal, *Vie de Henry Brulard*, ed. H. Martineau (Paris, 1927), p. 1). On the Gianicolo's reputation as one of the 'worst' Roman locations (with S. Giovanni Laterano, Forum, ancient Velabrum, banks of the Tiber, Trastevere, Janiculum to St Peter's, Vatican), see T.H. Burgess, *Climate of Italy in relation to Pulmonary Consumption …* (London, 1852), p. 186.

105 'la *malaria* menaçait d'arriver bientôt avec son cortège de fièvres, et Bertin, n'osant plus travailler dans la campagne de Rome, m'annonça un jour qu'il allait s'installer à la Riccia' (Amaury-Duval, *L'Atelier d'Ingres* (Paris, 1924), p. 124).

106 'le moment le plus dangereux pour cette fièvre qui ne nous quitte plus jamais …une précieuse maquette faite à tatons, car la nuit avait jeté son voile sur mes pinceaux' (Théodore Gudin, *Souvenirs du Baron Gudin, peintre de la marine (1820–1870)* (Paris, n.d.), pp. 93–4). A copy by the Baronne de Montaran of Gudin's *Marais pontins* (90 × 120 cm, Musée des beaux-arts, Caen), was destroyed in the war. Gudin's picture was described as 'the gem of the exhibition' (the 1833 Salon) in *The Court Journal: Court Circular and Fashionable Gazette*, vol. 5, 1833, p. 682. See also Sue, 'Peintres contemporains', p. 226.

107 'Ruins of the town of Nympha', in Middleton, *Grecian Remains*, pp. 35–6; plate 15, opp. p. 35, in chapter VII, 'Of Nemi, the lake, and its environs', p. 26. He notes that 'swarthy women of Norba' take water from the lake. The view chosen by Middleton was also adopted by Robert Macpherson approximately 50 years later (see Richard Wrigley, *Ruination: Photographs of Rome* (Djanogly Art Gallery, University of Nottingham, 2008), p. 26, cat. no. 15).

108 As summarised by Kim Sloan: 1. Sketch from life; 2. Enlarge the parts at home; 3. Correct these enlarged parts from life; 4. Correct the whole from these parts with ink at home; 5. Shade the whole with lead; 6. Finish with Indian ink at home; 7. Colour from life with dry colours and leather stumps (Kim Sloan, *Alexander and John Cozens: The Poetry of Landscape* (New Haven and London, 1986), p. 13).

109 Tobias Smollett, *Travels through France and Italy*, ed. F. Felsenstein ([1766] Oxford, 1979), pp. 245–6.

110 See Bianca Riccio's comments on *Les Marais Pontins* p. 353 (cat. no. 218), in *Paysages d'Italie*, p. 532. This may have exacerbated a painful eye condition perhaps brought on by sun light (Vahan D. Barooshian, *The Art of Liberation: Alexander A. Ivanov* (New York and London, 1987), p. 23).

111 M.V. Alpatov, *A.A. Ivanov: Zizn' I tvorcestvo*, 2 vols (Moscow, 1956), vol. 2, p. 291, cit. Iris Blochel, *Aleksandr Ivanov (1806–1858): Vom 'Meisterwerk' zum Bilderkreis* (Berlin, 2004), p. 103.

112 Tolstoy mentions the picture as a work of the character Golenishtchev in *Anna Karenina*.

113 Two works which focus more on later nineteenth-century art are *Paludi Pontine e Agro Romano nella pittura dell'ottocento* (Rome, 1981), and Renato Mammucari and Rigel Langella, *I Pittori della malaria dalla Campagna romana alle Palude pontine* (Rome, 1999).

114 Painting (Museo di Roma, Palazzo Braschi) and print: *Pius VI visiting the Drainage Works at the Pontine Marshes*, c.1784–5, coloured etching, 24.8 ×

25.8 cm, Goethe Museum, Düsseldorf ([Ducros], *Abraham-Louis-Rodolphe Ducros: A Swiss Painter in Italy* (Dublin, 2003), p. 13, fig. 12); *Pie VI au marais Pontins* (Pawlovsk, near St Petersburg), bought by Catherine the Great in 1792. Both illustrated and discussed in *Images of the Grand Tour: Louis Ducros 1748–1810* (Geneva, 1985), pp. 77–8, cat. no. 55. Ducros was commissioned by the pope. Pius visited the scheme every Easter between 1780 and 1796. The St Petersburg version (99 × 137 cm), shows a view facing south-west from heights bordering the Pontine marshes near Sezze looking towards Monte Circo and Isola Ponziane, with Terracina visible in the background on the left. In the Rome version (122 × 170 cm, n.d., 1786) the setting is at the bottom of Monte Circeo; Linea Pio and Terracina harbour are visible on the right. See also Cecilia Pericoli Ridolfino, 'Pio VI alle Paludi Pontine', *Bolletino dei musei communali di Roma*, vol. 22, nos 1–4, 1975, pp. 26–32.

115 For a listing of the incidence of Tivoli as a landscape subject in eighteenth-century Salons and between 1800 and 1833, see *Tivoli, variations sur un paysage au XVIIIe siècle* (Musée Cognac-Jay, Paris, 2010), pp. 26–7.

116 It is interesting to note that the first landscape subject suggested in N.G.H. Lebrun's *Essai sur le paysage, on Du Pouvoir des sites sur l'imagination* (Paris, 1822), produced after three years in Rome, is 'Un marais fétidè' (p. 17). Pierre-Jules Jollivet (1794–1871), *Paysans dans la campagne* or *Famille de paysans dans une charrette*, (117 × 90 cm), Musée de Soissons, bears a strong resemblance to Robert's painting, which it presumably post-dates; the Spanish costumes point to a date after the artist's trip to Spain in 1826; see also his similarly ambiguous *La Halte* (Daumier Leclere Saleroom, Marseille, 14 March 2009, lot 76).

117 Lajoye, *Paysage historique: Marius chassé de Rome précipite ses pas vers les marais de Minturne, apres avoir traversé dans sa fuite un gros [?] de cavaliers sans en être reconnu*, 1822 Salon, no. 762; Remond, *Paysage historique: Marius découvert par des soldats dans les marais à Minturne (M.I.)[?]*, 1827 Salon, no. 839; Vignes de Toulouse, *Vision d'un laboureur romain: L'étoile aux longs cheveux, signal de grands revers, / En sillons enflammés courut au bout des airs; / Du soc de la charrue, on dit qu'un laboureur / Entrou-*

vrit une tombe, et saisi d'épouvante, / Vit Marius lever la tête menaçante (Presage qui annonce la mort de César et la guerre civile à Rome), 1827 Salon, no. 2399).

118 See also Roger's *Une femme poursuivie par un buffle dans les marais pontins*, 1827–8 Salon; Reynolds, print, *La chasse aux marais*, after Horace Vernet, 1827 Salon, no. 1311; Horace Vernet, *Départ pour la chasse dans les marais Pontins*, Salon de 1831, no. 2085, and *Le départ pour la chasse (Environs de Rome)*, Exposition au profit des blessés du 27, 28, et 29 juillet 1830, no. 596 (1831); now National Gallery of Art, Washington, D.C., *Departure for the Hunt in the Pontine Marshes*, oil on canvas, 100 × 150.7 cm, 2004.38.1, where dated '1833'; see also Vernet's *Etudes de forêt: même numéro*, 1831 Salon, 6th supplément; 'Un cavalcatore conduisant ses boeufs', 2nd supplement no. 2879. See Ernest Legouvé, 'Campagne de Rome', in Norvins et al., *L'Italie pittoresque* (Paris, 1834), pp. 1–6, where Vernet's pictures are the occasion for anecdotal digression. Two plates of the *Forêt de Nettuno* and *Forêt de Porto Anzio* are included rather than the Salon pictures. On the *campagna* as a place for hunting in the seventeenth and eighteenth centuries, see Cesare de Cupis, *La Caccia nella Campagna Romana secondo la storia e i documenti* (Rome, 1922), pp. 114–36.

119 James Skene, *Italian Journey: Being Excerpts from the Pre-Victorian Diary of James Skene of Rubislaw* (London, 1937), p. 168. Skene was in Italy 1802–3. A print like Johan Christian Reinhardt's *View of the Tiber*, 1809, etching, British Museum, London, shows a man and dog looking into the landscape, as if this was a place for sport rather than more serious pursuits.

120 *Une femme et son enfant fiévreux consultant un ermite*; Ronmy, *Vue prise à Gensano près le lac de Nemi. Des pénitens portent une jeune fille à la terre*, 1817 Salon, no. 670; L. Robert, *Pèlerine avec son enfant mourant*, 1827 Salon, no. 88; Schnetz, *Une femme conduit une jeune fille malade dans une chapelle, et implore pour elle la Madone: Costumes de Rome et de l'île de Ischia*, 1827 Salon, no. 1737.

121 Painted for the Paris church of St-Etienne-du-Mont, entering the Musée du Luxembourg in 1856. See Bruno Foucart, *La Renouveau de peinture religieuse en France 1800–1860* (Paris, 1987).

122 'Jeune femme pleurant auprès de son mari. La moisson de la *campagna* de Rome, qui est inhabitée, se fait par des paysans qui viennent des montagnes, qui campent pendant tout le temps nécessaire à leurs travaux. La fièvre fait tous les ans beaucoup de victimes parmi les malheureux qui n'ont pas le temps d'être transportés dans les hôpitaux de Rome. On voit dans le fond les Fratelli della morte qui viennent chercher le mort', 1845 Salon no. 1512 (see [Schnetz], *Jean-Victor Schnetz 1787–1870: Couleurs d'Italie* (Musée du Château de Flers, 2000), p. 189, cat. no. 116 'non localisé'; and Bruno Foucart, 'Quelques peintres français devant les marais Pontins', in *Aux rives de l'incertain: Histoire et représentation des marais occidentaux du Moyen Âge à nos jours* (Paris, 2002), pp. 236–7). Other examples include: E. Dubois, *Une jeune italienne implore une madone en vénération pour la guérison de son frère malade, et la supplie d'agréer son voeu'*, 1831 Salon, no. 607; Trezel, *'Jeune femme de l'Achaie, effrayé du progrès de la maladie de son enfant qu'elle voue à la Vierge'*, 1833 Salon, no. 280. François Montessuy, *Voeu à la Madone dans la chambre d'une pauvre malade à Cervara*, 1848, Musée des beaux-arts, Agen. The confraternity is also visible in Carolus Duran's *Souvenir de la Campagne romaine* (1865, 1866 Salon, Palais des Beaux-Arts, Lille, inv. P. 582), which shows a murdered man recovered from the *campagna*.

123 Wheelock Whitney, *Géricault in Italy* (New Haven and London, 1997), pp. 54–8; Thomas, 'Cimetiere du bourg St Esprit', *Un an à Rome*, plate 53 (28.2 × 20.4 cm,); Haudebourg-Lescot, 1831 Salon, no. 1059.

124 Lee Munder Collection, Palm Beach; see *Maestà di Roma da Napoleone all'unità d'Italia, Da Ingres a Degas artisti francesi a Roma* (Rome, 2003), pp. 395–6, cat. no. 19. The subject is from *Culex*, formerly attributed to Virgil. Mooney gives 'gnat' for *culex* (Virgil, *The Minor Poems of Vergil: Comprising the Culex, Dirae, Lydia, Moretum, Copa, Priapeia, and Catalepton*, trans. J. Mooney (Birmingham, 1916)).

125 The festival had been used as a subject in the later eighteenth century by, for example, Pietro Fabris (1754–1804), *Villagers preparing to depart for the Festival of the Madonna dell'Arco* (1773), Sotheby's, Old Master Paintings New York, 5 June 2008, lot 143.

126 'le caractère sérieux et mélancholique' (Pierre Gassier and Maryse Schmidt-Surdez (eds), *Léopold Robert-Marcotte d'Argenteuil: Correspondance 1824-1835* (Neuchâtel, 2005) [henceforward *Robert-Marcotte*], Robert to Marcotte, 8 Aug. 1825, p. 3).

127 'une maladie grave et qui arrive fréquemment aux malheureux habitants de la campagne; son enfant a pris un accès de fièvre pernicieuse, elle est au moment de la perdre' (*Robert-Marcotte*, Robert to Marcotte, 15 Jan. 1826, p. 7).

128 'les quatre saisons de l'Italie....Le premier sera la représentation des restes des fêtes de Flore à Naples, le second celles de Cérès dans l'État romain, le troisième, qui sera le dernier fait, celles de Bacchus en Toscane et le dernier les Saturnales [Saturnalia] de Venise' (*Robert-Marcotte*, Robert to sister Adèle, 24 Oct. 1829, p. 218).

129 Letter (27 June 1822), 550 MS Neuchâtel, cit. *Maestà di Roma*, pp. 549–51, cat. no. 106.

130 'leurs vêtements pittoresques et sauvages...montagnes les plus sauvages...cette simplicité et cette noblesse...un trait conservé de ses aïeux' (3 Oct. 1822, Clément, *Léopold Robert*, p. 190). In 1858, Degas noted the 'Roman savagery', compared to Florentine grace, of pretty women and girls (1858 notebook, Richard Kendall, *Degas by Himself* (London, 1987), p. 15).

131 In 1827, he had noted his desire to work in the 'environs de Rome...pour avoir plus de choix pour trouver une belle tête et surtout le caractère italien sans mélange; nous le voyons disparaître tous les jours ici à Rome' (*Robert-Marcotte*, Robert Marcotte, 10 March 1827, p. 18). The way that the area's unhealthiness had preserved the population from any 'mélange' was also remarked on by Alfred Rivoire (*Essai sur la topographie et le climat de Rome et du bassin romain* (Montpellier, 1853, p. 50).

132 'Les marais Pontins m'ont donné le sujet: il sera d'un caractère assez sévère, quoiqu'il ait quelque rapport au premier [tableau]. Je trouve que la terre de Naples est tout à fait poétique et ses habitants rappellent incontestablement les Grecs, leurs fêtes et leurs usages. L'État pontifical me paraît avoir un aspect différent: les Romains ont quelque chose de plus sérieux et qui est en rapport avec l'idée que généralement on se fait de leurs ancêtres. Je désirerais faire voir, s'il est possible, la différence que je trouve entre ces deux peuples et, pour cela, il faut des sujets à peu près semblables' (*Robert-Marcotte*, Robert to Marcotte, 11 March 1828, p. 25).

133 'Pour mettre un cachet plus positif à ce que je vais entreprendre, j'aimerais bien m'installer à la campagne et c'est ce que je ferais si je peux m'y placer d'une manière convenable pour travailler. C'est dans les marais Pontins que nous allons; quoique je ne redoute pas la fièvre, il sera peut-être imprudent de s'y fixer pour y passer les mois que l'on appelle malsains'. He had already explored such areas and survived despite ignoring received wisdom: a certain Romantic bravura creeps into his selfimage: 'It seems that there are some temperaments which are safe from the pestilential influences of the country'. 'Il paraît qu'il y a des tempéraments qui sont à l'abri des influences pestilentielles du pays' (*Robert-Marcotte*, Robert to Marcotte, 16 Feb. 1829, p. 62).

134 'le courage de vivre la vie et de la nourriture de ces pâtres, pour étudier les travaux d'assainissement qu'il avait conçu, et qu'il aurait eu la gloire d'exécuter sans la chute de l'Empire français' (Norvins et al., *Italie*, p. 21). See Gaspard de Prony, *Description hydrographique et historique des marais Pontins*, 2 vols (Paris, 1822–3).

135 See Peter Funnell, 'The Symbolical Language of Antiquity', in Michael Clarke and Nicholas Penny (eds), *The Arrogant Connoisseur: Richard Payne Knight 1751–1824* (Manchester, 1982). Andrea De Jorio collected gestures, catalogued in his *Mimica degli antichi* (Naples, 1832), in the belief they were survivals from ancient forebears. On De Jorio see Francis Haskell, *History and its Images: Art and the Interpretation of the Past* (New Haven and London, 1993), pp. 155–8; Giancarlo Carabelli suggestively presents De Jorio in the context of contemporary Neapolitan writings on antiquity and its contemporary *Nachleben* (*In the Image of Priapus* (London, 1996), pp. 95–106); A. Schnapp, 'Antiquarian Studies in Naples at the End of the Eighteenth Century: From Comparative Archaeology to Comparative Religion', in G. Imbruglia (ed.), *Naples in the Eighteenth Century: The Birth and Death of a Nation State* (Cambridge, 2000). De Jorio's fusion of antiquarian learning and nascent social anthropology is to some extent anticipated in Revd. John James Blunt, *Vestiges of Ancient Manners and Customs Discoverable in Modern Italy and Sicily* (London, 1823).

136 '[E]spérant d'aller moissonner en voyant les moissonneurs....J'ai couru les environs et j'ai été cher-cher les moissonneurs jusque dans leurs tentes....qui compte trois mille bêtes....un de ces chars immenses,....c'est presque le motif de mon tableau, ou plutôt c'est le détail le plus considérable....j'ai vu des choses extrêmement pittoresques et je suis certain que mon tableau ne me demandera pas le quart de temps de l'autre et peut-être (au moins je l'espère) il sera beaucoup mieux, parce que je le sens mieux. J'ai déjà dessiné une esquisse peinte depuis mon retour et j'ai dessiné tout mon tableau et je vais l'ébaucher' (Robert to Adèle, *Robert-Marcotte*, mid-June 1829, p. 218). See G. M. Lancisi on the debate on Cisterna in chapter 4.

137 'portent sur leur figure l'empreinte d'une santé parfaite, quand autrefois on n'y voyait que des teints jaunes et livides' (*Robert-Marcotte*, Robert to Marcotte, 10 Aug. 1829, p. 67).

138 'c'est ma folie que les marais Pontins; je crois que j'y passerais ma vie' (Clément, *Léopold Robert*, July 1829, pp. 289–92).

139 'je suis heureux dans ces endroits presqu'inhabités, et je trouve que le caractère en est bien autrement vierge que dans les environs de Rome plus rapprochés' (ibid., to M. de Meuron, 27 Sept. 1829, p. 314).

140 'bien funeste pour tous les individus qui travaillent habituellement dans les campagnes des environs. La mortalité a été beaucoup plus grande que les années précédentes, les hôpitaux, qui sont ici en grand nombre, sont remplis; avec cela le nombre des étrangers étant moins grand que les hivers derniers, la misère se fera sentir plus que de coutume....Un ciel pur et le soleil méridional leur donnent une gaité et un attrait pour la vie qui est peu concevable pour nous qui apportons toujours dans les plus beaux lieux un principe de mort....Il me semble pourtant qu'elles ont toujours quelque chose de matériel, pour la plus grande partie, et que le résultat ordinaire est l'annonce d'un bonheur terrestre véritable, même dans leurs afflictions' (*Robert-Marcotte*, Robert to Marcotte, 21–22 Dec. 1829, p. 73).

141 'le climat, au lieu de m'être contraire, m'est extrêmement favorable' (Feuillet de Conches, *Léopold Robert*, p. 59, 3 Oct. 1822 to Brandt).

142 *Robert-Marcotte*, Marcotte to Robert, 9 July 1829, pp. 65–6; Robert to Marcotte, 10 Aug. 1829, p. 67; Robert to Marcotte, 21–22 Dec. 1829, p. 73.

143 Stephen Bann, 'Léopold Robert and the Afterlife of Antiquity', in Richard Wrigley (ed.), *Regarding Romantic Rome* (Oxford, 2007).

144 Victor Schoelcher remarked on the '[b]eauté raphaëlesque' he found in the painting (*L'Artiste*, 10 July 1831, pp. 94–5, cit. Nicos Hadjinicolaou, 'L'Exigence de Réalisme au Salon de 1831', *Histoire et critique des arts*, nos. 4–5 May 1978, p. 30).

145 'c'est l'idylle de l'humanité dans son premier Eden, devant le Créateur; idylle transposée aujourd'hui sous le soleil, dans ce monde de travail et de sueur, mais pleine encore de toute la félicité que cette terre corrompue peut offrir à l'homme'; 'Raphael a fait la Transfiguration d'un Dieu, les *Moissonneurs* sont la Transfiguration de la terre' (Lamartine, *Cours familier de littérature*, vol. 7, 1859, pp. 26, 42).

146 Delaunay was in Rome between 1857–1861. On Raymond Balze and his brother Jules, see Michel Baudat, 'Deux Arlésiens élèves d'Ingres: Les Frères Balze', *Bulletin des amis du vieil Arles pour la protection de son patrimoine historique et esthétique*, no. 141, June 2009.

147 Florian Reymond, 'Les Bêtes à cornes et l'art pictural', *Histoire et sociétés rurales*, vol. 30, no. 2, 2008, and his *L'Élevage bovin: De l'Agronome au paysan (1700–1850)* (Rennes, 2010).

148 Charles Coleman specialised in *campagna* and marsh imagery, focusing above all on livestock, producing *A Series of Subjects peculiar to the Campagna of Rome and Pontine Marshes* (Rome, 1850). See Pier Andrea De Rosa, 'Colemaniana', in Pier Andrea De Rosa and Paolo Emilio Trastulli (eds), *La Campagna Romana da Hackert a Balla* (Rome, 2002).

149 François Fossier, 'Il Lazio e i pittori francesi fra il 1840 e 1870', in *Maestà di Roma*, p. 94, fig. 10. However, Fossier strangely asserts that 'la poetica delle paludi' was a concern for German artists.

150 *L'Art dans la rue et dans le Salon* (Paris, 1859), p. 208. G.F. Watts, *Peasants in the Campagna*, whose centrepiece is a decorated ox, uses an upward view to decontextualise the scene, but this is Tuscan.

151 Bartoccini, *Roma nell'Ottocento*, p. 235.

152 Gross, *Rome in the Age of Enlightenment*, p. 156.

153 Ibid., p. 158. Celli gives 137 in 1803, falling to 70 by 1871 (*History of Malaria*, p. 2). Ashby notes that by 1914 more than half the *campagna* belonged to 44 owners (*Roman Campagna*, p. 51).

154 Giorgio Rossi, *L'Agro di Roma tra '500 e '800: Condizioni di vita e lavoro* (Rome, 1988), p. 9.

155 See Beneš, 'Pastoralism in the Roman Baroque villa', on agricultural practices.

156 A good indication of the limitations of images' ability to translate text is Charles Eastlake's prints for Maria Graham, *Three Months passed in the Mountains East of Rome, during the Year 1819* (London, 1821), which seem almost caricaturally schematic and insubstantial. Graham herself claimed 'to show the peasants of the hills as they are, and as they probably have been, with little change, since "Rome was at her height" ' (p. iv).

157 'une chaleur à faire calciner la terre….Cette partie des États du Pape est déplorable. L'air est très malsain. On croiroit en Arabie' (Montesquieu, *Œuvres complètes*, 2 vols (Paris, 1949–51), vol. 2, p. 760).

158 Nibby, *Analisi topografico-antiquaria*, vol. 1, p. 464.

159 'forêt étrange, sauvage, sombre…les forêts vierges de l'Amérique. Rien de plus beau, de plus poétique, de plus primitif, que cette forêt' (Norvins et al., *L'Italie pittoresque*, 4th edn (Paris, 1850), p. 129). As Broers points out, Norvins had earlier spent time in St-Domingo, an experience which informed his views of nature and race (*Napoleonic Empire in Italy*, pp. 227–31).

160 '[e]ffrayantes solitudes….On est réellement en Afrique; on voit les kraals des Hottentots. D'immondes reptiles et de myriades d'insectes altérées de sang complètent cette hideuse ressemblance' (Norvins, et al., *Italie* (1850), p. 20).

161 'Ces forêts vierges ont toute la majesté et toute l'horreur d'une nature primitive, dont elles conservent la sauvage indépendance. Nuit et jour elles retentissent du bruit des vents et des tempêtes, mêlés aux rugissements des animaux et aux cris farouches des pâtres, comme aussi des douces et vives mélodies des oiseaux, qui, à l'abri de l'homme, sous leurs impénétrables ombrages, y célèbrent la paix et les douceurs d'un tel asile; mais, ainsi que dans les bois consacrés aux divinités du Styx, les echoes de ces forêts n'ont jamais répétés des chants de joie, de poésie et d'amour' (ibid., p. 20).

162 'La race qui prenait possession de ce sol empesté était une race forte, rustique; elle se couvrit de la laine des ses troupeaux comme font aujourdhui les

pâtres de la *Campagna*; elle alluma des feux dans ses forêts, où le bois ne lui manquait point: elle s'établit sur les hauteurs d'où chaque jour elle descendit pour cultiver les endroits qu'elle avait défrichés, ainsi que le pratiquent encore les habitants des petites villes de l'État romain, qu'on voit tous les matins aller à plusieurs milles se livrer aux travaux de la campagne et le soir remonter à la ville portant la serpe et le hoyau' (Ampère, *Histoire romaine à Rome*, vol. 2, pp. 71–2). Ampère was nonetheless entirely candid about the poisoned atmosphere of the *campagna*, whatever its enduring signs of antique life.

163 C. Tournon, *Études statistiques sur Rome et la partie occidentale des états romains*, 2 vols ([1831] Paris, 1855), vol. 1, p. 299.

164 'l'aspect sauvage des steppes marécageux de l'Asie ou des llanos de l'Orénoque' (A.J.C.A. Dureau de la Malle, *Économie politique des romains*, 2 vols (Paris, 1840), vol. 2, p. 18).

165 'un'infingardaggine, uno squallore, una sporcizia, una mendicità nauseanti' (von Reumont, *Della Campagna Romana*, p. 63).

166 'germes d'abondance et de fécondité....Des germes corrompus dans le sein de la terre / S'exhalent vers les cieux en vapeur délétère;.../ Des miasmes impures condensés en nuage, / Comme un voile jaloux, couvrent le marécage, / Et lui cachent les feux des soirs et des matins; / Ainsi la politique a ses marais pontins' ('Ibrahim-Pacha', *La Pandore*, no. 1425, 13 April 1827, pp. 1–2).

167 The classic study is Louis Madelin, *La Rome de Napoléon: La Domination française 1809–1814* (Paris, 1906), a synthesis of diplomatic and political developments; recent studies have explored social and cultural history. R. De Felice, 'L'inchiesta napoleonica per I dipartimenti romani (1809–1810)', *Rassegna degli Archivi di Stato*, vol. 27, 1968; F. Sofia, 'Recueillir et mettre en ordre: Aspetti della politica amministrativa di J.M. de Gerando a Roma', *Roma moderna e contemporanea*, vol. 1, no. 1, 1994. Ph. Boutry, F. Pitocco and C.M. Travaglini (eds), *Roma negli anni di influenza e dominio francese* (Rome, 1989). For a general account see Susan Vandiver Nicassio, *Imperial City: Rome, Romans and Napoleon, 1796–1815* (Chicago, 2005), reprinted in 2009 as *Imperial City: Rome under Napoleon*.

168 Michael Broers, 'Cultural Imperialism in a European Context? Political Culture and Cultural Politics in Napoleonic Italy', *Past & Present*, vol. 170, 2001; also his *Napoleonic Empire in Italy*.

169 Tournon, *Études statistiques*, vol. 1, pp. 247–53. See Bruno Foucart (ed.), *Camille de Tournon: Le Préfet de la Rome napoléonienne 1809–1814*, (Rome, 2001).

170 'On dirait le type des Apollons et des Bacchus....quelque chose de sauvage qui harmonisent parfaitement avec les peaux de chèvres ou de moutons dont ils se vêtissent....on croit voir le sang des terribles Herniques couler dans leurs veines....'c'est là que se trouvent, mais en petit nombre, les plus beaux hommes de la province, et on se plait à les considérer comme les représentants de la noble Étrurie....ne seraient-ils pas les fils des compagnons de Tatius et de Numa?' (Tournon, *Études*, vol. 1, p. 249).

171 See Massimo Cattaneo, *La sponda sbagliata del Tevere: Mito e realtà di un'identità popolare tra antico regime e rivoluzione* (Naples, 2004).

172 'déesses descendues de leur piédestal' (Tournon, *Études statistiques*, vol. 1, p. 250).

173 Ibid., vol. 1, p. 251.

174 'abâtardissement et l'appauvrissement de l'espèce....La laideur des rares habitans de cette plaine est extrême, et leur débilité plus grand encore. La teigne, les hernies, le rachitisme portée à un tel degré que plusieurs malheureux n'atteignent pas à la taille d'un mètre, enfin l'obstruction des viscères et l'ulcération des jambes, désolent et détruisent cette population' (ibid., vol. 1, p. 252). He did, however, note some healthy types, e.g. at Sacco.

175 'Tel est l'état physique d'un peuple qui en grande partie vit sous un ciel le plus pur, parfumé par les émanations les plus suaves. Le mauvais air peut-il expliquer tous ces phénomènes?' (ibid., vol. 1, p. 253).

176 'longues colonnes de moissonneurs qui descendent en chantant de leurs salubres rochers, pour venir affronter une mort sans gloire sur un terrible champ de bataille' (ibid., vol. 1, p. 312).

177 Ibid., vol. 1, pp. 361–3.

178 'la forme de vêtements, de visages, des habitudes, celle même des besoins de la vie, tout vous est étranger....Plus de verdure, plus d'arts, plus de

fleurs, plus de marbres, plus de gaîté aussi, et plus de bien-être....Les haillons de la plus sale misère, qui est celle de mendians du pape et de ceux du grand turc, ont remplacé les gracieux costumes de l'Étrurie' (Norvins, 'L'État romain', in Norvins et al., *Italie* (1850), p. 2).

179 'de grands troupeaux de boeufs, gris de lin, à longues cornes, de la race antique des taureaux de Clitumne....gardien...manoir rustique....semblable à un ancien roi Sabin...avec ses pièces et ses caissons...l'attirail rural le plus étonnant, le plus beau que j'eusse vue de ma vie. Tout est grandiose, gigantesque, presque sublime dans ce pays romain....troupes de sauvages des Abruzzes ou des Calabres, esclaves nés de la terre romaine....Ces hommes caniculaires, presque nus, bronzés par le soleil, d'une taille gigantesque, présentant la race mêlée du sauvage et du brigand, portant des faucilles et des fourches, véritable pandémonium rural' (ibid., pp. 28–30).

180 'Je me vis réellement transporté de l'enfer au paradis. J'avais soif d'ombrage et de fraîcheur, et aussi de revoir des êtres complètement humains. Les fiévreux d'Ostie et de Terracine, les brigands de Fondi, les postillons spectres des marais Pontins, les buffles, les sangliers, les Calabrois [harvesters] de la princesse Caetani, et la canicule de la moisson et celle de la messe, me poursuivaient comme d'insupportables vampires, et me tenaient, tout éveillé que j'étais, sous la torture d'un véritable cauchemar' (ibid., p. 31). For Hazlitt, Genzano was the *ne plus ultra* of Roman beauty: 'The young women that come here from Gensano and Albano, and that are known by their scarlet boddices and white head-dresses and handsome good-humoured faces, are the finest specimens I have ever seen of human nature. They are like the creatures that breathed the air of Heaven, till the sun has ripened them into perfect beauty, health, and goodness' (*Notes of a Journey through France and Italy* ([1826] New York, 1983), p. 236); elsewhere he described them as 'Goddesses of health and good temper' (Hazlitt, 'English Students', p. 222). However, Genzano's reputation was dented when the Prussian ambassador died there in 1864 (K. Schlözer, *Römische Briefe* (Berlin, 1914), cit. Celli, *History of Malaria*, p. 124).

181 Pascal Griener, '"Un genre qu'on ne connaît pas encore...": Léopold Robert et l'élévation du genre sous la monarchie de Juillet', *Kunst+Architektur in der Schweiz*, no. 4, 1994; Stephen Bann, 'Il popolo, dall'eroico al pittoresco', in *Maestà di Roma*, pp. 245–7, and his 'Léopold Robert and the Afterlife of antiquity'.

182 Horace de Viel Castel, 'Cromwell par M. Delaroche', *L'Artiste*, vol. 1, 1831, p. 269, cit. Bann, 'Léopold Robert and the Afterlife of Antiquity', pp. 85–6.

183 'Les personnages sont des paysans; ils ont leur beauté propre: la vigueur, l'élégance énergique, la solidité du teint, la belle proportion des formes; on voit qu'ils sont capables de l'œuvre pénible qu'ils ont à accomplir; on voit qu'ils sont les hôtes naturels de cette campagne ardente que recouvre un ciel si chaud qu'il écraserait quiconque ne serait pas constitué pour lutter contre lui, comme un mortel qui aurait pénétrer dans les forges de Vulcain aurait été consommé [*sic?*] à l'instant même.' 'Il n'y a peut-être pas dans tout ce que nous reste de l'antiquité grecque et romaine une figure plus belle de mouvement, de pose, de contour, de naturel et de style que le bouvier qui se repose entre ses deux buffles suants' (Auguste Jal, *Ébauches critiques: Salon de 1831* (Paris, 1831), pp. 156–7).

184 'Vu de près, *les Moissonneurs* sont [est] un tableau qui fait penser, comme ces précieux vestiges de l'art antique que la terre nous rend quelquefois' (ibid., p. 157).

185 Charles Lenormant, 'Léopold Robert: Notice sur la vie et les ouvrages de cet artiste par M.L.J. Delécluze', in *Beaux-arts et voyages*, 2 vols (Paris, 1861), vol. 1.

186 'Le père de famille, qui habite l'une de ces villes si pittoresquement logées sur la chaîne majestueuse de montagnes par laquelle les marais Pontins sont bornés à l'orient, est parti de Piperno, de Cora et de Sezze, pour les champs qu'il possède dans la plaine; quand il arrive le soir au centre de ses moissons, le soleil, qui s'abaisse derrière les sommets de la presqu'île de Circé, ne dore plus d'une vive lumière que les corps placés à un certain hauteur, et déjà l'ombre se grave en traits noirs sur la figure des moissonneurs et dans les plis de leurs vêtements' (Charles Lenormant, *Les*

Artistes contemporains: Salon de 1831 (Paris, 1833), pp. 102–3, originally published in *Le Temps* as 25 articles between 4 May and 17 August). Lenormant (1802–59) was to die of malarial fever in Greece, as Prosper Merimée put it, 'victime de son amour pour la science', having insisted on exploring the marsh of Epidaurus despite the risk to his health (*Portraits historiques et littéraires* (Paris, 1874), p. 271). See also Lenormant's *Léopold Robert, essai d'appréciation critique* (Paris, 1838).

187 'et par-dessus de tout, un dessin d'une correction achevée, des airs de tête comme personne n'en trouve plus, une pantomime forte comme le Poussin et naïve comme Holbein' (Lenormant, *Artistes contemporains*, p. 104).

188 'qui ébauchait au couteau, sur les murs de son atelier, des motifs dignes de la frise du Parthénon' (ibid., p. 107).

189 'Nous avions des imitations sublimes comme Poussin en savait faire et comme David en rêvait, nous avons la *Psyché* de M. Gérard et l'*Endymion* de Girodet, mais il n'y a que Robert qui rentre dans le sentiment antique sans passer par les statues. Pour arriver à ce point, il se place au milieu des mêmes hommes et sous le même ciel; au lieu d'un peuple tout entier à peine sorti de la barbarie, et tout plein encore de la vigueur qu'elle communique, il ne trouve plus que des souvenirs de l'état primitif, ou des retours à la vie ancienne, dans cette classe d'hommes que la vie des champs et des montagnes a mis à l'abri de toutes les révolutions sociales; ces hommes, il ne les torture pas, il ne cherche pas à voir en eux ce qu'ils n'ont jamais pu être; mais il lit dans leur conformation, dans leurs traits, dans leurs habitudes, ce cachet d'une nature forte et simple, que nous autres races dégénérées, prenons par amour-propre pour des rêves d'une imagination exaltée, quand nous le retrouvons dans les œuvres de l'art' (ibid., pp. 107–8). Writing on the *Pêcheurs de l'Adriatique* in 1836, Guyot de Fère seems to echo this passage: 'Une telle peinture, qui rentre dans le sentiment de l'antique sans passer par la statuaire, qui reproduit le vrai, qui copie avec naïveté, sans perdre de vue la belle nature, qui est remplie de poésie, tout en peignant l'homme des classes laborieuses, une telle peinture pourrait être un type pour notre école actuelle' (*Journal des beaux-arts et de la littérature*, no. 11, 27 March 1836, p. 164, cit. Bann, 'Léopold Robert and the Afterlife of Antiquity', p. 71). Enthusiasm for an image of a society which still existed 'dans les pays qui ne sont pas corrodés par une dévorante civilisation' was expressed in *La Mode*, vol. 8, 7th livraison, 13 August 1831, p. 148, cit. Hadjinicolaou, 'L'Exigence de Réalisme', p. 30.

190 'la pensée de l'antiquité…ce que les vieilles populations de l'Italie avaient conservé de la physiognomie antique' (Lenormant, 'Léopold Robert', vol. 1, pp. 173, 186).

191 'À voir la naïveté qui règne dans les gestes de tous les personnages du tableau des Moissonneurs, et lorsque l'on se sent saisi par cette air de puissance, par cette haute beauté et ce grandiose, empreints sur la figure calme de tous ces paysans, on ne sait réellement pas de quel temps est cet ouvrage où l'on retrouve toute la gravité de la statuaire antique, jointe à cette soudaineté que présentent seules les productions inspirées par la nature, et copiées en quelque sorte d'après elle' (E.J. Delécluze, *Notice sur la vie et les ouvrages de Léopold Robert* (Paris, 1838), from 'Description des quatre tableaux de ce peintre', which follows (p. 108).

192 Ambroise Tardieu, *Annales du musée et de l'ecole moderne des beaux-arts, ou recueil des principaux tableaux, statues et bas-reliefs exposés au Louvre depuis 1808…par C.P. Landon: Salon de 1831; Recueil de pièces choisies parmi les ouvrages de peinture et de sculpture exposés pour la première fois au Louvre, le 1er mai 1831* (Paris, 1831), p. 113. Precisely the opposite view is found in *Le Correspondant*, where a home-grown version of the same scene located in Beauce or Champagne was thought 'triviale et grotesque' (29 July 1831, n.p., cit. Hadjinicolaou, 'L'Exigence de Réalisme', p. 30).

193 'plusieurs des attitudes manquent de naturel; il y a de la prétention à l'héroïque dans quelques-unes d'elles; ses paysans sont de trop noble allure. Après une espèce de voyage et par une chaleur dont l'imitation si parfaite brûle le regard, l'établissement des tentes et l'empressement au repos ne devraient-ils pas être le premier besoin de cette troupe de cultivateurs à idées plus animales et positives que poétiques?' (ibid., p. 114).

194 'les types rustiques d'Italie, dont il a idéalisé la beauté par son style élégant et pur' (cit. James

Kearns, *Théophile Gautier, Orator to the Artists: Art Journalism during the Second Republic* (London, 2007), p. 151.

195 'pensée profondément plébéienne' and their 'la majesté, la grâce, l'énergie' ('Beaux-arts: Gravure', *Revue du Progrès*, 15 Feb. 1839, p. 146, on the publication of Prévost's print, cit. Neil McWilliam, *Dreams of Happiness: Social Art and the French Left, 1830–1850* (Princeton, 1993), pp. 274–5).

196 'C'est qu'il a poétisé la nature humaine dans le peuple, en racontant le travail et les périls, les joies et les douleurs, sous les hasards de l'existence commune. C'est qu'il a réhabilité les inférieurs, en les douant de beauté, d'intelligence et de vertu. Et non seulement il a mis dans le peuple la beauté et les nobles passions mais il a idéalisé la nature' (Théophile Thoré, 'Léopold Robert, *Beaux-arts*, 1843–44', in *Robert-Marcotte*, p. 658).

197 'la passion du naturel, exploitée trop en détail, séduit l'imagination de l'artiste à n'être plus qu'une mosaïque plus ou moins ingénieuse....Il y a, qu'on me passe l'expression, abus de la nature' (Planche, *Salon de 1831*, pp. 93–4). Planche maintained his dismissive attitude to Robert, and the *Harvesters*, which lacked 'la naïveté, ni l'ardeur primitive, ni la gigantesque simplicité des épopées grecques' (*Études sur l'école française (1851–1852): Peinture et sculpture*, 2 vols (Paris, 1855), vol. 1, p. 169).

198 'Mais dans les marais Pontins, voici ce qui me détruit tout le tableau. Pourquoi, dites-vous? Ah! Pourquoi. Où est la fièvre? – Qu'est-ce que c'est? – Il me faut la fièvre, la fièvre des Marais Pontins qui tue les voyageurs, et rend freles et pâles les misérables habitans de ce lieux. La guénille de l'Italien, son couteau avec lequel il se saigne lui-même la matin, une figure hâve, des regards hébétés, des taureaux amaigris, et je suis dans les Marais Pontins: ôtez-moi donc les Marais Pontins et je trouve ce tableau ravissant' (*Le Voleur*, 30 June 1831, cit. Hadjinicolaou, 'L'Exigence de Réalisme', p. 31). It is interesting to note the similarity of this formulaic evocation of the fever-ridden marshes to the painting which Delacroix produced while remaining in Paris: 'Un pâtre de la campagne de Rome, blessé mortellement, se traîne au bord d'un marais pour se désaltérer' (1827 Salon *livret*) (c.1825, 32.5 × 40 cm, Öffentliche Kunstsammlung, Kunstmuseum, Basel; painted for Du Som-

merard); 'Brigand blessé' and 'La Mort du brigand' were used as titles on different states of the Mouilleron lithograph published during Delacroix's lifetime; see Lee Johnson, *The Paintings of Eugène Delacroix: A Critical Catalogue*, 6 vols (Oxford, 1981–9), vol. 1, pp. 171–2, cat. no. 162).

199 *Les Musées de France: Paris, guide et memento de l'artiste et du voyageur* (Paris, 1860), p. 278. Marie-Claude Chaudonneret also mistitles the picture 'Retour' from the Pontine marshes (*L'État et les artistes: De la Restauration à la monarchie de Juillet (1815–1833)* (Paris, 1999), pp. 85–6).

200 Gudin, *Souvenirs du Baron Gudin*, p. 94.

201 See [Bodinier], *Guillaume Bodinier*, p. 10 note 22, where two related works are noted *Le pâtre et ses chèvres* (1853), and *Les deux pâtres* (1855) (ibid., p. 12 note 21).

202 [Anon.], 'Beaux-arts: Salon de 1831', p. 233.

203 *Sixte Quint bénit les marais Pontins*, 1846 Salon, no. 1022: 'Dans les montagnes volsques, là où elles viennent se perdre dans les marais pontins, entre Sezze et le fameux nid de brigands Sonnino, se trouve un rocher détaché que le peuple appelle encore de nos jours: Il sasso di papa Sisto (le rocher du pape Sixte V); de ce point d'œil découvre les montagnes de Terracina, le cap Circe et la mer qui borde cette plaine désolée. C'est là qu'alla se placer Sixte-Quint, lorsqu'après avoir fait exécuter d'immenses travaux de déssechement, il vint en grande pompe, accompagné de toute sa cour papale, consacrer son œuvre par une bénédiction solennelle. A la nouvelle de cette cérémonie, unique dans ces contrées, accourut la foule des habitants de tous les environs. Les brigands, qui alors plus qu'aujourd'hui infestaient ces pays là, attirés par l'espoir d'une absolution, vinrent rendre les armes avec les objets volés'. Leon Rosenthal notes the picture as a sequel to Robert's *Moissonneurs*, but gives the 1847 Salon (*Du Romantisme au Réalisme: Essai sur l'evolution de la peinture en France de 1815 à 1830* (Paris, 1914), p. 209).

204 Jean-Baptiste Clésinger, *Vue des marais pontins*, oil on acajou, 9 × 32.5 cm, Sale at, Hôtel Drouot, Paris, 29 October 2010. lot 278; Clésinger was in Rome from 1856.

205 1846 Salon; Clermont Ferrand; see *Les Années romantiques: La Peinture française de 1815 à 1850* (Paris, 1995), p. 391.

206 See Annick Opinel, *Le Peintre et le mal (France XIXe siècle)* (Paris, 2005); Nina Athanassoglou-Kallmyer, 'Blemished Physiologies: Delacroix, Paganini, and the Cholera Epidemic of 1832', *Art Bulletin*, vol. 83, no. 4, 2001, reprinted in Frances S. Connelly (ed.), *Modern Art and the Grotesque* (Cambridge, 2003); another work of art which associates Rome and disease is Jules Delaunay, *Peste à Rome* (1869, Musée d'Orsay, Paris).

207 Edward Lear (with vignettes by Penry Williams), *Illustrated Excursions in Italy*, 2 vols (London, 1846). The assertion that Lear's approach to the sites in *Views in Rome* is 'conventional' is mistaken (Allan Staley et al., *Impossible Picturesqueness: Edward Lear's Indian Watercolours, 1873–1875* (Wallach Art Gallery, New York, 1988), p. 109); Lear introduced the images in *Illustrated Excursions* with the claim that 'with the exception of Isola Farnese, Castel Fusano, and Caprarola', these were 'but seldom seen by Tourists' (*Illustrated Excursions*, vol. 1, preface); he includes a map (vol. 2, following p. 45) locating the distribution of his sites.

208 Ibid., pp. 20/21, plate 11, 30.3 × 15.9 cm; vignette, wood engraving J. Bastin, 19 × 7.5 cm. Ninfa was abandoned and covered in vegetation by 1681; Ameti's 1693 map gives 'Ninfa dirruta'; see Tomassetti, *La Campagna romana*, vol. 2, pp. 470–1.

209 Lear, *Illustrated Excursions*, vol. 2, p. 21.

210 Middleton, *Grecian Remains* (1812), pp. 36–7, plate 15, M. Dubourg sculpt. Middleton often used a camera obscura, adding to his role as prototype for photographic imagery. Macpherson also photographed the adjacent site of 'Sermoneta, with Norma, Ninfa and the Volscian Maremma', no. 209 in his December 1871 catalogue, *Macpherson's Photographs*.

211 The picture was bought by the state for 5,000 francs and exhibited in the Musée du Luxembourg; see *Le Musée du Luxembourg en 1874: Peintures* (Paris, 1974), pp. 98–9.

212 'On ne peut écrire ce mot [malaria] sans penser tout d'abord au beau et pathétique tableau de M. Hébert' (Ampère, *Histoire romaine à Rome*, vol. 2, p. 72). Gustave Planche, referring to Robert's works in general, regretted the fact they were 'si populairement comprises, mais si incomplètement exécutées, d'une beauté tellement officielle et systématique' (*Études sur l'école française*, vol. 1, p. 169).

213 Pierre Larousse, *Grand Dictionnaire universel du XIXe siècle*. 15 vols (1866–1879), vol. 10, p. 999.

214 'Après Schnetz, après Léopold Robert, il présentait l'Italie sous un aspect original et vrai; au pittoresque se joignait le sentiment. Ce n'étaient plus ces types bronzés, découpés nettement dans une lumière crue, mais une grâce malade, un charme languissant, une mélancholie énervée, une poésie triste, qui vous allaient au cœur....L'âme rêveuse du peintre y est tout entière' (Théophile Gautier, *Des Beaux-arts en Europe en 1855*, 2 vols (Paris, 1855), vol. 1, p. 233).

215 Kearns, *Théophile Gautier*, p. 175.

216 See the discussion ibid., p. 175.

217 'Si *La Mal'aria* est une belle œuvre, c'est que la fièvre émane de la toile et qu'on éprouve le poids du ciel, de l'eau, de l'air, on se sent oppressé par l'atmosphère pestilentielle; l'artiste a littéralement peint le mauvais air' (Joseph Péladan, *Ernest Hébert, son œuvre et son temps* (Paris, 1910), p. 88).

218 Other works which use 'malaria' as a title are: Emile Lecomte-Vernet, *L'aria cattiva / Malaria* (Musée d'Aubénas); Jean-Antoine Injalbert's bronze statuette, *Malaria: Par le froid et la malaria*, c.1878 (Musée des beaux-arts, Béziers).

219 See René P. d'Unkermann, *Ernest Hébert 1817–1908* (Paris, 1982), pp. 62–6. See also *Maestà di Roma*, p. 270, cat. no. XII.5.

220 Inv. 151, 'Campagne romaine, marais mise en place d'un mat dans....'; inv. 97, 'Campagne romaine, marais bovins sur un rivage lagune....'; inv. 96, 'Campagne romaine'; inv. 81, 'Campagne romaine, avancée d'eau dans des dunes marécageuses', Musée Hébert, Paris.

221 *Salon de 1850–1851*, (Paris, 1851), pp. 26–7.

222 Bernard Terlay, 'Les Portraits de Granet', *Impressions du Musée Granet, Association des amis du musée Granet*, Aix-en-Provence, no. 7, 1992. Denis Coutagne dates it 'entre 1802 et 1810' (*François-Marius Granet 1775–1849: Une Vie pour la peinture* (Paris, 2008), p. 111, fig. 76).

223 Coutagne, *François-Marius Granet*, pp. 80 (1806–24), 234–7 (1827–47).

224 *François-Marius Granet: Watercolours from the Musée Granet at Aix-en-Provence*, with the 'Memoirs of the Painter Granet', trans. and ed. Joseph Focarino (Frick Collection, New York, 1988), pp. 21–2.

225 *François-Marius Granet*, p. 33.

226 The sobriety of his painting may be contrasted with the contrived Gothic horror of Desboicheaux's *Cimetière des Capucins à Rome* (1831 Salon, 2nd supplement, no. 2717), in which a monk, surrounded by the skeletons for which the Capucins' crypt was celebrated, died of fright thinking his habit was being held by a bony hand, having accidentally nailed his sleeve to the wall.

227 See Neil MacGregor, 'Girodet's Poem *Le Peintre*', *Oxford Art Journal*, vol. 4, no. 1, 1981.

6 'IT WAS DIRTY, BUT IT WAS ROME'

1 Tobias Smollett, *Travels through France and Italy*, 2 vols (London, 1766), vol. 2, p. 103.

2 James Johnson, *Change of Air*, 3rd edn (London, 1835), p. 163.

3 Charles Dickens, *Pictures from Italy* (London, 1846), p. 215.

4 For the Renaissance see Loren Partidge, 'Urbanism: Rotting Cadavers and the New Jerusalem', in *The Renaissance in Rome 1400–1600* (London, 1996).

5 Richard Krautheimer, *The Rome of Alexander VII 1655–1667* (Princeton, 1985), pp. 126–30.

6 See David Atkinson, 'Totalitarianism and the Street in Fascist Rome', especially the section 'Planning Fascist Streets: pathologies of the city', in Nicholas R. Fyfe (ed.), *Images of the Street: Planning, Identity, and Control in Public Space* (London, 1998), which includes a photograph of road inspectors (*cantonieri*) in a parade at the time of the Exhibition of Fascist Revolution, taken from an article by I. Vandone in *Le Strade*, vol. 17, no. 2, 1935, pp. 66–72; and more generally Spiro Kostof, *The Third Rome 1870–1950: Traffic and Glory* (Berkeley, 1973).

7 See Orietta Verdi, 'Da ufficiali capitolini a commissari apostolici: I maestri delle strade e degli edifici di Roma tra XIII e XVI secolo', in L. Spezzaferro and M.E. Tittoni (eds), *Il Campidoglio e Sisto V* (Rome, 1991); Emilio Re, 'Maestri di Strada', *Archivio della società romana di storia patria*, vol. 43, 1920; Daniele Manacorda, 'Su "Mondezzari" di Roma tra Antichità e età Moderna', in Xavier Dupré Raventós and Josp-Anton Remolà (eds), *Sordes Urbis: La Eliminación de residuos en la ciudad romana* (Rome, 2000); Katherine Wentworth Rinne, *The Waters of Rome. Aqueducts, Fountains and the Birth of the Baroque City* (New Haven and London, 2010), pp. 193–218, Renato Sansa, 'Istituzioni e politica dell'ambiente a Roma: Dalle magistrature capitoline alla Presidenza Pontificia', in G. Cascio Pratilli and L. Zangheri (eds), *Legislazione medicea sull'ambiente*, vol. 4, *Scritti per un commento* (Florence, 1998).

8 Renato Sansa, 'La pulizia delle strade a Rome nel XVII secolo: Un problema di storia ambientale', *Archivio della società romana di storia patria*, vol. 114, 1991. Similar tensions between occupants of the street and administrators as manifest in France have been studied by Arlette Farge, *La Vie fragile: Violence, pouvoirs et solidarités à Paris au XVIIIe siècle* (Paris, 1986), *Vivre dans la rue au XVIIIe siècle* (Paris, 1979), and Olwen Hufton, *The Poor of Eighteenth-Century France 1750–89* (Oxford, 1974). In *Nettezza Urbana* (1948), Antonioni represented Roman street cleaners in a way which shifts from a perspective of aestheticisation associated with the spectacle of Rome's public spaces to a social identity closely tied to marginal impoverishment.

9 On Freud's metaphor of Rome's historic layers and the human psyche made in *Civilisation and its Discontents*, see Donald Kuspit, 'A Mighty Metaphor: The Analogy of Archaeology and Psychoanalysis', in Lynn Gamwell and Richard Wells (eds), *Sigmund Freud and Art: His Personal Collection of Antiquities* (London, 1989). See also the discussion in Anne Janowitz, *England's Ruins: Poetic Purpose and the National Landscape* (Oxford, 1990), pp. 50–3.

10 'E' una città vissuta di spoglie, poi di rovine, oggi di rifiuti' (*Roma interrotta* (Rome, 1978), p. 11).

11 Mary Douglas, *Purity and Danger: An Analysis of the Concepts of Pollution and Taboo* (London and New York, 1966), p. 35. Mary Douglas had agreed to be the plenary speaker at a conference which I organised with Mark Bradley; alas, her death meant that the event became something of a tribute to the influence of her work. Mark edited the proceedings: *Rome, Pollution and Propriety: Dirt, Disease and Hygiene in the Eternal City from Antiquity to Modernity* (Cambridge, 2012).

12 A fruitful parallel here is Jérôme Monnet's *La Ville et son double: La Parabole de Mexico* (Paris, 1999), which discusses the ambiguous way in which the old city was a model for its modern successor. Thanks to Tom Gretton for this comparison.

Monnet has been criticised for reproducing a certain official discourse and neglecting popular interventions and appropriations; see Bernard Lepetit's review in *Annales: ESC*, vol. 50, no. 6, 1995, pp. 1380–1.

13 Joseph Forsyth, *Remarks on Antiquities, Arts, and Letters, during an Excursion in Italy in the Years 1802 and 1803*, 4th edn (London, 1835), p. 124. In a note it was observed that Forsyth's reproaches were no longer entirely merited, 'though there is still room for improvement'.

14 Lady Morgan, *Italy*, 3 vols (London, 1821), vol. 2, p. 234. She uses the word repeatedly in her account of Rome (vol. 2, pp. 409, 444). However, it is worth noting that, despite the way in which Morgan is associated with an excessive inclination to damn Rome for its filth, as if this was a matter of personal animadversion, her book also contained an appendix by Sir Charles T. Morgan, 'On the state of Medicine in Italy, with brief notices of some of the universities and hospitals', (vol. 1, pp. 311–48).

15 'il m'est venu dans l'esprit que, de toutes les antiquités romaines, l'ordure est ce qu'il y a de plus antique; car il ne paraît pas qu'elle ait jamais été enlevée' (Louis Simond, *Voyage eu Etalie et en Sicile*, 2 vols (Paris, 1828), vol. 1, p. 316).

16 'Delle cloache', in Nicola Maria Nicolai, *Sulle presidenze delle strade ed acque e su giurisdizione economica*, 2 vols (Rome, 1829), vol. 2, pp. 139–41, where he notes the plan of 10 August 1820 to make a 'pianta di tutti le condotti sotterranei'.

17 A.J.C.A. Dureau de la Malle, *Économie politique des romains*, 2 vols (Paris, 1840), vol. 2, pp. 479–82, 'Impots sur les egouts et les matières fécales'. See Mark Bradley, 'Roman Sewers and the Politics of Cleanliness', *Omnibus*, no. 51, January 2006. Philippe Maudry, 'Vivre à Rome, ou le mal d'être citadin: Réflexions sur la ville antique comme espace pathogène', in *Nomen Latinum: Mélanges de langue, littérature et civilisation latines offerts au professeur Andre Schneider à l'occasion de son départ à la retraite* (Neuchâtel, 1977). Walter Scheidel, 'Germs for Rome', in Catharine Edwards and Greg Woolf (eds), *Rome the Cosmopolis* (Cambridge, 2003). On ambivalent ancient attitudes to sewers, Catharine Edwards, *Writing Rome: Textual Approaches to the City* (Cambridge, 1996), pp. 105–9. More generally see Bradley (ed.), *Rome, Pollution, and Propriety*.

18 Augustus von Kotzebue, *Travels through Italy, in the Years 1804 to 1805*, 4 vols (London, 1806), vol. 4, pp. 112–13. Kotzebue here misrepresents Cloacina, the goddess who presided over the Cloaca Maxima, that is, a major means to maintain hygiene. Rome's reputation for filth, and the inefficacy of the plaques, was adapted by Gautier in his remarks on literary reputations: 'Il est vrai qu'un chien peut regarder un évêque, et que Saint Pierre de Rome, tout géant qu'il soit, ne peut empêcher que les Transtéverins ne le salissent par en bas d'une étrange sorte; mais je n'en crois pas moins qu'il serait fou d'écrire au long de certaines monumentales. DÉFENSE DE DÉPOSER DES ORDURES ICI' (Théophile Gautier, *La Préface de Mademoiselle de Maupin*, ed. Georges Matoré (Paris, 1946), p. 48).

19 As in the title of chapter 97 (Kotzebue, *Travels*, vol. 4): 'Some ruins which are only interesting by virtue of the memories which they recall'. Tommaso Landolfi notes that Gogol embraced Rome as his true *patrìa* precisely because of its contrast to St Petersburg, which for him 'was no more than a dream' (review of Daria Borghese, *Gogol a Roma* (Florence, 1957), in *Gogol' a Roma* (Milan, 2002), p. 390.

20 'Though much yet remains to be done, perhaps we might compare the state of modern London to that of ancient Rome for cleanliness and the preservation of the public health....unquestionably the health of the [Roman] people was preserved by the formation of regular cloacae to drain and receive the filth of the city' (Dr Armstrong, 'Lectures on the Principles and Practice of Physic', *The Lancet*, vol. 7, no. 7, 21 May 1825, pp. 199–200).

21 Johnson, *Change of Air* (1835), pp. 34–8. On Roman sewers as less good than those of Paris, and even less so London, 'on dit', E. Viollet-le-Duc, *Lettres d'Italie 1836–1837, adressées à sa famille* (Paris, 1971), p. 192, letter 13 Nov. 1836. See also David S. Barnes, *The Great Stink of Paris and the Nineteenth-Century Struggle against Filth and Germs* (Baltimore 2006), pp. 15, 29, 36, 47.

22 Sarah Uwins, *A Memoir of Thomas Uwins*, 2 vols (London, 1858), vol. 1, p. 120, cit. Edward Morris, *French Painting in Nineteenth-Century Britain* (New Haven and London, 2005), p. 23.

23 James Whiteside, *Italy in the Nineteenth Century*, 3 vols (London, 1848), vol. 2, p. 4.

24 Douglas, *Purity and Danger* p. 2.

25 James Johnson, *Change of Air, or The Pursuit of Health; An Autumnal Excursion through France, Switzerland and Italy in…1829* (London, 1831), p. 274. A similar view can be found in Henry Matthews, *The Diary of an Invalid, being the Journal of a Tour in Pursuit of Health in Portugal, Italy, Switzerland and France in the Years 1817, 1818, and 1819*, 2 vols (London, 1820), vol. 1, p. 72, and Morgan, *Italy*, vol. 2, p. 375.

26 Owsei Temkin, *Galenism: Rise and Decline of a Medical Philosophy* (Ithaca and London, 1973).

27 George Augustus Sala, *Rome and Venice with other Wanderings in Italy, in 1866–67* (London, 1869), p. 448, cit. Michael Meyer, *Ibsen* (London, 1967), p. 232.

28 Andreina de Clementi, *Vivere nel Latifondo: Le comunità della campagna laziale fra '700 e '800* (Milan, 1989), pp. 190–4.

29 William Wetmore Story, *Roba di Roma*, 2 vols (London, 1863), vol. 1, p. 5. This quotation is noted in William L. Vance, *America's Rome*, vol. 2, *Catholic and Contemporary Rome* (New Haven and London, 1989), p. 139. On Story and James, see James Buzard, *The Beaten Track: European Tourism, Literature, and the Ways to 'Culture', 1800–1918* (Oxford, 1993) pp. 206–7.

30 Henry James, *Transatlantic Sketches* (Boston, 1875), p. 127, cit. Buzard, *Beaten Track*, pp. 206–7.

31 *Fors Clavigera*, vol. 2, in John Ruskin, *The Works of John Ruskin*, ed. E.T. Cook and A. Wedderburn, 39 vols (London, 1903–12), vol. 27, p. 312. In his memoir, Ruskin alluded to Edinburgh but without the explanation of extreme filthiness: 'the pillars of the Forum I saw were on a small scale, and their capitals rudely carved, and the houses above them nothing like so interesting as the side of any close in the "Auld toun" of Edinburgh' (John Ruskin, *Praeterita* (New York, London and Toronto, 2005), p. 241). I should like to thank Karen Gunterman, my research assistant whilst I was a visiting scholar at the Getty Research Institute, for her invaluable help with looking into Ruskin and Rome. Lady Eastlake, *Journals and Correspondance of Lady Eastlake*, ed. Charles Eastlake Smith, 2 vols (London, 1895), vol. 2, pp. 105–6, 13 Oct. 1858.

32 Sala, *Rome and Venice*, p. 448. See Jean-Pierre Albert, *Odeurs de sainteté : La Mythologie chrétienne des aromates* (Paris, 1990). For Catholics, Rome was indeed spiritually fragrant: thus Louis Veuillot entitled his study *Le Parfum de Rome*, 2 vols (Paris, 1862); by contrast, the smells of Paris remained notoriously raw, hence his alternatively titled companion volume, *Les Odeurs de Paris* (Paris, 1867).

33 'Il faudrait du temps pour bien se reconstruire dans la tête la Rome antique, encrassée de l'encens de toutes les églises. Il y a des quartiers, pourtant, sur les bords du Tibre, de vieux coins pleins de fumier, où l'on respire un peu' (Gustave Flaubert, *Correspondance*, 5 vols (Paris, 1973), vol. 1, p. 779, 4 May 1851 to Louis Bouilhot). Scavengers and nightmen were thought to owe their health to their proximity to excrement, hence the eighteenth-century medical encouragement to visit stables, farmyards and slaughterhouses (John Charles Atkinson, *Change of Air: The Fallacies Regarding It* (London, 1848), pp. 59–61).

34 'Choses et gens: tout est ici un peu comme l'odeur de la rue de Rome, où l'on ne sait pas trop ce que l'on sent si c'est la merde ou la fleur d'oranger' (Edmond de Goncourt, *Journal: Mémoires de la vie littéraire*, 9 vols (Paris, 1887–96), vol. 3 (1866–1870), pp. 91–2, May 1867).

35 William Hazlitt, *Notes of a Journey through France and Italy* ([1826] New York, 1983), p. 232.

36 *Promenades* (1996), pp. 400–1.

37 Ibid., p. 12.

38 Cit. Yves-Marie Bercé, *Le Chaudron et la lancette: Croyances populaires et médecine préventive 1798–1830* (Paris, 1984), p. 232.

39 Dr J. Parkinson, 'Journal of a Tour through France and Italy', manuscript, 4 vols, 1783–4, Brinsley Ford Archive, Paul Mellon Centre for British Art, London (Rome, 6 Feb. 1784), file RBF/5/23. Parkinson notes Sir William Murray's advice to use a plant called 'Maragetta/Musagettas [?] which was an effective antidote for the taint of perfume in clothes. See also PRO 30/9/43, journal of Sara Bentham, Rome, 5 Jan. 1794, on Roman aristocrats being made to feel ill by the company of perfumed English ladies (PMCBA loc. cit.).

40 Hester Lynch Piozzi, *Observations and Reflections made in the Course of a Journey through France, Italy, and Germany* (Dublin, 1789), pp. 291–2.

41 Parkinson, 'Journal', vol. 4, p. 253, 13 Jan. 1784.

42 Thomas Watkins, *Travels through Europe 1787–1789*, 2 vols (London, 1794), vol. 1, p. 296, 10 Nov. 1787. Alain Corbin cites the *Encyclopédie* to the effect

that 'ambre, civette, musc sont tombés de mode depuis que nos nerfs sont devenus plus delicats' (*Encyclopédie*, 1765, 'parfum', in *Le Miasme et la jonquille: L'Odorat et l'imaginaire social XVIIIe et XIXe siècles* (Paris, 1982), p. 87).

43 Luigi Martorelli, *Dissertazione sugli odori usati degli antichi romani* (Rome, 1812), pp. 14–15.

44 'una permanente dibolezza nel sistema de'nervi dei modern'. Giuseppe Maria Querci, *Del gusto degli antichi romani per gli odori* (Rome, 1764). Querci queried if climate or people had changed (p. 25); if fashion changed, would perfumes return, whatever the state of the atmosphere? (p. 31). See also Giuseppe Fantini, *De danni che arreca alla salute del bel sesso l'uso continuo de'belletti e l'abuso degli odori nelle toelette* (Macerata, 1781).

45 Johnson, *Change of Air* (1831), pp. 273–4.

46 Jean-Baptiste Michel, *Recherches médico-topograph-iques sur Rome et l'Agro romano* (Rome, 1813), p. 16.

47 Ibid., p. 17; he cites Giuseppe Calanchelli and Andrea Conti, *Opuscoli Astronomici* (Rome, 1813) on climate (p. 18), as well as Giuseppe Matthaeis.

48 'dans un mode de prédisposition pathologique' (ibid., p. 31).

49 'maladies nerveuses…se plaignent d'affections hystériques et redoutent même les odeurs dont le parfum recherché avoit si souvent ailleurs flatté l'odorat' (ibid., p. 30).

50 'substances odorantes…ces odeurs masquent les vapeurs infectes; et que loin de purifier l'air, elle le vicient.…l'éducation physique et morale' (ibid., p. 30. All comments on this topic in Simond, *Voyage*, vol. 2, pp. 38–9, are lifted without acknowledgement from Michel's *Recherches*).

51 'che volete! non e questo un palazzo?'; 'il y a un coin de grandioso caché sous l'ordure d'un palais romain'; 'Le grandiose de la saleté' (Simond, *Voyage*, vol. 1, p. 237). See also Whiteside, *Italy*, vol. 2, p. 60, on the protocol for delaying one's entry into a vestibule and Pizzi, *Observations*, 2 vols (London), vol. 1, pp. 419–20.

52 Smollett, *Travels*, vol. 2, p. 95. Smollett's remark is discussed within a wide-ranging article by Clare Brant, 'Fume and Perfume: Some Eighteenth-Century Uses of Smell', *Journal of British Studies*, vol. 43, no. 4, Oct. 2004, p. 458. Lady Morgan makes the same disgusted point about the need to tread care-

fully when entering palaces and ascending their stairs (*Italy* vol. 2, p. 408).

53 'les immondices de la Ville. Ils les mettent dans un lieu par lequel l'eau du Tibre passe. Elle laisse les choses de quelque valeur qui peuvent etre dans les immondices, comme pièces d'argent, bijoux perdus, pièces antiques, et emporte l'ordure' (Montesquieu, 'Voyage de Gratz à La Haye', in *Œuvres complètes*, 2 vols (Paris, 1949–51), vol. 1, p. 708).

54 *Encyclopédie*, vol. 14, p. 438.

55 Mariana Starke, *Letters from Italy between the Years 1792 and 1798*, 2 vols (London, 1800), vol. 1, p. 332.

56 Whiteside, *Italy*, vol. 2, p. 170.

57 Pierre-Jean Grosley, *New Observations on Italy and its Inhabitants*, written in French by two Swedish gentlemen, trans. Thomas Nugent, 2 vols (London, 1769), vol. 2, pp. 60–1.

58 1605–23 (0.66); 1623–39 (0.86); 1639–55 (1.0); 1655–67 (1.0); 1667–76 (2.01); *Regesti di bandi editti notificazioni e prevvedimenti diversi relativi alla citta di Roma ed allo stato pontificio*, 7 vols (Rome, 1920–68).

59 See Francesco Palermo, *Monsignore Illustrissimo: Antichi mondezzari nelle strade romane; Eccelenti norme inutili contro l'abuso inveterato di tenere Roma 'non pulita'* (Rome, 1980).

60 Nicolai, *Sulle presidenze delle strade* vol. 2, pp. 88–9, 97–104.

61 Kotzebue, *Travels*, vol. 4, pp. 112–13; Johnson, *Change of Air* (1831), p. 178: 'The eye of the stranger is attracted by a notice in the corner, and often many other parts of the street, "IMMONDEZZAIO" throw dirt into the street'; in 1837, Viollet-le-Duc claimed Rome was perhaps 'la ville la plus sale, l'immondezzaio le plus infect de la terre' (*Lettres*, p. 278).

62 Hazlitt, however, claimed that trees were not planted 'on account of their bad effects on the air' (*Notes of a Journey*, p. 233).

63 Anna Lia Bonella, 'In Attesa del colera: Istituzioni pontificie e politica sanitaria nell'età della Restaurazione', in Anna Lia Bonella, Augusto Pompeo and Manola Ides Venzo (eds), *Roma fra la Restaurazione e l'Elezione di Pio IX: Amministrazione, economia, società e cultura* (Rome, Freiburg and Vienna, 1997). Margaret Pelling shows that it was fever (in general) rather than cholera which was the driving force behind public health policies developed in Victorian Britain, and that many of these ideas and

some policies were generated in the Enlightenment military services (*Cholera, Fever, and English Medicine, 1825–1865* (Oxford, 1978), cit. W.F. Bynum, 'Cullen and the Study of Fevers in Britain, 1760–1820', in W.F. Bynum and V. Nutton (eds), *Theories of Fever from Antiquity to the Enlightenment, Medical History* supplement no. 1 (London, 1981), p. 141). It is surely significant that, in the context of a compendious account of European public strategies for combatting disease and managing public health, Peter Baldwin makes no mention of Rome (*Contagion and the State in Europe 1830–1930* (Cambridge, 1999)).

64 Laura Megua, '"Acque e immonditie del fiume": Inondazioni del Tevere e smaltimento dei rifiuti a Roma tra Cinque e Settecento', *Mélanges de l'École française à Rome*, vol. 118, no. 1, 2006.

65 Nicolai, *Sulle presidenze delle strade*, vol. 2, pp. 88–9, 97–104. Lancisi supported the practice of using mud on fields by means of which harmful exhalations could be transformed into life-giving growth (*De noxiis* (1942) pp. 101–2). Tournon, ever alive to the need to improve productivity through the proper use of local resources, noted disapprovingly that not enough use was made of Rome's 'immondices': 'presque les seuls amendemens que reçoivent les terres sont l'incinération des chaumes, les sémis de lupin et leur enfouissement par la charrue au moment de la floraison, enfin et surtout le parcage des moutons, qui est conduit avec beaucoup d'intelligence' (C. Tournon, *Études statistiques sur Rome et la partie occidentale des états romains*, 2 vols ([1831] Paris, 1855), vol. 1, p. 302). In 1870, Emmanuele Lisi, founder of 'colonie agrarie' in Umbria for abandoned poor girls, negotiated with the Roman municipality to collect rubbish and sell it to Roman farmers once it had rotted down to form fertilizer (Emiliano Bertoloni and Marco De Nicolò, *Il municipio anemico: Il Campidoglio nell'ultimo decennio pontificio* (Rome, 2000), pp. 290–1). See Erland Mårald, 'Everything Circulates: Agricultural Chemistry and Recycling Theories in the Second Half of the Nineteenth Century', *Environment and History*, vol. 8, 2002, and David L. Pike, 'Sewage Treatments: Vertical Space and Waste in Nineteenth-Century Paris and London', in William A. Cohen and Ryan Johnson (eds), *Filth: Dirt, Disgust, and Modern Life* (Minneapolis and London, 2004).

66 Tournon, *Études* (1831), vol. 2, p. 164.

67 Whiteside, *Italy*, vol. 2, p. 86.

68 Norvins et al., *L'Italie pittoresque* (Paris, 1834), p. 83.

69 Preface, 'Prometheus Unbound', in P.B. Shelley, *The Complete Poetical Works of Percy Bysshe Shelley* (Oxford, 1960), p. 205.

70 Byron, *Childe Harold's Pilgrimage* (1818), IV, xxvi. Lamartine envisaged more of a struggle between man and nature: in the Colosseum: 'Là, le lierre jaloux de l'immortalité, / Triomphe en possédant ce que l'homme a quitté' (Alphonse de Lamartine, 'La Liberté', in *Œuvres poétiques complètes* (Paris, 1963), p. 168). Flaubert connected human virility and natural fertility: 'Je t'envoie des fleurs que j'ai cueillies dans un lupanar sur la porte duquel se dressait un phallus érectant. Il y avait dans cette maison plus de fleurs que dans aucune autre. Les spermes des vis antiques, tombés à terre ont peut-être fécondé le sol' (Flaubert, *Correspondance*, vol. 1, p. 773, 4 May 1851 to Louis Bouilhot).

71 'Rien de plus singulier que le commerce de cette vieille capitale du monde chrétien. Les vaisseaux qui amènent des vivres à Rome n'ont pour retour que des haillons, dont la destinée est brillante: car les Genois les portent aux pieds de leurs orangers, où ils font naître des fleurs, des fruits et des parfums délicieux. La pouzzolane, cette terre volcanique qui rend le mortier presque indestructible, compose, avec les haillons et les antiquités, l'unique exportation de Rome. Le temps présent est le seul qui ne rende rien à cette ville, dont la moitié des habitants ne vit que des ruines des siècles passés, tandis que l'autre fait le commerce exclusif de la vie future' (Charles Victor Bonstetten, *Voyage sur le scène des six derniers livres de l'Énéide* (Geneva, 1971), p. 37).

72 'Les medailles, figurines, etc., s'y vendre comme les fruits, les légumes et autres produits du sol....La seule exportation de Rome, c'est la terre même, les haillons, et les antiquités....Les medailles, figurines, etc., s'y vendre comme les fruits, les légumes et autres produits du sol' (Jules Michelet, *Introduction à l'histoire universelle*, 2nd edn ([1831] The Hague, 1835), pp. 47, 146). Theodora Scharten, *Les Voyages et séjours de Michelet en Italie: Amitiés italiennes* (Paris, 1934), p. 31, gives the main quotation but without the note. I am grateful to Michelle Hannoosh for help with Michelet.

73 'Ces plantes parasites se glissent dans les tombeaux, décorent les ruines, et semblent là seulement pour honorer les morts. On dirait que l'orgueilleuse nature a repoussé tous les travaux de l'homme, depuis que les Cincinnatus ne conduisent plus la charrue qui sillonnait son sein; elle produit des plantes au hasard, sans permettre que les vivants se servent de sa richesse. Ces plaines incultes doivent déplaire aux agriculteurs, aux administrateurs, à tous ceux qui spéculent sur la terre, et veulent l'exploiter pour les besoins de l'homme; mais les âmes rêveuses, que la mort occupe autant que la vie, se plaisent à contempler cette campagne de Rome, ou le temps present n'a imprimé aucune trace; cette terre qui chérit ses morts, et les couvre avec amour des inutiles fleurs, des inutiles plantes qui se trainent sur le sol, et ne s'élèvent jamais assez pour se séparer des cendres qu'elles ont l'air de caresser' (Madame de Staël, *Corinne ou l'Italie* (Paris, 1861), p. 89).

74 'La campagne de Rome, partout sillonée par d'énormes crevasses, souvent par des [restes] d'aqueducs à perte de vue, privée de végétation, déserte, aride, inculte, ressemble à une vaste sépulture. L'*aria cattiva*, qui, pendant une partie de l'été, ravage un tiers de la ville, a frappé de mort son vaste territoire: la peur en a chassé tout ce qu'a épargné la fièvre....sur cette vivifiante poussière de l'antiquité, quelques débris des arts et de l'opulence des temps modernes attirent encore le voyageur, et lui présentent un spectacle digne de toute son imagination' (Anne-Louis Girodet, *Œuvres posthumes de Girodet-Trioson, suivies de sa correspondance*, ed. Pierre A. Coupin, 2 vols (Paris, 1829), vol. 1, p. 243).

75 'aria della piu mal sana' (Nicola Maria Nicolai, *Memorie, leggi, ed osservazioni sulle campagne e sull'annona di Roma*, 3 vols (Rome 1803), p. 130).

76 'il semble qu'il y ait en réserve, dans cette terre, une force occulte qui, mise à jour par la moindre culture, sera aussi propice au développement des plantes que funeste à l'homme....puissance toxique' (Léon Colin, *Traité des fièvres intermittentes* (Paris, 1870), pp. 17–20).

77 Corrado Tommasi-Crudeli, *The Climate of Rome and the Roman Malaria*, trans. C. Cramond Dick (London, 1892), p. 119.

78 See Quatremère de Quincy, *Lettres à Miranda sur le déplacement des monuments de l'art de l'Italie*, ed. Édouard Pommier ([1796] Paris, 1989). See Humboldt in chapter 4 on censure of the disengagement of monuments from earth.

79 Tournon, *Études statistiques* vol. 2, p. 259. Tournon is careful to distinguish between 'l'irruption spoliatrice et révolutionnaire qui eût lieu en 1798' and the later occupation of 1809–14. The latter, 'malgré son injustice flagrante, et la politique maladroite et colérique qui la conseilla', he asserted, behaved with a completely different, more constructive attitude to their adminstration of the city and its people.

80 For a detailed account of the work on the Colosseum, see Ron Ridley, *The Eagle and the Spade: Archaeology in Rome during the Napoleonic Era* (Cambridge, 1992), pp. 109–23.

81 'Memoirs of the Painter Granet', ed. and trans. Joseph Focarino, in Edgar Munhall, *François-Marius Granet: Watercolours from the Musée Granet at Aix-en-Provence* (Frick Collection, New York, 1988), p. 48, as noted by Sarah Faunce, in P. Conisbee et al., *In the Light of Italy: Corot and Early Open Air Painting* (National Gallery of Art, Washington, D.C., 1996), p. 63.

82 The 'old friend' was in all probability the Swiss landscapist and long-time Roman resident François Kaesermann (Rembrandt Peale, *Notes on Italy Written during a Tour in the Years 1829 and 1830* (Philadelphia, 1831), pp. 105–6, cit. C.R. Mack and L. Robertson (eds), *The Roman Remains: John Izard Middleton's Visual Souvenirs of 1820–1823* (Columbia, S.C., 1997), p. 100).

83 T.H. Burgess, *Climate of Italy in Relation to Pulmonary Consumption...*(London, 1852), pp. 175–6.

84 C.E. Hallé, *Notes from a Painter's Life, including the Founding of Two Galleries* (London, 1909), p. 36.

85 Antonio Sebastiani, *Romanorum plantarum, fasciculus alter: Accedit Enumeratio plantarum sponte nascentium in ruderibus Amphiteatri Flavii* (Rome, 1815); Richard Deakin, *Flora of the Colosseum of Rome, or, Illustrations and Descriptions of Four Hundred and Twenty Plants growing spontaneously upon the Ruins of the Colosseum of Rome* (London, 1855), p. vi. Deakin was also the author of a meteorological chart of Rome. Chloe Chard notes Hugh

William Williams's observation that there were 261 varieties of plant growing on the Colosseum, of which 148 were native British (*Travels in Italy, Greece, and the Ionian Islands*, 2 vols (London, 1820), vol. 1, pp. 389–99, cit. Chloe Chard, *Pleasure and Guilt on the Grand Tour: Travel Writing and Imaginative Geography, 1600–1830* (Manchester, 1999), p. 229). Williams also includes two plates which show pressed leaves from Greece (vol. 2, pp. 282–3). See William L. Vance, 'The Colosseum: American Uses of an Imperial Image', in Annabel Patterson (ed.), *Roman Images* (Baltimore and London, 1984). *Frondose arcate: Il Colosseo prima dell'archeologia*, eds Italo Insolera, Denis Coutagne, Giulia Caneva, Simona Ceschin and Bernard Terlay (Palazzo Altemps, Rome, 2000). G. Caneva, A. Pacini, L. Celesti Grapow and S. Ceschin, 'The Colosseum's Use and State of Abandonment as analysed through its Flora', *International Biodeterioration & Biodegradation*, vol. 51, no. 3, April 2003; Giulia Caneva (ed.), *Amphitheatrum naturae: Il Colosseo, storia e ambienti letti attraverso la sua fauna* (Milan, 2004). See also Keith Hopkins and Mary Beard, *The Colosseum* (London, 2005), pp. 7–8, 177–80.

86   As Janet Delaine kindly pointed out to me, certain plants do indeed thrive on a combination of lime-rich mortar and water-retaining building materials.

87   *The Italian Journal of Samuel Rogers*, ed. J.R. Hale (London, 1956), p. 66. Michelet took Colosseum flowers to send home (Scharten, *Les Voyages et séjours de Michelet* p. 22). Others include James Holman, *The Narrative of a Journey*...(London, 1822), p. 157. Edward Lear promised to make a 'dry collection' of Colosseum plants for the Earl of Derby, (Edward Lear, *Selected Letters*, ed. Vivien Noakes (Oxford, 1990), p. 39, 14 Feb. 1838. The Romantic pathos of such mementoes is well expressed in 'A une fleur sêchée dans un album (1827)' (an orange blossom from a garland which had been given to a woman who had then placed it on a ruin) (Lamartine, *Œuvres poétiques complètes*, pp. 1197–8).

88   Mary Keele (ed.), *Florence Nightingale in Rome: Letters written by Florence Nightingale in Rome in the Winter of 1847–1848* (Philadelphia, 1981), p. 259, 28 Feb. 1848.

89   Wetmore Story, *Roba di Roma*, vol. 1, p. 7.

90   Chard, *Pleasure and Guilt*, pp. 229–30.

91   Ilaria Bignamini and Clare Hornsby (eds), *Archives and Excavations: Essays on the History of Archaeological Excavations in Rome and Southern Italy, from the Renaissance to the Nineteenth Century* (London, 2004).

92   Elisabetta Pallottino, 'La ricostruzione della basilica di San Paolo fuori le mura (1823–1854)', in *Maestà di Roma, da Napoleone all'unità d'Italia: Universale ed eterna; Capitale delle arti* (Milan, 2003). Mary Bergstein, 'The Mystification of Antiquity under Pius IX: Rome 1846–1878', in Geraldine A. Johnson (ed.), *Sculpture and Photography: Envisioning the Third Dimension* (Cambridge, 1998).

93   Marita Jonsson, 'La cura dei monumenti alle origini', in *Restauro e scavo dei monumenti antichi a Roma 1800–1830* (Stockholm, 1986), and her *Monumentvrdens begynnelse: Restaurering och friläggning av antika monument I Rom 1800–1830* (Uppsala, 1976).

94   Hans Andersen, *The True Story of my Life*, trans. Mary Howitt (London, 1847), p. 284.

95   *Rome in Early Photographs: The Age of Pius IX; Photographs 1846–1878 from Roman and Danish Collections* (Thorwaldsen Museum, Copenhagen, 1977), p. 9. It is somewhat ironical that Ibsen owned 'A View of the Portico of Octavia' by Hjalmar Petersen (Ibsen House Museum, Oslo), since this monument housed a fish-market and was adjacent to the ghetto, commonly thought to be the dirtiest place in Rome. On post-unification policies in 'Roma capitale', see Taina Syrjämaa, *Constructing Unity, Living in Diversity: A Roman Decade* (Helsinki, 2006).

96   'Letters to a College Friend', 27 September 1841, in Ruskin, *Works*, vol. 1, p. 457, with further reference to William Wetmore Story's disapproval of the periodical scraping of Roman ruins (*Roba di Roma*, vol. 2, chapter 4).

97   On pulmonary invalids' difficulty in getting lodgings, and the burning of furniture used and fumigation of the room inhabited, see Matthews, *Diary of an Invalid*, vol. 1, p. 217; A.P. Oppé (ed.), 'The Memoirs of Thomas Jones', *The Walpole Society*, vol. 32, 1951, pp. 118–19, 2 Nov. 1782.

98   James Clark, *Medical Notes, on Climate, Diseases, Hospitals, and Medical Schools, in France, Italy, and Switzerland*...(London, 1820).

99 P.B. Shelley, *The Letters of Percy Bysshe Shelley*, ed. F.L. Jones, 2 vols (Oxford, 1964), vol. 1, p. 34.

100 Les juifs de Rome sont pauvres pour la plupart et tout pauvre étant pour l'ordinaire malpropre, il s'ensuit que leur quartier est le plus puant de toute la ville' (Michel de Rotrou, *Le Voyage d'Italie récit de 1763* (Paris, 2007), pp. 387–9). See Johnson, *Change of Air* (1831), pp. 77, 122; Michel, *Recherches médico-topographiques*, p. 140; John Macculloch, *On Malaria* (London, 1827), pp. 292–3; on the absence of malaria but the presence of almost every other kind of disease, see W. North, *Roman Fever* (London, 1896), p. 24, and Tournon, *Études statistiques*, vol. 1, p. 232.

101 Montesquieu, *Œuvres complètes*, vol. 2, p. 757; Louis Valentin, *Voyage en Italie fait en l'année 1820: Deux-ième édition, corrigée et augmentée de nouvelles observations faits dans un second voyage en 1824* (Paris, 1826), p. 100.

102 Jeremiah Donovan, *Rome, Ancient and Modern: And its Environs*, 4 vols (London, 1842–4), vol. 3, pp. 906–8 (discussed in Kenneth Stow, *Theater of Acculturation: The Roman Ghetto in the Sixteenth Century* (Seattle, 2001), p. 126). Attilio Milano, *Il ghetto di Roma: Illustrazioni storiche* (Rome, 1964) notes three estimates between 1709 and 1720: Gibbon, 9,000 (Whiteside says Gibbon gives 10,000 for 1765 (*Italy*, vol. 2, p. 42); Schudt, 7,000–8,000; Basnage, 12,000–15,000; 1732 official statistics give 12,000, but this was in reality more like 6,000–7,000. The 1809 census gives 3,076, explained by some emigration after civil rights were granted (Milano, *Il ghetto*, pp. 97–100, 114). He also gives the following figures for 1829: 3,500 inhabitants, of whom 1,600 live in absolute indigence, 300 in shameful poverty (p. 16). Donovan gives 3,600 for 1842.

103 Sala, *Rome and Venice*, p. 448.

104 Johnson, *Change of Air*, pp. 161–6; on the ghetto, p. 168.

105 Macculloch, *Malaria*, pp. 292–3.

106 'pour rendre aux humeurs leur fluidité, et aux membres leur souplesse ordinaire…l'intempérie de l'air' (Abbé Jérôme Richard, *Description histo-rique et critique de l'Italie, ou nouveaux mémoires sur l'état actuel de son gouvernement, des sciences, des arts, du commerce, de la population et de l'histoire naturelle*, 6 vols (Paris, 1766), vol. 5, pp. 298–9. Tommasi-Crudeli referred to a proposal to plant sunflowers on the *campagna* so that the wings of birds attracted to them would agitate the air and thus improve its quality (*Roman Malaria*, p. 121).

107 'Arrivés sur le boulevard Poissonnière, Pons avait repris de couleurs, en respirant cette atmosphère des boulevards où l'air a tant de puissance; car, où la foule abonde, le fluide est si vital, qu'à Rome on a remarqué le manque de *mala aria* dans l'infect Ghetto où pullulent les juifs' (Balzac, *Cousin Pons* ([1848] Paris, 1962), pp. 97–8).

108 Augustus Hare, *Walks in Rome*, cit. Jacqueline Boudard, *Rome au XIXe siècle vue à travers les guides de l'époque* (Moncalieri, 2002), p. 145; Keele, *Florence Nightingale in Rome*, p. 128, 24 Dec. 1847.

109 Keele, *Florence Nightingale in Rome*, p. 259. Gates were removed in 1848, too late for Florence Nightingale. Palazzo Cenci had been annexed in 1836 following its use as a cholera hospital, as if being relinquished to the ghetto by virtue of its contaminated state (Daniela Di Castro, *Arte ebraica e Roma e nel Lazio* (Rome, 1994), p. 83).

110 Dickens, *Pictures from Italy*, p. 215.

111 'Les Juifs qui fourmillent dans le palais Orsini, ont consacré ce monticule à une singulière branche d'industrie, celle de transformer de vieux habits en habits neufs. Le vétéran, étendu au soleil, est soigneusement regratté avec la carde à foulon, afin d'arracher au drap rapé un faux duvet de jeunesse qui trompe l'ignorant acheteur' (Simond, *Voyage*, vol. 1, p. 317). The interior of the Palazzo Orsini had a 'monticule' formed from 'décombres' of the Theatre of Marcellus. Simond is unusual in giving a physical characterisation of Rome's Jews: 'La race rabougrie des Juifs, habitants de ce quartier, se fait remarquer par une grosse tête et des jambes greles'; this knowledge was, he noted, all too well documented as a consequence of the process of conscription: 'leurs conscrits étaient sujets à des maladies toutes particulières' (ibid.). He also noted that the gates had been reinstated, after having been opened in 1798, according to the wishes of elders.

112 Grosley, *New Observations on Italy*, vol. 2, p. 70 note u.

113 Boudard, *Rome au XIXe siècle*, p. 143. See Marcella Corsi, 'Il mercato del pesce al Portico d'Ottavia (con qualche nota su uso, abuso, disuso, riuso di un monumento antico dal medioevo al secondo

278

dopoguerra)', in L. Francescangeli and O. Rispoli (eds), *Le memorie dei mercati. Fonti e documenti sulla storia dell'annona dei mercati di Roma* (Rome, 2006), pp. 55–88.

114 Excavated 1926–32. The campanile was restored in the nineteenth century, after a previous Romanesque one had collapsed in 1660. Carlo Pietrangeli (ed.), *Guide rionale di Roma: Rione XI, S. Angelo* (Rome, 1976), p. 35. He notes that the *rione*'s stemma had a fish on it.

115 Kotzebue, *Travels*, vol. 4, p. 7.

116 Starke, *Letters*, vol. 1, pp. 375–6.

117 Charlotte Eaton, *Rome in the Nineteenth Century*, 5th edn, 2 vols (London, 1860), vol. 1.

118 'air infecte de ce repaire de la misère' (Simond, *Voyage*, vol. 1, p. 316). See Bonstetten, *Voyage*, p. 32, on the practice of a whole naked family occupying the same bed.

119 Robert J. Morris, 'Photography, Environment and Improvement in Scottish Cities 1860–1900', *Mélanges de l'École française à Rome*, vol. 116, no. 2, 2004. See *Paesaggi della Memoria. Gli aquarelli romani di Ettore Roesler Franz del 1876 al 1895* (Rome, 2008).

120 For the 1880s photographs, see *Roma nelle fotografie della raccolta Ceccarius, presso la Bibliotheca Nazionale di Roma* (Rome, 1991), pp. 187–200, and Salvatore Fornari, *La Roma del Ghetto* (Rome, 1984); on Roesler Franz, see *Paesaggi della Memoria: Gli acquerelli romani di Ettore Roesler Franz dal 1876 al 1875. Landscapes of Memory: The Roman Landscapes of Ettore Roesler Franz, 1876–95* (Rome, 2008). An anticipation of the archaeological clearing away of modern accretions to the Portico is the cork model by Antonio Chichi, made between 1777 and 1782; see *Antike Bauten. Korkmodelle von Antonio Chichi 1777–1782* (Kassel, 1986), pp. 76–7.

121 See Marina Caffiero, *Battesimi forzati: Storie di ebrei, cristiani e convertiti nella Roma dei papi* (Rome, 2005); Maria Margarita Segarra Lagunes, 'I problemi del Ghetto degli Ebrei e l'ampliamento promosso da Sisto V', in *Il Tevere e Roma: storia di una Simbiosi* (Rome, 2004), pp. 229–35.

122 Dupaty (1785), pp. 338–9. Norvins noted approvingly the earlier abolition of humiliating rituals which had been part of the Carnival's annual spectacle, such as having Jews race in sacks or weighed

down with rocks (Norvins et al., *L'Italie pittoresque*, 4th edn (Paris, 1850), p. 115).

123 Stow, *Theater of Acculturation*, p. 4.

124 Rose Marie San Juan, *Rome: A City Out of Print* (Minneapolis and London, 2001), pp. 152–60.

125 Pietrangeli, *Guide*, p. 48. 'Fountain in Piazza Giudea via del Progresso. Erected in 1591 by Giacomo della Porta in the Piazza Giudea at the centre of the ghetto, in front of the Portico of Octavia' (Anthony Blunt, *Guide to Baroque Rome* (St Albans, 1982), p. 233.

126 *Rome éternelle: Dessins et gravures panoramiques du XVe au XIXe siècle* (Charleroi, 2003), p. 100. A 'Vue de la Portique d'Octavie, soeur d'Auguste', is included in Jean Barbault's *Les Plus beaux monuments de Rome ancienne* (1761), illustrated in *Pour l'Amour de l'art. Artistes et amateurs français à Rome au XVIIIe siècle* (Milan, 2011), p. 157.

127 See Fornari, *Roma del Ghetto*, p. 16. However, the stone slabs on which fish were displayed were owned by noble families (Pietrangeli, *Guide*, pp. 37–8).

128 *Italian Scenery; representing the Manners, Customs, and Amusements of the Different States of Italy; containing Thirty-Two Coloured Engravings by James Godby; from Original Drawings by P. van Leberghi. The Narrative by M. Buonaiuti* (London, 1806), p. 29, plate XIV.

129 Fornari states that the via della Pescheria was only partially included in the ghetto as part of an extension in 1823, but also that there was a gate in the portico, implying it pre-dated this. Rossini's print, dated 1819, suggests the gate was indeed in place before this extension (Fornari, *Roma del Ghetto*, p. 24).

130 In another print (1817), Rossini shows via della Fiumara (Calcographia) (Fornari, *Roma del Ghetto*, p. 161). Other ghetto images: H. Willson, *Henry Willson's Fugitive Sketches in Rome, Venice &c.* (London, 1838), plate VI, 'Fish Market Portico d'Ottavia, Rome'; a ghetto image from Comtesse Eugénie Mistral Dutheil de la Rochère, *Rome: Souvenirs religieux, historiques, artistiques de l'expédition française en 1849 et 1850* (Tours, 1854), illustrated by Rouargue and Girardet: 'Le ghetto à Rome', ill. Fornari, *Roma del Ghetto*, pp. 160–1, was reused in Paul-Edme de Musset, *Voyage pittoresque en Italie* (Paris, 1855) (see Attilio Brilli, *Il Viaggio in Italia: Storia di una grande*

tradizione culturale dal XVI al XIX secolo (Milan, 1987), p. 166.

131 See Clare Hornsby, *Nicolas-Didier Boguet (1755–1839): Landscapes of Suburban Rome; Disegni dei contorni di Roma* (Rome, 2002), pp. 102–3, cat. no. 33.

132 For example, it is included in Alexander Ellis's *Italy Daguerreotyped* (unidentified photographer, National Media Museum, Bradford, R 70); De Bonis made another view, which shows the wall across the arch, a stall but no clothes (Musée d'Orsay, 'vers 1865', 24.3 × 18.2 cm). This image is close to the photogravure used in Robert Burn, *Rome and the Campagna: An Historical and Topographical Description of the Sites, Buildings and Neighbourhood of Ancient Rome* (London, 1876), p. 308. The Robert Macpherson photograph of the portico (Bruce Lundberg Collection), showing the exterior view from the south-west, may correspond to 'The Fishmarket in the Ghetto', no. 304 in Macpherson's 1871 catalogue of his photographs.

133 Piranesi's print was the model for Hubert Robert, *The Octavian Gate and Fish Market* (1784), Frances Lehman Loeb Art Center, Vassar College, Poughkeepsie, N.Y.. Charles-Louis Clérisseau made a watercolour (38.3 × 30.4 cm, British Museum, AN239531001). J. M. W. Turner made two drawings: St Peter's sketchbook, D16246, D16245, Tate Britain. Léopold Robert produced a scene with a laughing monk, etc. (Pierre Gassier and Maryse Schmidt-Surdez (eds), *Léopold Robert-Marcotte d'Argenteuil; Correspondance 1824–1835* (Neuchâtel, 2005), p. 142). On Bierstadt's elaborate genre painting, see the interesting discussion in William Vance, *America's Rome*, 2 vols (New Haven and London, 1989), vol. 2, pp. 153–6, and Paul A. Manoguerra, 'Anti-Catholicism in Albert Bierstadt's *Roman Fish Market, Arch of Octavius*', *Nineteenth-Century Art Worldwide: A Journal of Nineteenth-Century Visual Culture*, vol. 2, no. 1, Winter 2003, www. 19thc-artworldnide. org, accessed 11 Sept. 2012 [e-journal]. Jan Miel's drawing (*c*.1664, Albertina, Vienna) seems to be the earliest representation (Pietrangeli, *Guide*, p. 3). Interestingly, the photographer James Anderson produced an outline drawing (itself perhaps after a print) of the portico (*Rom 1846–1870: James Anderson und die Maler-Fotografen: Sammlung Siegert* (Munich, 2005), p. 18).

134 As regards paintings or drawings which show Jews in the ghetto, Henri Zerner suggests Léopold Robert perhaps drew in the Roman ghetto, but the reference is clearly to the Venetian ghetto. Henri Zerner, 'The Modern Pastoral', in Margaret Stuffmann and Werner Busch (eds) *Zeichnen in Rome 1790–1830* (Cologne, 2001), p. 237, referring to Robert's correspondance with Marcotte; the letter (14–17 Sept. 1832) is published in Gassier and Schmidt-Surdez, *Léopold Robert*, pp. 226–9.

135 It is possible that Bierstadt is alluding to the inclusion by Piranesi, in his interior view of the portico, of a similar seated figure in the shady left foreground.

136 In 'Notes on Prout and Hunt (1879–1880)', Ruskin, *Works*, vol. 14, p. 432.

137 A similar viewpoint is used by Benoist in the print illustrated in Pietrangeli, *Guide*, p. 33.

138 This was later reproduced in slighty revised form in *The Amateur's Portfolio of Sketches* (1844). See the discussion by Robert Hewison in his chapter 'Ruskin and the Picturesque', in *John Ruskin: The Argument of the Eye* (London, 1976), p. 38 and figs 12–13. Ruskin said of his sketches during the winter of 1840–1 that they were made partly in imitation of Prout and also David Roberts (*Modern Painters* (London, 1906), vol. 2, p. 247). On Ruskin's approbatory attitude to Prout, see Richard Lockett, *Samuel Prout (1783–1852)* (London, 1985), pp. 61–5. Relevant publications by Prout are *The Landscape Annual for 1831* (steel engravings after Prout's drawings, text by Thomas Roscoe), and the lithograph series, *Sketches in France, Switzerland and Italy* (1839).

139 Diary, 1 Dec. 1840, in Ruskin, *Works*, vol. 1, p. lvii.

140 William Gilpin, *Three Essays: on Picturesque Beauty; on Picturesque Travel; and an sketching landscape*, 3rd edn (London, 1808), p. 40. This is perhaps what Henry James had in mind when he spoke of the 'old Italian sketchability' or 'that element of the rich and strange – as to visible and reproducible "effect", I mean – for the love of which one revisits Italy' (*Italian Hours* (New York, 1979), pp. 114–15). In addition to Hewison (note 138 above), see John Dixon Hunt, 'John Ruskin and the Picturesque', in *Gardens and the Picturesque: Studies in the History of Landscape Architecture* (Cambridge, Mass. and London, 1997), pp. 193–212; Harold L. Shapiro, 'The

Poetry of Architecture: Ruskin's Preparation for *Modern Painters*', *Renaissance and Modern Studies*, vol. 15, 1971.

141 See Anne Janowitz, *England's Ruins: Poetic Purpose and the National Landscape* (Oxford, 1990); John Macarthur, *The Picturesque: Architecture, Disgust, and other Singularities* (London and New York, 2007), pp. 96–103. Macarthur (p. 108) notes the work of Nigel Henderson, who, inspired in part by his wife Judith Stephens's anthropological studies in East London, took documentary photographs of backyards, which the Smithsons referred to in designing their shed-like 'Pavilion' in *This is Tomorrow* at the Whitechapel Art Gallery in 1956; we might also compare this to a filmwork mentioned by André Bazin, made up of a series of Venetian courtyards (*Qu'est-ce que le cinéma?*, vol. 4, *Une Esthétique de la réalité: Le Néoréalisme* (Paris, 1962)).

142 See note 125 above on the fountain's relocation. The drawing was at Brantwood according to Cook and Wedderburn (Ruskin, *Works*, vol. 1, p. lvii); the plate illustrated in *Works* (vol. 1, p. 382) is a lithograph from *The Amateur's Portfolio of Sketches*, 1844, published for J.P. Walton by Colnaghi.

143 Ruskin, *Praeterita*, p. 244.

144 Anon., *View of Portico of Octavia*, 1860–70, albumen, 314 × 236 mm, Archivio Fotografico Comunale AF 6667, ill. *Rome au XIXe siècle: Photographies inédites*, ed. A. Margiotta and S. Tozzi (Rome, 1999), pp. 39–40.

145 'in the later half of the sixteenth century, the streets were "socially cleansed" by moving Jewish residents into their own walled ghetto, and "morally cleansed" as individuals engaged in shameful or suggestive activity such as prostitutes and laundresses were systematically sequestered in undesirable or remote areas' (Katherine W. Rinne, 'The Landscape of Laundry in Late Cinquecento Rome', *Studies in the Decorative Arts*, vol. 9, no. 1, Fall–Winter 2001–2, p. 55).

146 These works are most conveniently gathered together in *J. H. Fragonard e H. Robert a Roma* (Académie de France à Rome, Villa Medici, Rome, 1990). Titles of works by Fragonard (JHF) and Robert (HR) are given here in Italian following this catalogue, with reference to its catalogue entries and illustrations of unexhibited works.

147 JHF, *Le lavandaie*, 1760, Louvre, Paris, p. 20, fig. 1; HR, *Le lavandaie*, 1758–9, Museum of art and history, Sepoukhov, cat. no. 15.

148 JHF, *Veduta di Ronciglione* 1761, British Museum, London, cat. no. 96; HR, *Le lavandaie di Ronciglione*, 1761, Musée des beaux-arts, Valence, cat. no. 97; HR, *Le lavandaie di Ronciglione*, oil, private collection, cat. no. 98.

149 HR, *Veduta di Villa Madama* 1760[?], Hermitage, St Petersburg, cat. no. 53.

150 HR, *Le lavandaie*, Musée de Picardie, Amiens, cat. no. 30; JHF, *Le lavandaie*, or *Stenditoio* / drying rack, 1759–60, Musée des beaux-arts, Rouen, cat. no. 35; JHF, *Le lavandaie alla fontana*, private collection, New York, illustrated *J.H. Fragonard H. Robert* (1990) p. 90, fig. 36a; HR, *La guardaroba*, 1761, Clark Art Institute, Williamstown, ibid,. p. 44, fig. 9.

151 HR, *Lavandaie in una galleria in rovina*, 1760[?], Hermitage, St Peterburg, cat. no. 55.

152 HR, *Architettura colossale di fantasia, presso il colonnato di San Pietro*, 1760[?], private collection, cat. no. 51, ill. p. 136, fig. 83b; HR *Capriccio architettonico con il Pantheon e il Porto di Ripetta*, 1782, Palazzo Barberini, Rome.

153 Henk van Os notes that Poelenburch's picture of the Campo Vaccino, formerly in the collection of the duc de Noailles, was transferred to the Louvre in 1794 (*Dreaming of Italy* (Mauritshuis, The Hague, 2006), pp. 57–8). Robert, who joined the curatorial staff in 1795, could therefore have seen it.

154 However, Poelenburch again provides a precedent: *Baigneuses près de ruines antiques*, oil on panel, 16 × 22 cm, Louvre, Paris, INV. 1696.

155 For example, Jean François Charles André, known as Comte Frédéric Flacheron, *The Foca Column and the Arch of Septimius Severus, the Church of SS. Luca e Martina*, 1849, wet paper negative, 34 × 25.3 cm, Musée d'Orsay, PHO 1987 22 1, ill. *Roma 1850: Il circolo dei pittori fotografi del Caffè Greco* (Rome, 1984), p. 81, fig. 1.15.

156 'Les provisions de linge qui sèchent le long des maisons et des palais, font croire aux étrangers qu'ils entrent dans la capitale de la blanchisserie' (Edmond About, *Rome contemporaine* (Paris, 1861), p. 92).

157 Lear, *Selected Letters*, p. 43, 3 May 1838.

158 'Letters to a College Friend', Rome, 3 Dec. 1840, in Ruskin, *Works*, vol. 1, p. 433. In *Praeterita* he

acknowledged that the *campagna*'s bad air and 'the life of Rome', which entailed constant 'artificial excitement', was 'the worst [his parents] could have chosen' to restore his health (p. 263). Indeed, in reference to a later trip, Ruskin's father was to compare his son's excitement, depression and exhaustion to malarial infection (H.L. Shapiro (ed.), *Ruskin in Italy: Letters to his Parents, 1845* (Oxford, 1972), p. 168, cit. Robert Casillo, *The Empire of Stereotypes: Germaine de Staël and the Idea of Italy* (London, 2006), p. 314 note 115).

159 *Amours de Voyage* (1849), canto I, line 10, in A.H. Clough, *The Poems of Arthur Hugh Clough*, ed. F.L. Mulhauser (Oxford, 1974), p. 95. Tony Hughes kindly drew this source to my attention. Clough perhaps echoes Cassius in *Julius Caesar*, I, iii, 108–9: 'What trash is Rome, / What rubbish and what offal, When it serves / For the base matter to illuminate / So vile a thing as Caesar!'.

160 Ruskin, *Works*, vol.1, pp. 112–13

161 Diary entry for 5 April 1841, in Ruskin, *Works*, vol. 1, pp. 381–2. Prosper Mérimée's story, 'Il viccolo [*sic*] di Madama Lucrezia' (1846), which appeared in his *Dernières Nouvelles*, is a ghost story which makes no mention of dirt (*Romans et nouvelles* (Paris, 1951), pp. 680–701).

162 Walter Benjamin, *The Arcades Project*, ed. Rolf Tiedemann, trans. Howard Eiland and Kevin McLaughlin (Cambridge, Mass. and London, 1999), p. 417. I am grateful to Kathrin Yacavone for pointing out to me that this remark first appears in Benjamin's review of Franz Hessel, *Spazieren in Berlin* (Lepzig and Vienna, 1929); see the translation in Walter Benjamin, *Selected Writings*, vol. 2 (1927–1934), trans. Rodney Livingstone et al., ed. Michael W. Jennings, Howard Eiland, and Gary Smith (Cambridge Mass, 1999), p. 263.

163 'He [Colyar] took us by all sorts of windings to avoid the Corso which is our abhorrence' (*Florence Nightingale in Rome*, p. 260).

164 See Richard Wrigley, 'Loitering with Intent: The Political Origins of the Parisian Flâneur', forthcoming.

165 Oppé (ed.), *Memoirs of Thomas Jones, Memoirs*, p. 53, 14 Dec. 1776.

166 William Beckford, *Dreams, Waking Thoughts and Incidents* (Stroud, 2006), p. 157.

167 Hazlitt, *Notes of a Journey*, p. 232.

168 Sala, *Rome and Venice*, p. 442.

169 Ibid., p. 443.

170 Ibid., p. 444. This is almost an anticipation, albeit differently motivated, of Pasolini's phrase 'a Rome that was no longer Rome' to describe the peripheral shanty-towns that were the preferred location for his fiction and films of the 1960s (Enzo Siciliano, *Pasolini* (London, 1987), p. 225).

171 Angela Emanuel (ed.), *A Bright Remembrance: The Diaries of Julia Cartwright 1851–1924* (London, 1989), p. 118, Friday 15 Oct. 1880.

172 'Letters to Dale', Rome, 31 Dec. 1840, in Ruskin, *Works*, vol. 1, pp. 381–2. For a different angle on fever fear and fever as an experience, see Candace Ward, '"Cruel Disorder": Female Bodies, Eighteenth-Century Fever Narratives, and the Sentimental Novel', *Studies in Eighteeth-Century Culture*, vol. 32, 2003, and the author's *Desire and Disorder: Fever, Fictions, and Feeling in English Georgian Culture* (Lewisburg, Penn., 2007).

173 Repulsed at this level of physical interaction, he resorted to a catalogue of Rome's endemic woes: 'Rome…is the bluest place conceivable. Everybody in it looks like a vampyre; the ground is cold and church-like; the churches are full of skeletons' ('Letters to a College Friend' (Naples), in Ruskin, *Works*, vol. 1, p. 445).

174 Ibid.

175 Williams, *Travels*, vol. 1, p. 296.

176 William Bemrose, *The Life of Joseph Wright A.R.A., commonly called 'Wright of Derby'* (London and Derby, 1885), p. 32, 22 May 1774.

177 'Trovandomi io seco un giorno a vedere alcune ruine di Roma con un forastiere curiosissimo di portare alla patria qualche rarità antica: dissegli Nicolò io vi voglio donare la piu bella antichità che sappiate desiderare, & inclinando la mano, raccolse fra l'herba, un poco di terra, e calcigni con minuzzoli di porfidi, e marmi quasi in polvere, poi disse: eccovi Signore, portate nel vostro Museo e dite questa è Roma antica' (Giovanni Pietro Bellori, *Le vite de' pittori, scultori et architetti moderni* (Rome 1672), p. 441), cit. A.F. Blunt (ed.), *Nicolas Poussin: Lettres et propos sur l'art* (Paris, 1964), p. 192. This story was doubted by Hazlitt (*Notes of a Journey*, p. 232). A further story recounted by Valenciennes associated Poussin, cerebral painter par excellence, with an emotionally intense manifestation of

tactile engagement: 'Poussin 'à son arrivée à Rome [returning from a trip to France] alloit embrasser avec transport les colonnes de la Rotonde' (On his arrival in Rome…Poussin went to embrace ecstatically the columns of the Pantheon) (P.H. Valenciennes, *Éléments de perspective pratique à l'usage des artistes, suivis de réflexions et conseils à un élève sur la peinture et particulièrement sur le genre du paysage* (Paris, 1799), p. 597).

178 'Ce n'est pas sans frémissement que la main, en les approchant, touche, pour ainsi dire, le siècle de Néron, ou celui de Constantin' (C.V. Bonstetten, *L'Homme du Midi, l'homme du nord* (Lausanne, 1992), p. 16).

179 Dans ses sacrés tombeaux Rome m'a vu descendre; / Des mânes les plus saints troublant la froid repos, / J'ai pesée dans mes mains la cendre des héros. / J'allais redemander à leur vaine poussière / Cette immortalité que tout mortel espère!
From *Nouvelles Méditations poétiques* in Lamartine, *Œuvres poétiques complètes*, p. 7). T.S. Eliot, *The Wasteland*: 'I will show you fear in a handful of dust' depends on 'What's become of man's great extent and proportion, when himself shrinks himself and consumes himself to a handful of dust' (John Donne, *Meditations*, IV). In his will, Henri de Montherlant asked that his ashes be spread on the streets of Rome (Julien Gracq, *Autour des sept collines* (Paris, 1988), pp. 7–8). One might also recall here Jacob Bronowski's final gesture – of homage and lamentation – in *The Ascent of Man*, bending to scoop up a handful of the ash-impregnated soil at Auschwitz, thus connecting himself with his murdered ancestors.

180 George Keate, *Ancient and Modern Rome* (London, 1755), cit. David Solkin, *Richard Wilson: The Landscape of Reaction* (Tate Gallery, London, 1982), p. 47.

181 Charles Eliot Norton, *Notes of Travel and Study in Italy* (Boston, 1860), pp. 227–8, on his first 1855 visit, cit. Mack and Robertson, *Roman Remains*, p. 18.

182 'La Poussière de Rome contient plus d'or et plus pur plus de sang et plus noble que les autre spoudres de l'occident' (Joseph Péladan, *Ernest Hébert, son œvre et son temps* (Paris, 1910), p. 53).

183 Hazlitt, *Notes of a Journey*, pp. 230–1.

184 S. Kierkegaard, 'La Répétition', in *Œuvres complètes*, trans. P. H. Tisseau and E. M. Jacquet-Tissau (Paris, 1972), p. 67, cit. David Howes (ed.), *Empire of the Senses: The Sensual Culture Reader* (Oxford, 2005), p. 7 (Introduction).

185 Hester Lynch Piozzi, *Observations and Reflections made in the Course of a Journey through France, Italy and Germany*, ed. Herbert Burrows (Ann Arbor, Mich., 1967), pp. 212–13.

186 James Boswell, *The Journal of a Tour to the Hebrides with Samuel Johnson*, cit. Donovan, *Rome Ancient and Modern*, vol. 1, p. 10.

187 J. I. Middleton, *Grecian Remains in Italy: A Description of Cyclopian Walls, and of Roman Antiquities…*(London, 1812), pp. 49–50.

187 As the Julliens point out in their study of Corot: 'à l'époque où Corot voyage en Italie, les routes de Rome aux Castelli romani sont, comme aujourd'hui, à peu près les voies antiques' (A. and R. Jullien, 'Corot dans les Castelli romani', *Gazette des beaux-arts*, vol. 110, 1987).

189 Byron, *Childe Harold*, Canto IV, stanza LXXVIII, lines 5–12. This passage is discussed by Timothy Webb, '"City of the Soul": English Romantic Travellers in Rome', in Michael Liversidge and Catharine Edwards (eds), *Imagining Rome: British Artists and Rome in the Nineteenth Century* (London, 1996).

190 ' L'émigrant même a beau secouer la poussière du sol de la patrie qui s'attache à ses pieds, il en reste toujours quelque chose, et ce quelque chose est pêtrie dans le substance de son organisme' (E. Carrière, *Fondements et organisation de la climatologie médicale* (Paris, 1869), p. 28).

190 Samuel Rogers, *Italy, a Poem* (London, 1842), p. 147.

192 Monument écroulé, que l'écho seul habite! / Poussière du passé, qu'un vent stérile agite! / Terre, où les fils n'ont plus le sang de leurs aïeux, / Où sur le sol vieilli les hommes naissent vieux,… / Je vais chercher ailleurs (pardonne, ombre romaine! / Des hommes, et non pas de la poussière humaine!
(Lamartine, *Œuvres complètes*, 2 vols. (Paris, 1834), vol. 2, pp. 238–40, cit. Carolyn Springer, *The Marble Wilderness: Ruins and Representation in Italian Romanticism 1775–1850* (Cambridge, 1987), p. 14). Springer discusses Italian outrage at Lamartine's censure, which eventually took the form of Giusti's poetic riposte 'La terra dei morti' (1842). On the earlier use of a vocabulary of dust and memory, see Margaret M. McGowan, *The Vision of Rome in Late Renaissance France* (New Haven and London, 2000), p. 212.

193 Rome! Te voilà donc! Ombre des Césars! / J'aime à fouler aux pieds tes monuments épars. / 'La Liberté, ou une nuit à Rome', in Lamartine, *Œuvres poètiques complètes*, p. 169.

194 Nicolai, *Sulle presidenze delle strade*, vol. 1, p. 11.

195 Byron, *Childe Harold*, Canto IV, stanza CVII, lines 1–15.

196 Morgan, *Italy*, vol. 2, p. 336.

197 Ibid., vol. 2, p. 339.

198 The example runs counter to the argument of Ava Aradt that there was a comprehensive shift from the visual to touch by the late eighteenth century ('Touching London: Contact, Sensibility and the City', in Alexander Gowan and Jill Seward (ed), *The City and the Senses. Urban Culture since 1500* (Aldershot, Burlington Vt, 2007). Patrizia Di Bello and Gabriel; Koureas (eds), *Art History and the Senses: 1830 to the Present* (Burlington Vt, 2010), especially the introduction 'Other than the Visual: Art History and the Senses', pp. 1–17.

CONCLUSION

1 Paolo Liverani, 'The Museo Pio-Clementino at the time of the Grand Tour', *Journal of the History of Collections*, vol. 12, no. 2, 2000, pp. 151–9.

2 Paul Valéry, 'Le problème des musées' (1923), in *Œuvres*, 2 vols (Paris, 1957–60), vol. 2, pp. 1290–3, first published in *Le Gaulois*, 4 April 1923.

3 T. Adorno, 'Valéry, Proust, Museum', in *Prisms*, trans. Samuel and Shierry Weber (London, 1967), p. 175. For a study of the status of the museum as imagined institution, see Peter McIsaac, *Museums of the Mind. German Modernity and the Dynamics of Collecting* (University Park, Pa., 2007), and Michaela Giebelhausen (ed.), *The Architecture of the Museum: Symbolic Structures and Urban Contexts* (Manchester, 2003), especially her introduction on the problematic relations between cities and museums and their respective structuring of historical layers and materials.

4 Angela Windholz, *Et in Academia Ego: ausländische Akademien in Rom zwischen künstlerischer Standortbestimmung und nationaler Repräsentation* (Regensburg, 2008).

BIBLIOGRAPHY

Brinsley Ford Archive, Paul Mellon Centre for British Art, London.

[Anon.], 'Beaux-arts: Salon de 1831; Réouverture. Léopold Robert', *L'Artiste*, vol. 1, 1831, p. 233.

[Anon.], 'Blue Gum', in Royal Botanic Gardens Kew, *Bulletin of Miscellaneous Information*, 1903, no. 1, pp. 1–10.

[Anon.], *A Comparative Sketch of England and Italy, with Disquisitions on National Advantages*, 2 vols (London, 1793).

[Anon.], *Discours sur l'origine et l'état actuel de la peinture* (Paris, 1785).

[Anon.], *The Florence Miscellany* (Florence, 1785).

[Anon.] 'Photographs of Rome', *The Art-Journal*, new series, vol. 1, 1862, p. 227.

[Anon.], 'Ibrahim-Pacha', *La Pandore*, no. 1425, 13 April 1827, pp. 1–2.

About, Edmond, *Rome contemporaine* (Paris, 1861).

Adams, Steven, *The Barbizon School: The Origins of Impressionism* (London, 1994).

Adorno, Theodor W., *Prisms* trans. Samuel and Shierry Weber (London, 1967).

The Age of Neoclassicism (London, 1972).

Aisenberg, Andrew R., *Contagion: Disease, Government, and the 'Social Question' in Nineteenth-Century France* (Stanford, Calif., 1999).

Albert, Jean-Pierre, *Odeurs de sainteté: La Mythologie chrétienne des aromates* (Paris, 1990).

Alfieri, Vittorio, *Tragedie di Vittorio Alfieri*, 6 vols (Pisa, 1819).

Algarotti, Francesco, *Essai sur la peinture et sur l'Académie de France établie à Rome* (Paris, 1769).

—, *Saggio sopra l'Accademia di Francia che è in Roma* (Livorno, 1763).

Alpatov, M.V., *A. A. Ivanov: Zizn' I tvorcestvo* (Moscow, 1956).

Amaury-Duval, *L'Atelier d'Ingres* (Paris, 1924).

Ampère, Jean-Jacques, *Histoire romaine à Rome*, 4 vols (Paris, 1862–4).

Andersen, Hans C., *The True Story of my Life*, trans. Mary Howitt (London, 1847).

Andrews, Malcolm, *Landscape and Western Art* (Oxford, 1999).

Les Années romantiques: La Peinture française de 1815 à 1850 (Paris, 1995).

Antike Bauten, Korkmodelle von Antonio Chichi 1777–1782 (Kassel, 1986).

Aradt, Ava, 'Touching London: Contact, Sensibility and the City' in Alexander Gowan and Jill Seward (eds), *The City and the Senses. Urban Culture since 1500* (Aldershot and Burlington Vt., 2007), pp. 95–104.

Apollonio, Umberto, *Futurist Manifestoes* (London, 1973).

Arbelet, Paul, *L'Histoire de la peinture en Italie et les plagiats de Stendhal* (Paris, 1914).

Armstrong, Dr, 'Lectures on the Principles and Practice of Physic', *The Lancet*, vol. 7, no. 7, 21 May 1825, pp. 193–204.

Arnault, A.V., *Souvenirs d'un sexagénaire*, 4 vols (Paris, 1833).

L'Art dans la rue et dans le Salon (Paris, 1859).

Art in Rome in the Eighteenth Century, ed. Edgar Peters Bowron and Joseph J. Rishel (Philadelphia and London, 2000).

Ashby, Thomas, *The Roman Campagna in Classical Times* (London, 1927).
   Some Italian Scenes and Festivals (London, 1929).

Athanassoglou-Kallmyer, Nina, 'Blemished Physiologies: Delacroix, Paganini, and the Cholera Epidemic of 1832', *Art Bulletin*, vol. 83, no. 4, 2001, pp. 686–701; reprinted in Frances S. Connelly (ed.), *Modern Art and the Grotesque* (Cambridge, 2003).

Atkinson, David, 'Totalitarianism and the Street in Fascist Rome', in Nicholas R. Fyfe (ed.), *Images of the Street: Planning, Identity, and Control in Public Space* (London, 1998), pp. 13–30.

Atkinson, John Charles, *Change of Air: The Fallacies Regarding It* (London, 1848).

Aubrun, Marie-Madeleine, *Théodore Caruelle d'Aligny 1798–1871: Catalogue raisonné de l'œuvre peint, dessiné, gravé* ([Paris] 1988).

Baccelli, G. 'La Malaria di Roma', *Monografia della città di Roma e della campagna romana presentata all'Esposizione universale di Parigi del 1878*, 4 vols (Rome, 1879), vol. 1, pp. 149–96.

Baedeker, Karl, *Italy: Handbook for Travellers, First Part, Northern Italy* (Leipzig and London, 1877).

Baglivi, Giacomo, *The Practice of Physick* (London, 1723).

Bailly, Etienne-Martin, *Traité anatomico-pathologique des fièvres intermittentes simples et pernicieuses, fondé sur des observations cliniques, sur des faits de physiologie et de pathologie comparées, sur des autopsies cadavériques, et sur des recherches statistiques, recueillies en Italie; et principalement à l'Hopital du Saint-Esprit de Rome, pendant les années 1820, 1821, et 1822* (Paris, 1825).

Bajou, Valérie, *Monsieur Ingres* (Paris, 1999).

Baker, Thomas Herbert, *On Malaria and Miasmata and their Influence in the Production of Typhus and Typhoid Fevers, Cholera, and the Exanthemata* (London, 1868).

Baldwin, Peter, *Contagion and the State in Europe 1830–1930* (Cambridge, 1999).

Balestra, Pietro, *L'Hygiène dans la ville de Rome et dans la campagne romaine* (Paris, 1876).
   —, *L'Igiena nella campagna e città di Roma* (Rome, 1875).

Balfour, Francis, *A Treatise on the Influence of the Moon in Fevers* (Calcutta, 1784; Edinburgh, 1785).

Balley, François, *Endémo-epidémie et météorologie de Rome: Étude sur les maladies dans leurs rapports avec les divers agents météorologie* (Paris, 1863).
   —, *Météorologie et météorographie, pathogénie et nosographie, ou, Eléments de recherches sur la connexion entre les divers agents météorologiques et la pathogénie civile et militaire à Rome, de 1850 à 1861: Atlas* (Paris, 1863).

Balzac, Honoré de, *Cousin Pons* ([1848] Paris, 1962).

Bann, Stephen, 'Envisioning Rome: Granet and Gibbon in Dialogue', in Catharine Edwards (ed.), *Roman Presences: Receptions of Rome in European Culture, 1789–1945* (Cambridge, 1999), pp. 35–52.
   —, 'Il popolo, dall'eroico al pittoresco', in *Maestà di Roma, da Napoleone all'unità d'Italia: Da Ingres a Degas artisti francesi a Roma*, ed. Oliver Bonfait (Rome, 2003), pp. 245–7.
   —, 'Léopold Robert and the Afterlife of Antiquity', in Richard Wrigley (ed.), *Regarding Romantic Rome* (Oxford, 2007), pp. 69–90.

Barnes, David S., *The Great Stink of Paris and the Nineteenth-Century Struggle against Filth and Germs* (Baltimore, 2006).

Barooshian, Vahan D., *The Art of Liberation: Alexander A. Ivanov* (New York and London, 1987).

Barrett, Francis, *The Magus or Celestial Intelligencer* (London, 1801).

Barrett, Frank A., 'Finke's 1792 Map of Human Diseases: The First World Disease Map?', *Social Science and Medicine*, vol. 50, nos. 7–8, April 2000, pp. 915–20.

Bartoccini, Fiorella, *Roma nell'Ottocento*, Storia di Roma, vol. xvi (Bologna, 1985).

Barzellotti, Giacomo, *Avvisi agli stranieri che amano di viaggiare in Italia o dimorarvi per conservare o recuperare la salute* (Florence, 1838).

Baschet, Robert (ed.), *Journal de Delécluze 1814–1828* (Paris, 1948).

Bashford, Alison and Claire Hooker, *Contagion: Historical and Cultural Studies* (London, 2001).

Baudat, Michel, 'Deux Arlésiens élèves d'Ingres: Les Frères Balze', *Bulletin des amis du vieil Arles pour la protection de son patrimoine historique et esthétique*, no. 141, June 2009, pp. 3–32.

Bauer, Linda Freeman, 'Oil Sketches, Unfinished Paintings, and the Inventories of Artists' Estates', in Hellmut Hager and Susan Scott Munshower (eds), *Light on the Eternal City: Observations and Discoveries in the Art and Architecture of Rome* (Philadelphia, 1987), pp. 93–107.

Baxandall, Michael, *Patterns of Intention* (New Haven and London, 1985).

Bazin, André, *Qu'est-ce que le cinéma?*, vol. 4, *Une Esthétique de la réalité: Le Néoréalisme* (Paris, 1962).

Beaunier, André, 'Quelques lettres de Charles Gounod', *La Revue hebdomadaire*, vol. 12, Dec. 1908, p. 469.

Beaven, Lisa, 'Cardinal Camillo Massimo and Claude Lorrain: Landscape and the Construction of Identity in Seicento Rome', *Storia dell'Arte*, no. 112, April 2006, pp. 23–36.

Beckford, William, *Dreams, Waking Thoughts and Incidents* (Stroud, 2006).

Becq, Annie, *Genèse de l'esthétique moderne: De la Raison classique à l'imagination créatrice, 1680–1814*, 2 vols (Pisa, 1984).

Becq de Fouquères, L., *Isidore-Alexandre Auguste Pils: Sa vie et ses œuvres* (Paris, 1876).

Beddoes Thomas, *Considerations on the Medicinal Uses and on the Production of Factitious Airs* (Bristol, 1795).

Bellori, Giovanni Pietro, *Le vite de' pittori, scultori et architetti moderni* (Rome, 1672).

Bemrose, William, *The Life and Works of Joseph Wright A.R.A., commonly called 'Wright of Derby'* (London and Derby, 1885).

Beneš, Mirka, 'Pastoralism in the Roman Baroque Villa and in Claude Lorrain: Myths and Realities of the Roman Campagna', in Mirka Beneš and Dianne Harris (eds), *Villas and Gardens in Early Modern Italy and France* (Cambridge, 2001), pp. 88–113.

Benjamin, Walter, *The Arcades Project*, ed. Rolf Tiedemann, trans. Howard Eiland and Kevin McLaughlin (Cambridge, Mass., and London, 1999).

—, *Selected Writings*, vol. 2 (1927–1934), ed. M. W. Jennings, H. Eiland, and G. Smith, trans. Rodney Livingstone et al., (Cambridge Mass, 1999), p. 263.

Bérard, Dr, 'De l'hygiène de Rome, ou quelques avis utile à la santé des étrangers qui visitent cette ville', *Journal des connaissances médico-chirurgicales*, no. 5, Nov. 1847, p. 201.

Bercé, Yves-Marie, *Le Chaudron et la lancette: Croyances populaires et médicine préventive 1798–1830* (Paris, 1984).

—, 'Influence de la maladie sur l'histoire événementielle du Latium, XVI–XIXe siècles', in Neithard Bulst and Robert Delort (eds), *Maladies et société (XIIe–XVIIIe siècles): Actes du colloque de Bielefeld, Novembre 1986* (Paris, 1989), pp. 235–45.

Bergeret de Grancourt, *Voyage d'Italie, 1773–1774: Lettres écrites par M. Bergeret de Grancourt au cours de son voyage en compagnie de Fragonard*, ed. Jacques Wilhelm (Paris, 1948).

Bergstein, Mary, 'The Mystification of Antiquity under Pius IX: Rome 1846–1878', in Geraldine A. Johnson (ed.), *Sculpture and Photography: Envisioning the Third Dimension* (Cambridge, 1998), pp. 35–50.

Berlinguer, Giovanni, *Malaria romana: Patologia delle metropoli* (Milan, 1976).

Berlioz, Hector, *The Memoirs of Hector Berlioz, Member of the French Institute, including his Travels in Italy, Germany, Russia and England 1803–1865*, trans. and ed. David Cairns (London, 1970).

Bertoloni, Emiliano, and Marco De Nicolò, *Il municipio anemico: Il Campidoglio nell'ultimo decennio pontificio* (Rome, 2000).

Bertrand, Gilles, *Le Grand Tour revisité: Pour une archéologie du tourisme; Le Voyage des Français en Italie (milieu XVIIIe siècle–début XIXe siècle)* (Rome, 2008).

Bignamini, Ilaria, and Clare Hornsby (eds), *Archives and Excavations: Essays on the History of Archaeological Excavations in Rome and Southern Italy, from the Renaissance to the Nineteenth Century* (London, 2004).

Bindman, David, *Ape to Apollo: Aesthetics and the Idea of Race in the Eighteenth Century* (Ithaca, N.Y., 2002).

Biondi, Luigi, *Osserva del conte Luigi Biondi marchese di Badino sull'opera di S.E.R. Niccola Maria Nicolai uitore generale della C.R. intorno alla presidenza delle strade ed acque* (Rome, 1829).

Black, Jeremy, *The British Abroad: The Grand Tour in the Eighteenth Century* (Stroud, 1992, new edn 2003).

—, *Italy and the Grand Tour* (New Haven and London, 2003).

Blochel, Iris, *Aleksandr Ivanov (1806–1858): Vom 'Meisterwerk' zum Bilderkreis* (Berlin, 2004).

Bloom, Harold, *The Anatomy of Influence: Literature as a Way of Life* (New Haven and London, 2011).

—, *The Anxiety of Influence: A Theory of Poetry* (Oxford, 1973, 2nd edn 1997).

Blunt, Anthony, *Guide to Baroque Rome* (St Albans, 1982).

— (ed.), *Nicolas Poussin: Lettres et propos sur l'art* (Paris, 1964).

Blunt, Revd. John James, *Vestiges of Ancient Manners and Customs Discoverable in Modern Italy and Sicily* (London, 1823).

Boccamazza, Domenico, *Della caccia* (Rome, 1548).

[Bodinier], *Guillaume Bodinier: Paysages d'Italie, dessins de 1823 a 1826* (Musée des beaux-arts, Angers, 2004).

Les Bois sacrés: Actes du colloque international organisé par le centre Jean Bérard, Naples, 1989 (Naples, 1993).

Boissier de Sauvage, *Dissertation où l'on recherche comment l'air suivant ses différent qualités agit sur le corps humain* (Bordeaux, 1753).

Bonaparte, Marie, Anna Freud and Ernst Kris (eds), *The Origins of Psychoanalysis: Letters to Wilhelm Fliess, Drafts, Notes, 1887–1902 by Sigmund Freud* (London, 1954).

Bonella, Anna Lia, 'In Attesa del colera: Istituzioni pontificie e politica sanitaria nell'età della Restaurazione', in Anna Lia Bonella, Augusto Pompeo and Manola Ides Venzo (eds), *Roma fra la Restaurazione e l'Elezione di Pio IX: Amministrazione, economia, società e cultura* (Rome, Freiburg and Vienna, 1997), pp. 221–48.

—, 'Gli Ospedali romani nell'età della Restaurazione,' in *Archivi e archivista a Roma dopo l'Unità. Genesi storicah, ordinamenti, interrelazioni* (Rome, 1994), pp. 485–503.

Bonnard Georges A. (ed.), *Gibbon's Journey from Geneva to Rome: His Journal from 20 April to 2 October 1764* (London, 1961).

Bonstetten, Charles Victor, *L'Homme du midi et l'homme du nord, ou l'influence du climat* (Geneva and Paris, 1824).

—, *L'Homme du Midi, l'homme du nord* (Lausanne, 1992).

—, *Voyage dans le Latium* (Geneva, an III [1795]).

—, *Voyage sur la scène des six derniers livres de l'Énéide* (Geneva, 1971).

—, *Voyage sur la scène des six derniers livres de l'Énéide suivi de quelques observations sur le Latium moderne* (Geneva, an XIII [1805]).

Boott, Francis, *Memoir of the life and medical opinions of John Armstrong; to which is added an enquiry into the facts connected with those forms of fever attributed to malaria or marsh effluvium* (London, 1833–4).

Bordini, Silvia, 'Un'ipotesi di razionalizzazione tardo-illuminista: I "villaggi agrari" della *campagna romana*', *Quaderni sul Neoclassico*, vol. 3, 1975 (Miscellanea), pp. 64–96.

Borghese, Daria, *Gogol a Roma* (Florence, 1957).

Boudard, Jacqueline, *Rome au XIXe siècle vue à travers les guides de l'époque* (Moncalieri, 2002).

Bouffey, Louis Dominique Amable, *Recherches sur l'influence de l'air dans le développement, le caractère et le traitement des maladies* (Paris, 1813).

Bourgeois, Constant, *Vues et fabriques d'Italie* (Paris, 1803).

Boutry, Ph., F. Pitocco and C.M. Travaglini (eds), *Roma negli anni di influenza e dominio francese* (Rome, 1989).

Bouvier, Beatrice, and François Fossier (eds), *Procès-Verbaux de l'Académie des Beaux-Arts, Volume 3: 1821–25* (Paris, 2003).

Bradley, Margaret, 'Prony the Bridge Builder: The Life and Times of Gaspard de Prony, Educator and Scientist', *Centaurus*, vol. 37, no. 3, July 1994, pp. 230–68.

Bradley, Mark, 'Roman Sewers and the Politics of Cleanliness', *Omnibus*, no. 51, Jan. 2006, pp. 3–5.

— (ed.), *Rome, Pollution and Propriety: Dirt, Disease and Hygiene in the Eternal City from Antiquity to Modernity* (Cambridge, 2012).

Brant, Clare, 'Fume and Perfume: Some Eighteenth-Century Uses of Smell', *Journal of British Studies*, vol. 43, no. 4, Oct. 2004, pp. 444–63.

Braudel, Ferdinand, *The Mediterranean and the Mediterranean World in the Age of Phillip II*, 2 vols (French edn 1949; Princeton, 1995).

Breislak, Scipion, *Voyages physiques et lythologiques dans la Campanie: Suivi d'une mémoire sur la constitution physique de Rome*, 2 vols (Paris, an IX [1801]).

Brilli, Attilio, *Il 'Petit Tour': Itinerario minori del viaggio in Italia* (Milan, 1988).

—, *Il Viaggio in Italia: Storia di una grande tradizione culturale dal XVI al XIX secolo* (Milan, 1987).

Brocchi, Giovanni Battista, *Dello stato fisico del Suolo di Roma* (Rome, 1820).

Brockliss, Laurence, and Colin Jones, *The Medical World of Early Modern France* (Oxford, 1997).

Broers, Michael, 'Cultural Imperialism in a European Context? Political Culture and Cultural Politics in Napoleonic Italy', *Past & Present*, vol. 170, 2001, pp. 152–80.

—, *The Napoleonic Empire in Italy, 1796–1814: Cultural Imperialism in a European Context?* (Basingstoke, 2005).

Brookner, Anita, *The Genius of the Future* (London, 1971).

Brosses, Abbé Charles de, *Lettres familières écrites d'Italie en 1739 et 1740*, 2 vols (Paris, n.d.).

Bruce-Chwatt, L.J., 'Ague as Malaria', *Journal of Tropical Medicine and Hygiene*, vol. 79, 1976, pp. 168–76.

Burgess, T.H., *Climate of Italy in Relation to Pulmonary Consumption: With Remarks on the Influence of Foreign Climates upon Individuals* (London, 1852).

Burn, Robert, *Rome and the Campagna: An Historical and Topographical Description of the Sites, Buildings and Neighbourhood of Ancient Rome* (London, 1876).

Bush, Anne, 'The Roman Guidebook as a Cartographic Space', in R. Wrigley (ed.), *Regarding Romantic Rome* (Oxford, 2007), pp. 181–204.

Buzard, James, *The Beaten Track: European Tourism, Literature, and the Ways to 'Culture', 1800–1918* (Oxford, 1993).

Bynum, W.F., 'Cullen and the Study of Fevers in Britain, 1760–1820', in W.F. Bynum and V. Nutton (eds), *Theories of Fever from Antiquity to the Enlightenment, Medical History*, supplement no. 1 (London, 1981), pp. 135–47.

Byron, Baron, *Childe Harold's Pilgrimage*, 2 vols (Brussels, 1829).

Cabanis, P.J.G., *Coup d'œil sur les révolutions et sur la réforme de la médecine* (Paris, 1804).

—, *Rapports du physique et du moral de l'homme* (Paris, 1802).

Caffiero, Marina, *Battesimi forzati: Storie di ebrei, cristiani e convertiti nella Roma dei papi* (Rome, 2005).

Cagnati, Marsilio, 'De Romani aeris salubritate' (1599), in *Opuscula varia* (Rome, 1603).

Cairns, David, *Berlioz: The Making of an Artist 1803–1832* (London, 1989).

Calanchelli, Giuseppe, and Andrea Conti, *Opuscoli Astronomici* (Rome, 1813).

Cancellieri, Francesco, *Lettera di Francesco Cancellieri al Ch. Sig. Dottore Koreff, Professore di Medicina nell'Universita di Berline sopra il tarantismo, l'aria di Roma, e della sua campagna ed. i Palazzi Pontificij entro e fuori di Roma, con le Notizie di Castel Gandolfo, di Paesi circonvicini* (Rome, 1817).

Caneva, Giulia (ed.), *Amphitheatrum naturae: Il Colosseo, storia e ambienti letti attraverso la sua fauna* (Milan, 2004).

Caneva, G., A. Pacini, L. Celesti Grapow and S. Ceschin, 'The Colosseum's Use and State of Abandonment as analysed through its Flora', *International Biodeterioration & Biodegradation*, vol. 51, no. 3, April 2003, pp. 211–19.

Cantinelli, Richard, *Jacques-Louis David* (Paris, 1930).

Carabelli, Giancarlo, *In the Image of Priapus* (London, 1996).

Carlin, Claire L. (ed.), *Imagining Contagion in Early Modern Europe* (Basingstoke, 2005).

Carpentier, Paul, 'Notice sur M. De Montabert, peintre et homme de lettres', in Paillot de Montabert, *L'Artistaire* (Paris, 1855), pp. i–xxviii.

Carrière, E., *Le Climat de l'Italie sous le rapport hygiénique et médical* (Paris, 1849).

—, *Fondements et organisation de la climatologie médicale* (Paris, 1869).

Carter, H.W., *A Short Account of some of the Principal Hospitals of France, Italy, Switzerland and the Netherlands, with Remarks upon the Climate and Diseases of these Countries* (London, 1819).

Cartwright, Julia [Mrs Ady], *The Painters of Florence: From the Thirteenth to the Sixteenth Century*, 2nd edn (London, 1910).

Casillo, Robert, *The Empire of Stereotypes: Germaine de Staël and the Idea of Italy* (London, 2006).

Cattaneo, Massimo, *La sponda sbagliata del Tevere: Mito e realtà di un'identità popolare tra antico regime e rivoluzione* (Naples, 2004).

Caviglia-Brunel, Susanna, *Charles-Joseph Natoire (1700–1777)* (Paris, 2012).

Cavina, Anna Ottani, and Emilia Calbi (eds), *La pittura di paesaggio in Italia: Il settecento* (Milan, 2005).

Celli, Angelo, *The History of Malaria in the Roman Campagna from Ancient Times*, ed. Anna Celli-Fraentzel (London, 1933).

Celoni, Tommaso Maria, *Ragionamento sull'aria del Vaticano di Arenio Triense P.A., recitato in una general Adunanza tenuta degli Arcadi nella sala del Serbatojo* (Rome, 1780).

Chancerel, Lucien, *Influence hygiénique des végétaux sur le climat et leur action spéciale sur la malaria et le tuberculose* (Paris, 1896).

Chaney, Edward, *The Grand Tour and the Great Rebellion: Richard Lassels and 'The Voyage of Italy' in the Seventeenth Century* (Geneva, 1985).

—, *The Evolution of the Grand Tour* (London, Portland OR, 1998).

Chard, Chloe, 'Nakedness and Tourism: Classical Sculpture and the Imaginative Geography of the Grand Tour', *Oxford Art Journal*, vol. 18, no. 1, 1995, pp. 111–28.

—, *Pleasure and Guilt on the Grand Tour: Travel Writing and Imaginative Geography, 1600–1830* (Manchester, 1999).

—, and Helen Langdon (eds), *Transports: Travel, Pleasure, and Imaginative Geography, 1660–1830* (New Haven and London, 1996).

Chastel, André, 'L'Aria: Théorie du milieu à la Renaissance', in *Fables, formes, figures*, 2 vols (Paris, 1978), vol. 1, pp. 393–405 (originally in *L'uomo e il suo ambiente*, Quaderni di S. Giorgio, no. 34, Florence, 1973, pp. 161–79).

—, 'Michel-Ange en France', in *Fables, formes, figures*, 2 vols (Paris, 1978), vol. 1, pp. 189–207.

Chateaubriand, François-René, Vicomte de, *Correspondance*, ed. P. de Raynal (Paris, 1862).

—, *Lettre à M. de Fontanes sur la campagne romaine*, ed. J. M. Gautier (Geneva, 1951).

—, *Lettre à M. de Fontanes sur la campagne romaine*, ed. J. M. Gautier, new edn (Geneva and Paris, 1961).

—, *Mémoires d'outre-tombe*, 3 vols (Paris, 1951).

—, *Œuvres complètes*, 26 vols (Paris, 1826–31).

—, *Œuvres romanesques et voyages*, ed. Maurice Regard, 2 vols (Paris, 1969).

Chaudonneret, Marie-Claude, *L'État et les artistes: De la Restauration à la monarchie de Juillet (1815–1833)* (Paris, 1999).

Christensen, Allen Conrad, *Nineteenth-Century Narratives of Contagion: 'Our Feverish Contact'* (London, 2005).

Clark, James, *Medical Notes on Climate, Diseases, Hospitals, and Medical Schools, in France, Italy, Switzerland, comprising an Inquiry into the Effects of a Residence in the South of Europe in Cases of Pulmonary Consumption, and illustrating the Present State of Medicine in these Countries* (London, 1820).

—, *The Sanative Influence of Climate*, 3rd edn (London, 1841).

Clark, Ronald W., *Freud: The Man and the Cause* (London, 1980).

Clarke, Michael, *Corot and the Art of Landscape* (London, 1991).

Clément, Charles, *Géricault: Étude biographique et critique* (Paris, 1868).

—, *Léopold Robert d'après sa correspondance inédite* (Paris, 1875).

—, *Prud'hon: Sa Vie, ses œuvres et sa correspondance* (Paris, 1872).

Clough, Arthur Hugh, *The Poems of Arthur Hugh Clough*, ed. F.L. Mulhauser (Oxford, 1974).

Cochin, Charles-Nicolas, *Lettre à un jeune artiste peintre, pensionnaire à l'Académie royale de France à Rome par M. C.* (Paris, 1773–4).

[Cogniet, Léon] *Léon Cogniet 1794–1880* (Musée des beaux-arts, Orléans, 1990).

Cohen, William B., 'Malaria and French Imperialism', *Journal of African History*, vol. 24, 1983, pp. 23–36.

Coleman, Charles, *A Series of Subjects Peculiar to the Campagna of Rome and Pontine Marshes* (Rome, 1850).

Colin, Léon, *Traité des fièvres intermittentes* (Paris, 1870).

Conisbee, Philip, et al., *In the Light of Italy: Corot and Early Open Air Painting* (National Gallery of Art, Washington, D.C., 1996).

Corbin, Alain, *Le Miasme et la jonquille: L'Odorat et l'imaginaire social XVIIIe–XIXe siècles*, (Paris, 1982).

Corot par lui-même, 2 vols (Paris, 1924).

Correspondance de François Gérard, peintre d'histoire, ed. Henri Gérard, 2 vols (Paris, 1867).

Correspondance des directeurs de l'Académie de France à Rome, new series, ed. Georges Brunel and Isabelle Julia, vol. 2, Directorat de Suvée 1795–1807 (Rome, 1984).

Corsi, Marcella, 'Il mercato del pesce al Portico d'Ottavia (con qualche hota su uso, abuso, disuso, riuso di un monument antico dal medioevo al secondo dopoguerra)', in L. Francescangeli and P. Rispoli (eds), *Le Memoire dei mercati. Fonti e documenti sulla storia dell'annono dei mercati di Roma* (Rome, 2006).

Cosmacini, Giorgio, *Soigner et réformer: Médecine et santé en Italie de la grande peste à la première guerre mondiale*, trans. Françoise Felce (Paris, 1992) [originally published as *Storia della medicina e della sanità in Italia: Dalla peste europea alla guerra mondiale, 1348–1918* (Rome and Bari, 1978)].

Coutagne, Denis, *François-Marius Granet 1775–1849: Une Vie pour la peinture* (Paris, 2008).

Creuzé de Lesser, Auguste, *Voyage en Italie et en Sicile fait en 1801 et 1802* (Paris, 1806).

Cropper, Elizabeth, *The Domenichino Affair: Novelty, Imitation, and Theft in Seventeenth-Century Rome* (New Haven and London, 2005).

Crouzet, Michel, *Stendhal et l'italianité: Essai de mythologie romantique* (Paris, 1982).

Crow, Thomas, *Emulation: Making Artists for Revolutionary France* (New Haven and London, 1995).

Cunningham, Allan, *The Life of Sir David Wilkie*, 3 vols (London, 1843).

Curtin, Philip D., *Disease and Empire: The Health of European Troops in the Conquest of Africa* (Cambridge, 1998).

Cuzin, Jean-Pierre, *Jean-Honoré Fragonard: Life and Work; Complete Catalogue of the Paintings* (New York, 1988).

Dacier, Madame, *Des Causes de la corruption du goût* (Paris, 1715).

Dagognet, F., 'La Cure d'air: Essai sur l'histoire d'une idée en thérapeutique', *Thalès*, vol. 10, 1959, pp. 75–98.

Dancel, Jean-François, *De l'Influence de voyages sur l'homme et sur les maladies* (Paris, 1846).

D'Argens, Marquis, *Mémoires du marquis d'Argens* (Paris, 1807).

—, *Réflexions critiques sur les différentes écoles de peinture* (Paris, 1752).

Darmon, Pierre, *L'Homme et les microbes XII–XXe siècle* (Paris, 1999).

David a Roma (Académie de France à Rome, Rome, 1981).

David, Jules, *Le Peintre Louis David: Souvenirs et documents inédits*, 2 vols (Paris, 1880–2).

Deakin, Richard, *Flora of the Colosseum of Rome, or, Illustrations and Descriptions of Four Hundred and Twenty Plants growing spontaneously upon the Ruins of the Colosseum of Rome* (London, 1855).

Decaisne, A.E.L., *Guide médicale et hygiénique du voyageur* (Paris, 1864).

De Clementi, Andreina, *Vivere nel Latifondo: Le comunità della campagna laziale fra '700 e '800* (Milan, 1989).

Décultot, Élizabeth, 'Le Cosmopolitisme en question: Goethe face aux saisies françaises d'œuvres d'art sous la Révolution et sous l'Empire', *Revue germanique internationale*, no. 12, 1999, pp. 161–78.

De Cupis, Cesare, *La Caccia nella Campagna Romana secondo la storia e i documenti* (Rome, 1922).

De Felice, Renzo, 'L'inchiesta napoleonica per I dipartimenti romani (1809–1810)', *Rassegna degli Archivi di Stato*, vol. 27, 1968, pp. 67–102.

De Jorio, Andrea, *Mimica degli antichi* (Naples, 1832).

Delacroix, Eugène, *Correspondance générale*, ed. André Jouin, 5 vols (Paris, 1935–8).

Delécluze, Etienne-Jean, *Carnet de route d'Italie (1823–1824). Impressions romaines*, ed. Robert Baschet (Paris, 1942).

—, *Notice sur la vie et les ouvrages de Léopold Robert* (Paris, 1838).

—, 'Sur l'exposition des ouvrages de peinture, sculpture, architecture et gravure des artistes vivans', *Le Lycée français*, 1819, vol. 1, pp. 269–78.

De Matthaeis, G., *Sul culto reso degli antichi romani alla dea Febbre* (Rome, 1814).

—, *Sulle infermerie degli antichi e loro differenza dai moderni ospedali: Dissertazione letta il Dì 24 Luglio 1828 nell'Accademia di archaeologia* (Rome, 1829).

Deperthes, Jean-Baptiste, *Histoire de l'art du paysage, depuis la Renaissance des Beaux-Arts jusqu'au dix-huitième siècle* (Paris, 1822).

De Rosa, Pier Andrea, and Paolo Emilio Trastulli (eds), *La Campagna Romana da Hackert a Balla* (Rome, 2002).

Deseine, Louis-Pierre, *Notices historiques sur les anciens académies royales de peinture, sculpture, et celle d'architecture: Suivies de deux écrits qui ont déjà été publiés, et qui ont pour l'objet la restitution des monumens consacrés à la religion catholique* (Paris, 1814).

—, *Opinion sur les musées où se trouvent retenus tous les objets d'arts, qui sont la propriété du temples consacrés à la religion catholique* (Paris, Floréal an XI [April 1801]).

Di Bello, Patrizia and gabrier Koureas (eds) *Art History and the Senses: 1830 to the Present* (Aldershot and Burlington Vt., 2010).

Di Castro, Daniela, *Arte ebraica e Roma e nel Lazio* (Rome, 1994).

Dickens, Charles, *Pictures from Italy* (London, 1846).

Diccy, Edward, *Rome in 1860* (Cambridge and London, 1861).

Dillon, Brian, *Tormented Hope: Nine Hypochondriac Lives* (London, 2009).

Ditlevsen, Jytte Walker, *Inspirations italiennes dans les œuvres de Chateaubriand, Stendhal, Barrès, Suarès* (Turin, 1962).

Dixon Hunt, John, *Gardens and the Picturesque: Studies in the History of Landscape Architecture* (Cambridge, Mass. and London, 1997).

Dobson, Mary, 'Bitter-sweet Solutions for Malaria: Exploring Natural Remedies from the Past', *Parassitologia*, vol. 40, nos 1–2, 1998, pp. 68–81.

—, *Contours of Death and Disease in Early Modern England* (Cambridge, 1997).

—, ''Marsh Fever' – The Geography of Malaria in England', *Journal of Historical Geography*, vol. 6, 1980, pp. 357–89.

Doni, Giovanni Battista, *De restituenda salubritate Agri Romani* (Florence, 1664).

Donovan, Very Revd. Jeremiah, *Rome, Ancient and Modern: And its Environs*, 4 vols (London, 1842–4).

Doran, John, *'Mann' and Manners at the Court of Florence, 1740–1786: Founded on the Letters of Horace Mann to H[orace] Walpole*, 2 vols (London, 1876).

Dorbec, Prosper, 'La Tradition classique dans le paysage au milieu du XIXe siècle', *Revue de l'art ancien et moderne*, vol. 24, no. 139, Oct. 1908, pp. 264–5.

Douglas, Mary, *Purity and Danger: An Analysis of the Concepts of Pollution and Taboo* (London and New York, 1966).

Douglas-Fairhurst, Robert, *Victorian Afterlives: The Shaping of Influence in Nineteenth-Century literature* (Oxford, 2002).

Dru, Alexander (ed.), *The Letters of Jacob Burckhardt* (London, 1955).

Du Bellay, Joachim, *Œuvres poétiques*, 2 vols (Paris, 1934).

Dubos, [J.B.], *Réflexions critiques sur la poésie et sur la peinture*, 7th edn, 3 vols (Paris, 1770).

[Ducros] *Abraham-Louis-Rodolphe Ducros: A Swiss Painter in Italy* (Dublin, 2003).

D'Unkermann, René P., *Ernest Hébert 1817–1908* (Paris, 1982).

Dupaty, Charles-Marguerite-Jean-Baptiste Mercier, *Lettres sur l'Italie en 1785* (Paris, 1788).

—, *Lettres sur l'Italie, en 1785*, 3rd edn (Paris, 1796).

Dureau de la Malle, A.J.C.A., *Économie politique des romains*, 2 vols (Paris, 1840).

Duro, Paul, 'The Lure of Rome: The Academic Copy and the Académie de France in the Nineteenth Century', in Rafael Cardoso Denis and Colin Trodd (eds), *Art and the Academy in the Nineteenth Century* (Manchester, 2000), pp. 133–49.

Eastlake, C.L., *Contributions to the Literature of the Fine Arts*, 2nd edn (London, 1870).

Eastlake, Lady, *Journals and Correspondance of Lady Eastlake*, ed. Charles Eastlake Smith, 2 vols (London, 1895).

Eaton, Charlotte, *Rome in the Nineteenth Century*, 5th edn, 2 vols (London, 1860).

—, *Rome in the Nineteenth Century containing a Complete Account of the Ruins of the Ancient City, the Remains of the Middle Ages, and the Monuments of Modern Times,…; in a Series of Letters Written during a Residence at Rome in the Years 1817 and 1818*, 3 vols (Edinburgh, 1820).

Edwards, Catharine, *Writing Rome: Textual Approaches to the City* (Cambridge, 1996).

—, *Roman Presences: Receptions of Rome in European Culture, 1789–1945* (Cambridge, 1999).

Ehrard, Jean, *L'Idée de nature en France dans la première moitié du XVIIIe siècle*, 2 vols (Paris, 1963).

Eliasson, Sabrina Norlander, *Portraiture and Social Identity in Eighteenth-Century Rome* (Manchester, 2009).

Eliot, George, *Middlemarch* (Harmondsworth, 1965).

[Elmes, James], *The Arts and Artists; or, Anecdotes and Relics of the Schools of Painting, Sculpture and Architecture*, 3 vols (London, 1825).

Elsden, Annamaria Formichella, *Roman Fever: Domesticity and Nationalism in Nineteenth-Century American Women's Writing* (Columbus, 2004).

Emanuel, Angela (ed.), *A Bright Remembrance: The Diaries of Julia Cartwright 1851–1924* (London, 1989).

Encyclopédie, ou dictionnaire des sciences, des arts et des métiers, ed. Denis Diderot and Jean Le Rond d'Alembert, 28 vols (Paris, 1751–72).

Escholier, Raymond, *Delacroix, peintre, graveur, écrivain* (Paris, 1926).

Espiard de La Borde, Abbé François Ignace, *Essais sur le génie et le caractère des nations*, 3 vols (Brussels, 1743).

Fabre, Gérard, *Épidémies et contagions; L'Imaginaire du mal en Occident* (Paris, 1998).

Faitrop-Porta, Anne Christine, *Rome au XIXe siècle, vu par les grands compositeurs pensionnaires à la Villa Médicis et par leurs contemporains* (Paris, 1996).

Falconer, William, *A Dissertation on the Influence of the Passions upon Disorders of the Body: Being the Essay to which the Fothergillian Medal Was Adjudged* (London, 1788).

—, *Remarks on the Influence of Climate, Situation, Nature of Country, Population, Nature of Food, and Way of Life on the Disposition and Temper, Manners and Behaviour, Intellect, Laws, Customs, Form of Government and Religion of Mankind* (London, 1781).

Fantini, Giuseppe, *De danni che arreca alla salute del bel sesso l'uso continuo de'belletti e l'abuso degli odori nelle toelette* (Macerata, 1781).

Farge, Arlette, *La Vie fragile: Violence, pouvoirs et solidarités à Paris au XVIIIe siècle* (Paris, 1986).

—, *Vivre dans la rue au XVIIIe siècle* (Paris, 1979).

Fea, Carlo, *Discorso intorno alle belli arte in Roma* (Rome, 1797).

Félibien, André, *Entretiens sur les vies et sur les ouvrages des plus excellens peintres anciens et modernes*, 2 vols (Paris, 1685–8).

Felsenstein Frank, 'The Splenetic Traveller and the Grand Tour', in Tobias Smollett, *Travels through France and Italy*, ed. F. Felsenstein ([1766] Oxford, 1979), pp. xv–xxv.

Fenimore Cooper, James, *Excursions in Italy*, 2 vols (1838).

[Ferber], *Lettres sur la minéralogie et sur les divers objets de l'histoire naturelle de l'Italie, écrites par Mr. Ferber à Mr. le Chev. De Born*, trans. B. De Dietrich (Strasbourg, 1776).

Feuillet de Conches, Félix-Sébastien, *Léopold Robert, sa vie, ses œuvres et sa correspondance* (Paris, 1848).

Flaubert, Gustave, *Correspondance*, ed. Jean Bruneau, 5 vols (Paris, 1973–2007).

Fleming, John, *Robert Adam and his Circle in Edinburgh and Rome* (London, 1962).

Fleres, Ugo, *La Campagna romana* (Bergamo, 1904).

Foissac, P., *De l'Influence des climats sur l'homme et des agents physiques sur le moral* (Paris, 1867).

—, *De la Météorologie dans ses rapports avec la science de l'homme et principalement avec la médecine et l'hygiène publique*, 2 vols (Paris, 1854).

Fontaine, André (ed.), *Vies des artistes du XVIIIe siècle* (Paris, 1910).

Fontenelle, *Œuvres*, 3 vols (The Hague, 1728–9).

Fornari, Salvatore, *La Roma del Ghetto* (Rome, 1984).

Forsyth, Joseph, *Remarks on Antiquities, Arts, and Letters, during an Excursion in Italy in the Years 1802 and 1803* (London, 1813).

—, *Remarks on Antiquities, Arts, and Letters, during an Excursion in Italy in the Years 1802 and 1803*, 4th edn (London, 1835).

Fossier, François, 'Il Lazio e i pittori francesi fra il 1840 e 1870', in *Maestà di Roma, da Napoleone all'Unità d'Italia, Da Ingres a Degas artisti francesi a Roma*, ed. Oliver Bonfait (Rome, 2003) pp. 89–94.

Foucault, Michel, *The Archaeology of Knowledge* (New York, 1972).

Foucart, Bruno (ed.), *Camille de Tournon: Le Préfet de la Rome napoléonienne 1809–1814* (Rome, 2001).

—, 'Quelques peintres français devant les marais Pontins', in *Aux Rives de l'incertain: Histoire et représentation des marais occidentaux du Moyen Âge à nos jours* (Paris, 2002).

—, *Le Renouveau de peinture religieuse en France 1800–1860* (Paris, 1987).

Fournel, Etienne, *Bodin, prédécesseur de Montesquieu* (Paris, 1896).

François Boucher, 1703–1770 (Metropolitan Museum of Art, New York, 1986).

François-Marius Granet: Watercolours from the Musée Granet at Aix-en-Provence, trans. and ed. Joseph Focarino (Frick Collection, New York, 1988).

Fried, Michael, *Manet's Modernism, or The Face of Painting in the 1860s* (Chicago, 1996).

—, 'Manet's Sources: Aspects of his Art 1859–1869', *Artforum*, vol. 7, no. 7, March 1969, pp. 28–82.

Frondose arcate: Il Colosseo prima dell'archeologia (Palazzo Altemps, Rome, 2000).

Funnell, Peter, 'The Symbolical Language of Antiquity', in Michael Clarke and Nicholas Penny (eds), *The Arrogant Connoisseur: Richard Payne Knight 1751–1824* (Manchester, 1982), pp. 65–81.

Gaehtgens, Thomas W., and Jacques Lugand, *Joseph-Marie Vien, peintre du Roi (1716–1809)* (Paris, 1988).

Gage, John, *J. M. W. Turner: 'A Wonderful Range of Mind'* (New Haven and London, 1987).

—, '"More French than the French": British Romantics and the Roman Landscape', in *Corot, un artiste et son temps* (Paris, 1998), pp. 527–37.

Galassi, Peter, *Corot in Italy: Open Air Painting and the Classical Landscape Tradition* (New Haven and London, 1996).

Garlick, Kenneth, *Lawrence: A Complete Catalogue of the Oil Paintings* (London, 1831).

Garlick, Kenneth, and Angus Macintyre (eds), *The Diary of Joseph Farington*, vol. 3 (New Haven and London, 1979).

Gassier, Pierre, and Maryse Schmidt-Surdez (eds), *Léopold Robert-Marcotte d'Argenteuil: Correspondance 1824–1835* (Neuchâtel, 2005).

Gaudenti, A. Canaletti, *La politica agraria e annonaria dello Stato Pontificio da Benedetto XIV a Pio VII* (Rome, 1947).

Gautier, Théophile, *Des Beaux-Arts en Europe en 1855*, 2 vols (Paris, 1855).

—, *Italia* (Paris, 1852).

—, *La Préface de Mademoiselle de Maupin*, ed. Georges Matoré (Paris, 1946).

Gell, Sir William, *The Topography of Rome and its Vicinity*, revised and enlarged by E.H. Bunbury (London, 1846).

Gerbet, Philippe Olympe, *Esquisse de Rome chrétienne*, 3 vols (Paris, 1844–50).

Giannini, Giuseppe, *Della natura delle febbri, e dei metodi di curarle*, 2 vols (Naples, 1817).

Gibson-Wood, Carol, *Jonathan Richardson: Art Theorist of the English Enlightenment* (New Haven and London, 2000).

Giebelhausen, Michaela (ed.), *The Architecture of the Museum: Symbolic Structures and Urban Contexts* (Manchester, 2003).

Gilii, Filippo Luigi, *Agri Romani historia naturalis tres in partes divisa, sive methodica synopsis naturalium rerum in agro Romano existentium Pars I. Regnum animale*, vol. 1, *Ornithologia, in qua de priori avium classe* (Rome, 1781).

Gilpin, William, *Three Essays: On Picturesque Beauty; On Picturesque Travel; and on Sketching Landscape*, 3rd edn (London, 1808).

Gimbert (de Cannes), Dr, *Étude sur l'influence des plantations d'"Eucalyptus globulus" dans les pays fiévreux et sur le traitement des accidents intermittents par ce végétal, par le Dr Gimbert,... Mémoire présenté à la Société de médecine de Paris* (Paris, 1875).

—, *L'Eucalyptus globulus, son importance en agriculture, en hygiène et en médecine* (Paris, 1870).

Giovanni, G. de, *Difesa del Popolo romano sull'abandono della campagna del. Can. Gioacchino de Giovanni parroco di S. Marco* (Rome, 1848).

Girodet, Anne-Louis, *Œuvres posthumes de Girodet-Trioson, suivies de sa correspondance*, ed. Pierre A. Coupin, 2 vols (Paris, 1829).

Glacken, Clarence J., *Traces on the Rhodian Shore: Nature and Culture in Western Thought from Ancient Times to the End of the Eighteenth Century* (Berkeley, 1967).

Goethe, Johann Wolfgang von, *Goethes Werke: Hamburger Ausgabe*, ed. Erich Trunz, 14 vols (Munich, 1988).

—, *Italian Journey, 1786–1788*, trans. W.H. Auden and Elizabeth Mayer (Harmondsworth, 1970).

Golinski, Jan, *British Weather and the Climate of Enlightenment* (Chicago and London, 2007).

Goncourt, Edmond and Jules de, *Journal: Mémoires de la vie littéraire*, 9 vols (Paris, 1887–96).

Gotlieb, Marc J., *The Plight of Emulation: Ernest Meissonier and French Salon Painting* (Princeton, 1996).

Gould, Cecil, *Trophy of Conquest: The Musée Napoleon and the Creation of the Louvre* (London, 1965).

Gracq, Julien, *Autour des sept collines* (Paris, 1988).

Graham, Maria, *Three Months passed in the Mountains East of Rome, during the Year 1819* (London, 1821).

Griener, Pascal, '"Un Genre qu'on ne connaît pas encore…": Léopold Robert et l'élévation du genre sous la monarchie de Juillet', *Kunst+Architektur in der Schweiz*, no. 4, 1994, pp. 346–55.

—, *La République de l'œil: L'Expérience de l'art au siècle des Lumières* (Paris, 2010).

Grosley, Pierre-Jean, *New Observations on Italy and its Inhabitants*, written in French by two Swedish gentlemen, trans. Thomas Nugent, 2 vols (London, 1769).

Gross, Hanns, *Rome in the Age of Enlightenment: The Post-Tridentine Syndrome and the Ancien Régime* (Cambridge, 1990).

Grosskurth, Brian, review of Norman Bryson, *Tradition and Desire: From David to Delacroix* (Cambridge, 1984), in *Burlington Magazine*, vol. 127, no. 989, August 1985, pp. 539–40.

—, 'Solitude as Style', in Richard Wrigley (ed.), *Regarding Romantic Rome* (Basel and Oxford, 2007), pp. 59–68.

Gudin, Théodore, *Souvenirs du Baron Gudin, peintre de la marine (1820–1870)* (Paris, n.d.).

Guinan Laoureins, J.B., *Tableau de Rome vers la fin de 1814* (Brussels, 1816).

Guislain, Joseph, *Lettres médicales sur l'Italie, avec quelques renseignements sur la Suisse: Résumé d'un voyage fait en 1838* (Ghent, 1840).

Guyot de Fère, *Journal des beaux-arts et de la littérature*, 27 March 1836, no. 11, p. 164.

Hadjinicolaou, Nicos, 'L'Exigence de Réalisme au Salon de 1831', *Histoire et critique des arts*, nos 4–5, May 1978, pp. 21–33.

Hallé, Charles E., *Notes from a Painter's Life, including the Founding of Two Galleries* (London, 1909).

Halliday, Tony, *The Temperamental Nude: Class, Medicine, and Representation in Eighteenth-Century France*, Studies on Voltaire and the Eighteenth Century (Oxford, 2010).

Hamilton, James, *Turner and Italy* (Edinburgh, 2009).

A Handbook of Rome and its Environs; Forming Part II of the Handbook for Travellers in Central Italy, 5th edn (London, 1858).

Hare, Augustus, *Walks in Rome*, 13th edn, 2 vols (London, 1893).

—, *Walks in Rome*, 15th edn, 2 vols (London and New York, 1902).

Haskell, Francis, *History and its Images: Art and the Interpretation of the Past* (New Haven and London, 1993).

—, *Patrons and Painters: Art and Society in Baroque Italy*, 2nd edn (New Haven and London, 1980).

Hautecoeur, Louis, *Louis David* (Paris, 1954).

Hayley, William, *The Life of Romney* (London, 1809).

Hazlitt, William, 'English Students at Rome', in *Criticisms on Art* (London, 1844), pp. 203–22.

—, *Notes of a Journey through France and Italy* ([1826] New York, 1983).

—, *The Complete Works of William Hazlitt*, ed. P.P. Howe, 21 vols (London, 1930–4).

Hedley, Jo, *François Boucher: Seductive Visions* (London, 2004).

Hennequin, Ph. A., *Mémoires de Ph. A. Hennequin, écrits par lui-même* (Paris, 1933).

Henner, John, *Sketches of Medical Topography of the Mediterranean: Comprising an Account of Gibraltar, the Ionian Islands, and Malta; To which is prefaced a Sketch of a Plan for Memoirs on Medical Topography* (London, 1830).

Hercenberg, Bernard, *Nicolas Vleughels: Peintre et directeur de l'Académie de France à Rome 1668–1737* (Paris, 1975).

Herrmann, Wolfgang, *Laugier and Eighteenth-Century French Theory* (London, 1962).

Hersant, Yves (ed.), *Italies: Anthologie des voyageurs français aux XVIIIe et XIXe siècles* (Paris, 1988).

Hewison, Robert, *John Ruskin: The Argument of the Eye* (London, 1976).

'Histoire de Julien de Parme racontée par lui-même' (1794), *L'Artiste*, 1862, new period, vol. 1, 15 Feb., p. 85.

Holman, James, *The Narrative of a Journey undertaken in the Years 1819, 1820, 1821 through France, Italy, Savoy, Switzerland, parts of Germany bordering on the Rhine, Holland, and the Netherlands; Comprising incidents that occurred to the author, who has long suffered under a total deprivation of sight; with various points of information collected on his tour* (London, 1822).

Hoolihan, Christopher, 'Health and Travel in Nineteenth-Century Rome', *Journal of the History of Medicine and Allied Sciences*, vol. 44, no. 4, 1989, pp. 479–84.

Hopkins, Keith and Mary Beard, *The Colosseum* (London, 2005).

Hornsby, Clare, *Nicolas-Didier Boguet (1775–1839): Landscapes of Suburban Rome; Disegni dei contorni di Roma* (Rome, 2002).

Houël, Jean-Pierre-Laurent, *Voyage pittoresque des isles de Sicile, de Malte et de Lipari; où l'on traicte des antiquités qui s'y trouvent encore, des principaux phénomènes que la nature y offre, du costume des habitans, et de quelques usages*, 4 vols (Paris, 1782–7).

Howes, David (ed.), *Empire of the Senses: The Sensual Culture Reader* (Oxford, 2005).

Hufton, Olwen, *The Poor of Eighteenth-Century France 1750–1789* (Oxford, 1974).

Hume, David, 'Of National Characters', in *Essays Moral, Political, and Literary*, ed. T. H. Green and T. H. Grose, 2 vols (London, 1898), vol. 1, pp. 244–58.

—, 'On the Populousness of Ancient Nations', in *Essays Moral, Political, and Literary*, ed. Eugene F. Miller (Indianapolis, 1985).

Humphreys, Noel, *Rome and its Surrounding Scenery* (London, 1840).

Hunt, Leigh, *Lord Byron and some of his Contemporaries; With Recollections of the Author's Life*, 2 vols (London, 1828).

Ilvento, Arcangelo, *Storia delle grandi malattie epidemie con speciale riguoardo alla malaria* (Rome, 1936; anno XVI).

Images of the Grand Tour: Louis Ducros 1748–1810 (Geneva, 1985).

Ingamells, John, and John Edgecumbe (eds), *The Letters of Joshua Reynolds* (New Haven and London, 2000).

Italian Scenery: Representing the Manners, Customs, and Amusements of the Different States of Italy; Containing Thirty-Two Coloured Engravings by James Godby, from Original Drawings by P. van Leberghi. The Narrative by M. Buonaiuti (London, 1806).

Jal, Auguste, *Ébauches critiques: Salon de 1831* (Paris, 1831).

—, 'Notes sur Louis David, peintre d'histoire', *Revue étrangère*, vol. 55, Sept. 1845, pp. 623–31 and 701–10.

James, Henry, *Transatlantic Sketches* (Boston, 1875).

—, *Daisy Miller* ([1878] Harmondsworth, 1978).

—, *Italian Hours* (New York, 1979).

—, *Letters*, vol. 1, 1843–1875 , ed. Leon Edel (London, 1974).

Jameson, Anna, *Diary of an Ennuyée* (London, 1826; Boston, 1846).

Janković, Vladimir, *Confronting the Climate. British Airs and the making of Environmental Medicine* (New York and Basingstoke, 2010).

Janowitz, Anne, *England's Ruins: Poetic Purpose and the National Landscape* (Oxford, 1990).

Jarcho, Saul, 'A Cartographic and Literary Study of the Word *Malaria*', *Journal for the History of Medicine*, vol. 25, no. 1, 1970, pp. 31–9.

—, *The Concept of Contagion in Medicine, Literature and Religion* (Malabar, Fl., 2000).

Jean-Germain Drouais, 1763–1788 (Musée des Beaux-Arts, Rennes, 1985).

J. H. Fragonard e H. Robert a Roma (Académie de France à Rome, Villa Medici, Rome, 1990).

Joannides, Paul, 'Delacroix and Modern Literature', in Beth S. Wright (ed.), *The Cambridge Companion to Delacroix* (Cambridge, 2001), pp. 130–53.

Johns, Christopher M.S., *Antonio Canova and the Politics of Patronage in Revolutionary and Napoleonic Europe* (Berkeley, Los Angeles, London, 1998).

—, 'The Roman Experience of Jacques-Louis David, 1775–80', in Dorothy Johnson (ed.), *Jacques-Louis David: New Perspectives* (Newark, 2006), pp. 58–70.

—, Johnson, James, *Change of Air, or The Pursuit of Health; An Autumnal Excursion through France, Switzerland, and Italy; in the Year 1829 with Observations and Reflections on the Moral, Physical, and Medicinal Influence of Travelling-Exercise, Change of Scene, Foreign Skies, and Voluntary Expatriation* (London, 1831).

—, *Change of Air*, 3rd edn (London, 1835).

—, *The Recess, or Autumnal Relaxation in the Highlands and Lowlands: Being the Home Circuit versus Foreign Travel; A Tour…to the Highlands and Hebrides* (London, 1834).

Johnson, Lee, *The Paintings of Eugène Delacroix: A Critical Catalogue*, 6 vols (Oxford, 1981–9).

Jones, F.L. (ed.), *The Letters of Percy Bysshe Shelley*, 2 vols (Oxford, 1964).

Jones, W.H.S., and Ronald Ross, *Malaria: A Neglected Factor in the History of Greece and Rome* (London, 1907).

Jonsson, Marita, 'La cura dei monumenti alle origini', in *Restauro e scavo dei monumenti antichi a Roma 1800–1830* (Stockholm, 1986), pp. 178–9.

—, *Monumentvårdens begynnelse: Restaurering och friläggning av antika monument I Rom 1800–1830* (Uppsala, 1976).

Jouin, Henri-Auguste, *David d'Angers, sa vie, son œuvre, ses écrits et ses contemporains*, 2 vols (Paris, 1878).

Jouy, Etienne de, *L'Hermite en Italie*, 4 vols (Paris, 1824).

Julia, Isabelle, *La Campagne romaine à propos d'un tableau d'Hébert 'La Mal'aria'*, Petit Journal des Grandes Expositions, new series, no. 93, 1980, Musée Hébert, Paris.

Julien, Pierre, 1731–1804 (Somogy, Musée Crozatier, Le Puy-en-Velay, 2004).

Jullien, André and Renée, 'Les Campagnes de Corot au nord de Rome (1826–1827)', *Gazette des beaux-arts*, vol. 99, May–June 1982, pp. 179–202.

—, 'Corot dans les Castelli romani', *Gazette des beaux-arts*, vol. 110, Oct. 1987, pp. 109–30.

—, 'Corot dans les montagnes de la Sabine', *Gazette des beaux-arts*, vol. 103, May–June 1984, pp. 179–97.

Kearns, James, *Théophile Gautier, Orator to the Artists: Art Journalism during the Second Republic* (London, 2007).

Keate, George, *Ancient and Modern Rome* (London, 1755).

Keele, Mary (ed.), *Florence Nightingale in Rome: Letters written by Florence Nightingale in Rome in the Winter of 1847–1848* (Philadelphia, 1981).

Kendall, Richard, *Degas by Himself* (London, 1987).

Keysler, J. G., *Travels through Germany, Bohemia, Hungary, Switzerland, Italy and Lorrain*, trans. from 2nd edn of German original, 4 vols (London, 1756–7).

Kierkegaard, S., 'La Répétition', in *Œuvres complètes*, trans. P.-H. Tisseau and E.-M. Jacquet-Tissau (Paris, 1972).

Knowles, John (ed.), *The Life and Writings of Henry Fuseli*, 3 vols (London, 1831).

Koerner, Joseph, 'Albrecht Dürer: A Sixteenth-Century *Influenza*', in Giulia Bartrum et al., *Albrecht Dürer and his Legacy: The Graphic Works of a Renaisssance Artist* (Princeton, 2002), pp. 18–36.

Koller, Armin Hajman, *The Abbé Dubos: His Advocacy of the Theory of Climate; A Precursor to Johann Gottfried Herder* (Champaign, Ill., 1937).

Kostof, Spiro, *The Third Rome 1870–1950: Traffic and Glory* (Berkeley, Los Angeles, London, 1973).

Kotzebue, Augustus von, *Travels through Italy, in the Years 1804 to 1805*, 4 vols (London, 1806).

Kraus, Rosalind, 'The Future of an Illusion', *AA Files*, no. 13, Autumn 1986, pp. 3–7.

Krautheimer, Richard, *The Rome of Alexander VII 1655–1667* (Princeton, 1985).

Krüdener, Baron Alexis von, *Voyage en Italie en 1786: Note sur l'Italie, la Savoie, Lyon et la Suisse*, trans. and ed. Francis Ley (Paris, 1983).

Kudlick, Catherine J., *Cholera in Post-Revolutionary Paris. A Cultural History* (Berkeley, Los Angeles, London, 1996).

Kuspit, Donald, 'A Mighty Metaphor: The Analogy of Archaeology and Psychoanalysis', in Lynn Gamwell and Richard Wells (eds), *Sigmund Freud and Art: His Personal Collection of Antiquities* (London, 1989), pp. 133–52.

La Condamine, Charles Marie de, *An Extract from the Observations made in a Tour to Italy, by the Chevalier La Condamine, translated by a Fellow of the Royal Society* (London, 1767).

Lacroix, Lucien-Prosper, *Une Idée nouvelle sur la manière d'envisager les fièvres intermittentes, ou Considérations générales sur le rôle que joue l'élimination séreuse dans les diverses manifestations de l'intoxication tellurique, par le Dr Lacroix (des Rousses)* (Paris, 1854).

La Font de, Saint-Yenne, Etienne, *Réflexions sur quelques causes de l'état présent de la peinture en France avec un examen des principaux ouvrages exposés au Louvre le mois d'Août 1746* (The Hague, 1747).

Lagunes, Maria Margarita Segarra, *Il Tevere e Roma: Storia di una Simbiosi* (Rome, 2004).

Laing, Alastair, 'Boucher: The Search for an Idiom', in *François Boucher, 1703–1770* (Metropolitan Museum of Art, New York, 1986), pp. 56–72.

Lalande, Joseph Jérôme le Français de, *Voyage d'un français en Italie*, 10 vols (Paris, 1786).

Lamartine, Alphonse de, *Cours familier de littérature*, 28 vols (Paris, 1856–69).

—, *Œuvres complètes*, 2 vols (Paris, 1834).

—, *Œuvres poétiques complètes* (Paris, 1963).

La Mettrie, Julien Offray de, *L'Homme-plante* (Potsdam, n.d.).

Lancisi, Giovanni Maria, *Dissertatio de nativis atque adventitiis coeli qualitatibus: Cui accidit historia epidemiae rheumaticae que per hyemem anni 1709 vagata est* (Rome, 1711).

—, *De noxiis paludum effluviis, eorumque remediis*, in *Opera*, 3 vols (Geneva, 1718).

—, *De noxiis paludum effluviis eorumque remediis*, trans. Elvira Valentini (Milan and Rome, 1942).

Landolfi, Tommasi, *Gogol' a Roma* (Milan, 2002).

Lane, Laura D., 'Malaria: Medicine and Magic in the Roman World', in David and Noelle Soren (eds), *A Roman Villa and a Late Roman Infant Cemetery: Excavation at Poggio Gramignano Lugnano in Teverna* (Rome, 1999), pp. 633–51.

Langdon, Helen, 'The Imaginative Geographies of Claude Lorrain', in Chloe Chard and Helen Langdon (eds), *Transports: Travel, Pleasure, and Imaginative Geography* (New Haven and London, 1996), pp. 151–78.

Lapauze, H., *Histoire de l'Académie de France à Rome*, 2 vols (Paris, 1924).

—, *Le Roman d'amour de M. Ingres* (Paris, 1910).

Larousse, Pierre, *Grand Dictionnaire universel du XIXe siècle*, 15 vols (Paris, 1866–1879).

Lear, Edward, *Illustrated Excursions in Italy*, 2 vols (London, 1846).

—, *Selected Letters*, ed. Vivien Noakes (Oxford, 1990).

Leavis, Q.D., 'A Note on Literary Indebtedness: Dickens, George Eliot, Henry James', *The Hudson Review*, vol. 8, no. 3, Autumn 1955, pp. 423–8.

Leblanc, Abbé, *Observations sur les ouvrages de MM. de l'Académie de peinture et de sculpture exposés au Sallon du Louvre en l'année 1753* (Paris, 1753).

Lebrun, N.G.H., *Essai sur le paysage, on Du Pouvoir des sites sur l'imagination* (Paris, 1822).

Lenoir, Alexandre, 'Fragonard', in *Biographie universelle et moderne* (Paris, 1816), pp. 419–21.

Le Normand, Antoinette, *La Tradition classique et l'esprit romantique: Les Sculpteurs de l'Académie de France à Rome de 1824 à 1840* (Rome, 1981).

Lenormant, Charles, *Les Artistes contemporains: Salon de 1831* (Paris, 1833).

—, *Léopold Robert, essai d'appréciation critique* (Paris, 1838).

—, 'Léopold Robert: Notice sur la vie et les ouvrages de cet artiste par M.E.J. Delécluze', in *Beaux-arts et voyages*, 2 vols (Paris, 1861), vol. 1, pp. 153–86.

Lettres inédites de Jean-Victor Schnetz à François-Joseph Navez: Une Amitié italienne (Flers, 2000).

Liverani, Paolo, 'The Museo Pio-Clementino at the time of the Grand Tour', *Journal of the History of Collections*, vol. 12, no. 2 (2000), pp. 151–9.

Lockett, Richard, *Samuel Prout (1783–1852)* (London, 1985).

Locquin, Jean, *La Peinture d'histoire en France de 1747 à 1785* (1912, reprint Paris, 1976).

Lodolino, Elio, 'Il brigantaggio nel Lazio meridionale (1814–1825)', *Archivio della società romana di storia patria*, vol. 83, 1960, pp. 189–268.

—, 'Le "selve" nello Stato pontificio (secc. XV–XVIII): Legislazione e fonti archivistiche', in Simonetta Cavaciocchi (ed.), *L'uomo e la foresta: Secc. XIII–XVIII* (Florence, 1996), pp. 521–32.

Lombard, Alfred, *L'Abbé Dubos, un initiateur de la pensée moderne, 1670–1742* (Paris, 1913).

Lombardi, Jean, *Le Compagnon des voyages de Freud* (Paris, 1988).

Lullin de Châteauvieux, Frédéric, *Lettres écrites d'Italie en 1812 et 1813 à Mr Charles Pictet, l'un des rédacteurs de la Bibliothèque britannique* (Geneva and Paris, 1820).

Macarthur, John, *The Picturesque: Architecture, Disgust, and other Singularities* (London, 2007).

McClellan, Andrew, *Inventing the Louvre: Art, Politics, and the Origins of Modern Museum Culture in Eighteenth-Century Paris* (Cambridge, 1994).

Macculloch, John, *On Malaria: An Essay on the Production and Localities of the Places by which it is produced; With an Enunciation of the Diseases caused by it, and the Means of Preventing or Diminishing Them, both at Home, and in the Naval and Military Service* (London, 1827).

McCully, Marilyn (ed.), *A Picasso Anthology: Documents, Criticism, Reminiscences* (London, 1981).

McGann, Jerome, 'Rome and its Romantic Significance', in Annabel Patterson (ed.), *Roman Images: Selected Papers of the English Institute, 1982* (Baltimore, 1984), pp. 83–104.

McGowan, Margaret M., *The Vision of Rome in Late Renaissance France* (New Haven and London, 2000).

MacGregor, Neil, 'Girodet's Poem *Le Peintre*', *Oxford Art Journal*, vol. 4, no. 1, July 1981, pp. 26–30.

McIsaac, Peter, *Museums of the Mind. German Modernity and the Dynamics of Collecting* (University Park P., 2007).

Mclauchlan, Kathy, 'French Artists in Rome 1815–1863' (Ph.D. Courtauld Institute of Art, University of London, 2001).

Macphail, Eric, *The Voyage to Rome in French Renaissance Literature*, Stanford French and Italian Studies (Saratoga, Calif., 1990).

McWilliam, Neil, *Dreams of Happiness: Social Art and the French Left, 1830–1850* (Princeton, 1993).

Mack, Charles R., and Lynn Robertson (eds), *The Roman Remains: John Izard Middleton's Visual Souvenirs of 1820–1823* (Columbia, S.C., 1997).

Madelin, Louis, *La Rome de Napoléon: La Domination française 1809–1814* (Paris, 1906).

Maestà di Roma, da Napoleone all'unità d'Italia: Universale ed eterna; Capitale delle arti, ed. Sandra Pinto, Liliana Barroero, Fernando Mazzocca, Giovanna Capitelli and Matteo Lafranconi (Milan, 2003).

Maestà di Roma: da Napoleone all'unità d'Italia: Da Ingres a Degas artisti francesi a Roma, ed. Olivier Bonfait (Rome, 2003).

Magherini, Graziella, *Le Syndrome de Stendhal: Du Voyage dans les villes d'art* (Paris, 1989).

Mahon, Denis, *Studies in Seicento Art and Theory* (London, 1947).

[Maihows, Dr], *Voyage en France, en Italie…trad. de l'anglais de M. de Puisieux*, 4 vols (Paris, 1763).

Malone, E., *The Works of Joshua Reynolds, Knt., Late President of the Royal Academy*, 5th edn, 2 vols (1819).

Mammucari, Renato, and Rigel Langella, *I Pittori della malaria dalla Campagna romana alle Palude pontine* (Rome, 1999).

Manacorda, Daniele, 'Su "Mondezzari" di Roma tra Antichità e età Moderna', in Xavier Dupré Raventós and Josep-Anton Remolà (eds), *Sordes Urbis: La Eliminación de residuos en la ciudad romana* (Rome, 2000), pp. 63–75.

Mannlich, Johann Christian von, *Histoire de ma vie*, ed. K.H. Bender and H. Kleber, 2 vols (Trier, 1989–93).

Manoguerra, Paul A., 'Anti-Catholicism in Albert Bierstadt's *Roman Fish Market, Arch of Octavius*', *Nineteenth-Century Art Worldwide: A Journal of Nineteenth-Century Visual Culture*, vol. 2, no. 1, Winter 2003 [e-journal]. www.19thc-artworldwide.org, accessed 11th Sept. 2012.

Mårald, Erland, 'Everything Circulates: Agricultural Chemistry and Recycling Theories in the Second Half of the Nineteenth Century', *Environment and History*, vol. 8, 2002, pp. 65–84.

Marchand, Leslie A. (ed.), *'So late into the night': Byron's Letters and Journals*, vol. 5, 1816–1817 (London, 1976).

Martins, Luciana, 'The Art of Tropical Travel 1768–1830', in Miles Ogborn and Charles W.J. Withers (eds), *Georgian Geographies: Essays on Space, Place and Landscape in the Eighteenth Century* (Manchester, 2004), pp. 72–91.

Martorelli, Luigi, *Dissertazione sugli odori usati degli antichi romani* (Rome, 1812).

Matthews, Henry, *The Diary of an Invalid, being the Journal of a Tour in Pursuit of Health in Portugal, Italy, Switzerland and France in the Years 1817, 1818, and 1819*, 2 vols (London, 1820).

Matthews, T., *The Biography of John Gibson R.A., Sculptor* (London, 1911).

Maudry, Philippe, 'Vivre à Rome, ou le mal d'être citadin: Réflexions sur la ville antique comme espace pathogène', in *Nomen Latinum: Mélanges de langue, littérature et civilisation latines offerts au professeur Andre Schneider à l'occasion de son départ à la retraite* (Neuchâtel, 1977), pp. 99–108.

Mead, Richard, *A Treatise concerning the Influence of the Sun and the Moon upon Human Bodies, and the Disease Thereby Produced* (London, 1748).

—, *De imperio solis ac lunae in corpora humana et morbis inde oriundis* (London, 1704).

Megua, Laura, '"Acque e immonditie del fiume": Inondazioni del Tevere e smaltimento dei rifiuti a Roma tra Cinque e Settecento', *Mélanges de l'École française à Rome*, vol. 118, no. 1, 2006, pp. 21–34.

Mendini, Dr, *Doctor Mendini's Hygienic Guide to Rome*, translated from the Italian and edited with an additional chapter on 'Rome as a Health Resort' by John J. Eyre (London, 1897).

Mercier, Louis-Sébastien, *Le Nouveau Tableau de Paris*, 6 vols (Paris, 1797).

Mercier, R., 'La Théorie des climats des *Réflexions critiques à L'Esprit des lois*', *Revue d'histoire littéraire de la France*, vol. 53, Jan.–March, April–June 1953, pp. 17–37, 159–74.

Mérimée, Prosper, *Portraits historiques et littéraires* (Paris, 1874).

—, *Romans et nouvelles* (Paris, 1951).

Metaxa, Luigi, *Monografia de'serpenti di Roma e suoi contorni* (Rome, 1823).

Meyer, Michael, *Ibsen* (London, 1967).

Michea, R., 'Quelques détails inédits sur le voyage en Italie de Greuze et de Gougenot', *Études italiennes*, vol. 4, 1934, pp. 137–54.

Michel, Christian, 'Les Relations artistiques entre l'Italie et la France (1680–1750): La contradiction des discours et de la pratique', *Studiolo*, no. 1, 2002, pp. 11–19.

— (ed.), *Le Voyage d'Italie de Charles-Nicolas Cochin (1758)* (Rome, 1991).

Michel, Jean-Baptiste, *Recherches médico-topographiques sur Rome et l'agro romano* (Rome, 1813).

Michel, Olivier, and Pierre Rosenberg (eds), *Subleyras, 1699–1749* (Paris, 1987).

Michel, Régis (ed.), *Géricault*, 2 vols (Paris, 1996).

Michelet, Jules, *Introduction à l'histoire universelle*, 2nd edn ([1831] The Hague, 1835).

Middleton, John Izard, *Grecian Remains in Italy: A Description of Cyclopian Walls, and of Roman Antiquities; With Topographical and Picturesque Views of Ancient Latium* (London, 1812).

Milano, Attilio, *Il ghetto di Roma: Illustrazioni storiche* (Rome, 1964).

Minzi, Giuseppe, *Sopra la genesi della febbri intermittenti* (Rome, 1844).

Misan, Jacques, *L'Italie des doctrinaires, 1817–1830: Une Image en élaboration* (Florence, 1978).

Monnet, Jérôme, *La Ville et son double: La Parabole de Mexico* (Paris, 1999).

Montaigne, Michel de, *Journal de voyage en Italie par la Suisse et l'Allemagne en 1580 et 1581*, ed. Maurice Rat (Paris, 1955).

Montesquieu, *Œuvres*, 3 vols (Amsterdam and London, 1758).

—, *Œuvres complètes*, 2 vols (Paris, 1949–51).

—, *Œuvres complètes*, 3 vols (Paris, 1870).

—, *Œuvres complètes*, 3 vols (Paris, 1950–55).

Moore, Thomas, *The Life of Byron* (Philadelphia, 1851).

Morgan, Sir Charles, 'On the State of Medicine in Italy, with brief notices of some of the universities and hospitals', in Lady Morgan, *Italy*, 2 vols (London, 1821), vol. 1, pp. 311–48.

Morgan, Lady, *Italy*, 2 vols (New York, 1821).

Morichini, Domenico, *Raccolti di scritti editti ed ineditti del Cavaliere D. Morichini*, 2 vols (Rome, 1857).

Moroni, Gaetano, *Dizionario di Erudizione storico-ecclesiastica*, 103 vols (Venice, 1840–61).

Morris, Edward, *French Painting in Nineteenth-Century Britain* (New Haven and London, 2005).

Morris, Robert J., 'Photography, Environment and Improvement in Scottish Cities 1860–1900', *Mélanges de l'École française à Rome*, vol. 116, no. 2, 2004, pp. 787–95.

Mortier, Roland, *La Poétique des ruines en France: Ses Origines, ses variations de la Renaissance à Victor Hugo* (Geneva, 1974).

Mosca, Giuseppe, *Dell'aria e de' morbi dall'aria dipendenti*, 2 vols (Naples, 1746–9).

Moskal, Jeanne, 'Politics and the Occupation of a Nurse in Mariana Starke's *Letters from Italy*', in Amanda Gilroy (ed.), *Romantic Geographies: Discourse of Travel, 1775–1844* (Manchester, 2000), pp. 150–64.

Moulard, Jacques (ed.), *Lettres inédites du comte Camille de Tournon, préfet de Rome, 1809–1814, 1ere partie: La Politique et l'esprit publique* (Paris, 1914).

Mount, Harry, 'Reynolds, Chiaroscuro and Composition', in Paul Taylor and François Quiviger (eds), *Pictorial Composition from Medieval to Modern Art* (London and Turin, 2001),

Munhall, Edgar, *François-Marius Granet: Watercolors from the Musée Granet at Aix-En-Provence* (Frick Collection, New York, 1988).

Le Musée du Luxembourg en 1874: Peintures (Paris, 1974).

Les Musées de France: Paris, guide et memento de l'artiste et du voyageur (Paris, 1860).

Musset, Paul-Edme de, *Voyage pittoresque en Italie, partie septentrionale* (Paris, 1855).

Myrone, Martin, *Bodybuilding: Reforming Masculinities in British Art 1750–1810* (New Haven and London, 2005).

Naves, R., 'Un Adversaire de la théorie des climats au XVIIe siècle, Adrien Baillet', *Revue d'histoire littéraire de la France*, vol. 43, no. 3, 1936, pp. 430–3.

Negro, Silvio, *Seconda Roma, 1850–1870* (Vicenza, 1966).

Nibby, A., *Analisi topografico-antiquaria della carta de dintorni di Roma*, 3 vols (Rome, 1837).

Nicassio, Susan Vandiver, *Imperial City: Rome, Romans and Napoleon, 1796–1815* (Chicago, 2005), reprinted in 2009 as *Imperial City: Rome under Napoleon*.

Nicholson, Kathleen, 'Turner, Claude, and the Essence of Landscape', in David Solkin (ed.), *Turner and the Masters* (London, 2009), pp. 57–71.

Nicolai, Nicola Maria, *Memorie, leggi, ed osservazioni sulle campagne e sull'annona di Roma*, 3 vols (Rome, 1803).

—, *Sulla presidenza delle strade ed acque e su giurisdizione economica*, 2 vols (Rome, 1829).

Nisbet, H.B. (ed.), *German Aesthetic and Literary Criticism: Winckelmann, Lessing, Hamann, Herder, Schiller, Goethe* (Cambridge, 1985).

Noakes, Vivien, *Edward Lear: The Life of a Wanderer*, rev. edn (Stroud, 2004).

— (ed.), *Edward Lear: Selected Letters* (Oxford, 1990).

Nolhac, Pierre de, *Souvenirs d'un vieux romain* (Paris, 1921).

North, W. *Roman Fever: The Results of an Inquiry during Three Years' Residence on the Spot into the Origin, History, Distribution and Nature of the Malarial Fevers of the Roman Campagna, with Especial Reference to their Supposed Connection with Pathogenic Organisms* (London, 1896).

Northcote, James, *The Life of Sir Joshua Reynolds*, 2nd edn, 2 vols (London, 1819).

Norton, Charles Eliot, *Notes of Travel and Study in Italy* (Boston, 1860).

Norton, J.E. (ed.), *The Letters of Edward Gibbon to Edward Gibbon Sen.*, 3 vols (London, 1956).

Norvins, Baron Jacques Marquet de Montbreton, et al., *L'Italie pittoresque* (Paris, 1834).

—, *L'Italie pittoresque*, 4th edn (Paris, 1850).

Nutton, Vivian, *Ancient Medicine* (London and New York, 2004).

O'Donovan, Denis, *Memories of Rome* (London, 1859).

O'Keeffe, Paul, *A Genius for Failure: The Life of Benjamin Robert Haydon* (London, 2009).

Opinel, Annick, *Le Peintre et le mal (France XIXe siècle)* (Paris, 2005).

Oppé, A.P. (ed.), 'The Memoirs of Thomas Jones', *The Walpole Society*, vol. 32, 1951.

Oswald, Stefan, *Italienbilder: Beiträge zur Wandlung der deutschen Italienauffassung 1770–1840* (Heidelberg, 1985).

Pace, Claire, 'Claude the Enchanted: Interpretations of Claude in England in the earlier Nineteenth Century', *Burlington Magazine*, vol. III, no. 801, Dec. 1969, pp. 733–40.

Paesaggi della Memoria: Gli acquerelli romani di Ettore Roesler Franz dal 1876 al 1895. Landscapes of Memory: The Roman Landscapes of Ettore Roesler Franz, 1876–95 (Rome 2008).

Paillot de Montabert, [J.N.], *Traité complet de la peinture*, 9 vols (Paris, 1829–51).

Palermo, Francesco, *Monsignore Illustrissimo: Antichi mondezzari nelle strade romane; Eccelenti norme inutili contro l'abuso inveterato di tenere Roma 'non pulita'* (Rome, 1980).

Pallottino, Elisabetta, 'La ricostruzione della basilica di San Paolo fuori le mura (1823–1854)', in *Maestà di Roma, da Napoleone all'unità d'Italia: Universale ed eterna; Capitale delle arti* (Milan, 2003), pp. 484–501.

Palsky, Giles, *Des chiffres et des cartes. Naissance de la cartographic quantitative Français au XIXe siècle* (Paris, 1996)

Paludi Pontine e Agro Romano nella pittura dell'ottocento (Rome, 1981).

Panarolo, Domenico, *Aërologia o discorso dell'aria* (Rome, 1642).

[Papillon de la Ferté, Denis Pierre], *Extrait des différens ouvrages publiés sur les vies des peintres par M. P. D. L. F.*, 2 vols (Paris, 1776).

Partridge, Loren, 'Urbanism: Rotting Cadavers and the New Jerusalem', in *The Renaissance in Rome 1400–1600* (London, 1996).

Paxton, Frederick S., 'Liturgy and Healing in an Early Medieval Saint's Cult: The Mass *in honore sancti Sigismundi* for the Cure of Fevers', *Traditio*, vol. 49, 1994, pp. 23–44.

Paysages d'Italie: Les Peintres du plein air (1780–1830) (Paris, 2001).

Peale, Rembrandt, *Notes on Italy Written during a Tour in the Years 1829 and 1830* (Philadelphia, 1831).

Pease, William H., and Jane H. Pease (eds), *The Roman Years of a South Carolina Artist: Caroline Carson's Letters Home, 1872–1892* (Columbia, S.C., 2003).

Pecori, Dr G., 'La malaria dell'Urbe nei tempi passati e la sua salubrita attuale', *Capitolium*, vol. 2, 1925–6, pp. 505–9.

Péladan, Joseph, *Ernest Hébert, son œuvre et son temps* (Paris, 1910).

Pelling, Margaret, *Cholera, Fever, and English Medicine, 1825–1865* (Oxford, 1978).

Pemble, John, *The Mediterranean Passion: Victorians and Edwardians in the South* (Oxford, 1987).

Pernoud, Emmanel, *Corot: Peindre comme un ogre* (Paris, 2009).

Peter, Jean-Pierre, 'Malades et maladies à la fin du XVIIIe siècle', *Annales ESC*, vol. 22, no. 4, 1967, pp. 711–51.

Petherbridge, Deanna, *The Primacy of Drawing: Histories and Theories of Practices* (New Haven and London, 2010).

Petroni, Alexander, *Del vivere delli Romani et di conservare la sanità* (Rome, 1592).

Petronius, Alexander, *De victu Romanorum et de sanitate tuenda* (Rome, 1581).

Petrucci, Marina, 'Alberi e venti: La vertenza di Cisterna e Sermoneta nel secolo XVIII', in Fondazione Lelio e Lisli Basso-Issoco, *L'Ambiente nella storia d'Italia: Studi e immagini* (Venice, 1989), pp. 115–29.

Pick, Daniel, *Rome or Death: The Obsessions of General Garibaldi* (London, 2005).

Pierre Julien 1731–1804 (Musée Crozatier, Le Puy-en-Velay, 2004)

Pietrangeli, Carlo (ed.), *Guide rionali di Roma: Rione XI, S. Angelo* (Rome, 1976).

Pike, David L., 'Sewage Treatments: Vertical Space and Waste in Nineteenth-Century Paris and London', in William A. Cohen and Ryan Johnson (eds), *Filth: Dirt, Disgust, and Modern Life* (Minneapolis and London, 2004), pp. 51–77.

Piles, Roger de, *Cours de peinture par principes* ([1708] Paris, 1989).

Pine-Coffin, R. S., *Bibliography of British and American Travel in Italy to 1860* (Florence, 1974).

Piozzi, Hester Lynch, *Observations and Reflections made in the Course of a Journey through France, Italy and Germany* (Dublin, 1789).

—, *Observations and Reflections made in the Course of a Journey through France, Italy and Germany*, ed. Herbert Burrows (Ann Arbor, Mich., 1967).

Piscitelli, E., *La riforma di Pio VI e gli scrittori economici romani* (Milan, 1958).

Planche, Gustave, *Études sur l'école française (1851–1852): Peinture et sculpture*, 2 vols (Paris, 1855).

—, *Salon de 1831* (Paris, 1831).

—, 'Géricault', *Revue des deux mondes*, vol. 2 (Paris, 1851), pp. 502–31.

Pommier, Édouard, *L'Art de liberté: Doctrines et débats de la Révolution française* (Paris, 1991).

Pope, William Bissell (ed.), *The Diary of Benjamin Robert Haydon*, 5 vols (Cambridge, Mass., 1960–3).

Poulot, Dominique, '*Surveillir et s'instruire*': *La Révolution française et l'intelligence de l'héritage historique* (Oxford, 1996).

Pour l'amour de L'Art. Artistes et amateurs français à Rome an XVIIIe Siècle (Milan, 2011).

Poynter, Eleanor Frances, *Madame de Presnel*, 2 vols (London, 1885).

Powell, Cecilia, *Turner in the South: Rome, Naples, Florence* (New Haven and London, 1987).

Prampolini, Enrico, 'Incontro con Picasso', in *Cinquanta Disegni di Pablo Picasso (1905–1938)* (Novara, 1943), pp. 11–13.

Prat, Louis-Antoine, '"Cortone, hélas…": Sur deux dessins de Jacques-Louis David', in Olivier Bonfait, Véronique Gerard Powell and Philippe Sénéchal (eds), *Curiosité: Études d'histoire de l'art en l'honneur d'Antoine Schnapper* (Paris, 1998), pp. 177–80.

Promenades italiennes: Études d'Ernest Hébert (La Tronche, Grenoble, 2006).

Prony, Gaspard de, *Description hydrographique et historique des marais Pontins*, 2 vols (Paris, 1822–3).

Quatremère de Quincy, 'Essai historique sur l'art du paysage à Rome', *Archives littéraires de l'Europe*, vol. 10 (Paris, 1806), pp. 193–208, 376–91.

—, *Lettres à Miranda sur le déplacement des monuments de l'art de l'Italie*, ed. Édouard Pommier ([1796] Paris, 1989).

Quennell, Peter, *Byron, the Years of Fame: Byron and Italy* (London, 1974).

Querci, Giuseppe Maria, *Del gusto degli antichi romani per gli odori* (Rome, 1764).

Quincy, John, *Loimologia: or, An Historical Account of the Plague in London in 1665; To which Is Added, An Essay on the Different Causes of Pestilential Diseases, by J. Quincy*, trans. Nathaniel Hodges (London, 1720).

Radisich, Paula Rea, 'Eighteenth-Century Plein-Air Painting and the Sketches of Pierre-Henri de Valenciennes', *Art Bulletin*, March 1982, pp. 98–104.

Ramage, Crauford Tait, *The Nooks and By-Ways of Italy: Wanderings in Search of its Ancient Remains and Modern Superstitions*, in *Ramage in South Italy*, ed. Edith Clay (London, 1965).

Ramsden E.H. (ed. and trans.), *The Letters of Michelangelo*, 2 vols (London, 1963).

Rand, Richard, *Claude Lorrain: The Painter as Draftsman: Drawings from the British Museum* (New Haven and London, 2006).

Rao, Anna Maria, *Esule: L'emigrazione politica in Francia 1792–1802* (Naples, 1992).

Re, Emilio, 'Maestri di Strada', *Archivio della società romana di storia patria*, vol. 43, 1920, pp. 5–102.

Regesti di bandi editti notificazioni e prevvedimenti diversi relativi alla citta di Roma ed allo stato pontificio, 7 vols (Rome, 1920–68).

Reumont, Alfred von, *Della Campagna romana* (Florence, 1842).

Reymond, Florian, 'Les Bêtes à cornes et l'art pictural', *Histoire et sociétés rurales*, vol. 30, no. 2, 2008, pp. 31–66.

—, *L'Élevage bovin: De l'Agronome au paysan (1700–1850)* (Rennes, 2010).

Reynolds, Sir Joshua, *Discourses on Art*, ed. R. Wark (New Haven and London, 1997).

Richard, Abbé Jérôme, *Description historique et critique de l'Italie, ou nouveaux mémoires sur l'état actuel de son gouvernement, des sciences, des arts, du commerce, de la population et de l'histoire naturelle*, 6 vols (Paris, 1766).

—, *Histoire naturelle de l'air et de ses météores*, 10 vols (Paris, 1770–1).

Richardson (senior and junior), Jonathan, *An Account of some of the Statues, Bas-reliefs, Drawings and Pictures in Italy, &c. with Remarks* (London, 1722).

Ridley, Ron, *The Eagle and the Spade: Archaeology in Rome during the Napoleonic Era* (Cambridge, 1992).

Ridolfino, Cecilia Pericoli, 'Pio VI alle Paludi Pontine', *Bolletino dei musei communali di Roma*, vol. 22, nos 1–4, 1975, pp. 26–32.

Riley, James C., *The Eighteenth-Century Campaign to Avoid Disease* (Basingstoke and London, 1987).

Rinne, Katherine W., 'The Landscape of Laundry in Late Cinquecento Rome', *Studies in the Decorative Arts*, vol. 9, no. 1, Fall–Winter 2001–2, pp. 34–60.

—, *The Waters of Rome. Aqueducts, Fountains and the Birth of the Baroque City* (New Haven and London, 2010), pp. 193–218

Rivoire, Alfred J. B., *Essai sur la topographie et le climat de la ville de Rome et du bassin romain* (Montpellier, 1853), pp. 35, 50.

—, *The Waters of Rome. Aqueducts, Fountains and the Birth of the Baroque City* (New Haven and London, 2010).

Robaut, Alfred, *L'Œvre de Corot*, 4 vols (Paris, 1905).

Robson-Scott, William Douglas, *The Younger Goethe and the Visual Arts* (Cambridge, 1981).

Rochère, Comtesse Eugénie Mistral Dutheil de la, *Rome: Souvenirs religieux, historiques, artistiques de l'expédition française en 1849 et 1850* (Tours, 1854).

Rogers, Samuel, *Italy, a Poem* (London, 1842).

—, *The Italian Journal of Samuel Rogers*, ed. J.R. Hale (London, 1956).

Rom 1846–1870: James Anderson und die Maler-Fotografen; Sammlung Siegert (Munich, 2005).

Roma 1840–1870: La fotografia, il collezionista e lo storico; Fotografie della collezione Orsola e Filippo Maggia (Modena, 2008).

Roma 1850: Il circolo dei pittori fotografi del Caffè Greco (Rome, 1984).

Roma interrotta (Rome, 1978).

Roma nelle fotografie della raccolta Ceccarius, presso la Bibliotheca Nazionale di Roma (Rome, 1991).

Rome au XIXe siècle: Photographies inédites, ed. A. Margiotta and S. Tozzi (Rome, 1999).

Rome éternelle: Dessins et gravures panoramiques du XVe au XIXe siècle (Charleroi, 2003).

Rome in Early Photographs: The Age of Pius IX; Photographs 1846–1878 from Roman and Danish Collections (Thorwaldsen Museum, Copenhagen, 1977).

Rose, William Stewart, *Letters from the North of Italy, addressed to Henry Hallam* (London, 1819).

Rosenberg, Pierre, 'The Mysterious Beginnings of the Young Boucher', in *François Boucher, 1703–1770* (Metropolitan Museum of Art, New York, 1986), pp. 41–55.

—, and Udolpho van de Sandt, *Pierre Peyron, 1744–1814* (Paris, 1983).

Rosenthal, Léon, *Du Romantisme au Réalisme: Essai sur l'évolution de la peinture en France de 1815 à 1830* (Paris, 1914).

Rossi, Giorgio, *L'Agro di Roma tra '500 e '800: Condizioni di vita e lavoro* (Rome, 1988).

Rossi, Laura, 'Appunti per una storia della malaria nell'Agro Romano nella seconda metà dell'Ottocento', in Maria Luisa Betri and Ada Gigli Marchetti (eds), *Salute e classi lavoratrici in Italia dell'Unità al fascismo* (Milan, 1982), pp. 227–53.

Rotrou, Michel de, *Le Voyage d'Italie récit de 1763* (Paris, 2007).

Rousseau, Jean-Jacques, *Confessions*, 2 vols (Paris, 1968).

Rupke, Nicholaas A. (ed.), *Medical Geography in Historical Perspective*, *Medical History*, supplement no. 20 (London, 2000).

Ruskin, John, *Praeterita* (New York, London and Toronto, 2005).

—, *The Works of John Ruskin*, ed. E.T. Cook and Alexander Wedderburn, 39 vols (London, 1903–12).

[Russel, James], *Letters from a Young Painter Abroad to his Friends in England*, 2 vols (London, 1750).

Russell Barrington, Mrs, *The Life and Letters of Frederic Baron Leighton of Stretton*, 2 vols (London, 1906).

Rustin, J., and J.P. Schneider, 'Le Motif de l'arrivée à Paris dans les romans français du XVIIIe siècle', *Images de la ville au XVIIIe siècle* (Strasbourg, 1984), pp. 47–157.

Saint-Yves, C.L. de, *Observations sur les arts* (Paris, 1748).

Sala, George Augustus, *Rome and Venice with other Wanderings in Italy, in 1866–67* (London, 1869).

Sallares, Robert, *Malaria and Rome: A History of Malaria in Ancient Italy* (Oxford and New York, 2002).

San Juan, Rose Marie, *Rome: A City Out of Print* (Minneapolis and London, 2001).

Sanquirico, Paolo, *Parere dell'aere di Borgo* (Rome, 1670).

Sansa, Renato, 'Istituzioni e politica dell'ambiente a Roma: Dalle magistrature capitoline alla Presidenza Pontificia', in G. Cascio Pratilli and L. Zangheri (eds), *Legislazione medicea sull'ambiente*, vol. 4, *Scritti per un commento* (Florence, 1998), pp. 209–24.

—, *L'Oro verde: I boschi nello stato pontificio tra XVIII e XIX secolo* (Bologna, 2003).

—, 'La pulizia delle strade a Rome nel XVII secolo: Un problema di storia ambientale', *Archivio della società romana di storia patria*, vol. 114, 1991, pp. 127–60.

Schaffer, S., 'Measuring Virtue: Eudiometry, Enlightenment and Pneumatic Medicine', in A. Cunningham and R. French (eds), *The Medical Enlightenment in the Eighteenth Century* (Cambridge, 1990), pp. 281–318.

Scharten, Theodora, *Les Voyages et séjours de Michelet en Italie: Amitiés italiennes* (Paris, 1934).

Scheidel, Walter, 'Germs for Rome', in Catharine Edwards and Greg Woolf (eds), *Rome the Cosmopolis* (Cambridge, 2003), pp. 158–76.

Scher, Steven Paul, 'Mignon in Music', in Gerhart Hoffmeister (ed.), *Goethe in Italy, 1786–1986* (Amsterdam, 1988), pp. 188–69.

Schiff, Gert, *Johann Heinrich Füssli, 1741–1825*, 2 vols (Zurich and Munich, 1973).

[Schirmer] *Johan Wilhelm Schirmer und seine Zeit: Landschaft im 19. Jh. zwischen Wirklichkeit und Ideal* (Kunsthalle Karlsruhe/Suermont-Ludwig-Museum Aachen, Heidelberg, 2002).

—, *Johan Wilhelm Schirmer: Von Rheinland in die Welt*, ed. Marcell Perse et al. (Petersberg, 2010).

Schlözer, K., *Römische Briefe* (Berlin, 1914).

Schnapp, A., 'Antiquarian Studies in Naples at the End of the Eighteenth Century: From Comparative Archaeology to Comparative Religion', in G. Imbruglia (ed.), *Naples in the Eighteenth Century: The Birth and Death of a Nation State* (Cambridge, 2000), pp. 154–66.

Schnapper, Antoine, *Jacques-Louis David, 1746–1824* (Paris, 1989).

[Schnetz] *Jean-Victor Schnetz 1787–1870: Couleurs d'Italie* (Musée du Château de Flers, 2000).

Schorske, Carl E., *Fin-de-siècle Vienna: Politics and Culture* (London, 1980).

Schoy, Auguste, *Histoire de l'influence italienne sur l'architecture des Pays-bas* (Brussels, 1879).

Sebastiani, Antonio, *Romanorum plantarum, fasciculus alter: Accedit Enumeratio plantarum sponte nascentium in ruderibus Amphiteatri Flavii* (Rome, 1815).

Sehnsucht Italien: Corot und die frühe Freilicht 1750–1850 (Baden, 2004).

Senebier, Jean, *Recherches sur l'influence de la lumière solaire pour métamorphoser l'air fixe en air pur par la végétation* (Geneva, 1783).

Sérieys, Antoine (ed.), *Voyage en Italie de M. l'Abbé Barthélemy*, 2nd edn (Paris, 1802).

Shackleton, Robert, 'The Evolution of Montesquieu's Theory of Climate', *Revue internationale de philosophie*, 1955, vol. 9, nos 33–4, pp. 317–29.

—, *Montesquieu: A Critical Biography* (Oxford, 1961).

Shapiro, Harold L., '*The Poetry of Architecture*: Ruskin's Preparation for *Modern Painters*', *Renaissance and Modern Studies*, vol. 15, 1971, pp. 70–84.

—, *Ruskin in Italy: Letters to his Parents, 1845* (Oxford, 1972).

Sharp, Samuel, *Letters from Italy* (London, 1766).

Shearman, John, 'A Functional Interpretation of Villa Madama', *Römisches Jahrbuch fur Kunstgeschichte*, vol. 20, 1983, pp. 313–27.

Shelley, Percy Bysshe, *The Complete Poetical Works of Percy Bysshe Shelley* (Oxford, 1960).

—, *The Letters of Percy Bysshe Shelley*, ed. F.L. Jones, 2 vols (Oxford, 1964).

Shields, James G., 'Stendhal et Cabanis: Le Mythe italien à travers le prisme de physiologie', in V. Del Litto and J. Dérens (eds), *Stendhal, Paris et le mirage italien: Colloque pour le cent-cinquantième anniversaire de la mort de Stendhal* (Paris, 1992), pp. 123–40.

Siciliano, Enzo, *Pasolini* (London, 1987).

Siegel, Jonah, *Desire and Excess: The Nineteenth-Century Culture of Art* (Princeton, 2000).

—, *Haunted Museum: Longing, Travel and the Art-Romance Tradition* (Princeton and Oxford, 2005).

Siler, Douglas (ed.), *James Pradier, Correspondance*, 2 vols (Geneva, 1984).

Silvestre, T., *Histoire des artistes vivants français et étrangers: Études d'après nature* (Paris, 1855–6).

Simmons, Lawrence, *Freud's Italian Journey* (Amsterdam, 2006).

Simond, Louis, *Voyage en Italie et en Sicile*, 2 vols (Paris, 1828).

Skene, James, *Italian Journey: Being Excerpts from the Pre-Victorian Diary of James Skene of Rubislaw* (London, 1937).

Sloan, Kim, *Alexander and John Cozens: The Poetry of Landscape* (New Haven and London, 1986).

Smollett, Tobias, *Travels through France and Italy*, 2 vols (London, 1766).

—, *Travels through France and Italy*, ed. F. Felsenstein ([1766] Oxford, 1979).

Snowden, Frank, *The Conquest of Malaria: Italy, 1900–1962* (New Haven and London, 2006).

Sofia, F., 'Recueillir et mettre en ordre: Aspetti della politica amministrativa di J.M. de Gerando a Roma', *Roma moderna e contemporanea*, vol. 1, no. 1, 1994, pp. 105–24.

Solkin, David, *Richard Wilson: The Landscape of Reaction* (Tate Gallery, London, 1982).

Sontag, Susan, *Illness as Metaphor* (New York, 1988).

Sorsby, Arnold, *A Short History of Opthalmology* (London, 1933).

Spacks, Patricia Meyer, '"Splendid falsehoods": English Accounts of Rome, 1760–1798', *Prose Studies*, vol. 3, no. 3, 1980, pp. 203–16.

Spear, Richard E., *Domenichino*, 2 vols (New Haven and London, 1982).

Springer, Carolyn, *The Marble Wilderness: Ruins and Representation in Italian Romanticism 1775–1850* (Cambridge, 1987).

Staël, Anne-Louise Germaine, Madame de, *Corinne ou l'Italie* (Paris, 1861).

—, *Corinne ou l'Italie* (Paris, 1872).

—, *De la littérature considérée dans ses rapports avec les institutions sociales*, 2 vols (Paris, 1959).

Stafford, Barbara Maria, *Voyage into Substance: Art, Science, Nature, and the Illustrated Travel Account, 1760–1840* (Cambridge, Mass., 1984).

Staley, Allan, et al., *Impossible Picturesqueness: Edward Lear's Indian Watercolours, 1873–1875* (Wallach Art Gallery, New York, 1988).

Starke, Mariana, *Letters from Italy, between the Years 1792 and 1798, containing a View of the Revolutions in that Country, from the Capture of Nice by the French Republic to the Expulsion of Pius VI from the Ecclesiastical State*, 2 vols (London, 1800).

Stendhal, *Correspondance*, 10 vols, ed. H. Martineau (Paris, 1933–4).

—, *Correspondance de Stendhal, 1800–1842*, 3 vols (Paris, 1908).

—, *Correspondance de Stendhal* (Paris, 1967).

—, *Journal*, 4 vols ([1811] Paris, 1932).

—, *Œuvres intimes* (Paris, 1955).

—, *Œuvres posthumes: Journal d'Italie*, ed. Paul Arbelet (Paris, 1911).

—, *Promenades dans Rome*, 2 vols (Paris, 1829).

—, *Promenades dans Rome*, 3 vols (Paris, 1958).

—, *Promenades dans Rome* (Paris, 1973).

—, *Promenades dans Rome* (Paris, 1996).

—, *Vie de Henry Brulard*, ed. H. Martineau (Paris, 1927).

—, *Vies de Haydn, Mozart, et Métastase* (Paris, 1928).

Stevenson, Christine, *Medicine and Magnificence: British Hospital and Asylum Architecture, 1660–1815* (New Haven and London, 2000).

Stow, Kenneth, *Theatre of Acculturation: The Roman Ghetto in the Sixteenth Century* (Seattle, 2001).

Suard, J.B.A., *Correspondance littéraire de Suard avec la margrave de Bayreuth, fragments inédits* [1773], ed. G. Bonno, University of California Publications in Modern Philology, vol. 18, no. 2 (Berkeley, 1934).

Sue, Eugène, 'Peintres contemporains – Louis et Théodore Gudin', *Revue de Paris*, vol. 1, 1833 [pub. 1835], p. 226.

Sullin de Châteauvieux, Jacob Frédéric, *Lettres écrites d'Italie en 1812 et 13 à C. Pictet*, 2 vols (Paris, 1816).

Syrjämaa, Taina, *Constructing Unity, Living in Diversity: A Roman Decade* (Helsinki, 2006).

Szambien, Werner, 'Le Musées tueront-ils l'art? A propos de quelques animadversions de Deseine', in Jacques Guillerme (ed.), *Les Collections: Fables et programmes* (Paris, 1993), pp. 335–40.

Tardieu, Ambroise, *Annales du musée et de l'ecole moderne des beaux-arts, ou recueil des principaux tableaux, statues et bas-reliefs exposés au Louvre depuis 1808…par C. P. Landon: Salon de 1831; Recueil de pièces choisies parmi les ouvrages de peinture et de sculpture exposés pour la première fois au Louvre, le 1er mai 1831* (Paris, 1831).

Taussig, G., *The Roman Climate, its Influence on Health and Disease, Serving as an Hygienical Guide* (Rome, 1870).

Temkin, Owsei, *Galenism: Rise and Decline of a Medical Philosophy* (Ithaca and London, 1973).

Le Temps des passions: Collections romantiques des musées d'Orléans (Orléans, 1997).

Terlay, Bernard, 'Les Portraits de Granet', *Impressions du Musée Granet, Association des amis du musée Granet, Aix-en-Provence*, no. 7, 1992, pp. 6–14.

Thomas, Keith, *Man and the Natural World: Changing Attitudes in England 1500–1800* (London, 1983).

Thomas, Richard W., 'Photography in Rome', *The Art-Journal*, May 1852, p. 159.

Thomas, Sophie, *Romanticism and Visuality: Fragments, History, Spectacle* (London, 2007).

Thompson, Carl, *The Suffering Traveller and the Romantic Imagination* (Oxford, 2007).

Thoré, Théophile, 'Léopold Robert', '*Beaux-arts, 1843–44*', in Pierre Gassier and Maryse Schmidt-Surdez (eds), *Léopold Robert-Marcotte d'Argenteuil: Correspondance 1824–1835* (Neuchâtel, 2005).

Thouin, André, *Voyage dans la Belgique, la Hollande et l'Italie* (Paris, 1841).

Thouvenel, Pierre, *Traité sur le climat de l'Italie considéré sous ses raports* [sic] *phisiques météorologiques et médicinaux*, 4 vols (Verona, 1797–8).

Thuillier, Jacques, '"Il se rendit en Italie": Notes sur le voyage à Rome des artistes français au XVIIe siècle', in *'Il se rendit en Italie': Études offertes à André Chastel* (Rome, 1987), pp. 321–36.

Tivoli, variations sur un paysage au XVIIIe siècle (Musée Cognac-Jay, Paris, 2010).

Tobin, J.J. (M.D.), *Journal of a Tour made in the Years 1828–1829, through Styria, Carniola, and Italy, whilst accompanying the late Sir Humphrey Davy* (London, 1832).

Todorov, Tzvetan, *Nous et les autres: La Réflexion française sur la diversité humaine* (Paris, 1989).

Toghotti, Eugenia, 'La carta della malaria d'Italia (1880–82)', *Quaderni internazionali di storia dell a medicina e della sanità*, vol. 1, no. 2, 1992, pp. 23–34.

Tomassetti, Giuseppe, *La Campagna romana antica, medioevale e moderna*, ed. Luisa Chiumenta and Fernando Bilancia, 4 vols ([1910] Rome, 1975–6).

Tommasi-Crudeli, Corrado, *The Climate of Rome and the Roman Malaria*, trans. C. Cramond Dick (London, 1892).

Tomory, P., *The Life and Art of Henry Fuseli* (London, 1972).

Tooley, Marian J., 'Bodin and the Medieval Theory of Climate', *Speculum*, vol. 28, 1953, pp. 64–83.

Torelli, Luigi, *L'Eucalyptus e l'agro romano* (Rome, 1878).

Tournon, Camille, comte de, *Études statistiques sur Rome et la partie occidentale des états romains*, 2 vols ([1831] Paris, 1855).

Travaglini, Carlo M., *Il dibattito sull'agricultura romana nel secolo XIX (1815): Le Accademie e le società agrarie* (Rome, 1981).

Trelawny, Edward, *Records of Shelley, Byron and the Author* (Harmondsworth, 1973).

Ure, Andrew, *The General Malaria of London and the Peculiar Malaria of Pimlico Investigated, and the Means of their Economical Removal Ascertained* (London, 1850).

Uwins, Sarah, *A Memoir of Thomas Uwins*, 2 vols (London, 1858).

Valenciennes, P.H., *Éléments de perspective pratique à l'usage des artistes, suivis de réflexions et conseils à un élève sur la peinture et particulièrement sur le genre du paysage* (Paris, au VIII [1799–1800]).

Valentin, Louis, *Voyage en Italie fait en l'année 1820: Deuxième édition, corrigée et augmentée de nouvelles observations faits dans un second voyage en 1824* (Paris, 1826).

Valéry, Paul, *Œuvres*, 2 vols (Paris, 1957–60).

Vance, William L., *America's Rome*, 2 vols (New Haven and London, 1989).

—, 'The Colosseum: American Uses of an Imperial Image', in Annabel Patterson (ed.), *Roman Images* (Baltimore and London, 1984), pp. 105–40.

Vander Burght, R., *Joseph François, peintre belge: Émule de David 1759–1851; Les Manuscrits de ses deux voyages en Italie; Les Lettres du Prince Louis et de la princesse Pauline d'Arneberg* (Brussels, 1948).

Van Os, Henk, *Dreaming of Italy* (Mauritshuis, The Hague, 2006).

Vasari, Giorgio, *Lives of the Painters, Sculptors and Architects*, 4 vols (London, 1963).

—, *Le vite de' più eccellenti pittori, scultori e architettori*, Club del Libro, 9 vols (Milan, 1962–6).

Vaughan, William, '"David's Brickdust" and the Rise of the British School', in Alison Yarrington and Kelvin Everest (eds), *Reflections on Revolution: Images of Romanticism* (London, 1993), pp. 134–58.

Venuti, Ridolfino, *Risposta alle reflessioni critiche sopra le diferenti scuole di pittura del sig. marchese d'Argens* (Lucca, 1755).

Verdi, Orietta, 'Da ufficiali capitolini a commissari apostolici: I maestri delle strade e degli edifici di Roma tra XIII e XVI secolo', in L. Spezzaferro and M.E. Tittoni (eds), *Il Campidoglio e Sisto V* (Rome, 1991), pp. 54–62.

Verdi, Richard, 'Poussin's Critical Fortunes: The Study of the Artist and the Criticism of his Works from c.1690 to c.1830 with Particular Reference to France and England', Ph.D. thesis, University of London, 1976.

Veuillot, Louis, *Les Odeurs de Paris* (Paris, 1867).

—, *Le Parfum de Rome*, 2 vols (Paris, 1862).

Viel Castel, Horace de, 'Cromwell par M. Delaroche', *L'Artiste*, vol. 1, 1831, p. 269.

Vieusseux, André, *Italy and the Italians in the Nineteenth Century*, 2 vols (London, 1824).

Viollet-le-Duc, E., *Lettres d'Italie 1836–1837, adressées à sa famille*, ed. Geneviève Viollet-le-Duc (Paris, 1971).

Virgil, *The Minor Poems of Vergil: Comprising the Culex, Dirae, Lydia, Moretum, Copa, Priapeia, and Catalepton*, trans. J. Mooney (Birmingham, 1916).

Volney, Constantin François de, *Œuvres complètes* (Paris, 1846).

Wallace-Hadrill, A., L. Haselberger and J. Humphrey, 'Roman Topography and the Prism of Sir William Gell', in L. Haselberger and J. Humphrey (eds), *Imaging Ancient Rome: Documentation, Visualization, Imagination* (Postsmouth, R.I., 2006), pp. 285–96.

Ward, Candace, '"Cruel Disorder": Female Bodies, Eighteenth-Century Fever Narratives, and the Sentimental Novel', *Studies in Eighteenth-Century Culture*, vol. 32, 2003, pp. 93–121.

—, *Desire and Disorder: Fever, Fictions, and Feeling in English Georgian Culture* (Lewisburg, Penn., 2007).

Waterhouse, Ellis, *Three Decades of English Art 1740–1770* (Philadelphia, 1964).

Watkins, Thomas, *Travels through Europe 1787–1789*, 2 vols (London, 1794).

Webb, Timothy, '"City of the Soul": English Romantic Travellers in Rome', in Michael Liversidge and Catharine Edwards (eds), *Imagining Rome: British Artists and Rome in the Nineteenth Century* (London, 1996), pp. 20–37.

Weinglass, David (ed.), *The Collected English Letters of Henry Fuseli* (New York and London, 1982).

Weston, Helen, 'Prud'hon in Rome: Pages from an Unpublished Sketchbook', *Burlington Magazine*, vol. 126, no. 970, Jan. 1984, pp. 6, 8–19.

[Weston, Stephen] *Viaggiana: Or Detached Remarks on the Buildings, Pictures and Statues, Inscriptions, &c. of Ancient and Modern Rome, with Additional Observations*, 3rd edn (London, 1797).

Wetmore Story, William, *Roba di Roma*, 2 vols (London, 1863).

White, Barbara Ehrlich, 'Renoir's Trip to Italy', *Art Bulletin*, vol. 60, December 1969, pp. 333–51.

Whiteside, James, *Italy in the Nineteenth Century*, 3 vols (London, 1848).

Whitley, W., *Artists and their Friends in England 1700–1799*, 2 vols (London, 1928).

Whitney, Wheelock, *Géricault in Italy* (New Haven and London, 1997).

Wildenstein, Daniel and Guy, *Louis David: Recueil de documents complémentaires au catalogue complet de l'œuvre de l'artiste* (Paris, 1973).

Williams, D.E., *The Life and Correspondence of Sir Thomas Lawrence*, 2 vols (London, 1831).

Williams, Hugh William, *Travels in Italy, Greece, and the Ionian Islands*, 2 vols (London, 1820).

Willson, Henry, *Henry Willson's Fugitive Sketches in Rome, Venice &c.* (London, 1838).

Winckelmann, Johann Joachim, *History of the Art of Antiquity*, trans. Harry Francis Mallgrave (Los Angeles, 2006).

Windholz, Angela, *Et in Academia Ego: ausländische Akademien in Rom Zwischen Künstlerischer Standortbestimmung und nationaler Repräsentation* (Regensburg, 2008).

Wine, Humphrey, *The Seventeenth-century French Paintings*, National Gallery catalogues (London, 2001).

Wittkower, Margot and Rudolph, *Born under Saturn: The Character and Conduct of Artists; A Documented History from Antiquity to the French Revolution* (London, 1963; reissued New York, 2007).

Wood, Jeremy, *Rubens. Copies and Adaptations from Renaissance and Later Artists*, Corpus Rubenianum Ludwig Burchardt, XXVI (2), 3 vols (London and Turnhout, 2010–11).

Worboys, Michael, 'From Miasma to Germs: Malaria 1850–1879', *Parassitologia*, vol. 36, nos 1–2, Aug. 1994, pp. 61–8.

—, *Spreading Germs: Disease Theories and Medical Practice 1865–1900* (Cambridge, 2000).

Worley, Michael Preston, *Pierre Julien: Sculptor to Queen Marie-Antoinette* (New York, 2003).

Wrigley, Richard, 'The Afterlife of an Academician', in Nicola Kalinsky (ed.), *Courage and Cruelty: Le Brun's Horatius Cocles and the Massacre of the Innocents* (Dulwich Picture Gallery, London, 1990), pp. 29–43.

—, *Ruination: Photographs of Rome* (Djanogly Art Gallery, University of Nottingham, 2008).

Yarrington, Alison, '"Made in Italy": Sculpture and the Staging of National Identities at the International Exhibition of 1862', in Manfred Pfister and Ralph Hertel (eds), *Performing National Identities: Anglo-Italian Cultural Transactions* (Amsterdam, 2008), pp. 75–99.

Young, Arthur, *Voyage en Italie pendant l'année 1789*, trans. François Soules (Paris, 1796).

Young, David, *Rome in Winter, the Tuscan Hills in Summer* (London, 1880).

Zerner, Henri, 'The Modern Pastoral', in Margaret Stuffmann and Werner Busch (eds), *Zeichnen in Rome 1790–1830* (Cologne, 2001), pp. 232–46.

INDEX

PICTURE CREDITS

In most cases illustrative material has been provided by the owners or custodians of the works. Those for which further credit is due are listed below.